Buddhism

A Modern Perspective

List of Contributors

Stefan Anacker, University of Illinois
Stephan V. Beyer, University of Wisconsin
Francis H. Cook, University of California, Riverside
Roger J. Corless, Duke University
Douglas D. Daye, Bowling Green State University
Mark A. Ehman, Springfield College
Lewis R. Lancaster, University of California, Berkeley
Charles S. Prebish, The Pennsylvania State University

BUDDHISM:

A Modern Perspective

EDITED BY

CHARLES S. PREBISH

THE PENNSYLVANIA STATE UNIVERSITY PRESS
UNIVERSITY PARK AND LONDON

Printed in the United States of America
Designed by Andrew Vargo

Library of Congress Cataloging in Publication Data

Prebish, Charles S
Buddhism—a modern perspective.

Bibliography: p. 311
1. Buddha and Buddhism. I. Title.
BQ4012.P73 1975 294.3 74-26706
ISBN 0-271-01185-8

Contents

Foreword

This book is a valuable addition to the literature on Buddhism. It presents a basic and accurate survey of the tremendous variety of traditions and practices associated with Buddhism throughout the world.

In the past half century Buddhist ideas have been introduced to Western Countries in very impure forms due to the particular viewpoints of the adventurers and translators who interpreted them. It is especially unfortunate that Buddhism has been presented as a theistic religion, whereas in fact it is a non-theistic spiritual philosophy, psychology, and way of life. In recent decades the practice of Zen meditation has become well known in the West. While this is an improvement over the ways in which Buddhism was presented earlier, there is still very little clear presentation of other forms that meditation practice can take, or of the philosophy which is an essential part of the study of Buddhism.

The value of this book, then, lies in the care and scholarship which the authors have shown in outlining the doctrines in a simple and straightforward way, and in providing ample resources for further study. It is a beginning step in the vast amount of work which needs to be done if Buddhism is to take a firm root in American soil.

Chögyam Trungpa, Rinpoche

volume, composed of contributions only from Professor Robinson's former students, and now a rather fitting vehicle seemed to emerge. What better way to reveal the manner in which this brilliant scholar's genius had become manifest than to utilize the writings of his former students to actualize that to which Richard Robinson dedicated his life?

When I had completed what I felt to be a list of scholars with the comprehensive talents necessary for such an undertaking, and had secured their affirmative responses, I submitted a preliminary prospectus of lecture topics to each. Within a relatively short time span, the precise topics were agreed upon and work began.

Of course the primary issue, at the outset, is how the lecture topics were chosen. In this regard, our objectives were manifold. We wanted to present a comprehensive study on the introductory level, but we also felt it advisable to include several topics previously untouched in introductory books. We began with basics, for no introductory text would be complete without the usual background materials: a treatment of Buddha's life, the early history of the Buddhist order, basic doctrines, mention of the Hīnayāna sects, a section on Aśoka, the rise and basic doctrines of Mahāyāna, brief mention of some Mahāyāna sects, several references to the Buddhist literary tradition, nirvāṇa, meditation, and a survey of Buddhism in China, Tibet, and Japan, as well as India. As a group, we felt that even these topics could be improved upon if the work was done with care. Consequently, we decided to expand this usual treatment. Traditionally, Buddhist councils are discussed with early Buddhist history. We felt, due to the extreme importance of the councils in terms of their implications for the sectarian movement in early Buddhism, that this topic should be dealt with separately. Likewise, since the Hīnayāna sects provide the ground from which later forms of Buddhism arose, several of the most important groups should also merit their own section. Here we included lectures on the Mahāsāṃghikas, Theravādins, and Sarvāstivādins. Kaniṣka, so important and so overlooked in Buddhist history, was cited for special reference. No book on Buddhism, and certainly no discussion of early Buddhism, would be complete without ample reference to the Tripiṭaka or Buddhist canon. Nevertheless, most of the prior works mention the divisions of the canon hardly at all, or only at the end of the volume. We felt it imperative to devote a full lecture to each of individual baskets. Basic Mahāyāna is allotted three full lectures: its rise, its literature, and its doctrines. However, as Mahāyāna developed and a vast, new literature emerged in the process, it was essential to emphasize the impact of these new texts by including lectures on several of the most important sūtras. As with the Hīnayāna, Mahāyāna sects had to be taken into account. The problem here is that the two primary Mahāyāna schools, Mādhyamika and Yogācāra, not only provide great difficulty for the beginning student but also for many scholars. In this regard, most literature on the subject is quite sophisticated, aimed for the knowledgeable few, or quite incorrect and useful to nobody. Further, literature on the subject is rarely in English. In the lectures on each of these schools, we feel that we have provided readings that are both accurate and understandable. The concluding lectures on Indian Buddhism discuss areas rarely dealt with in detail, or at all, in introductory books: cosmology, logic, nirvāṇa, and meditation. This latter topic is extremely important to provide in fullness, for as one of my colleagues noted, "There is no Buddhism without the experiential methods of meditation."

In coming to terms with Buddhism outside of India, we have weighted our lectures most heavily on China and Japan. Nevertheless, we have taken great pains not to exclude Ceylon, Tibet, Southeast Asia, and Korea from proper treatment. In addition, the latter two areas are hardly ever more than simply mentioned in introductory works. The unique feature of our lectures on Buddhism outside of India is that we try to direct some attention, much needed at that, to Buddhism in the modern world. Previously, one had to resort to quite specialized readings to uncover information on Chinese Buddhism and Communism, religion in modern-day Japan or Korea, and Buddhism in the West. For this final lecture, we have also added an Appendix locating various Buddhist groups in the United States. Since the groups listed are from diverse geographic areas in America, it is quite likely that many of those utilizing this text might have the opportunity to visit Buddhist groups in their area, and of course the study of Buddhism in America is truly the newest aspect of Buddhology to emerge.

Lest any volume be falsely accused, it seems appropriate to devote at least a few words to that which we have omitted. We have clearly made a studied omission of lectures on specific Hīnayāna texts. Perhaps ideally we might have included lectures on the Visuddhimagga, Milindapañha, and Abhidharmakośa. The Visuddhimagga has been omitted as a separate entry primarily because it forms the substance of the lecture on Hīnayāna meditation. Both Stephan V. Beyer (the author of that lecture) and I feel that its most important aspects are fully dealt with under that heading. While the Milindapañha is not specifically dealt with, the implications of its many pronouncements, as well as its doctrinal affinities, are implicit in many lectures in the text. The Abhidharmakośa too is dealt with both in the lectures on Sarvāstivāda and the Abhidharma Piṭaka. Certainly, on the textual question, we had considered making references in our Suggested Readings to anthologies containing scriptural collections. We opted for omission on this point primarily because we wanted to provide the greatest flexibility for our readers. Rather than choosing one of the many fine anthologies (e.g., those of de Bary, Conze, or Beyer), we felt it most appropriate to leave that choice open to those utlilizing the volume. We do, however, make reference to many translations of specific texts, thus reflecting our own textual concern as well as providing a guide for ambitious students. We would like to have included a section on popular Buddhism. The experience of the contributors has been that these studies are most often entertained by anthropologists with imperfect training in Buddhology or Buddhologists with imperfect training in anthropology. In either case, the results are usually disastrous. Indeed, with very few exceptions, literature on popular Buddhism has not lived up to the highest standards. A lecture on Buddhist art also would have been valuable. Certainly, other topics not mentioned here could have been included, but limits and restrictions (particularly length) had to be considered.

The format for the lectures has been dictated solely on the basis of pragmatic concerns. This is a book designed to provide basic input for beginners, and we wanted to adopt a format that would promote rather than frustrate study of this difficult topic. Consequently, the basic outline format provides the most simple, direct, and *organized* fashion for structuring one's study. In addition, key words (whether they be technical terms in the various Buddhist languages or critical signposts in English) have been italicized on their first appearance in each lecture and elsewhere in the lecture where they are critical to understanding a given topic. In addition, Suggested Readings are provided at the conclusion of each lecture. These readings should not be construed to be a complete bibliography on the lecture but rather a sampling of that literature which the author of the lecture feels would enhance the understanding of the reader. The entries from the Suggested Readings section of each lecture have been gathered together and presented in a complete bibliography at the conclusion of the text. We feel that this bibliography represents the most ambitious and complete collection of books ever presented in an introductory text. Since the text is filled with many Buddhist technical terms, place names, names of famous texts and persons, etc., we have compiled a glossary containing brief definitions or identifications for the most important of these. To include them all would prove neither practical nor useful. Nevertheless, since one's introductory study of Buddhism is often confounded by repeated exposure to this sometimes overwhelming new vocabulary, we hope that our glossary, again the most complete such enterprise in an introductory volume, will lessen the pains and bewilderment so often apparent in beginners.

To prepare a complete list of acknowledgments for this volume would obviously be impossible. However, several persons cannot be overlooked. Joseph Elder, whose *Lectures in Indian Civilization* provided the take-off point for this volume, both in format and effectiveness, must be singled out for thanks by each contributor. Luther H. Harshbarger, who was instrumental in aiding me obtain a grant which helped defray some of the costs involved in bringing the project to completion, and who is uncanny in constantly providing profitable suggestions, must receive the special thanks of the editor. In this regard, I am particularly grateful to The Pennsylvania State University for providing those monies mentioned above. To our students, who were often unaware that they were our trial audience, and who in a very real sense shaped the entire volume by their inquiries, problems, and frustrations, we offer our gratitude. Like all education, the study of Buddhism is indeed the proverbial "two-way street," and without our students to teach us, there would be no *Buddhism: A Modern Perspective*. Finally, the greatest thanks must go to Professor Richard H. Robinson. Although his life and career were cut short at the height of productivity, we all sincerely hope that this volume will be but one manifestation of the myriad ways in which Richard has influenced Buddhology. Hardly a sincere student of Buddhism emerges who has not been influenced by Richard Robinson in a very profound way. Often we hear of "schools" of Buddhist scholarship growing up around a great professor: the students of Thomas W. Rhys Davids, the students of Th. Stcherbatsky, or the students of Louis de La Vallée Poussin. What all these great scholars and schools shared was a common question, however variously it may have been asked. And one can be sure of hearing of the students of Richard H. Robinson, including those who have not contributed here. Nevertheless, something significant seems to have changed, for Richard H. Robinson, in his own fashion, rewrote the rulebook. Richard found new questions to ask, and with the asking has changed the face of Buddhology. If he could see the new face, there are no doubts it would be grinning.

PART I

Indian Buddhism

1

The Background to Buddhism

Stephan V. Beyer

THE INDUS VALLEY CIVILIZATION

In the third millenium B.C., peoples from the neolithic cultures of Baluchistan moved into the fertile flood plains of the Indus River and established cities at *Harappā*, *Mohenjodaro*, and other sites. They engaged in considerable trading as far as Mesopotamia; the southern city at *Lothal* had a sophisticated drydock system. The well laid-out streets, consistent city plans, almost modern sanitation facilities, centralized food storage areas, and the presence of citadels in the hearts of the cities all suggest a strong and conservative system of government.

This Indus Valley Civilization developed its own writing system, which is as yet undeciphered, although there has been some fruitful speculation that it was used to write a *proto-Dravidian* language. This writing is found in short inscriptions on beautifully carved seals, probably giving the name of the owner, with well-conceived and naturalistic pictures of animals and what may well be gods. Another clue to the religious life of these people is found in the presence of large ritual baths associated with the central city and indicating a profound concern for bodily purity—a concern reflected also in the sophisticated sewage system.

By the time this civilization had reached its full growth, it covered a territory over a thousand miles long, greater than that of any other ancient civilization. By around 1200 B.C. the cities were dying: craftsmanship and organization were disappearing, and huddled skeletons with crushed skulls in the most recent levels suggest either invasions or internecine warfare. The Indus River seems to have no longer been under control, perhaps because of a shift in its flow, and there may have been excessive floods. It is debated whether the Indo-European invaders from the northwest were the actual destroyers of the cities; but in any case they probably found a civilization in the final process of decay.

THE INDUS RELIGION

From the seals and the baths we can make some uncertain inferences about the religion of the cities. They seem to have shared in the general Near Eastern cult of the *Mother Goddess*, producing terracotta figurines of female figures, nude except for a short skirt. This goddess, as represented on the seals, seems often to have been associated with horned animals, even being represented herself as a theriomorph. We find scenes of religious processions approaching what seem to be sacred trees, occasionally with a goddess—or a tree spirit—depicted in the branches; one seal depicts a female figure, upside down, with a tree growing from between her parted legs.

Several figures are shown sitting in what came to be called a yogic posture, with legs tightly crossed and the hands placed on the knees, often being paid homage by others. Here too we may mention the ritual baths, and the extreme importance that seems to have been laid upon bodily purity and the proper disposal of human wastes: water itself seems to have carried considerable religious significance. We find, finally, large numbers of seemingly phallic objects, perhaps presented as offerings to the goddess as part of rituals of growth and fertility.

THE INDUS INHERITANCE

We may speculate on the elements of this religious culture that were passed on to its scattered descendants and absorbed into the mainstream of Indian religion. The Mother Goddess especially reappears in later Hinduism, but played almost no role at all in the Buddhist cult. But we find local spirits of trees and streams as central figures in early Buddhism: these are the *yakṣas* and serpent-like *nāgas* who appear constantly in the canonical texts. The sacred tree, too, appears in Buddhism as the tree of enlightenment. There are, for example, any number of Buddhist representations of the Buddha seated cross-legged beneath the tree, protected by the giant hood of the serpent *Mucilinda*. The three basic elements in the portrayal may all be derived from the Indus Civilization.

The Indus emphasis on purity of the body and the presence of what may have been yogic practices give some evidence of a basically transcendent perspective in Indus religion. We may postulate the presence of a sacerdotal class who ran the sacred baths and interceded with the goddess for the fertility of the crops. But even more, there may well have been a special class of religious practitioners whose aim lay in the induction of trance-like states of bodily immobility, and the impenetrability of the body to pollution. The entire yogic ideal of absolute withdrawal from sensory input cannot easily be traced to Indo-European antecedents; but in the Indus concern for the integrity of the bodily integument and in their representation of figures in cross-legged immobility, we may find a clue to what would become a major element of Indian religion.

THE VEDIC CULTURE

The Indo-European invaders who trod upon the warm corpse of the Indus Civilization were, by their own account, a hard-drinking, hard-riding band of stalwart warriors, who used with considerable efficacy their own invention of war, the horse-drawn chariot. They brought with them a pantheon of sky gods, families of professional reciters of hymns and performers of ritual, and a substance called *soma* that produced states of divine ecstacy and magical power.

This soma may well have been the psychotropic mushroom *Amanita muscaria*. The religious professionals—the technicians of the sacred—opened up the shining world of the gods, and in their rituals of offerings and praise asked boons of the *devas*, the shining ones. Yet in their ecstatic power they were able to control even the gods themselves, and the rituals grew with time into complex magical simulacra for the processes of the entire cosmos, owned and controlled by human agency.

This growing homologization of the ritual to the universe took place as the secret of soma was being lost among the priests. But the ideal of ecstatic trance and magic power continued to be expressed, and paradox and metaphor became the vehicles for a literary alteration of consciousness. The magical correspondences of the ritual were expanded, and even in the latest hymns we find the sacrificer still flying in space, his spirit among the gods, while mortals see only his body here below.

VEDIC LITERATURE

The Basic Texts. This visionary tradition was early formulated into orally transmitted texts. The priestly families kept collections of their own inherited hymns, and shortly before the first millenium B.C. these were in turn collected into an anthology known as the *Ṛg-veda*. As the rituals grew more complex, specialized functions were introduced. A priest was appointed specifically to handle the physical actions of the sacrifice and to manipulate the sacred implements, each of which had to be empowered by the recitation of stereotyped magical formulas. The utterances of this performance were then collected into another anthology, the *Yajur-veda*. Again, another specialized priest took on the role of cantor, and chanted the sacred verses to special melodies, and these verses were collected, along with their musical notation, in the *Sāma-veda*.

In addition to these texts, the *threefold sacred knowledge*, a fourth collection of hymns called the *Atharva-veda* was made specifically for the magical averting of evil. These rituals against death, disease, and hostile witchcraft seem to have been the property of less orthodox religious specialists who lived somewhat closer to the everyday life of the people.

The Expositions. Around 800 B.C. there began the composition of compendious prose expositions of the Vedic ritual. These *Brāhmaṇas* deal in sacerdotal detail with the homologies of the sacrifice and the cosmos, and there are the first hints of later doctrines of liberation. If the ritual granted magical power and control of the universe through the magic namings of the priest, then might there not be the single thing whose name is the name of all? There had already been some speculation that all the gods and the universe itself came from the *one*: if this one thing could be known, then the ultimate power, and the ultimate freedom, might be gained.

These doctrines were expanded upon in the *Āraṇyakas*, books whose secret and sacred lore could be learned only in the solitude of the forests. The archaic modes of ecstacy were turned to realization, and in meditations called *vidyās*, the practitioner internalized the cosmic dimensions of the ritual and could gain the knowledge and power of the ritual without its actual performance.

Very shortly before the time of the Buddha himself, there began to be composed the earliest prose *Upaniṣads*, teachings imparted only from a master to a disciple. Here the quest for the *one* was carried on in true earnest. Ritual elements increasingly disappear, and the secret and shockingly new truth of *transmigration* and its terror of repeated death becomes the central motivation for knowledge. The single thing whose name is the essence of the world process is identified as that which is changeless in the midst of change, the ultimate cause of all effects, that which cannot nonexist: to know it—and thus to possess it—is the key to liberation from death.

The one was approached from several directions. It was considered to be the substance of which all things were made, and thus the unchanging ground of phenomenal appearances. As such it was identified with the magic oral powers that created and sustained the cosmos, and was called the *Brahman*. Again, the one was sought within the individual, as that without which life and consciousness could not be, and was thus the unchanging ground of the transmigrating self. As such it was identified with earlier speculations upon the sustaining power of the breath and was called the *ātman*. A final step was taken in the most secret teaching of all, that in reality this Brahman and this ātman were the same.

This teaching is enshrined in the most sacred utterances of the Upaniṣads, the great sayings such as *Tat tvam asi* ("You are That") or *Brahmo 'ham*

("I am Brahman"). It was by meditation upon such sayings that the practitioner gained knowledge in a flash of realization; he perceived directly the unchanging reality that underlay the shifting panorama of experience, and his knowledge freed him forever from the terrible round of death.

THE VEDIC INHERITANCE

Such teachings were of paramount importance for developing Buddhism. Buddha's own enlightenment was a visionary and ecstatic experience in the mythic mode of the earliest Vedic tradition. The doctrine of transmigration is central to the Buddhist quest, and the idea of *nirvāṇa* would be unintelligible without it. The Buddhist process of insight meditation is a direct continuation of the meditations on the great sayings of the Upaniṣads, wherein the practitioner internalizes a concise doctrinal formula as a direct and personal realization of the truth. However much the metaphysical superstructure may have differed—and it differed considerably—the quest for freedom as a state of being within the phenomenal world, and the contemplative techniques used in the search, were inherited from the Vedic tradition.

THE AGE OF THE WANDERERS

For several centuries before the birth of the Buddha, a revolution had been under way in India. Iron technology had developed, creating a new type of military specialist and a new impersonal mode of warfare. Iron implements cleared great forests for cultivation and constructed the vast timber palisades of fortified cities. The iron-tipped plough produced a surplus economy that could support great governmental and religious institutions. And from the West came the new concept of the centralized imperium, the world-conquering monarch, and the uses of war for power rather than for gain.

There was vast social upheaval as rival kings sought to establish their empires, as religious ritual was increasingly turned to the support of centralized government, and as the family and tribal structures of earlier times dissolved under the pressures of impersonal imperialism. Independent tribal groups were swept up into larger political units, until by the time of the Buddha only sixteen city-states ruled over what had once been a vast series of independent peoples. Some tribal groups in the foothills of the Himalayas held to their independence, but the writing was clearly on the wall. Soon the state of *Magadha* would inaugurate a final solution to the tribal question.

THE TWO TRADITIONS

Opposition to these new forces took many forms, including miltary resistance. The philosophical quest for freedom was inextricably bound up with a new social movement, the wanderers (*parivrājakas*) who left home and family to seek a way of liberation in the world. Social anomie was expressed creatively in religious seeking, and it was from this movement that Buddhism directly derived. We may note that the movement was inherently conservative politically, a reaction against the release of new social forces; the Buddha himself modeled his monastic institution upon the old customs of the independent tribes.

We may distinguish two main religious postures in the wanderer movement itself. Some sought freedom in transcendence, in an enstatic withdrawal from all sensory input, and in total immobility of the body, the breath, and the mind. Progressive states of trance gradually drew the meditator further and further from the realm of phenomena, until he achieved a state of isolation and monadic impenetrability. This practice was closely bound up with concepts of purity and pollution, for action was seen as a sort of defiling substance that weighted the soul and bound it to the world. The process of trance was often viewed as a means of burning away impurities. If our speculations concerning the Indus Valley religion are valid, we have a clear source for these ideas and practices. The basic functional term would seem to be inviolability: the purity of body is a way of preserving its unitary integrity, establishing the skin as the ultimate ego-boundary, just as the immobility of the mind becomes a means of transcending the defilements of sensory input. Other wanderers sought freedom in immanence, in the visionary and ecstatic experience that rendered all things new, and in the magic knowledge that granted power over the world. The quest was for insight rather than for isolation, for the infinite maneuverability available to the one who knew how the universe worked. Here was the direct continuation of the Vedic tradition, which was to culminate in the vision of the Upaniṣads.

THE PHILOSOPHICAL PROBLEMATIC

The above is a much simplified view of a complex phenomenon. Although transcendence and immanence remained the basic polarities of the entire Indian contemplative tradition, there was considerable borrowing of *techniques* from one tradition to the other. We shall see later how Buddhism dealt with the implicit contradictions of its dual contemplative inheritance. These contradictions further generated an entire series of philosophical problems that both Buddhism and Hinduism had to deal with. If ultimate reality is immanent, then there arises the epistemological question of why the practitioner has not realized it already. The choice of transcendence raised ontological problems, and the choice of immanence raised epistemological ones.

What is the relationship between the body and the soul? If the soul is a permanent and unchanging entity somehow trapped within the phenomenal world in spite of its transcendence, then what is the historical process by which this ontological fall took place? Or if the soul participates in change, then what is the psychological process by which it enters into an epistemological relation with an unchanging reality? We must account for personal change and the possibility of spiritual progress on the one hand and for personal continuity and the persistence of memory on the other. If the soul is permanent and unchanging, then how can it be said to transmigrate?

Problems such as these were early put in specifically Buddhist terms. The problem of *karma* remained a central issue for over a thousand years, for the Buddhist maintained that there was no permanent entity within the personality: how then can we say that it is the same person who suffers for his past deeds, or who attains enlightenment? The problem of perception remained equally central: how can one impermanent entity perceive another that is already past?

But even more important were the most fundamental soteriological issues raised by the implicit contradictions of the tradition. What is the moral value of action in the world? What happens to an enlightened person when he dies? The Buddha is taken for the model for all religious action, but what was the central act of his life—the enlightenment or the nirvāṇa?

The entire history of Buddhist thought can be seen as a search for answers to these questions.

SUGGESTED READING

Basham, A.L. *The Wonder That Was India.*

Jaini, Padmanabh. "*Śramanas*: Their Conflict with Brāhmaṇical Society." In Joseph Elder, ed., *Chapters in Indian Civilization*, vol. 1, pp. 39–81.

Robinson, Richard H. "Classical Indian Philosophy." In Joseph Elder, ed., *Chapters in Indian Civilization*, vol. 1, pp. 127–227.

Wasson, R. Gordon. *Soma, Divine Mushroom of Immortality.*

2
Life of the Buddha

Charles S. Prebish

SOURCES

In trying to explicate a complete biography of *Siddhārtha Gautama*, the historical Buddha, the Three Baskets of the Buddhist canon (*Tripiṭaka*) offer us precious little. Apart from presentation in an unconnected fashion, these piecemeal accounts focus primarily on the two great events in Buddha's life: his attainment of enlightenment and his passing into final *parinirvāṇa*. The details surrounding his forty-five year ministry remain shrouded in mystery and uncertainty. Nevertheless, several noncanonical legends of the life of the Buddha emerge from the growing corpus of Buddhist literature in the centuries following the parinirvāṇa, and it is from these that a more unified portrait of Buddha's career begins to make itself visible. Of these, five are worthy of mention: the *Mahāvastu* or "Great Account," written in Buddhist Hybrid Sanskrit and belonging to the *Lokottaravādin* subsect of the *Mahāsāṃghika* school of Buddhism; the *Lalitavistara* or "Detailed Account of the Sports (of the Buddha)," a *Sarvāstivādin* text; the *Nidāna-kathā* or "Connected Story," attributed to the great *Theravādin* exegete *Buddhaghosa* and forming the introduction to the *Pāli Jātakas;* the *Buddhacarita* or "Acts of the Buddha," a portion of which remains in Sanskrit and is attributed to the first-century (A.D.) poet *Aśvaghoṣa*; and the *Abhiniṣkramaṇa-sūtra* or "Discourse of the Great Renunciation," lost in the original but preserved in translation and attributed to the *Dharmaguptaka* school.

FAMILY AND BIRTH

Preliminary to his appearance in the world and attainment of enlightenment the future Buddha or *Bodhisattva* underwent a long series of rebirths, the substance of which form the core of the *Jātaka* tales or stories of the Buddha's previous lives. In one of these he is overwhelmed by the quiescence and munificence of the Buddha of that world cycle (identified as *Dīpaṅkara* in the Nidānakathā) and awakens the thought of enlightenment (*bodhicitta*), transforming his entire personality and resulting in his taking a vow (*praṇidhāna*) to attain complete perfect enlightenment. After receiving a prediction (*vyākaraṇa*) from the current Buddha regarding the actualization of the vow, he begins to practice many perfections (*pāramitās*) so as to build a great stock of merit, aiding him in his noble task. After countless lives, the Bodhisattva is born as lord of the gods in the *Tuṣita* heaven. From this vantage point, he makes three determinations regarding his birth into the world: time, place, and family. The time, sixth century B.C., seems to be one filled with moral decay, as the world cycle is declining. India, called *Jambu-dvīpa*, appears to be the best of the continents and he centers on the middle country. With regard to family, he chooses the highest class of the time, the *Kṣatriyas*, finally selecting the *Śākya* tribe of the *Gautama* clan, a petty kingdom ruled over by *Śuddhodana* and his queen, *Māyā*.

The story of his conception and birth, fraught with mythic elements, involves Māyā conceiving in a dream in which a six-tusked white elephant, after circumambulating her seven times, enters directly into her right side. After carrying the fetus for ten months, Māyā gives birth to the infant while standing in *Lumbinī* garden grasping the branch of a tree. Being no ordinary child, the Bodhisattva steps down from her right side pure and undefiled. After being washed by a stream of water furnished by a deity (as was the mother), the child steps in each of the directions proclaiming that he will be the highest creature in each of them. As with all mothers of Buddhas, Māyā dies on the seventh day following the delivery, whereupon Suddhodana marries her sister *Mahāprajāpatī*, furnishing his son with a foster mother. A sage comes to the kingdom and, after examining the marks on the child's body (i.e., the thirty-two major and eighty minor marks of a superman), declares that the child shall become either a universal monarch (literally, turner of the wheel of the law or *cakravartin*) or a Buddha. Thus the child was named *Siddhārtha* or "he whose aim will be accomplished."

INFANCY AND YOUTH

Growing up in luxury, as befitting the son of a ruler, Siddhārtha enjoyed all the pleasures of his position. One day, however, while watching the ploughing festival, he inadvertently attained a meditational experience or *samādhi* as he was seated under a tree. The recollection of the spontaneity of this experience, at a later stage in his life, was to make a profound impression on his approach to attaining full enlightenment.

In the course of time Siddhārtha was married to *Yaśodharā*. Some time after his marriage the young prince took a chariot ride through the countryside, seeing, in the course of his ride, an old man. His charioteer, inspired by the gods, explained to his master that such was the way of all life: impermanent. Psychologically depressed, Siddhārtha returned to the palace. When his father was informed of the event, he strengthened the guard around the palace, remembering the sage's prediction and fearful that his son would renounce the world. On three successive days the youth slips out of the palace (presumably aided by the gods) and sees a sick man, a corpse, and a religious ascetic. When he learns that the ascetic is one seeking liberation from the perpetual existence in *saṃsāra*, his heart leaps and he begins to formulate his plan to renounce the world. When he shortly thereafter learns that his wife has given birth to a son, his despondency is overwhelming, resulting in his declaration that "A fetter has been born." Thus he names his son *Rāhula*, the fetter.

RENUNCIATION AND ENLIGHTENMENT

Although his intent to renounce the world and seek to overcome old age, sickness, death, and rebirth is strong, he desires his father's approval, and when it is not obtained, he is forced to take matters into his own hands. Stealing a last look at his young son, he goes to the edge of the forest, dons the robes of an ascetic, and goes forth from the world as a religious recluse. He is now twenty-nine years old.

Seeking a teacher, he first studies with *Ārāḍa Kālāma.* After mastering the system and experiencing the state of the sphere of nothingness (*akiṃcanyāyatana*), he is offered status equal to Ārāḍa, but declines, realizing that this is not enlightenment. His second teacher, *Udraka Rāmaputra*, teaches the attainment of the sphere of neither perception nor non-perception (*naivasaṃjñānāsaṃjñāyatana*), and here too Siddhārtha finds the experience lacking and leaves. Shortly thereafter he begins to practice austerities with five other ascetics, each hoping that one of them breaks through to enlightenment, in order to teach it to the others. After six years of severe austerities, the Bodhisattva surveys his emaciated body and concludes that this path, like the luxurious pleasure seeking he experienced as a boy, also falls short of enlightenment. Remembering his childhood experience during the ploughing festival, he decides to steer a middle course through these two extremes. After he has taken nourishment to strengthen his body, the five ascetics leave in disgust branding him a "backslider." Upon regaining his strength, he sits beneath a tree (later to be called the Tree of Awakening or *Bodhi Tree*) and resolves not to rise from this spot until he attains complete perfect enlightenment. During that night he experienced all four of the transic states (*dhyānas*). In the first watch of the night he surveys his own previous existences. In the second watch he surveys the death and rebirth of other living beings, and during the third watch he destroys the *āsravas* (outflows, impurities): *kāma* or sensual desire, *bhava* or desire for existence, *dṛṣṭi* or false views, and *avidyā* or ignorance. Thus as dawn bursts forth, by seeing things as they really are (*yathābhūtaṃ*), Siddhārtha Gautama has become *samyaksaṃbuddha*, completely and perfectly enlightened. In other words, he has become the *Buddha* (Awakened One), the *Jina* (Conqueror), the *Arhant* (Worthy One), the *Tathāgata* (Thus-Come). Corollary to his experience, it is generally agreed that Buddha, in his enlightening experience, also perceived the two doctrines which later become the cornerstone of his teaching: the Four Noble Truths (*ārya satyas*) and Dependent Origination (*pratītya-samutpāda*).

CAREER

After attaining enlightenment, Buddha spent several weeks in the general vicinity of the Bodhi Tree. During this period two merchants (*Trapuṣa* and *Bhallika*) offered him food and later took refuge in him, thus becoming the first male lay disciples (*upāsakas*). Buddha also allowed *Sujātā*, the woman who had offered him food when he abandoned his austerities, to take refuge in him, thus becoming the first female lay disciple (*upāsikā*). Nevertheless, Buddha had doubts about preaching his doctrine or *Dharma*, as he felt that it was too deep and subtle for the common people to understand. At the entreaty of *Brahmā* (the chief deity), however, he decides to preach the Dharma for the benefit of mankind. A deity informs him that his two previous teachers, Ārāḍa Kālāma and Udraka Rāmaputra have died, so he sets off to seek his five ascetic cohorts who he discerned with his divine eye to be dwelling in the Deer Park at *Sārnāth*. Although they saw him coming in the distance and planned simply to ignore the "backslider," on closer observance they at once recognized a calm, tranquil visage quite different from their old friend Gautama. They addressed him in the usual manner and were scolded in so doing, for Buddha explained that he had become a Tathāgata and was going to preach Dharma to them. On hearing the First Sermon (*Dharmacakrapravartana-sūtra*), espousing the futility of the two extremes of pleasure seeking and strict asceticism, and outlining the Four Noble Truths of suffering (*duḥkha*), the cause of suffering (*samudaya*), the cessation of suffering (*nirodha*), and the path leading to the cessation of suffering (*mārga*), one of the disciples, *Ājñāta Kauṇḍinya*, became enlightened and received ordination as a monk (*bhikṣu*) by the simple formula "Come, O monk" (*ehi bhikṣu*). Thus the monastic community or *Saṃgha* was founded. Upon hearing a sermon on the marks of the not-self (*Anātma-*

lakṣaṇa-sūtra), the other four ascetics became enlightened and were ordained as monks.

The Saṃgha grew by leaps and bounds, soon including the main characters who were to play the largest roles in early Buddhist religious history: *Śāriputra*, *Maudgalyāyana*, *Upāli*, and *Ānanda*. At Ānanda's insistence and clever use of argument, an order of nuns (*bhikṣuṇīs*) was started. Although our records provide little more information, there is much indication that early Buddhism received royal patronage and the support of many wealthy merchants. We also know that of the Buddha's forty-five year ministry, the last twenty-five rainy seasons were spent in *Śrāvastī*.

BUDDHA'S DEATH

As Buddha approached the ripe old age of eighty, he became gravely ill while dwelling at *Vaiśālī*. He said to Ānanda, who was his personal servant throughout the last twenty-five years of his ministry, that he could live for a *kalpa* if he wished. Ānanda, however, having been so busy attending to Buddha's personal matters that he had not had time to fully understand and actualize the Dharma, did not pick up the cue and request it. Then when the demon *Māra* approached, suggesting that Buddha enter into parinirvāṇa or final nirvāṇa, Buddha acquiesced, much to Ānanda's dismay (for he now realized his error). Buddha decided to enter parinirvāṇa in *Kuśinagara* three months hence. Shortly before his death Buddha took a meal at the home of a blacksmith, resulting in a severe stomach disorder. Painfully pressing on to Kuśinagara, Buddha received one final convert into the Saṃgha and addressed the monks: "Impermanent are all conditioned things; Work out your own salvation with diligence." Ascending the trance states, *Śākyamuni*, the sage of the Śākyas, entered parinirvāṇa. Thereafter, on the seventh day following his death, Buddha was cremated with the relics being distributed and memorial mounds (*stūpas*) constructed over them.

SUGGESTED READING

Bareau, André. *Recherches sur la biographie du Buddha dans les Sūtrapiṭaka et les Vinayapiṭaka anciens: de la quête du l'Éveil à la conversion de Śāriputra et de Maudgalyāyana.*

Cowell, E.B., tr. "The Buddha-Carita of Aśvaghoṣa." In *Buddhist Mahāyāna Texts.*

Foucher, Alfred. *La Vie du Bouddha.* English translation available as *The Life of the Buddha According to the Ancient Texts and Monuments of India.*

Jones, J.J., tr. *The Mahāvastu, translated from the Buddhist Sanskrit.*
Renou, Louis, and Filliozat, Jean. *L'Inde Classique.* Tome 2, pp. 463–94.
Rhys Davids, Thomas W., tr. *Buddhist Birth Stories.*
Rockhill, W., tr. *The Life of the Buddha and the Early History of His Order.*
Thomas, Edward J. *The Life of the Buddha as Legend and History.*

3

Early History of the Buddhist Order

Charles S. Prebish

IMPORTANT DISCIPLES

During the time period immediately following Buddha's attainment of enlightenment, many disciples became an integral part of the early history of Buddhism. The most significant of these should be mentioned, classified under the headings monks and laymen, the latter group being subdivided into wealthy members of society and royal patrons.

MONKS

Yaśas. Shortly after Buddha had converted the five ascetics in the Deer Park at *Sārnāth*, *Yaśas*, the son of a wealthy merchant, being disgusted with worldly life, left his home, eventually coming upon Buddha. Yaśas's father set out to find him and when he too came across Buddha, the Tathāgata made Yaśas invisible, so as not to be discovered. Buddha preached to Yaśas's father who was overwhelmed and became a layman (*upāsaka*). When Buddha made Yaśas visible, he discovered that Yaśas, in hearing Buddha's discourse, became an *arhant*. Returning to Yaśas's home, his wife and mother became laywomen (*upāsikās*) by taking refuge in the three jewels (*triratna*) and professing the five moral precepts (*pañcaśīla*). Soon, fifty-four of Yaśas's friends became enlightened, bringing the number of arhants to sixty, excluding Buddha.

The Three Kāśyapas. Buddha eventually, after leaving Benares, wanders to *Uruvilvā* where he takes residence with three *jaṭilas* or matted-hair ascetics: *Uruvilvākāśyapa* (with 500 disciples), *Nadīkāśyapa* (with 300 disciples), and *Gayākāśyapa* (with 200 disciples). After Buddha performs a long series of miracles, the three ascetics and their disciples become monks (*bhikṣus*). Buddha then preaches the well-known "Fire Sermon," whereby all the new monks become arhants.

Śāriputra and Maudgalyāyana. One day *Śāriputra*, a follower of the wanderer

Sañjaya, meets a novice Buddhist monk named *Aśvajit*. Curious about the Buddha, Śāriputra asks Aśvajit to expound on Buddhist doctrine. Aśvajit explains that he is just a novice, but he states that the essence of the doctrine is that Buddha has explained the cessation of all things which are issued from a cause. Being spiritually advanced, Śāriputra perceives the true import of this statement and becomes an arhant. Śāriputra then recites this Dharma summary to his close friend *Maudgalyāyana* who also becomes enlightened. These two young men then become monks, eventually establishing themselves as two of Buddha's closest disciples. Śāriputra is often associated with the *Abhidharma* and Maudgalyāyana becomes proficient in miraculous powers.

Rāhula. Buddha eventually returns to *Kapilavastu* to visit his family. Buddha's former wife, *Yaśodharā*, sends their son, *Rāhula*, to receive his birthright. Buddha, however, makes the boy (who was seven years old) a novice (*śramaṇera*). Rāhula is later known as the chief of all the novices.

Ānanda. *Ānanda* was Buddha's cousin and was also converted during Buddha's visit to Kapilavastu. During the twentieth year of Buddha's ministry, Ānanda became Buddha's personal attendant, remaining so for the rest of Buddha's life. Most notable among his accomplishments were his recitation of all the *Sūtras* at the first council after Buddha's death and his role in helping to establish the order of nuns (*bhikṣuṇīs*) by coming to the aid of *Mahāprajāpatī* who became the first nun.

Devadatta. Also related to the Buddha, *Devadatta* became a monk but, unlike other followers, was a threat to the Order by constantly, toward the end of Buddha's ministry, trying to usurp leadership of the *Saṃgha*. After several unsuccessful attempts to murder Buddha, Devadatta founded his own Order based on more austere religious practices. When his followers left him to return to Buddha's Order, he spit up blood and died.

Upāli. Belonging to a barber's family, *Upāli* also became a monk at Kapilavastu, eventually becoming a master of the *Vinaya* and recited it at the first council.

LAYMEN

Wealthy Patrons. *Anāthapiṇḍika* was a wealthy banker of *Śrāvastī* in *Kośala*. Upon going to see Buddha he was afforded the benefit of some Dharma instruction, whereby he became a lay follower. He desired to build

Buddha a monastery in Śrāvastī. Śāriputra helped select the site and the *Jetavana* (Grove of Prince Jeta) monastery was erected. From the twentieth year of his ministry, Buddha spent all the rainy seasons in Jetavana.

Viśākhā was a banker's daughter. Born into a Buddhist family, she was, at marriageable age, married into a family who followed a rival religious system. Although instructed by her father-in-law to support this new system and its followers, she rebelled, eventually bringing her father-in-law to Buddhism. Viśākhā excelled in performing social services for the Saṃgha. Some of her activities included feeding many monks each day, providing robes for the monks, and offering medicine to the sick.

Royal Patrons. *Bimbisāra* ruled *Magadha* from his chief city of *Rājagṛha*. Having become a disciple of Buddha after hearing a Dharma discourse, Bimbisāra donated the first monastery to the Saṃgha: *Veṇuvana ārāma* (Bamboo Grove Park). Bimbisāra was also responsible for Buddha's adoption of the twice monthly confessional meeting (*poṣadha*), suggesting these periodic meetings after observing other sects in the wanderers' community gathering three times each month to preach their respective doctrines, resulting in a net gain of adherents. Bimbisāra was eventually caught in a court intrigue involving his son, Prince *Ajātaśatru*, and Devadatta. Devadatta won the support of Prince Ajātaśatru, who imprisoned his father. After one of Devadatta's unsuccessful attempts to murder Buddha, Ajātaśatru relented and expressed faith in Buddha.

Unlike Bimbisāra, *Prasenajit*, king of Kośala, did not give unqualified support to Buddha, although he did make gifts to the Saṃgha. The Pāli Canon states that he became a lay follower of Buddha and was respected by the Buddhists as a patron of the religion.

MONASTIC LIFE

During the early history of Buddhism, it existed as simply another sect in the community of wanderers (*parivrājakas*). One custom which seems to have been observed by all these sects was that of suspending the wandering life during the rainy season. While the *Jain* and *Brāhmaṇical* wanderers seemed to have no fixed regulations regarding the observance of this seasonal custom, the Buddhists used this temporary settling down to live together in concord, establishing careful rules for the observance of the rainy season (*varṣā*), thus differentiating themselves from the rest of the wanderers' community and establishing the rudiments of Buddhist monastic life.

Buddhist rainy season settlements were generally of two types: *āvāsas* or dwelling places which were determined, constructed, and kept up by the monks themselves, and *ārāmas* or parks which were donated and maintained by some wealthy patron. Within the āvāsas or ārāmas, huts called *vihāras* were constructed for monks' residences. Later, when the monastic dwellings became more fully developed, the term vihāra came to designate the whole monastery. Monks' accommodations were of the simplest kind. The only furniture provided was a board to recline on and a mat for sitting *śayanāsana*). Most monasteries were built on the outskirts of towns and villages. Their close proximity to the town made alms procurement easy but provided enough isolation so that the monks in meditation would not be disturbed by the hustle and bustle of city life.

The three months of enforced communal living quickly made a profound impact on the Buddhist Saṃgha. Various institutions within the Saṃgha began to emerge to mold the monastic unit into a cohesive body. The recitation of the code of monastic law (*Prātimokṣa*) was adopted on a twice monthly basis. The preparation and distribution of robes (*kaṭhina*) took on collective features, eventually becoming a distinct ceremony, as did the "Invitation" or *Pravāraṇā* held at the end of the varṣā residence and dealing with purity during the rainy season. Initial and full ordination (*pravrajyā* and *upasaṃpadā*) were administered by the Saṃgha rather than individual monks.

The monastery as a unit, however, was by definition a self-limiting institution at the outset. At the end of each rainy season the monks were to abandon the settlement and begin wandering once again. Nevertheless, monks did tend to return to the same monastic residence year after year. Eventually, blending motivations of self-preservation and usefulness to their lay communities, monks ceased to wander at all. Thus individual saṃghas grew up, such as the saṃgha of Śrāvastī. Gradually, as the wandering life became a fiction, the Buddhists established themselves as a distinct group, bound by the teaching and discipline of the Buddha and committed to their own attainment of nirvāṇa, as well as the spiritual uplift of the laity; but with the rise of distinct saṃghas, the maintenance of commonality became acute. As each saṃgha became increasingly more individualized and removed geographically from other saṃghas, the first seed of sectarianism was sown.

GEOGRAPHIC DISPERSAL

During Buddha's lifetime his religion did not spread far. Most of his preaching was conducted in and around the great regions of *Magadha* and *Kośala*. Within Magadha three places seem to be most noteworthy. First, the capital of the region, *Rājagṛha*. Here Bimbisāra's patronage resulted in the first gift of an ārāma to the Saṃgha. Also in Magadha, *Pāṭaliputra* was later to become the stronghold capital of perhaps the greatest king of Indian history, *Aśoka*. Besides these two cities, on the outskirts of Rājagṛha was *Nālandā*, later to become the seat of one of the most important early Buddhist universities. Magadha also marks the birthplace of the religion as it was in *Bodh-Gayā* that Buddha's enlightenment was attained. In Buddha's early wanderings he gained his largest group of followers in Magadha, most notably the three Kāśyapas. Kośala, ruled by Prasenajit, is most important for its capital of Śrāvastī. Here Buddha not only received two of his foremost early patrons, Anāthapiṇḍika and Viśākhā, but spent the last twenty-five rainy seasons of his ministry. Within the kingdom of Kośala was Kapilavastu, Buddha's home.

To the east of Kośala and north of Magadha were several other kingdoms which, although being strongholds of Brāhmaṇical tradition, felt Buddha's impact: the *Licchavis*, the *Videhas*, and the *Koliyas*, to name a few. Also to the east was the region of *Aṅga*, mentioned occasionally in early Buddhist texts, as is the city of *Kauśāmbī*. The west and north seem to have been much less frequented by the early Buddhists. Consequently, we can see from the above that during its earliest history Buddhism spread within some rather closely defined limits. The wide dispersal, both within India and outside its borders, belongs to a period several hundred years (at least) after Buddha's death.

SUGGESTED READING

Dutt, Nalinaksha. *Early History of the Spread of Buddhism and the Buddhist Schools*, pp. 1–194.

Dutt, Sukumar. *Buddhist Monks and Monasteries in India*.

———. *Early Buddhist Monachism*.

Lamotte, Étienne. *Histoire du Bouddhisme Indien des origines à l'ère Śaka*, pp. 58–129.

4

Buddhist Councils and Divisions in the Order

Charles S. Prebish

INTRODUCTION

Before Buddha died he made two statements to the monks which were to haunt Buddhism through its first several hundred years. On the one hand, Buddha advised his followers that they could, if they wished, abolish all the lesser and minor precepts. Unfortunately, he never identified exactly which precepts he had in mind. On the other hand, Buddha instructed the monks to work out their own salvation with diligence. It was of course obvious that each of these statements, apart from causing the bewilderment of the members of the *Saṃgha*, lent itself to various interpretations, thus highlighting the necessity for periodic meetings of the Saṃgha to reaffirm what it perceived Buddha's intentions, in these nebulous statements, to be. Since the unity of the Saṃgha depended on tacit agreement with regard to these points of discipline and doctrine in general, the literature surrounding these periodic "councils" becomes of extreme importance for understanding the sectarian movement which ultimately beset Buddhism during its first several hundred years.

SOURCES OF COUNCIL LITERATURE

During the first 250 years of Buddhist religious history, four major councils seem to have taken place: at *Rājagṛha*, immediately following Buddha's death; at *Vaiśālī*, 100 years later; at *Pāṭaliputra*, approximately 50 years after the previous council; and at *Pāṭaliputra*, around 250 B.C.

Information on the Rājagṛha and Vaiśālī councils is derived from the concluding chapters in the *Skandhaka* portion of the *Vinayas* of the various Buddhist schools. For information on the first Pāṭaliputra council, we refer primarily to the *Mahāprajñāpāramitāśāstra*, sometimes attributed to the great Buddhist philosopher *Nāgārjuna*, the *Samayabhedoparacanacakra* of *Vasumitra*, and the *Nikāyabhedavibhaṅgavyākhyāna* of *Bhavya*, as well as a host of other texts composed by Buddhist scholars such as *Paramārtha*,

Ki-tsang, *Bu-ston*, *Hsüan-tsang*, and *Tāranātha*. For information on the second Pāṭaliputra council we refer, almost exclusively, to four Pāli texts: *Dīpavaṃsa*, *Mahāvaṃsa*, *Mahābodhivaṃsa*, and *Samantapāsādikā*.

THE FIRST COUNCIL (RĀJAGṚHA)

The events of the first council may be outlined as follows:

1. *Kāśyapa* appears and relates the details of his journey. When informed of Buddha's death, the arhants understand that all is indeed impermanent, but the nonenlightened disciples grieve. *Subhadra* alone is overjoyed with the Buddha's death, for he believes that the bhikṣus will no longer be bound to Gautama's rigid discipline. Kāśyapa thus sets forth the notion to chant the *Dharma* and *Vinaya*.
2. Kāśyapa is selected to elect the attending monks and 499 are chosen. The monks plea for *Ānanda*, who has not yet attained arhantship, to be admitted. Kāśyapa reconsiders, Ānanda is included, and the total number is brought to 500.
3. A place for the council is sought and Rājagṛha is decided upon. The 500 monks agree to spend the rainy season there with no other monks in attendance.
4. The first month of the rainy season is spent repairing buildings, etc.
5. During the night previous to the convocation of the council, Ānanda becomes an arhant.
6. The council begins with Kāśyapa questioning *Upāli* on the Vinaya and Ānanda on the Dharma. Ānanda relates that Buddha assented to abolishing the lesser and minor precepts, but Kāśyapa, in fear of the Saṃgha falling into disrepute, decides to accept all of Buddha's preaching unconditionally.
7. Ānanda is reproached for several faults. Only reluctantly he confesses his transgressions.
8. *Purāṇa*, a monk who had been traveling, arrives at Rājagṛha as the council is concluding. He is asked to become one with the council, but refuses, stating that he chooses to retain the doctrine and discipline as he remembers it to have been spoken by the Buddha.
9. Ānanda relates that Buddha declared that after his death, the *Brahmadaṇḍa* penalty (i.e., social excommunication) was to be imposed on *Channa*, his childhood charioteer for renouncing the world like his master. When Ānanda finds this monk and imposes the penalty on him, Channa becomes an arhant, at which time the penalty is suppressed.
10. The account of the council concludes and is referred to as the *Vinayasaṃgīti*, "chanting of the Vinaya," or also as the council of 500.

In trying to interpret the meaning of this first council, at least six major points may be noted.

1. In terms of the essential function of the council we can delineate:
   a. *Mythic*—renewal of the cosmic and social order.
   b. *Practical*—affirmation of authority and solidarity now that the charismatic leader is dead.
   c. *Purification*—establish main intent by punishing both Ānanda and Channa for their transgressions; as a corollary, monastic law procedure is given a precedent with a specific penalty imposed on Channa.
2. Rājagṛha seems to be chosen because it was the capital of Magadha, a stronghold of early Buddhism where the monks could find adequate food and shelter.
3. In some accounts, as indicated above, Kāśyapa is the leader of the council, apparently chosen on the basis of his personal merit as a Buddhist. Other accounts, however, indicate the first arhant, *Ājñāta Kauṇḍinya*, as the leader, leaving the uncertainty as to whether merit or seniority was of prime interest.
4. The number of monks in attendance (500) is both artificial and convenient. The method of selection is not at all clear.
5. The compilation of the canon, apparently the chief motive for the council, is not described in any of the accounts. Several schools seem to compile a canon of two parts: Vinaya and Sūtras, while several other schools add the Abhidharma to these two.
6. The historicity of the council as described is questioned by almost all scholars. That a small group of Buddha's intimate disciples gathered after his death is not unlikely, but a council in the grand style described in the various texts is almost certainly a fiction.

THE SECOND COUNCIL (VAIŚĀLĪ)

The events of the second council may be outlined as follows:

1. About a century after the Buddha's parinirvāṇa, the *vṛjiputraka bhikṣus* at Vaiśālī allowed the practice of ten points.
2. On arriving in Vaiśālī, *Yaśas*, a monk, observes these practices, protests because he believes them to be unlawful, and is sentenced to a punishment requiring him to obtain the forgiveness of the offended parties.
3. He intends to comply but changes his mind and begins to convince the laymen that these monks are at fault.
4. When the monks learn of Yaśas's renewed actions, they banish him.

5. Yaśas goes to *Kauśāmbī*, explains the ten points to a learned monk named *Saṃbhūta Śāṇavāsin*, and enlists his support.
6. Additional support is sought from a venerable, well-respected monk named *Revata* who is also won over.
7. The vṛjiputraka bhikṣus, however, also gain adherents. The matter of the ten points is brought to a head, both parties deciding that a council at Vaiśālī is necessary for the resolution of the problem.
8. A new episode is recounted with Revata carrying on a dialogue with *Sarvagāmin*, an elder monk of Vaiśālī who had Ānanda as his teacher.
9. Śāṇavāsin questions Sarvagāmin on the ten points with the outcome being convocation of the council.
10. The council begins with Revata as its president. Sarvagāmin is questioned on each of the ten points, rejecting them in turn on the basis of various scriptures. When the ten points have been sufficiently explained, and condemned, the council is concluded, having been referred to as the chanting of Vinaya or the recital of 700 (the monks who attended).

In trying to interpret the second council, at least four major points may be noted.

1. The ten points in question (according to the Pāli tradition) are preserving salt in a horn; taking food when the shadow is beyond two fingers wide; after finishing one meal, going to another town for another meal; holding several confession ceremonies within the same monastic boundary; confirming a monastic act in an incomplete assembly; carrying out an act improperly, justifying it by its habitual performance in this way; after eating, drinking unchurned milk which is somewhere between the states of milk and curd; drinking unfermented wine; using a mat without a border; and accepting gold and silver.
2. Many scholars trace the first great schism (*mahābheda*) in Buddhism to this council, stating that it is here that the *Mahāsāṃghikas* and *Sthaviras* separate into two distinct groups. In other words, the Mahāsāṃghikas are characterized as the laxist disciplinary group. In their monastic confessional code or *Prātimokṣa*, the Mahāsāṃghikas only mention the tenth point. In fact, however, the other nine points are condemned elsewhere in their Vinaya. This has caused several scholars to conclude that accepting gold and silver was the only issue at this council, and since no Vinaya mentions any schism, that the great schism must have occurred later.
3. Despite the fact that the council smoothed over the existing differences in the Saṃgha, it appears that several tensions were beginning to make themselves felt; laxist versus rigorist tendencies, monastic versus lay

matters, and, more generally, the sacred versus the profane aspects of life.
4. Almost all scholars agree that this council was a historical event.

THE "SECOND" SECOND COUNCIL [PĀṬALIPUTRA]

The events of the "second" second council may be outlined as follows:

1. Some years after the second council (37 seems to be the figure most often agreed upon) the tensions outlined above become more severe.
2. By this time, a monk named *Mahādeva* was deprecating the arhant, stating that arhants were subject to temptation, may have a residue of ignorance, may have doubts, gain knowledge through others' help, and gain the path by an exclamation.
3. Coupled with monastic laxity, the problem of maintaining unity within these two factions was acute, and it was decided to hold a council mediated by the king of the time, *Mahāpadma Nanda*, in his capital of Pāṭaliputra.
4. Mahāpadma Nanda, being unqualified to make religious judgments, had but one choice open to him: to assemble the two parties and count the partisans in each.
5. With the vote taken, the majority party chose an appropriate name, indicative of their victory: Great Group-ists or *Mahāsāṃghikas*. The minority party, espousing their adherence to the "orthodox" religion, referred to themselves as Elders or *Sthaviras*.
6. Each group withdrew, tightening and strengthening their positions by modifying their canons.

In trying to interpret the "second" second council, at least five major points may be noted.

1. All the early sources consider this event the first true schism in the Saṃgha, separating into two groups.
2. Within given limits, all the early sources agree on the date.
3. The schism was due to Mahādeva's five theses which, although representing doctrinal issues, have direct bearing on monastic discipline (e.g., temptation).
4. The event is unquestionably an historic event.
5. Once the initial schism took place, each group, in the course of time, would fall prey to further internal subdivisions, ultimately resulting in the traditional eighteen *Hīnayāna* schools.

THE THIRD COUNCIL (PĀṬALIPUTRA).

The events of the third council may be outlined as follows:

1. During the seventeenth year of the reign of Aśoka, the Saṃgha was threatened by heretics entering the Order and degrading the Dharma.
2. A famous monk, *Moggaliputta Tissa*, is chosen to preside over a council of 1,000 monks in Aśoka's capital of Pāṭaliputra.
3. All the offending viewpoints are refuted, finally concluding that Buddha was a *Vibhajyavādin* (distinctionist).
4. The offenders were expelled from the capital.
5. The views discussed were recorded in an Abhidharma text, the *Kathāvatthu*.

In trying to interpret the third council, at least three major points may be noted.

1. Three edicts of Aśoka, those at *Sāñchī*, *Sārnāth*, and *Kauśāmbī*, clearly indicate a severe threat to the Buddhist community.
2. Aśoka, traditionally regarded as a pious Buddhist ruler, personally intervenes, to purify the Saṃgha.
3. Scholars react to this council, admittedly historical, in one of two ways: either to declare it simply as a "party meeting" among the Vibhajyavādins (later to give rise to the *Theravādins*), or to view it as the schism separating yet another school, the *Sarvāstivādins*, from the Sthavira proper.

SUGGESTED READING

Bareau, André. *Les premiers conciles bouddhiques.*

Demiéville, Paul. "À propos du concile de Vaiśālī," *T'oung Pao*, 40 (1951): 239–96.

Dutt, Nalinaksha. "The Second Buddhist Council," *Indian Historical Quarterly*, 35 (March 1959): 45–56.

Franke, R.O. "The Buddhist Councils as Rājagaha and Vesālī as Alleged in Cullavagga XI, XII" *Journal of the Pali Text Society* (1908): 1–80.

Hofinger, M. *Étude sur la concile du Vaiśālī.*

La Vallée Poussin, Louis de. "The Buddhist Councils." *Indian Antiquary*, 37 (1908): 1–18, 81–106.

Prebish, Charles. "A Review of Scholarship on the Buddhist Councils," *Journal of Asian Studies*, 33, 2 (February 1974): 239–54.

Przyluski, Jean. *Le Concile de Rājagṛha.*

5

Aśoka and the Missionary Activity of the Buddhists

Stefan Anacker

THE CONVERSION OF AŚOKA AND HIS REIGN OF DHARMA

The *Mauryan* Emperor *Aśoka* (reign: ca. 269–232 B.C.), ruler of most of north and peninsular India even at his accession, continued wars of expansion until the bloodiness of the conquest of *Kaliṅga* impelled him to become a Buddhist lay disciple (cf. Rock Edict No. XIII). Consequently, he embarked upon a "Reign of Dharma," attempting to inculcate moral precepts such as non-harming, respect for all religious teachers, and noncovetousness. Even Aśoka himself renounced all future use of force. He urged moderation in spending and accumulation of wealth, kind treatment of servants and slaves, tolerance of all religious sects, prohibition of the slaughter of animals, and various other maxims, all carved as edicts on numerous rocks and cave walls throughout his vast realm. He set up a system of giving donations to the needy, ordered the planting of shade and medicinal trees throughout the empire, and designated the digging of wells at fixed intervals. He appointed officers, called *dharma-mahāmātras* or Superintendents of Dharma, for the propagation of religions, and arranged for annual, triennial, and quinquennial preaching tours. He realized the effectiveness of propaganda over legislation, as shown in Pillar Edict No. VII, and himself preached the Dharma on occasion. He recommended certain texts of Dharma to the Saṃgha, some of which have versions in the present Pāli Canon (cf. Minor Rock Edict No. III). He arranged for the extensive enlarging and embellishing of *stūpas* (cf. Pillar Inscription No. II), and though particularly interested in Buddhism, he also patronized the *Jains* and *Ajīvakas*, and advocated complete tolerance.

THE MISSIONS

According to traditional accounts, corroborated in part by epigraphical evidence, Aśoka sent missionaries of Buddhism to *Kaśmīr*, *Karnataka*, *North Kanara*, *Koṅkan*, *Mahārāṣṭra*, the *Northwest Regions*, the *Himalayan*

Regions, *Suvarṇabhūmi* (probably here meaning Burma—the Talaing Buddhist community of Thaton claims its origin with Aśoka's mission), and *Ceylon* (this mission being headed by Aśoka's son, or brother, *Mahinda*). It is through these missionary efforts of Aśoka that Buddhism first becomes an "international" religion, and they served as a model for later Indian kings to send missionaries across the sea (e.g., *Ikṣvāku Vīrapuruṣadatta's* missionaries to Ceylon and Burma).

THE THIRD COUNCIL

Aśoka is said to have convened a council of all Buddhist communities, prompted by his preceptor *Upagupta* (also known as *Moggaliputta Tissa*), around 250 B.C. At this council, those holding heretical doctrines were expelled from the orthodox community of Buddhists at *Pāṭaliputra* (Aśoka's capital), thus indicating that Aśoka favored the traditional *Sthaviras* (or *Vibhajyavādins*). The expelled group migrated to the northwest and are thought by many to be the forerunners of the *Sarvāstivādin* sect of Buddhism.

THE LEGENDS OF AṢOKA

The *Aśokāvadāna* (ca. third century A.D.?) is the main source of the cluster of traditional stories concerning Aśoka. It makes much of the previous cruelty of the emperor, and how he was first attracted to Buddhism when a monk thrown into a cauldron refused to die. Other famous stories collected in the text include the account of how Aśoka converted his heretical brother *Vītāśoka*, how he built and embellished 84,000 stūpas, how his wife *Tiṣyarakṣitā* loved and finally hated her own son *Kuṇāla*, and how at the end of his reign the treasury was finally closed to Aśoka, as he had given away almost all of the realm's wealth to religious foundations. Thus he died in destitution.

The great question mark regarding Aśoka is how we can tally the traditional Buddhist accounts of this great Indian king, marking him as perhaps the most forceful ruler in terms of his service to the religion, with the accounts left by Aśoka himself in his various rock and pillar edicts—accounts which seem to place no special emphasis on Buddhism.

SUGGESTED READING

Gokhale, B. *Buddhism and Aśoka.*

Mookerji, R. *Aśoka.* Includes translations of the edicts.

Przyluski, Jean, tr. *La légende de l'empereur Aśoka dans les textes indiens et chinois.* Includes translations of the Aśokāvadāna.

Thapar, Romila. *Aśoka and the Decline of the Mauryas.*

6

Doctrines of the Early Buddhists

Charles S. Prebish

INTRODUCTION

The doctrines of the earliest Buddhists are not so easy to pinpoint as one might initially suspect. During Buddha's lifetime no methodical, written records were kept, and we owe whatever knowledge of these early doctrines that we have to a rather nebulous oral tradition, fraught with all the pitfalls inherent in this method of transmission. In spite of the hazards basic to investigating this early Buddhism, we can include here a discussion of those doctrines which seem to be fundamental: the Four Noble Truths (*ārya satyas*), the Three Marks (*lakṣaṇas*), the Five Aggregates (*skandhas*), Dependent Origination (*pratītya-samutpāda*), and the Stages of Sanctification.

THE FOUR NOBLE TRUTHS

When Buddha preached the first sermon, the *Dharmacakrapravartana-sūtra*, or "Discourse on the Turning of the Wheel of the Law," to his five ascetic friends near Benares, the Four Noble Truths (*ārya satyas*) formed the major substance of his instruction.

The first of the noble truths is that of suffering (*duḥkha*). Buddha states, "Birth is suffering, old age is suffering, disease is suffering, death is suffering, association is suffering, separation from what is pleasant is suffering, not obtaining that which one desires is suffering .... " By this rather negative statement, Buddha does not summarily dismiss all pleasure and happiness. Rather, he means to point out the transiency of all mental and physical pleasures. Consequently, suffering may be viewed as of three types: *duḥkha-duḥkhatā*—ordinary mental and physical suffering; *vipariṇāma-duḥkhatā*—suffering resulting from change (or pleasure transformed into suffering); *saṃskāra-duḥkhatā*—suffering due to conditioned states. These three types of suffering each have their manifestation in the three *lakṣaṇas*, or marks, described below.

The second of the noble truths is the cause (*samudaya*) of suffering. Buddha states the cause of suffering to be "that which is craving (*tṛṣṇā*) leading to rebirth, connected with pleasure and lust, finding delight here and there, namely: craving for sensual desires (*kāmatṛṣṇā*), craving for becoming (*bhava-tṛṣṇā*), and craving for nonexistence (*vibhavatṛṣṇā*)." The second truth is enhanced by Buddha's explanation of causation, to be discussed below.

The third of the noble truths is the cessation (*nirodha*) of suffering. In other words, through the proper understanding and discipline, suffering can be uprooted and *nirvāṇa* attained. Two types of cessation are outlined: *sa-upādiśeṣa nirodha*—cessation with a remnant, or that state experienced when an adept removes all his impurities in experiencing nirvāṇa while still in the body; *an-upādiśeṣa nirodha*—cessation without a remnant, or that which is attained when the enlightened adept lays down his body.

The fourth of the noble truths is the eightfold path (*aṣṭāṅgika mārga*) leading to the cessation of suffering. The eight steps are:

1. Right Understanding (*samyak dṛṣṭi*)—an understanding of the four noble truths. Dṛṣṭi may be alternatively translated here as views. In any case, the reasoning is clearly circular.
2. Right Thought (*samyak saṃkalpa*)—thought that is free from lust, ill-will, and cruelty. What is intended here is a proper "shaping together" (saṃkalpa) of one's mental framework.
3. Right Speech (*samyak vācā*)—essentially refraining from improper speech consisting of engaging in falsehood, malicious talk, or harsh and/or frivolous speech.
4. Right Action (*samyak karmānta*)—three primary actions to be avoided: killing, stealing, and general misconduct. It is here that the ethical dimension of Buddhism is perhaps most keenly felt.
5. Right Livelihood (*samyak ājīva*)—refraining from earning a living by such means as the use of astrology, magic spells, or interpreting dreams and omens, acting as a go-between, officiating at marriage ceremonies, and other improper careers (such as butcher).
6. Right Effort (*samyak vyāyāma*)—making an effort to cleanse one's mind of all existing evil thoughts, preventing new evil thoughts from arising, and, on the positive side, maintaining and increasing good thoughts.
7. Right Mindfulness (*samyak smṛti*)—maintaining mindfulness of one's body and mind, as well as of worldly things.
8. Right Concentration (*samyak samādhi*)—essentially, practicing meditation culminating in the four *dhyānas* or trance states, to be discussed later.

These eight members may be more comprehensible if they are organized into the following three main groups: *śīla* or morality, steps 3, 4, 5; *samādhi* or concentration, steps 6, 7, 8; and *prajñā* or wisdom, steps 1, 2. *Buddhaghosa*, a great *Theravādin* exegete, has stated that we may think of śīla and samādhi as the legs of Buddhism, while prajñā is its body.

THE THREE MARKS OF EXISTENCE

In his second discourse to the ascetics at Benares, Buddha preached a sermon which has come to be known as the *Anātmalakṣaṇa-sūtra* or "Discourse on the Marks of Not-Self." The main doctrinal content of this sermon, however, included not only statements about the self (*ātman*), but also about impermanence (*anitya*) and suffering (*duḥkha*).

The first mark (*lakṣaṇa*) is *anātman*, or not-self. Axiomatic to the *Brāhmaṇical* religion of the time was the notion that each living creature possessed a self which was pure, subtle, and eternal, and which carried *karmic* residues from one existence to the next. Buddha, recognizing the problems inherent in a belief in the existence in a self (*satkāyadṛṣṭi*), attacked the concept in two ways. First, he emphasized the necessity for nonattachment in the quest for nirvāṇa, eliminating the possibility of clinging to the ātman (i.e., if one was to progress toward nirvāṇa). Second, he stressed the illogic of the concept. How could something pure, subtle, and eternal (the ātman) associate itself with something as impure, gross, and impermanent as the body? In addition, for very early Buddhism there was only one unconditioned, permanent state: nirvāṇa. If ātman was eternal, this would result in a contradiction. Nevertheless, Buddhism accepted the notion of rebirth, and in spite of an abundance of literature on the subject, has never been able to explain the transference of karmic residues very satisfactorily. The manner in which they attempted an explanation is clear. They applied the law of dependent origination (*pratītya-samutpāda*) explained below. In the Buddhists' formulation of dependent origination, *saṃskāras*, or "mental constituents," are said to result from ignorance of the truth. They are, in effect, the karmic residues transmitted from one life to the next. They are, at the moment of death (in an unenlightened person), transmitted to the "rebirth consciousness" (*pratisandhi-vijñāna*), an artificial *Abhidharma* cover-term, and rebirth then occurs in a flowing stream (*santāna*). Of course this is dangerously close to positing rebirth consciousness as self, but with a different title. In addition, stream or santāna is only a metaphor to accommodate talk (within the realm of "ordinary" language) about the self. In fact, even for the unenlightened person, nothing is solved by this explanation. Nor is the question answered in the famous *Milindapañha* ("The Questions of King

Milinda") in which the clever and able monk *Nāgasena* asks King *Menander* whether the lamp which burns during one watch of the night produces the *same* flame during the middle or last watch of the night. When the wise king responds that the flame is not the same, Nāgasena replies, "Just so, Great King, is the continuity of states connected. One arises, another ceases; the continuity is as if simultaneous. . . ." The process is not explained. Further, the flame in the second watch is not the same but not different from the flame in the first watch. It is this perplexing problem which may explain why, in early Buddhism, a sect such as the *Pudgalavādins*, who posited an entity not unlike the Brāhmaṇical ātman (called the *pudgala* or "person"), gained a large measure of popularity in spite of its apparently heretical stance on this point.

The second mark of existence is impermanence (*anitya*). Buddhist doctrine divides all things (*dharmas*) into two categories, conditioned (*saṃskṛta*) and unconditioned (*asaṃskṛta*). For the earliest Buddhists, the only unconditioned dharma is nirvāṇa. As for the rest of existence, each dharma is subject to change in every moment of its existence, and thus is impermanent. Even each moment can be analyzed into origin (*utpatti*), duration (*sthiti*), and decay (*vināśa*). Consequently, only that which is permanent, unchanging (i.e., nirvāṇa) is worthy of our striving. The problem, of course, becomes more complicated with the rise of the various Buddhist schools, several of which posit more than one asaṃskṛta dharma.

The third mark of existence is suffering (*duḥkha*), and is essentially an expanded restatement of the first noble truth.

THE FIVE AGGREGATES

If all things are without self, what is it that we refer to as a "being" or "individual"? According to Buddha, all individuals are composed of five aggregates or *skandhas*. Literally, skandha means "heap" or "bundle," so each individual represents only a mass of these physical and mental bundles or energies. According to early Buddhism, there are two basic kinds of skandha, the physical (*rūpa*) and mental (*nāma*). Nāma is further subdivided into four groups to yield a total of five skandhas (*pañcaskandha*), attachment to which is described by Buddha to be suffering.

The first skandha, that of form (*rūpa*), denotes the four great elements (*mahābhūtas*)—earth (*pṛthivī*), water (*āp*), fire (*tejas*), and air (*vāyu*)—and their derivatives, the five sense organs and their physical counterparts. Thus the rūpa skandha includes all material objects of the past, present, and future, as well as that which is both internal and external, and that which is either gross or subtle.

The second skandha, that of feeling (*vedanā*), derives from the contact of our physical and mental organs with objects in the external world. All things experienced in the world are identified as good, bad, or neutral.

The third skandha, that of perception (*saṃjñā*), determines the characteristics of an object. Like the second skandha, it results from the contact of our physical and mental organs with the external world, and may be categorized as good, bad, or neutral. It differs from the second skandha in that it makes that which is felt known through its characteristics. Certainly, without perception there would be no consciousness.

The fourth skandha, that of mental constituents (*saṃskāra*), denotes the volitional aspects of the individual. Buddha has interpreted *karma* to represent volition (*cetanā*), and although feeling and perception represent the contact of our physical organs with the external world (just as saṃskāra does), they do not represent volitional actions and consequently do not produce karmic effects. This skandha, on the other hand, through volitional actions such as hatred and ignorance, produces karmic effects. We might say, then, that the skandha of mental constituents puts the mind in action.

The fifth skandha, that of consciousness (*vijñāna*), is the resultant activity when our physical and mental organs come into contact with objects in the external world. Thus we find six essential consciousnesses: eye, ear, nose, tongue, body, and mind. It should be emphasized that consciousness is not identification of an object but only awareness of it. The identification of an object (e.g., determining from the taste of a substance that it is salt) is a function of the third skandha.

Since practical Buddhism is so much concerned with meditation, and consequently the mind, as were later scholastic Buddhists, the latter four skandhas were of primary interest to each of these groups. Within the four skandhas describing the mind, consciousness became of particular interest, with various schools positing many individual kinds of specific consciousnesses.

DEPENDENT ORIGINATION

Dependent Origination (*pratītya-samutpāda*) or Buddha's theory of causation was meditated on by the Tathāgata, forward and backward, shortly after he attained enlightenment. In seeking to illustrate the dynamic, relational aspect of all existent things, this theory of causation is presented as twelve "links" (*nidānas*), arranged in a circle, and related to each other in the following way: "Because of this, that becomes; because of that, something else becomes"; etc. In other words, employing the actual links: because of ignorance (*avidyā*), mental constituents (*saṃskāras*) arise; because of mental constituents, consciousness (*vijñāna*) arises; because of consciousness, name and form (*nāmarūpa*) arises; because of name and form, the six sense organs (*ṣaḍāyatana*) arise; because of the six sense organs, contact (*sparśa*) arises; because of contact, feeling (*vendanā*) arises; because of feeling, craving (*tṛṣṇā*) arises; because of craving, grasping (*upādāna*) arises; because of grasping, becoming (*bhava*) arises; because of becoming, birth (*jāti*) arises; because of birth, old age and death (*jarāmaraṇa*) arise. Due to old age and death, ignorance arises and thus the wheel begins again. The circle of existence has no beginning or end or, for that matter, any reference to temporal or spatial matters. In striving to attain nirvāṇa, three links seem to be given great emphasis by the Buddha: the overcoming of ignorance, craving, and grasping. To eliminate these allows one, experientially, to break the causal cycle and taste the fruits of nirvāṇa. In any case, the theory of dependent origination dispels notions of the creation of the universe by a God or gods, predetermination, atomistic theories, etc.

STAGES OF SANCTIFICATION

In passing from existence as a common person (*pṛthagjana*) to experiencing nirvāṇa, several stages can be delineated. The first task is to become a member of the family of spiritually elect noble personages (*ārya pudgalas*). To do this one must first make himself fit to commence the practices that will make him an ārya pudgala. Even to begin this quest is significant, resulting in the stage of *gotrabhū* or member of the family (of āryas). From here, depending on temperament and capability, one of two courses is open: either the follower in faith (*śraddhānusārin*), for those with mild faculties, or the follower of Dharma (*Dharmānusārin*), for those of keen intellect. By progressively gaining insight into each of the four noble truths, one becomes, at the culmination of the process, a *srotāpanna* or "streamwinner," the first class of the ārya pudgalas. Having abandoned totally belief in the self, doubts about the Three Jewels (i.e., Buddha, Dharma, Saṃgha), and belief in the efficacy of rituals, the streamwinner is assured of no bad rebirths. All the while working to overcome the impurities or outflows (*āsravas*), he then becomes a *sakṛdāgāmin*, or "once returner," assured of enlightenment within one more lifetime. Progressing further still, the adept becomes an *anāgāmin* or "non-returner," assured of enlightenment during his current lifetime. When all negative qualities have been eradicated and the adept is pure in all respects, he is able to experientially realize nirvāṇa, thus becoming an *arhant*, and establishing himself as a true saint in Buddhism.

SUGGESTED READING

Dutt, Nalinaksha. *Early Monastic Buddhism*, pp. 133–47, 193–271.

Lamotte, Étienne. *Histoire du Bouddhisme Indien des origines à l'ère Śaka*, pp. 25–58.

Rāhula, Walpola. *What the Buddha Taught.*

Sangharakshita, Bhikshu. *A Survey of Buddhism*, pp. 100–11, 118–35, 171–87.

7

Major Schools of the Early Buddhists: Mahāsāṃghika

Charles S. Prebish

HISTORY

It has been noted earlier that at the time of the first of two Buddhist councils held at *Pāṭaliputra* during the reign of *Mahāpadma Nanda* (approximately 346 B.C.), the Buddhist Saṃgha divided itself into two groups, the *Sthaviras* and the *Mahāsāṃghikas*. Historically, our information on the second of these groups is scanty. The records of Chinese pilgrims who traveled to India (*Fa-hien* A.D. 399–414, *Hsüan-tsang* A.D. 629–645, *I-tsing* A.D. 671–695) seem to indicate that the Mahāsāṃghikas flourished in *Magadha* in general and Pāṭaliputra in particular. Views coincident with specific Mahāsāṃghika doctrines are recorded in the Pāli Abhidharma text of the *Kathāvatthu*, said to have been composed around 250 B.C. as a result of the council convened under *Aśoka*, and the phrase "some Mahāsāṃghikas" also appears in the text. Epigraphical evidence, dating as early as 120 B.C., has been found in the ancient city of *Mathurā*. As for the rest, it can only be inferred from a careful reading of the texts of the schools themselves and the secondary sources focusing on Buddhist sectarianism. Nevertheless, given certain limits, we can state with assurance that within several centuries the Mahāsāṃghikas divided internally, resulting in several subsects, the most important of which are the *Ekavyāvahārikas*, *Lokottaravādins*, *Gokulikas*, *Bahuśrutīyas*, *Prajñaptivādins*, and *Caitīyas*.

LITERATURE

The canon of the Mahāsāṃghikas includes:

A. *Vinaya Piṭaka*—Basket of Discipline

B. *Sūtra Piṭaka*—Basket of Discourses: 1. *Dīrgha Āgama*—Long Discourses; 2. *Madhyama Āgama*—Middle Length Discourses; 3. *Saṃyukta Āgama*—Linked Discourses; 4. *Ekottara Āgama*—Increased by One Discourses; 5. *Kṣudraka Āgama*—Miscellaneous Discourses

C. *Abhidharma Piṭaka*—Basket of Higher Philosophy

D. *Saṃyukta* or *Kṣudraka Piṭaka*—Basket of Miscellaneous Matters
E. *Dhāraṇī Piṭaka*—Basket of Mystical Formulas

Little of this canon is preserved today. We are told that Fa-hien discovered a manuscript of the Mahāsāṃghika Vinaya at Pāṭaliputra in A.D. 414 which he translated into Chinese. In 1934 several Sanskrit Vinaya fragments of this school were discovered in Tibet by Rāhula Sāṅkṛtyāyana. Of the Sūtra Piṭaka, only the Ekottara Āgama exists, in Chinese translation, and none of the other texts mentioned above are extant, although Fa-hien is recorded to also have found the Abhidharma piṭaka at Pāṭaliputra. We do have one complete text, the *Mahāvastu* (in Buddhist Hybrid Sanskrit), claiming to be the Vinaya of the Lokottaravādin subsect, but actually representing a detailed account of the life of the Buddha, as well as a storehouse for many doctrinal matters. Most scholars agree that the actual linguistic medium of the Mahāsāṃghikas was Prakrit, and on examination of the Sanskrit texts that have come down to us, this hypothesis seems likely.

DOCTRINES

We have already seen that the Mahāsāṃghikas held a thoroughly progressive view with regard to the arhants. They also represent the first school of Buddhism to speculate about the nature of the Buddha. The orthodox Buddhism of the time held Buddha to be a human being, but one who had distinguished himself among men by attaining full enlightenment, and as a corollary of this complete perfect enlightenment (*samyaksaṃbuddha*), omniscience. The docetic speculations of the Mahāsāṃghikas were founded in statements made by the Buddha:

He who sees the Dharma, sees me;
He who sees me, sees the Dharma.
Or, Victorious over all things, I am omniscient,
Unstained among all things,
Abandoning everything, released through the destruction of craving,
By knowing for myself, to whom should I point?

There is no teacher for me,
One like me does not exist in the world with its gods,
There is no one equal to me.

As a result of statements such as these, the Mahāsāṃghikas held Buddha to be supramundane and possessed of all perfections (*pāramitās*). As a result of his past stock of meritorious actions (*puṇyakarma*) and current attainments, they speculated that, for example, Buddha's material body was unlimited, as was his length of life and divine power. He could comprehend all things in a moment and was always plunged in meditation, never sleeping or dreaming. This speculation set the stage for the later development of the *Mahāyāna*, expressed first in the *Prajñāpāramitā-sūtras.*

In view of the previously mentioned deprecation of the arhant ideal, the Mahāsāṃghikas offered a new interpretation of the path to the goal. In orthodox doctrine there was only one *Bodhisattva*, or "Buddha to be" Siddhārtha Gautama. The Mahāsāṃghikas, however, note that others can follow this path and thus, in the Mahāvastu, establish a ten-step path for Bodhisattvas to follow. Although the stages outlined in the Mahāvastu do not all coincide with the ten Mahāyāna stages (*bhūmis*), they do represent a fundamental point of departure from which the Mahāyāna developed its mature Bodhisattva doctrine, emphasizing that all sentient creatures may strive for and attain complete perfect enlightenment.

Apart from some rather sophisticated notions concerning the doctrine of the act and the nature of Buddha's teaching, the above represents the main contributions of the Mahāsāṃghikas to early Buddhist doctrinal development. We can unequivocally state that in setting forth these progressive doctrinal statements, in emphasizing an attempt to live by the spirit of the law rather than its letter, monastically, the Mahāsāṃghikas played an extremely significant role in shaping the future of Buddhism.

SUGGESTED READING

Bareau, André. *Les Sectes Bouddhiques du Petit Véhicule*, pp. 56–109.

Dutt, Nalinaksha. *Buddhist Sects in India*, pp. 60–128.

———. *Early History of the Spread of Buddhism and the Buddhist Schools*, pp. 225–248.

8

Major Schools of the Early Buddhists: Theravāda

Charles S. Prebish

HISTORY

The *Theravāda* school of Buddhism, flourishing today in Ceylon, Burma, Thailand, Laos, and Cambodia, represents both the only surviving school of so-called *Hīnayāna* Buddhism and that school about which we have the most information. The name of the school, Theravāda in Pāli, corresponds exactly to the Sanskrit *Sthaviravāda*, the name of one of the two great schools separating at the time of the great schism around 346 B.C., and this small but significant detail has caused scholars more than a fair share of confusion. The logical tendency is to simply equate the two schools, but this is not the case. By the time of the council held by *Aśoka* around 250 B.C., the Sthavira school had split itself into primarily three groups: the *Vātsīputrīya-Sammatīyas*, the *Sarvāstivādins*, and the *Vibhajyavādins*. In the course of time (perhaps 100 years) the Vibhajyavādin school splintered into two primary schools: the *Mahīśāsakas* and the *Theravādins*.

One must then ask how this school managed to implement itself so strongly throughout Asia. King Aśoka, in his missionary zeal, sent his son *Mahinda* to the island of *Laṅkā* or Ceylon, establishing Buddhism as the state religion. Apparently, the form of Buddhism exported was the Vibhajyavāda. Ceylon, however, was constantly threatened in its early history by *Tamil* invasions from South India. When King *Duṭṭhagāmiṇī* of Ceylon, during the first century B.C., finally drove the Tamils from the island, Theravāda emerged and consolidated itself into a distinct school, dominant on the island. It is most probably this isolation in Ceylon which allowed Theravāda to prosper, while its continental counterpart, the Mahīśāsakas, eventually died out in India.

LITERATURE

The canon of the Theravādins includes:

A. *Vinaya Piṭaka*—Basket of Discipline: 1. *Suttavibhaṅga*—Analysis of a Sutta, including *Mahāvibhaṅga*—Great (or Monks') Analysis and *Bhikkhunīvibhaṅga*—Nuns' Analysis; 2. *Khandhaka*—Division, including *Mahāvagga*—Great Section and *Cullavagga*—Small Section; 3. *Parivāra*—The Accessory.

B. *Sutta Piṭaka*—Basket of Discourses: 1. *Dīgha Nikāya*—Long Discourses; 2. *Majjhima Nikāya*—Middle Length Discourses; 3. *Saṃyutta Nikāya*—Linked Discourses; 4. *Aṅguttara Nikāya*—Increased by One Discourses; 5. *Khuddaka Nikāya*—Miscellaneous Discourses.

C. *Abhidhamma Piṭaka*—Basket of Higher Philosophy: 1. *Dhammasaṅgaṇi*—Explication of Dhammas; 2. *Vibhaṅga*—Divisions; 3. *Dhātukathā*—Discourse on the Elements; 4. *Puggalapaññatti*—Descriptions of Persons; 5. *Kathāvatthu*—Subjects of Discussion; 6. *Yamaka*—Pairs; 7. *Paṭṭhāna*—Causal Relations.

We are fortunate to have the entire *Tripiṭaka* of the Theravādins preserved in Pāli, as presented above. The texts were committed to writing for the first time during the reign of *Vaṭṭagāmaṇī* in Ceylon (29–17 B.C.). Apart from the canonical literature of the Theravādins, their school provides us with a rich and full commentatorial tradition. For each text of the Pāli Canon there is a major commentary, usually attributed to either *Buddhaghosa* or his successor *Dhammapāla*, and a host of subcommentaries. In addition, there are several texts which serve as compendiums of doctrine, such as Buddhaghosa's *Visuddhimagga* ("Path of Purity") or the *Milindapañha* ("The Questions of King Milinda"), recording conversations between the learned monk *Nāgasena* and the Bactrian king *Menander*.

DOCTRINES

While accepting all the early doctrines outlined in lecture six, the Theravādins make a number of specific pronouncements with regard to items of contention between the various schools. With respect to Gautama the Buddha, the Theravādins maintain and stress his humanity. Although representing an example of perfection, he is only a man possessed of a physical body (*Rūpakāya*). The *Dharmakāya*, later to be metaphysically interpreted by the Sarvāstivādins as the "Body of Essence" or "Buddhahood" and by the *Mahāyānists* as "Ultimate Reality," represents for the Theravāda school only the sum total of Buddha's teachings; in other words, the "Body of Doctrine." For the Theravādins there is but one *Bodhisattva*, Gautama. Aspiring to complete perfect enlightenment is an option simply not open to all sentient beings. In Theravāda there is just one unconditioned state (*asaṃskṛta dharma*), *nirvāṇa*. All other things in the world of *saṃsāra* are conditioned (*saṃskṛta*). The past and future do not exist. In orthodox

Theravāda doctrine *arhants* are perfect in all respects. There is no chance of regression nor are they bound by the laws of *karma*. Further, they experience and enjoy the fruits of the four meditational states (*dhyānas*). For the unenlightened, rebirth occurs in a fluid, continuous stream with no intermediate existence (*antarābhava*) witnessed. Although the attainment of nirvāṇa is theoretically open to all Buddhists, and some examples of laymen attaining nirvāṇa are cited in the texts, it is virtually impossible for the non-monk to attain this highest achievement. The Theravādins, in summary, are conservative in all respects.

SUGGESTED READING

Bareau, André. *Les Sectes Bouddhiques du Petit Véhicule*, pp. 205–43.

Bechert, Heinz. *Buddhismus, Staat und Gesellschaft in den Ländern des Theravāda Buddhismus*. 2 vols.

Dutt, Nalinaksha. *Buddhist Sects in India*, pp. 226–33.

———. *Early History of the Spread of Buddhism and the Buddhist Schools*, pp. 249–65.

Law, Bimala Churn. *A History of Pāli Literature*. 2 vols.

9

Major Schools of the Early Buddhists: Sarvāstivāda

Charles S. Prebish

HISTORY

There is a great deal of mystery surrounding the rise and early development of the *Sarvāstivādin* school. On the one hand, we have the tradition of Aśoka's council, stating the schismatic group in the Saṃgha was expelled from Magadha, migrating to Northwestern India and evolving into the Sarvāstivādin school. On the other hand, we have the attempts of several scholars to ascribe the rise of the school to one of Aśoka's missions—that sending *Majjhantika* to *Gandhāra*, an early seat of the school. This episode corresponds well with one Sarvāstivādin tradition stating that *Madhyāntika* (the Sanskrit counterpart of the Pāli Majjhantika) converted the city of *Kaśmīr*, which seems to have close ties with Gandhāra. Still another tradition establishes a community of Sarvāstivādin monks at *Mathurā*, founded by the patriarch *Upagupta*. Be that as it may, until the reign of King *Kaniṣka*, around the turn of the Christian era, the history of the school is at best sketchy.

Upon his accession to power, Kaniṣka extended his rule over a substantial empire and in his own distinctive way set out to be a second Aśoka, i.e., a pious ruler, governing in accordance with the Dharma. During his reign yet another council was held, at Kaśmīr. This council marks the emergence of the Sarvāstivādins as a pervasive school in Buddhism. Some 500 monks gathered, under the presiding eye of the monk *Vasumitra*, with the majority being Sarvāstivādins. In addition to the canonical texts of the school being established, extensive commentaries on the Vinaya, Sūtras, and Abhidharma (the *Upadeśa-śāstra*, *Vinayavibhāṣā-śāstra*, and *Abhidharmavibhāṣā-śāstra*, respectively) were composed. These treatises, when completed, were written on copper plates and enclosed in a memorial mound or *stūpa*.

Strengthened by Kaniṣka's patronage, the Sarvāstivādins were to prosper for 1,000 years in India. Being located on the trade route between China and the West, this school was invariably responsible for much of the Buddhist literature finding its way into China, and consequently occupied a doubly important role in the religious history of Buddhism.

LITERATURE

The canon of the Sarvāstivādins includes:

A. *Vinaya Piṭaka*—Basket of Discipline. The Vinaya of the Sarvāstivādins is known as the "Vinaya in Ten Recitations" (*Daśādhyāya Vinaya*). The recitations are: 1–3. *Prātimokṣa*—Monastic Code; 4. *Saptadharma*—7 Sections; 5. *Aṣṭadharma*—8 Sections; 6. *Kṣudrakaparivarta*—Miscellaneous Points; 7. *Bhikṣuṇī Vinaya*—Nuns' Vinaya; 8. *Ekottaradharma*—Preceding Rules Arranged in Ascending Order, Adding One at a Time; 9. *Upāliparipṛcchā*—The Questions of Upāli (A Mahāyānist Vinaya Treatise); 10. *Kuśalapativarta*—Good Points (Preface to the Vinaya).

B. *Sūtra Piṭaka*—Basket of Discourses: 1. *Dīrgha Āgama*—Long Discourses; 2. *Madhyama Āgama*—Middle Length Discourses; 3. *Saṃyukta Āgama*—Linked Discourses; 4. *Ekottara Āgama*—Increased by One Discourses.

C. *Abhidharma Piṭaka*—Basket of Higher Philosophy: 1. *Jñānaprasthāna* of Ārya *Kātyāyanīputra*; 2. *Saingītiparyāya* of *Mahākauṣṭhila* (Tibetan tradition) or *Śāriputra* (Chinese tradition); 3. *Prakaraṇapāda* of *Vasumitra*; 4. *Vijñānakāya* of *Devaśarmā*; 5. *Dhātukāya* of *Pūrṇa* (Tibetan tradition) or *Vasumitra* (Chinese tradition); 6. *Dharmaskandha* of Ārya *Śāriputra* (Tibetan tradition) or *Mahāmaudgalyāyana* (Chinese tradition); 7. *Prajñapti-śāstra* of *Mahāmaudgalyāyana*.

One early Buddhist commentator, *Yaśomitra*, states that, regarding the Abhidharma, the Jñānaprasthāna can be compared to the body of a being and the other six texts to its legs.

The Sarvāstivādin canon was originally composed in Sanskrit. All that remains of these early Sanskrit texts are a few scattered fragments. Nevertheless, the whole of the canon has been faithfully preserved in Chinese, and several portions of it in Tibetan. Perhaps the most striking feature of the Sarvāstivādin canon is its extremely developed Abhidharma tradition. The Sarvāstivādin tradition is rich in its commentatorial literature, particularly on Abhidharma texts. Three texts, at least, are worthy of special mention. First, *Kātyāyanīputra's* own commentary of the *Jñānaprasthāna*, *Abhidharmavibhāṣāśāstra*. It is unfortunately incomplete, but another commentary on the Jñānaprasthāna, compiled by 500 arhants and called the *Abhidharmamahāvibhāṣāśāstra*, is not. These two texts seem to result in their adherents developing into another sect, the *Vaibhāṣikas*, having their home in Kaśmīr and making much headway in the Buddhist community. Finally,

Vasubandhu, probably one of the two greatest Buddhist commentators (with Buddhaghosa), wrote his magnificent Abhidharma treatise, the *Abhidharmakośa*, covering almost all the philosophical topics espoused in the Sarvāstivādin Abhidharma books and offering many refutations of Vaibhāṣika viewpoints. The Sarvāstivādins represent the chief exponents of "Hīnayāna Scholasticism," as attested to by their scriptures and commentaries.

DOCTRINES

Since the Sarvāstivādin doctrines are complicated and complex, we shall outline here only the main features of the school. The school takes its name from the Sanskrit phrase *sarvam asti*, or "all is," thus we translate their name to mean "those who hold the doctrine that all is." In other words, although usually understood as exponents of the doctrine of impermanence (*anitya*), which excludes the existence of the past and future, they do hold that the past is made manifest in the present and the future is latent in the present through the transmission of dharmas. These dharmas fall into five categories basic to all existents: form (*rūpa*)—11 items; mind (*citta*)—1 item; mental constituents (*caitasikas*)—46 items; things not associated with form or mind (*rūpacittaviprayuktasaṃskāras*)—14 items; and unconditioned states (*asaṃskṛta*)—3 items. These five major groups of dharmas, when applied to the present, seem to indicate that each presently existing object or being is the resultant of these persistent dharmas, while at the same time providing the potential for future events.

Although affirming with the other Sthaviras that Buddha was indeed but a mortal man possessed of a form-body (*Rūpakāya*), the Sarvāstivādins recognize a problem inherent after Buddha's death. While Buddha lived, taking refuge in the Three Jewels (*triratna*) provided no difficulty. What happens, however, when Buddha dies and there is no living leader? What does taking refuge in Buddha then mean? In the *Abhidharmakośa*, *Vasubandhu* responds to this problem in two ways. First, he states that *Dharmakāya*, previously referred to as simply the Body of Dharma or the totality of Buddha's teachings, actually represents the sum of all things constituting a Buddha, or more simply, the essence of Buddha. Second, Vasubandhu conceives of Dharmakāya as a foundation of pure dharmas, consonant with the doctrine that an individual is only a combination of physical and mental dharmas. Thus Vasubandhu has given the notion of Buddhahood a rather metaphysical interpretation, one which is carried to its radical conclusion by the *Mahāyānists*.

The Sarvāstivādins also provide us with an emphasis on the practice of the six *pāramitās* or perfections—charity or giving (*dāna*), morality (*śīla*), patience (*kṣanti*), vigor (*vīrya*), trance (*samādhi*), and wisdom (*prajñā*). The doctrine of the practice of the pāramitās was later to become one of the primary tenets of the Mahāyānists, thus we see that the Sarvāstivādins, like the Mahāsāṃghikas, provided much of the soil from which the Mahāyāna emerged. Just as the Mahāsāṃghikas expressed critical concern regarding the nature of the *arhant*, so did the Sarvāstivādins, going as far as to say that the arhant could regress. For this school the arhants were not free from their past karmic influence or dependent origination. Fortunately, however, while the arhant could fall back, the streamwinner could not, insuring at least no bad rebirths or loss of the path. In summary, we can say that on doctrinal matters the Sarvāstivādins added much to early Buddhism in both philosophical and practical matters.

SUGGESTED READING

Banerjee, Ankul Chandra. *Sarvāstivāda Literature.*

Bareau, André. *Les Sectes Bouddhiques du Petit Véhicule*, pp. 131–52.

Dutt, Nalinaksha. *Buddhist Sects in India*, pp. 134–83.

———. *Early History of the Spread of Buddhism and the Buddhist Schools*, pp. 266–96.

10
Kaniṣka

Stefan Anacker

KANIṢKA AND THE KUSHAN EMPIRE

Kaniṣka with his bushy beard, pointed hat, and curled-up shoes, looks at us from his coins with an expression both determined and bewildered. This fits in well with what tradition has to tell us of him.

Kaniṣka was a *Kushan*, from the stock of people called "*Yüeh-chi*" by the Chinese—those Yüeh-chi who first invaded Bactria because of the pressures brought to bear on them by the Huns. They have been called Turks by some scholars, *Tokharians* by others; clearly, they were Central Asiatic horse people, and they were certainly bedazzled by the cultures of the peoples with which they found themselves in contact. Kaniṣka, the third of the Kushan kings, extended his influence up to *Mathurā*, controlled *Sindh*, *Rajasthan*, *Malwa*, and the *Kathiawar* peninsula, and led a celebrated campaign against *Pāṭaliputra*, from where he brought the great Buddhist poet *Aśvaghoṣa* to his court.

CULTURE IN THE COURT OF KANIṢKA

The culture in the court of Kaniṣka shows a strange and inconsistent syncretism. Gods from India, Iran, and the Hellenistic world figure on his coins, and the formulas of protocol of all these areas, as well as those of China, existed side by side in his court rituals. His summer capital at *Begram* (*Afghanistan*) has revealed rich archeological finds, and though ivory work in Indian styles predominates, there are also Hellenistic and Chinese artifacts, attesting to the cosmopolitan nature of his court. The art styles of *Gandhāra* and Mathurā, which introduce the first Buddha images, are partly contemporaneous with Kaniṣka's reign. His court was graced by Aśvaghoṣa, the Buddhist teacher *Sangharakṣa* (author of the early *Yogācārabhūmi*), the great medical theorist *Caraka*, the Greek engineer *Agesilaus*, and the political strategist *Māṭhara*.

PERSONALITY OF KANIṢKA AND HIS RELATION TO BUDDHISM

One senses in Kaniṣka a yearning for understanding the religions of the people he subdued, and perhaps it was the impossibility of his being admitted into *Brāhmaṇical* religious rites that made him such a fervent, if not very understanding, patron of Buddhism. A clear understanding of his personality, and the nature of his support of Buddhism, can be gleaned from works such as Aśvaghoṣa's *Sūtrālaṅkāra*, the *Saṃyuktaratna-piṭaka-sūtra*, and the *Dharma-piṭaka-nidāna-sūtra*. In these works Kaniṣka appears as a fervent supporter of Buddhism, who never, however, has a very accurate idea of what is transpiring. There is the repeated story of Kaniṣka's venerating a *Jain stūpa*, and its breaking to pieces because of the Buddhistic hymns of praise uttered by him while circumambulating it.

Kaniṣka, unlike *Aśoka*, never allowed his interest in Buddhism to mitigate his basic bloodthirstiness; even the Buddhist works most sympathetic to the king mention his irrational massacres. Nonetheless, he was a devoted patron, building the great monastery at *Peshāwar* and munificently endowing existing institutions.

Kaniṣka's most famous contribution to Buddhism is the *Fourth Council*, which, according to some, was held in Gandhāra and, according to others, was held in *Kaśmir*. At the advice of the *Sarvāstivādin* master *Pārśva*, Kaniṣka issued invitations to all learned Buddhists of the realm, of which only 499 were finally selected to take part in great debates covering every aspect of Buddhist theory and practice. The *Bhadanta Vasumitra* became president of the council, and Aśvaghoṣa assisted him. The council thus contained *both Hīnayānists and Mahāyānists*, and can be characterized as a conference of peace and compromise. A new *Vinaya* was put into writing, and the results of all debates on theory was recorded in the *Mahāvibhāṣā*, the Great Book of Options.

The *Mahāvastu*, *Lalitavistara*, *Avadānaśataka*, *Divyāvadāna*, and *Saddharmapuṇḍarīka-sūtra* may date from about Kaniṣka's time. *Nāgārjuna* was a contemporary, though never associated with Kaniṣka's name, but rather with the Central/South Indian imperial dynasty of the *Andhra Śātavāhanas*. *Āryaśūra*, author of the *Jātaka-mālā*, is almost certainly a contemporary; some urge his identification with *Mātṛceṭa*, the famous writer of Buddhist hymns of praise. In fact, there exists a letter by Mātṛceṭa to a King Kaniṣka, or Kaniṣka the *Kanikalekha*. This young king, who is being advised by Mātṛceṭa on how to rule in Dharmic fashion, is probably not the great Kaniṣka, but probably Kaniṣka II.

THE END OF KANIṢKA

Insatiable in his greed for conquest, and in his sexual lusts, Kaniṣka decided to subdue the countries to the north of his realm. It was then that the people rebelled, tired of constant war, and, taking advantage of his sudden illness, smothered him in his blanket. Buddhist monks, to expiate for all the bloodshed caused by their benefactor, had gongs rung continually in the monasteries even long after Kaniṣka's death.

The big statue of Kaniṣka found at Mathurā has no head, and it looks almost as if it had been deliberately lopped off. It is clear, at any rate, that many people were relieved that he was dead.

The date of Kaniṣka has been the subject of vast controversy. Some say his first regnal year was the first year of the Śaka era, A.D. 78, and others, on evidence from Chinese accounts, prefer 103 or 130 or even later dates for the year of his accession.

SUGGESTED READING

Basham, A.L., ed. *Papers on the Date of Kaniṣka* (collected from the Conference on the Date of Kaniṣka, London, 1960).

Lévi, Sylvain. "Notes sur les Indo-Scythes." *Journal Asiatique*, 8 (Novembre-Décembre 1896: 444–84; 9 (Janvier-Fevrier 1897): 6–42.

11

The Vinaya Piṭaka

Charles S. Prebish

INTRODUCTION

The *Vinaya Piṭaka* is that portion of the Buddhist canon regulating the monastic life of the monks and nuns. Properly speaking, though, a consideration of the monastic aspect of Buddhist life must be taken in broad spectrum, focusing not just on that portion of the monastic law which was canonized, but on Vinaya literature in general, thus affording us an opportunity to view the developmental process going on within the early Buddhist community in the first few centuries after Buddha's death. For convenience, then, we arrive at the following schema:

Paracanonical Vinaya Literature
- *Prātimokṣa*
- *Karmavācanā*

Canonical Vinaya Literature
- *Sūtravibhaṅga*
- *Skandhaka*
- *Appendices*

Noncanonical Vinaya Literature
- *Commentaries*
- *Miscellaneous Texts*

PARACANONICAL VINAYA LITERATURE

PRĀTIMOKṢA

The *Prātimokṣa* is an inventory of offenses organized into several general categories classified according to the gravity of the offense. Many scholars now agree that Prātimokṣa, as a technical term in the Buddhist lexicon, seems to have undergone at least three related stages of development—as a simple confession of faith recited by the monks and nuns at periodic intervals, as a bare monastic code employed as a device insuring proper monastic discipline, and as a monastic liturgy, representing a period of relatively high organization and structure within the *Saṃgha*. We find the following classes of offenses within the monks' text:

1. *Pārājika dharmas*—offenses requiring expulsion from the Saṃgha.
2. *Saṃghāvaśeṣa dharmas*—offenses involving temporary exclusion from the Saṃgha while undergoing a probationary period.
3. *Aniyata dharmas*—undetermined cases (involving sexuality) in which the offender, when observed by a trustworthy female lay follower, may be charged under one of several categories of offenses.
4. *Naiḥsargika-Pāyantika dharmas*—offenses requiring forfeiture and expiation.
5. *Pāyantika dharmas*—offenses requiring simple expiation.
6. *Pratideśanīya dharmas*—offenses which should be confessed.
7. *Śaikṣa dharmas*—rules concerning etiquette.
8. *Adhikaraṇa-Śamatha dharmas*—legalistic procedures to be used in settling disputes.

The nuns' text contains only seven categories, the third being excluded. The number of rules cited varies in the texts of the diverse Buddhist schools from 218 to 263 for the monks and from 279 to 380 for the nuns (this latter figure being higher due to the insertion of many rules specifically designed for females). When formalized into the *Prātimokṣa-sūtra*, recited as a confessional at the twice monthly *Poṣadha* or fast-day ceremony (concurrent with the new and full moon days), three new features were added to the text: a series of verses preceding and following the text, praising the virtuous, disciplined life; a *nidāna* or introduction, used to call the Saṃgha together and instrument the confessional procedure; and an interrogatory formula, recited after each class of offenses, aimed at discovery of who was pure and who was not. Thus within a short time after the founder's death, the monks had provided themselves with an organizational tool for implementing purity in the monastic order.

KARMAVĀCANĀ

The *Karmavācanā* is the functional, legalistic device by which the communal life of the Saṃgha is regulated. We might say that what the Prātimokṣa represented to the individual monk or nun, the Karmavācanā represented to the Saṃgha. At least fourteen Karmavācanās are cited by scholars.

1. Admission into the Order (*pravrajyā*).
2. Full ordination of monks (*upasaṃpadā*).

3. Holding the confession ceremony (*poṣadha*).
4. Holding the invitation ceremony (*pravāraṇā*).
5. Residence obligation during the rainy season (*varṣopagamana*).
6. Use of leather objects (*carman*).
7. Preparation and use of medicines (*bhaiṣajya*).
8. Robe-giving ceremony (*kaṭhina*).
9. Discipline.
10. Daily life of monks.
11. Beds and seats, i.e., dwellings (*śayanāsana*).
12. Schisms in the order (*saṃghabheda*).
13. Duties of a student and teacher to one another.
14. Rules for nuns.

All of these acts are handled under a general procedure called *saṃgha-karma* (literally, an act of the saṃgha), arising either by a general requisition or a dispute. To be considered valid the proper number of competent monks must be assembled, all absentee ballots gathered, and a motion or *jñapti* set forth. The motion is then read aloud or proclaimed (this is the Karmavācanā or announcing the action) and a decision, positive or negative, obtained. On the basis of the decision, democratically elicited, the Saṃgha acts as a unified Order. It should be noted that since Karmavācanā nine concerns discipline, all breaches of the Prātimokṣa offenses are treated in this fashion and appropriate punishments inflicted.

CANONICAL VINAYA LITERATURE

SŪTRAVIBHAṄGA

The term *Sūtravibhaṅga* is literally translated as "analysis of a sūtra." Thus the Sūtravibhaṅga is a detailed analysis of the offenses recorded in the Prātimokṣa Sūtra. As we should expect, the Sūtravibhaṅga has the same general categories of offenses as the Prātimokṣa Sūtra. Regarding each of the Prātimokṣa rules, the Sūtravibhaṅga has a fourfold structure: 1. a story (or stories) explaining the circumstances under which the rule was pronounced; 2. the Prātimokṣa rule; 3. a word-for-word commentary on the rule; 4. stories indicating mitigating circumstances in which exceptions to the rule or deviations in punishment might be made. In addition to the Prātimokṣa offenses, several new terms are found in the Sūtravibhaṅga: *sthūlātyaya* or grave offense, *duṣkṛta* or light offense, and *durbhāṣita* or offense of improper speech. These new terms were added because by the time the Sūtravibhaṅga was compiled, the Prātimokṣa had become fixed (closed) with new rules considered inadmissible. To provide the flexibility of a situational ethics, the Sūtravibhaṅga expanded necessarily in this direction. Like the Prātimokṣa-sūtra, there is both a monks' and nuns' Sūtravibhaṅga.

SKANDHAKA

The *Skandhaka* contains the regulations pertaining to the organization of the Saṃgha. It functions on the basis of the acts and ceremonies dictated by the Karmavācanās. We might say that the Karmavācanās are to the Skandhaka what the Prātimokṣa is to the Sūtravibhaṅga. There are twenty sections in the Skandhaka, each referred to as a *vastu*.

1. *Pravrajyāvastu*—admission to the Saṃgha.
2. *Poṣadhavastu*—the monthly confession ceremony.
3. *Varṣāvastu*—residence during the rainy season.
4. *Pravāraṇāvastu*—the invitation ceremony at the end of the rainy season.
5. *Carmavastu*—use of shoes and leather objects.
6. *Bhaiṣajyavastu*—food and medicine for the monks.
7. *Cīvaravastu*—rules concerning clothing.
8. *Kaṭhinavastu*—rules concerning the production and distribution of robes.
9. *Kośāmbakavastu*—dispute between two groups of monks in Kauśāmbī.
10. *Karmavastu*—lawful monastic procedure.
11. *Pāṇḍulohitakavastu*—measures taken by the Saṃgha to correct disciplinary problems.
12. *Pudgalavastu*—ordinary procedure for simple offenses.
13. *Pārivāsikavastu*—behavior during the *parivāsa* and *mānatva* probationary periods.
14. *Poṣadhasthāpanavastu*—prohibiting a monk from participating in the poṣadha ceremony.
15. *Śamathavastu*—procedures to settle disputes.
16. *Saṃghabhedavastu*—schisms in the Saṃgha.
17. *Śayanāsanavastu*—monastic residences.
18. *Ācāravastu*—behavior of the monks (not discussed elsewhere).
19. *Kṣudrakavastu*—miscellaneous, minor matters.
20. *Bhikṣuṇīvastu*—rules specifically for nuns.

In addition to the twenty vastus, there is an introductory section discussing Buddha's genealogy, birth, and life history up to the conversion of *Śāriputra* and *Maudgalyāyana*, and also a concluding section covering Buddha's death, the council of *Rājagṛha*, the history of the patriarchs, and the council of *Vaiśālī*. Consequently, we can outline the structure of the Skandhaka in the following manner: 1. Introduction: Buddha's Early Life and Career; 2. Buddhist Monastic Institutions, chapters 1–4; 3. Daily Needs of the Monks, chapters 5–8; 4. Monastic Law, chapters 9–10; 5. Disciplinary Proceedings, chapters 11–13; 6. Miscellaneous Matters, chapters 14–20; 7. Conclusion: Buddha's Death and Afterwards.

APPENDICES

Appendices are attached to several Vinayas as a supplement. They serve two basic functions, providing summaries of the rules found in the Sūtravibhaṅga and Skandhaka, and providing interesting bits of monastic history.

NONCANONICAL VINAYA LITERATURE

Fortunately, a wide variety of Vinaya commentaries have come down to us, and their importance for the student of Vinaya literature need not be stressed here. It is clear that the most complete commentatorial traditions have been preserved in the *Theravādin* and *Mūlasarvāstivādin* schools, written in Pāli and Tibetan, respectively. We also possess Chinese translations for Vinaya commentaries in virtually all of the major Hīnayāna schools, but, unfortunately, we are almost totally lacking in Sanskrit Vinaya commentaries.

SUGGESTED READING

Frauwallner, Erich. *The Earliest Vinaya and the Beginnings of Buddhist Literature.*

Lamotte, Étienne. *Histoire du Bouddhisme Indien des origines à l'ère Śaka*, pp. 181–97.

Pachow, W. *A Comparative Study of the Prātimokṣa*. In *Sino-Indian Studies*, vol. 4, pts. 1–4 and vol. 5, pt. 1, 1951–1955.

Prebish, Charles S. *Buddhist Monastic Discipline: The Sanskrit Prātimokṣa Sūtras of the Mahāsāṃghikas and Mūlasarvāstivādins.*

———. "The Prātimokṣa Puzzle: Fact Versus Fantasy," *Journal of the American Oriental Society*, 94, 2 (April–June 1974): 168–76.

———. "Theories Concerning the Skandhaka: An Appraisal," *Journal of Asian Studies*, 32, 4 (August 1973): 669–78.

Thomas, Edward J. *The History of Buddhist Thought*, pp. 11–26.

12

The Sūtra Piṭaka

Francis H. Cook

INTRODUCTION

Buddhist sacred literature is generally divided into three types according to the dominant characteristic of the piece in question. The three types are *Vinaya*, which deals with the disciplinary regulations for the community of monks, *Sūtra*, comprising discourses or "sermons" delivered by the Buddha, and *Abhidharma*, scholastic texts which give detailed discussions of matters in Vinaya and Sūtra literature by way of definition of terms, lists of like terms, etc. Together, these three parts constitute the *Tripiṭaka* (literally, Three Baskets), which is the Buddhist canon. The sūtras are the essential teachings of Buddhism and are believed by most Buddhists to have been delivered by the Buddha at various times and places to his followers.

FORMAT

An item of Buddhist canonical literature is identifiable as a *sūtra* by its form. A sūtra always begins with the words, "Thus have I heard. At one time . . . " (in Sanskrit, *evam mayā śrutam ekasmin samaye* . . .), followed by the name of the place where the sermon was delivered, often followed by a list of names of people in the audience, and concluding with the actual sermon of the Buddha. This form reflects the historical circumstance of the meeting soon after the Buddha's death at which his disciples recited from memory all the sermons they could remember, in order to establish an orthodox, accurately transmitted teaching. Thus a monk would recite a sermon which he recalled, prefacing it with the foregoing stock phrase.

SOME CHARACTERISTICS OF SŪTRA LITERATURE

The sūtras are dogmatic, in the sense that there is little effort to demonstrate or prove statements made in them. The Buddha claims that this is the truth discovered by him in his enlightenment, and the listener may accept it or not as he wishes. Sūtras abound in various figures of speech, chiefly simile and metaphor. These are meant not only to embroider the text but to help in memorization, to emphasize, and occasionally to persuade by analogy. Sūtras, particularly those of the *Pāli Canon*, are extremely repetitious. This reflects the fact that for several centuries these texts existed only in oral form, and repetition, as well as stock phrases and figures of speech, helped the individual memorize them. Many sūtras, upon close study, reveal that they originally existed in much shorter form. The nuclear text has grown over time, chiefly through improvement by monks who added to it.

EXPLICATION

Sūtras composed in the Indian homeland of Buddhism, in several languages (Sanskrit, Pāli, and Prakrit), remain extant in fragments or whole, comprising complete *Sūtra Piṭakas* or fragments of once-existing Piṭakas, in either the original language, or in translations of countries into which Buddhism entered, and occasionally both.

The *Sutta Piṭaka* of the *Pāli Canon* is the collection of suttas recognized as authentic Buddha-discourse by the *Theravāda* tradition of present-day Śrī Laṅkā, Burma, Thailand, Laos, and Cambodia. It is also revered by *Mahāyānists* of all schools. The collection was committed to writing and closed in the first century before the Christian era after having been brought to Ceylon from India in oral form. All other Buddhist scriptures not included in the Pāli Canon, including those identified as Mahāyāna sūtras, are considered to be postcanonical, apocryphal, or corruptions of the real teaching, by present-day Theravādins. Following is a brief outline of the Pāli Sutta Piṭaka.

1. *Dīgha Nikāya*—"Collection of Long Discourses." 34 long suttas further divided into 3 groups (*vaggas*).
2. *Majjhima Nikāya*—"Collection of Suttas of Medium Length." 152 suttas subdivided into 15 vaggas.
3. *Saṃyutta Nikāya*—"Collection of Grouped Discourses." 5 vaggas subdivided into 56 more groups. The initial division into 5 vaggas is made on the basis of some unifying factor, such as dramatis personae, topic of discussion (such as the Eight-fold Path), etc.
4. *Aṅguttara Nikāya*—"Collection of Discourses Treating Enumerations Classed in Ascending Order." The name of this Nikāya is derived from the method of arranging the suttas, whereby the first of eleven groups concerns lists of single things, the second concerns lists of two things, and so on, up to the eleventh group, which discusses lists of eleven things.
5. *Khuddaka Nikāya*—"Collection of Minor Works." The Ceylonese

version contains 15 items in this nikāya, the Burmese adding 4 more. The Ceylonese Nikāya includes the following:

a. *Khuddaka-pātha*—"The Reading of Short Passages."
b. *Dhammapada*—"Stanzas on the Teaching."
c. *Udāna*—"Solemn Utterances."
d. *Itivuttaka*—"Thus it is Said" (from the introductory phrase to each sutta).
e. *Sutta-nipāta*—"Collection of Suttas."
f. *Vimāna-vatthu*—"Stories About Heavenly Palaces."
g. *Peta-vatthu*—"Stories About Hungry Ghosts."
h. *Thera-gāthā*—"Verses of the Elders."
i. *Therī-gāthā*—"Verses of the Nuns."
j. *Jātaka*—"Previous Lives of the Buddha."
k. *Niddesa*—"Exposition."
l. *Paṭisambhidā-magga*—"The Way of Analysis."
m. *Apadāna*—"Verse Accounts of the Lives of Certain Monks and Nuns."
n. *Buddhavaṃsa*—"The Lineage of the Buddha."
o. *Cariyā-piṭaka*—"Collection Concerning Conduct."

Besides the suttas constituting the Pāli Canon, there are a number of other scriptures belonging to various schools of *Hīnayāna* Buddhism. Along with these independently existing scriptures, there is evidence in Indian literature that there were other whole Tripiṭakas, including Sūtra Piṭakas, belonging to Hīnayāna schools existing alongside the Theravādins. The remains of these scriptures are now found only in foreign translations.

Whereas the suttas of the Pāli Canon represent the Theravāda tradition, which is only one form of so-called Hīnayāna Buddhism, there is also a vast collection of scriptures which belongs to *Mahāyāna* Buddhism and is not recognized by the Theravādins.

Whereas the Pāli Canon was closed and fixed in the first century before the Christian era, Mahāyāna sūtras continued to be composed for several centuries. It is now believed that the sūtras teaching the perfection of wisdom (*prajñāpāramitā*) appeared perhaps two hundred years before the Christian era and are presumably the first Mahāyāna sūtras. Some scholars believe that Mahāyāna teachings go back to the beginning of Buddhism.

Mahāyānists have traditionally classified their scriptures in several ways, but there is no evidence to show that Indian Mahāyānists ever had a closed canon similar to that of the more conservative Theravādins. New sūtras continued to be composed and accepted as Buddha-teaching over a period of several hundred years, as new religious insights developed in Mahāyāna. The great geographical dispersal of Mahāyāna also probably precluded any consensus on what was canonical and what was not.

The appearance of new sūtras reflected the development within Buddhism of a new strain of thought concerning the nature of a Buddha, the career of the *Bodhisattva*, and a view of things as empty (*śūnya*). Thus, although Mahāyānists continued to revere "Hīnayāna" scriptures as Buddha-discourse, they also criticized them as incomplete and shallow versions of the truth, accommodations to the immature understanding of the Buddha's listeners. The new sūtras were thought to present fuller versions of the Buddha's teaching.

1. The *Prajñāpāramitā-sūtra* (existing in several versions of various lengths) is marked by a new emphasis on the career of the Bodhisattva, a new emphasis of compassion (*karuṇā*), and a new view of existence called emptiness (*śūnyatā*).
2. The *Saddharmapuṇḍarīka-sūtra* ("Sūtra on the Lotus of the True Teaching") combated Hīnayāna doctrines as partial, shallow, and selfish and presented a view of the Buddha as eternal.
3. The *Avataṃsaka-sūtra* ("Flower-ornament Sūtra") gave an extensive portrayal of the Bodhisattva's search for enlightenment and offered a view of existence as one of complete identity and interdependence.
4. Several sūtras taught the existence of a Buddha named *Amitābha* (Infinite Light) and his paradise in Western space, as well as a doctrine of faith and devotion as a means of being reborn in that paradise.
5. Many Mahāyāna sūtras, regardless of type or class, taught the existence of numerous Buddhas and Bodhisattvas throughout the universe.

Indian sūtras were destroyed in large numbers by the elements, and by Muslim invaders, and many now exist only in the languages of other countries into which Buddhism entered.

1. Many sūtras no longer extant in the original languages are included in the Tibetan collection of scriptures, the *Kanjur*. This remains one of the best repositories for Indian Buddhist scriptural works. It is very valuable because of the excellence of the translation.
2. Sūtras began to arrive in China from India soon after the beginning of the Christian era, and many now extinct in India are preserved in Chinese translation. Scriptures representing both the Hīnayāna and Mahāyāna traditions in Sanskrit, Pāli, and Prakrit languages were collected, translated into Chinese, and published as a complete Sūtra Piṭaka several times. The most commonly used now is the edition made during the *Sung Dynasty*.
3. The Sung Dynasty edition of the scriptures was imported into Japan along with Chinese forms of Buddhism, and this has been published

several times in Japan. The most commonly used, and a basic source in the study of Buddhism, is the *Taishō shinshū daizōkyō*, the collection of scriptures published during the *Taishō* era (1912–1926). This has been augmented by the publication of the *Zokuzōkyō*, a collection of pieces not included in the former collection.

TRANSLATIONS

Buddhist sūtras, which are essential for any study of Buddhism, have been partially translated into English. The Pāli Canon of Theravāda Buddhism, including the Sutta Piṭaka, was translated into English by the Pali Text Society in the period from 1882 to 1927. Portions of the Sutta Piṭaka were also translated in the *Sacred Books of the Buddhists* series during the same period. Mahāyāna sūtras have been translated in a sporadic fashion by a number of scholars. Progress has been slow, due to the recent beginning of serious study of Mahāyāna, the great number of sūtras, and the imperfect understanding of many technical terms in the literature. A good beginning is the translation of the very important "wisdom literature" (Prajñā-pāramitā-sūtra) made by Edward Conze in various publications.

SUGGESTED READING

Conze, Edward. *Thirty Years of Buddhist Studies*, pp. 123–84, 191–206.
Lamotte, Étienne. *Histoire du Bouddhisme Indien des origines à l'ère Śaka*, pp. 167–81.
Law, Bimala Churn. *A History of Pāli Literature*. 2 vol.
Thomas, Edward J. *The History of Buddhist Thought*, pp. 265 ff.
Warren, Henry Clarke, tr. *Buddhism in Translations*.
Winternitz, Moriz. *A History of Indian Literature*, vol. 2, pp. 1–21, 34–165.

13

The Abhidharma Piṭaka

Stefan Anacker

THE ABHIDHARMA PIṬAKA

DEFINITION OF THE TERM AND POSITION OF THE LITERATURE

Adhidharma (Pāli: *Abhidhamma*), "that which is above Dharma" or "that which represents superior Dharma," is the explanation and genetic ordering of all key factors mentioned in the *sūtra* collections. The prefix *abhi* (above) carries the implication that the revelations of this manner of investigation are held to be more authoritative than the explanations in the sūtras themselves. In the *Vibhaṅga*, a Pāli Abhidharma text, there are, in fact, sūtra explanations and Abhidharma explanations, and the latter are held to be superior. To all schools that develop Abhidharmas, they become integral parts of their Canons. Because almost all entities are in Abhidharma discussed as factors of consciousness (materiality itself being discerned primarily by the tactile consciousness), Abhidharma comprises what we would call a psychological theory.

BACKGROUND FOR ABHIDHARMA

Meditations on the flow of bodily and mental factors are an essential part of the training of Buddhist monks, and it is probable that the impetus for Abhidharma lay in a desire to catalogue everything that was experienced in and out of mediation. At first there seems to have been only bare lists of all factors of personality occurring in meditative and nonmeditative states. These lists, or *Mātṛkās*, are the basis of all later Abhidharma literature. A special importance was attached to the lists containing those factors under which all other events were to be ordered: the five *skandhas* or aggregates making up personality, i.e., materiality (*rūpa*), feelings (*vedanā*), cognitions (*saṃjñā*), motivational dispositions (*saṃskāras*), and consciousness (*vijñāna*); the twelve *āyatanas* or sense-fields, i.e., eye, ear, nose, tongue, tactile body, and mental consciousness, plus their objects (visibles, sounds, smells, tastes, touch, and mentally cognizables or *dharmas*, respectively); the eighteen basic constituents of experience (*dhātus*), i.e., the sense fields plus their corresponding consciousnesses (visual, audial, olfactory, gustatory, tactile, and mental, respectively). At a somewhat later time, explanatory sections were added onto these Mātṛkās. The *Dhammasaṅgaṇi*, first book of the *Theravāda Abhidhamma*, follows this format, and may date in part from about 380 to 330 B.C.

EXTANT PIṬAKAS

Though Abhidharmas are attested to for a great many Buddhist sects, at present only three Abhidharma Piṭakas exist in their entirety. These are 1. the *Theravāda Abhidhamma*, in Pāli, 2. the *Sarvāstivāda Abhidharma*, originally in Sanskrit, and except for one fragment in the original and sections of the *Prajñapti-śāstra* in Tibetan, found only in Chinese translation, and 3. the *Dharmaguptaka* (?), *Śāriputrābhidharma*, in Chinese translation. In addition, an early treatise of the *Saṃitīyas*, the *Saṃmitīyanikāya-śāstra*, has come down to us in Chinese translation (and also what may well be an early *Mahāsāṃghika* Abhidharma text, the *Śāriputraparipṛcchā*, is found in Chinese translation).

Books of the Theravāda Abhidhamma and Their Contents.

a. *Dhammasaṅgaṇi*—an analysis of mental and bodily factors, in and out of meditation, categorized as to their ethicality.

b. *Vibhaṅga*—Sūtra and Abhidharma explanations of the skandhas, the overcoming of fetters, dependent origination, meditation, and types of knowledge, each followed by a catechetic question and answer section.

c. *Kathāvattu*—polemical treatise, traditionally said to be a result of Aśoka's council, upholding orthodox doctrinal views against those of other schools.

d. *Puggalapaññatti*—the analysis of personalities into three basic affliction types (lust, hatred, delusion) and their subdivisions.

e. *Dhātukathā*—the ordering of all factors under a skandha and an āyatana.

f. *Yamaka*—"the book of pairs," giving more precise determinations of ambiguous terms by a process of mutual exclusion.

g. *Paṭṭhāna*—the voluminous discussion, in full, of dependent origination.

Books of the Sarvāstivāda Abhidharma and Their Contents.

a. *Jñānaprasthāna* of *Kātyāyanīputra*—definitions of key psychological terms.

b. *Saṅgītiparyāya* of *Mahākauṣṭhila* (or *Śāriputra*)—commentary on the *Saṅgīti-sūtra*, where schisms in *Jainism* on the death of the *Jina* prompt

Śāriputra to lay down a résumé of the Buddha's teaching: Mātṛkās and explanations of all key terms in the sūtra.

c. *Dhātukāya* of *Pūrṇa* (or *Vasumitra*)—introduction of the concepts of *mahābhūmika-dharmas*, i.e., those psychological events which occur in every consciousness-moment (feelings, cognition, contact, mental attention, impulse, trust, memory, mindfulness, and discernment), *kleśa-mahābhūmikas*, i.e., those which are major factors causing afflictions (lack of faith, sloth, false memory, distraction, ignorance, nondiscernment, wrong mental attention, trust in what is false, arrogance, negligence), and *parīttakleśabhūmikas*, i.e., the minor factors causing affliction (anger, hypocrisy, hatefulness, envy, stinginess, falsehood, conceit, guile).

d. *Vijñānakāya* of *Devaśarman*—polemical treatise upholding the Sarvāstivāda doctrine of the existence of the past and future in the present moment and refuting the concept of "self" or "personality."

e. *Prakaraṇapāda* of *Vasumitra*—contains both manners of ordering events. The older one arranges all events under one or another of the skandhas, and the newer one divides all events into the categories of materiality (*rūpa*), consciousness (*citta*), factors associated with consciousness (*cittasaṃprayukta-saṃskāras*, *caitasikas*), conditioned events dissociated from consciousness (*cittaviprayuktasaṃskāras*), and unconditioned factors (*asaṃskṛta*), which always include space, the last formless meditations, and *nirvāṇa*. This text also orders all events mentioned in the *bhūmika*-list of the Dhātukāya as factors associated with consciousness, and it introduces a new division: the major factors of the beneficial (*kuśala-mahābhūmika*), i.e., faith, vigor, equanimity, shame, dread of blame, lack of greed, lack of hate, lack of harmful intent, confidence, and lack of confusion.

f. *Dharmaskandha* of *Śāriputra* (or *Maudgalyāyana*)—discussion of all practices preparatory to Buddhist sainthood, followed by a discussion of major and minor afflictions (*kleśa*, *upakleśa*), the 22 faculties, the sense-fields, and the skandhas.

g. *Prajñapti-śāstra* of *Maudgalyāyana*—cosmology and a discussion of the genesis of psychological events.

METHOD OF ANALYSIS

Abhidharma analyzes what is usually termed personality into a number of types of discrete but genetically related moment-events, without assuming any hypothetical wholes such as person, mind, etc. The elements or events (*dharmas*) which it considers are thus not divisions of something larger, but coordinated ultimates. One event may condition the next, and speaking metaphorically one can say that such related events form series (*saṃtāna*), but as truly present phenomena they are momentary. Thus when we might conventionally say, "He's really in a bad mood now," the Abhidharmika would perhaps analyze the situation as follows: "Associated with this materiality-series there are consciousness-moments accompanied by displeasurable feeling-moments with volition-moments stemming from impulse-moments resulting in recurrent anger-moments." One result of thinking like an Abhidharmika is that individuality, or self, is no longer held to and that there is a recognition that "self" and "others" are similar complexes of constantly changing phenomena.

The enumeration of all the different types of event possible within a state, and their definitions, are chief concerns of the Abhidharmika. At first, definitions are really amassments of synonyms (as in the Dhammasaṅgaṇi), but already in the Prajñaptiśāstra there are true definitions of the following type: Whatever has characteristics *A*, *B*, *C* is designated as *X*.

LATER ABHIDHARMA LITERATURE

THERAVĀDA

Between the last books of the Theravāda Abhidhamma Piṭaka and the great commentators of the fifth century A.D. lie such Abhidhamma treatises as the *Nettippakaraṇa* and *Peṭakopadesa of Mahākaccāna*, and the *Vimuttimagga* of *Upatissa*. Commentaries in Ceylonese upon the Abhidhamma, called *Aṭṭhakathās*, are known to have existed, and they may have been one of the reasons the teacher *Buddhaghosa* came to Ceylon.

In the fifth century A.D., there was a generation of commentators upon the Abhidhamma, who worked mostly in Ceylon. The interpretations of these men come to be the orthodox Theravāda position. *Buddhadatta*, author of the *Abhidhammāvatāra*, *Dhammakitti*, author of the *Saddhammasaṅgaha*, and particularly *Buddhaghosa*, with his *Visuddhimagga* describing the Theravāda path and his commentaries on all of the books of the Abhidhamma Piṭaka (*Aṭṭhasālinī* on the Dhammasaṅgaṇī, *Sammohavinodanī* on the Vibhaṅga, and *Aṭṭhakathās* on the Dhātukathā, Puggalapaññatti, Kathāvatthu, Yamaka, and Paṭṭhāna), shaped Theravāda doctrine as it exists today. A later Theravādin Abhidhamma work is the *Abhidhammaṭṭhasaṅgaha* of *Anuruddha* (eleventh century). It adopts many Sarvāstivāda Abhidharma concepts, such as atomism and the citta/caitasika method of analyzing psychological events. Theravāda Abhidhamma activity is by no means dead, having been cultivated throughout the centuries particularly in Burma and Ceylon, and even in this century there have been great Abhidhamma expositors (such as Burma's *Ledi Sadaw*).

SARVĀSTIVĀDA

The Mahāvibhāṣā and Its Masters. The second century A.D. is the most fertile for Sarvāstivāda Abhidharma, with such masters as *Dharmaśrī*, author of the *Abhidharmasāra*, who introduces atomism and establishes the citta/caitasika method of analysis as an indispensable tool. The second century is also the period of the compilation of the *Mahāvibhāṣā*.

According to traditional accounts, King *Kaniṣka* assembled a huge gathering of learned monks to determine which interpretations of Dharma were to be accepted, and the result of their debates was a tremendous compendium, ostensibly a commentary on the Jñanaprasthāna, but actually containing within itself all the controversies raised by the council. Its title, Mahāvibhāṣā, means the Great (Book of) Options, and its methodology is to list all opinions given by various masters on a point, and then perhaps to come to a well-argumented conclusion. Dharmaśrī's atomism is accepted, and different ways of explaining the past and future's manner of existing (remember that the Sarvāstivādins uphold the existence of the past and future in each present moment) are presented.

The four great masters of the Mahāvibhāṣā—the Bhadanta *Vasumitra* (author of the *Pañcavastuka*), *Ghoṣaka* (author of the *Abhidharmāmṛta*), the Bhadanta *Dharmatrāta*, and *Buddhadeva*—each evolved a different theory to explain the past and future's manner of existence. The Bhadanta Vasumitra said that the present moment differs from a past and future one in that it is in a different state (*avasthā*); i.e., it has a full efficacy (*karitvā*) Ghoṣaka said that the elements change their aspect (*lakṣaṇa*) of intensity in the present, the Bhadanta Dharmatrāta held that each present moment is different, but that there is an own-nature (*svabhāva*) for a dharma representing all potential appearances of the moment; and Buddhadeva maintained that all three are relative and contingent (*āpekṣā*) on one another —i.e., the present is past to the future, etc.

The creation of the Mahāvibhāṣā would have been unnecessary if serious differences had not arisen among Sarvāstivādin Abhidharmikas. So that the extent of individual thought in the Abhidharma of the Sarvāstivāda can be seen, some of the differences of opinion among Abhidharmikas of the second century regarding the *caitasikas* are presented here. Thus though Ghoṣaka accepts the mahābhūmikas (psychological events concomitant to every consciousness-moment), the Bhadanta Vasumitra does not, and accepts besides a subtle *citta* which exists in the highest meditation. *Śrīlāta*, one of the original masters of the *Sautrāntika* sect (a group which generally wished to discard Abhidharma interpretations and go back to the sūtras), says there are only three types of psychological event concomitant with every consciousness-moment—feelings, cognitions, and volitions—and *Hari-*

varman, author of the *Satyasiddhi-śāstra*, says there can be only one event concomitant to a citta, thus denying the mahābhūmikas. On the most radical end of the spectrum are the Bhadanta Dharmatrāta (in general this writer seems to have been something of a rebel), who accepts only three caitasikas (feelings, cognitions, volitions), and says no two dharmas are ever simultaneous in a consciousness-moment, and Buddhadeva, who finally denies the existence of caitasikas altogether, saying that they are only different forms of citta.

An entire school of thought was founded upon the Mahāvibhāṣā. Called *Vaibhāṣikas* after the text, they soon evolved fixed theories regarding points the Mahāvibhāṣā itself had left open, leaning most heavily on the opinions of the Bhadanta Vasumitra. Their two main centers of activity were in *Kaśmīr* and *Gandhāra* (the *Pāścatīyas*).

The Abhidharmakośa of Vasubandhu. In the fourth century controversies came to a head with the orthodox Vaibhāṣika *Saṅghabhadra* (author of the *Abhidharmanyāyānusāra*, an attempt to argue for all of the Vaibhāṣika categories), and the Sautrāntika-leaning *Vasubandhu*, who in his great *Abhidharmakośa* gives a beautiful exposition of the entire Vaibhāṣika system, and in his autocommentary completely demolishes it from a Sautrāntika viewpoint. Atomism, the existence of past and future, and of all kinds of categories the Vaibhāṣikas had devised to forge a coherent system (such as *prāpti*, a kind of metaphysical glue linking related but diverse elements), are all thrown out by Vasubandhu, who in his argumentation follows a principle somewhat like Occam's Razor ("If it is not an absolutely necessary category, throw it out!"). Saṅghabhadra and other orthodox Vaibhāṣikas responded in fury, but Vasubandhu's attack was so successful that soon the Vaibhāṣika became a dead school, studied only in universities like *Nālandā*, and even then only through the lens of Vasubandhu's Abhidharmakośa, which becomes the standard Abhidharma work for all Mahāyānists.

SUGGESTED READING

Aung, Shwe Zan, tr. *Compendium of Philosophy* (*Abhidhammaṭṭhasaṅgaha*), Introduction, pp. 1–76.

Lamotte, Étienne. *Histoire du Bouddhisme Indien des origines à l'ère Śaka*, pp. 197–210.

La Vallée Poussin, Louis de, tr. *L'Abhidharmakośa de Vasubandhu*. 6 vols.

Ñāṇatiloka Mahāthera. *Guide Through the Abhidhammapiṭaka*.

Stcherbatsky, Th. *The Central Conception of Buddhism and the Meaning of the Word "Dharma."*

14
The Rise of the Mahāyāna

Lewis R. Lancaster

INTRODUCTION

After the nirvāṇa of the Buddha, Buddhism continued to flourish and spread geographically, thus it is not surprising that differences arose and schisms appeared in the Saṃgha. Today there are two major divisions of Buddhism, the *Theravāda* of the South and Southeast Asian countries and the *Mahāyāna* in its various cultural forms among the Chinese, Koreans, Japanese, Vietnamese, and Tibetans.

INFORMATION ON EARLY MAHĀYĀNA

The importance of Mahāyāna today makes it surprising to discover that there is very little information about the earliest development of the movement. We have no record of a founder, no authors have placed their names on the early texts, and no written history of the Mahāyāna dates from those early centuries of its existence. In fact, it was not until the first century A.D. that a master of this school is known, the founder of the *Mādhyamika*, *Nāgārjuna*.

There is not even a final conclusion about the geographic location in which Mahāyāna emerged. Some scholars feel that it was in the Northwest of India, pointing out the strength of this form of Buddhism in that region and suggesting that certain aspects of its teaching may have had influences from the religions and cultures to the west of India. During the formative years of early Mahāyāna (second century B.C. to first century A.D.) these influences were strongest in the Northwest, an example being the impact of Western ideas on the making of the Buddhist image, where the Greco-Roman models were borrowed.

In opposition to this theory about the place of origin, other scholars point out that Nāgārjuna and many later masters came from the southern centers. There, also, contact with the cultures of the Western countries was not unknown in the maritime cities. In addition, the sūtras give an indication of the spread of Mahāyāna from the South to the North.

THE EARLY PERIOD

The great split between the *Mahāsāṃghikas* and the *Sthaviras* is the beginning of the story of Mahāyāna which can be traced with any degree of certainty. Within the Mahāsāṃghikas a number of internal schisms developed, such as the *Lokottaravādins* and the *Ekavyāvahārikas*, schools which held to certain ideas and doctrines found later in Mahāyāna. For example, the statements about the nature of the Buddha and the Bodhisattva are found to be similar to the doctrines expounded in the *Prajñāpāramitā-sūtra* in its oldest form. The important doctrine of *śūnyatā* (emptiness) in its less developed form is found among the Ekavyāvahārikas. It is possible that this group later joined with the Lokottaravādins and that their ideas passed on into the new Mahāyāna. Most of our information about these schools has been traced through documents that were translated by the Chinese but no longer exist in Sanskrit.

NEW LITERATURE

Since it is impossible to establish an exact beginning point or even a line of transmission, the first text produced and preserved by the Mahāyāna school is a primary document for the study of its development. In this case it is the philosophical and doctrinal texts called the Prajñāpāramitā-sūtras. Although many of the ideas in it can be traced in some form to the groups within the Mahāsāṃghikas, the systematization in the Prajñāpāramitā was a new format and the use of the doctrines presented by that text constituted a new school.

It is in this Prajñā sūtra that we find reference to both the *Śrāvakas* and *Pratyekabuddhas*, defined as those who do not know or follow the teachings of the Prajñāpāramitā and so they are given a degrading epithet of *Hīnayāna*, the lesser vehicle, as opposed to the followers of the Prajñā—the Mahāyāna or the great vehicle.

During the centuries which followed the appearance of the Prajñāpāramitā, a new form of Buddhist literature appeared, the *Vaipulya-sūtras* or "extended sūtras" which were said to be the "word" of the Buddha, using the exact formula of the *Nikāyas* or *Āgamas*.

The rationale for the literature is given at the beginning of the Prajñāpāramitā-sūtra, i.e., whatever is taught by a true disciple of the Buddha is indeed the word of the Buddha.

From this period of the development of Mahāyāna came a tremendous outpouring of literary works which included some of the best known and most widely used of all the Buddhist texts. There was the group of Prajñā-pāramitā-sūtras, including the *Diamond* and *Heart Sūtras*, the *Lotus Sūtra* (*Saddharmapuṇḍarīka-sūtra*), the *Daśabhūmika-sūtra*, the *Sukhāvatīvyūha-sūtra*, and many others.

Therefore, as with much of Indian history, we know little of the details of dates or events, but we have a great deal of information about the development of thought.

IDEAS AND DOCTRINES

Through these sūtras and texts, we can trace a movement that put forth new conceptions about such doctrines as the *Bodhisattva*, *śūnyatā* (emptiness), the six *pāramitās* (perfections), and *karuṇā* (compassion).

It is often said that the Mahāyāna was a triumph of the laity, since the texts recognize the potential of the son or daughter of a good family (Buddhist believers). But it should be borne in mind that the movement was mainly directed to those monks who were in training on the path of the Bodhisattva and this path is one of rigorous meditation, presupposing a monastic life at some time or other. The Mahāyāna goes to great length to reject the *Arhant* as the highest saint or *nirvāṇa* as the proper immediate goal of meditation, maintaining that out of compassion the Bodhisattva aids sentient beings and delays entering nirvāṇa. This act of compassion involves an action that is not limited to this mundane world or the laws which regulate it. It centered, as was later taught in the texts, on a turning over of merit to all beings, a supernormal ability to control future destinies of beings. Although the laity ultimately profits from this action, it does not imply that monks and laymen are considered on equal terms in these early Mahāyāna texts, or that a Bodhisattva is bound to act in accord with any set of social ethics. The Bodhisattva is directed only by his insight of the ultimate needs of men if they are to achieve an enlightened state. His skill in these matters is called *upāya* and can often appear in a form that seems to bear little direct relationship to the immediate needs or problems of men.

The necessity for having the training of a monk holds true even for the great layman *Vimalakīrti*, for his enlightened state is explained on the basis of his former lives and the fact that he in the past had gone through the training of a Bodhisattva.

SUGGESTED READING

Bareau, André. *Les Sectes Bouddhiques du Petit Véhicule*, pp. 55 ff.

Conze, Edward. *Buddhism: Its Essence and Development*, pp. 32–34, 69, 119–43.

Demiéville, Paul. "L'origine des sectes bouddhiques d'après Paramārtha," *Mélanges Chinois et Bouddhiques*, 1 (1931–1932): pp. 15–64.

Lamotte, Étienne. *Histoire du Bouddhisme Indien des origines à l'ère Śaka.*

Zürcher, Erik. *Buddhism, Its Origin and Spread in Words, Maps, and Pictures.*

15

The Prajñāpāramitā Literature

Lewis R. Lancaster

DEFINITION OF THE TERM

The Sanskrit compound *Prajñāpāramitā* is made up of *prajñā*, often translated as wisdom and sometimes as insight or awareness, and *pāramitā*, perfection or literally *pāram* other side or beyond and *itā* gone, i.e., gone beyond or gone to the other side. Since this world is said to be like a flooding river filled with troubles and dangers, one seeks the means to go across or beyond it to the other side where the anguish of birth and death no longer function.

THE FIRST MAHĀYĀNA LITERATURE

The Prajñāpāramitā was the literature resulting from the development of the Mahāyāna movement. It was in the process of being formulated from about the second century B.C.

At first there was no title except the name Prajñāpāramitā given to these texts. But as more sūtras bearing that name came into existence, it became necessary to make some distinction between them and so they were given names according to their length.

The earliest Prajñāpāramitā-sūtra that we know came to be called the "8,000 Line Sūtra" (*Aṣṭasāhasrikā-prajñāpāramitā-sūtra*). Not only is it the earliest known Mahāyāna sūtra, but it was the first philosophical text of this form of Buddhism to be translated into Chinese (A.D. 179). This translation, done by *Lokakṣema*, is the oldest extant version of any Mahāyāna sūtra and was the text most often used by those Taoists who first discovered in Buddhism an affinity with their own teachings.

The Chinese did not name the texts after their length, but having received some of them before distinctive titles were used on the manuscripts in India, they made a title by using the one given for the first chapter. Thus the "8,000 Line Sūtra" was known in China as the *Tao-hsing Ching* (the practice of the way sūtra) from the first chapter heading of "Tao-hsing."

EXPANDED PRAJÑĀPĀRAMITĀ

The Prajñāpāramitā-sūtras underwent a process of expansion in length after the introduction of the first text. The most important versions in this large group are the "25,000 Line" *Pañcaviṃśati-sāhasrikā-prajñāpāramitā-sūtra*, and the largest of all, i.e., the "100,000 Line" *Śatasāhasrikā-prajñāpāramitā-sūtra*. In addition, the "18,000 Line," *Aṣṭadaśa-sāhasrikā-prajñāpāramitā-sūtra*, is also preserved. These contain basically the same text, their length being determined by the amount of repetition.

SUMMARIES

After the period of lengthy expansions, there was an attempt to put together a shorter and more usable summary that would contain the essence of the teaching. The two main sūtras of this type are the *Vajracchedikā-prajñāpāramitā-sūtra*, commonly known as the "Diamond Sūtra," and the *Hṛdaya-prajñāpāramitā-sūtra*, translated as the "Heart Sūtra."

THE TANTRIC PRAJÑĀPĀRAMITĀ

The *Tantric* movement, which had great support from the seventh century on, helped to spark a new interest in the Prajñāpāramitā and new sūtras appeared containing *mantras* and the vocabulary of the Tantra. The extreme limit of abbreviation can be found among these, in the text which is composed of only one letter, "A," said to contain all the teachings.

COMMENTARIES

Scholastic traditions in Buddhism have provided important commentaries for these sūtras. Thus for the "8,000 Line" text there is the *Abhisamayālaṃkārāloka* by *Haribhadra*, and for the "25,000 Line" text the most famous of Chinese Buddhist commentaries, the *Ta Chih Tu Lun*, said to have been the work of *Nāgārjuna* and translated into Chinese by *Kumārajīva*. Of great help is the *Yogācāra* commentary, the *Abhisamayālaṃkāra* of *Maitreyanātha*, that sums up the contents of the *Large Sūtra* (25,000 Lines) in 273 verses.

THE FORMAT

The texts of the Prajñāpāramitā follow a format of a continuous dialogue between the Buddha and various disciples, as well as an audience of gods, spirits, and men, or occasionally speeches between the disciples themselves.

From these questions, answers, and comments, it is possible to rank each speaker according to his degree of insight. The disciple of highest development becomes *Subhūti*, a little known figure in the *Nikāyas* or *Āgamas*. On the other hand, a famous follower of the Buddha, *Śāriputra*, is downgraded to an inferior position, indicating that the Mahāyāna movement was no longer attempting to trace its roots back to the old establishment but was setting up a new tradition and line of transmission.

THE TEACHINGS

The main teaching of the sūtras is the emphasis on the six *pāramitās*, hence the name for the literature. These six are *dāna* (giving), *śīla* (morality), *kṣanti* (patience), *vīrya* (vigor), *samādhi* (trance), and *prajñā* (wisdom). These pāramitās are central to the development and training of the *Bodhisattvas*, who combine both wisdom and compassion. Thus they are able to accomplish the feat of vowing and working for the salvation of all beings while recognizing that no beings as such exist.

In the ontological realm all mental states, all elements which make up our world of experience—i.e., all *dharmas*—are empty and ultimately nonexistent. All dharmas are like a dream, not produced and not related to any other dharma. Through such insights, the Bodhisattva achieves wisdom of emptiness (*śūnyatā*), that not only is a person empty of an *ātman* (a self) as in the so-called *Hīnayāna* teachings, but the dharmas are also empty and thus there is no need to analyze and review these states in the manner of the schools which emphasized the *Abhidharma*.

SUGGESTED READING

Conze, Edward, ed. and tr. *Selected Sayings From the Perfection of Wisdom*, pp. 11–26.

———. *The Prajñāpāramitā Literature*.

Hikata, R., tr. *Suvikrāntavikrāmī-prajñāpāramitā-sūtra*.

Murti, T.R.V. *The Central Philosophy of Buddhism*, pp. 207 ff. (Chapter 8: "The Mādhyamika Conception of Philosophy as Prajñāpāramitā").

16

Doctrines of the Mahāyāna

Lewis R. Lancaster

INTRODUCTION

Those doctrines that may be said to be distinctly Mahāyāna are not easily set apart from those of earlier Buddhism, since the doctrinal material of Mahāyāna is not for the main part a discussion or introduction of new terms, but rather it is a new format for the ideas expressed. Thus the key to understanding Mahāyāna is finding that particular emphasis which is given in the teaching, for it is this which may make it peculiarly Mahāyāna.

SŪTRA GLORIFICATION

Sūtras had long been a part of the Buddhist canon, but the Mahāyānists developed a literature which they called sūtras or, more specifically, *Vaipulya-sūtras*. These texts introduced along with their teaching an account of the merit to be gained by preserving, reciting, and honoring the sūtra itself. This was carried to its ultimate form in such sūtras as the *Vajracchedikā-prajñā-pāramitā-sūtra* where we are told that the cultic activity directed toward the sūtra outranks all other efforts. For example, it is taught that the reciting of one verse from the sūtra is more meritorious than building enough *stūpas* to fill up the world systems in the ten directions. This procedure of praising the merit and worth of the Vaipulya-sūtras has been very successful and consequently in this group of texts are to be found the most famous of all Buddhist works, the Lotus, Diamond, Heart, and Perfect Wisdom *Sūtras*.

An indirect effect of the glorification of the sūtras can be seen in China where schools were formed in reliance on a single text. Even the anti-textual Ch'an group produced its own work, the *Platform Sūtra of the Sixth Patriarch*.

BODHISATTVAS, THE MAHĀSATTVAS

In early Buddhism, *Bodhisattva* (Enlightened Being) had been an interim term used for one who had been recognized as a future Buddha but had not yet achieved that state. This term was taken up by the Mahāyānists, who declared the Bodhisattva to be the ideal saint, vastly superior to the *Arhant* in that he chooses to remain in *Saṃsāra*, constantly undergoing rebirth for the sake of helping all sentient beings achieve enlightenment. The Bodhisattva was given a second title of *Mahāsattva* (Great Being), and a tradition of celestial Bodhisattvas became part of Buddhism. These Bodhisattvas, such as *Mañjuśrī* and *Avalokiteśvara*, gradually assumed greater importance and eventually their images were to be found on the altars along with the Buddha or even standing alone as the sole recipient of reverence from the worshipper in the shrine or monastery.

COMPASSION AND SKILL

Compassion (*karuṇā*) ascribed to the Buddha when he finally decided to preach the Dharma after his enlightenment was not a new item of Buddhist dogma, but again the Mahāyāna gave it a particular twist. It became the primary force behind the action of the Bodhisattvas, the Mahāsattvas, and it was this compassion which led them to make vows to save all sentient beings before entering the blissful state, or *nirvāṇa*. The many methods and techniques by which the Bodhisattva converts beings and secures their ultimate salvation is called his Skill-in-Means (*upāya*).

WISDOM

The arrangement of the six *pāramitās* as expounded by the *Prajñāpāramitā* was yet another example of the way in which the Mahāyāna managed to teach by making use of older terms in a new system. The pāramitās culminated in the sixth, *prajñā*, the insight or wisdom by which the Bodhisattva knows all things as they really are, i.e., Thusness (*tathatā*).

Emptiness. Through the prajñā-perfection, the Bodhisattva was able to see that not only is the person (*pudgala*) empty (*śūnya*) of a self (*ātman*), but also that those mental states (*dharmas*), said by some schools to be indivisible and constant, are in fact also empty of any own-being (*svabhāva*). This twofold doctrine of emptiness—the most important aspect of the teaching of the Prajñāpāramitā-sūtra—was the primary distinction between Mahāyāna and such "Hīnayāna" schools as the *Sarvāstivādins*.

STAGES OF DEVELOPMENT

In later Mahāyāna the procedure by which the Bodhisattva perfected himself was formalized in the doctrine of the Ten Stages (*daśa-bhūmi*). In the first stage (*pramuditā*) the Bodhisattva experiences joy since he knows that he will soon attain *bodhi*, the state of complete and perfect enlightenment.

From this intial stage he pursues a career of deepening his insight and reaches a final turning point at the seventh bhūmi. The completion of this seventh stage means that he will never again fall back into a lower stage, and so it is said that he becomes "irreversible." On the eighth stage he is capable of achieving nirvāṇa, and it is only by the knowledge (*jñāna*) he has acquired that he resists doing so. From this point, the Bodhisattva glides on effortlessly to the tenth stage without forsaking the world of birth-and-death.

CELESTIAL BUDDHAS

Following the earlier lead of the *Mahāsāṃghikas*, the Mahāyānists taught that the Buddha was transcendent, above all sensual desires and human weaknesses. Thus *Śākyamuni*, the historic Buddha of most recent time, was seen to be but one of the many manifested forms of the Buddha. Eternal Buddhas, who were later described as aspects of the eternal Buddha-nature, became important. The first one to be mentioned was *Akṣobhya* Buddha (in the *Aṣṭasāhasrikā-prajñāpāramitā-sūtra*). *Amitābha* Buddha became the most important of all these Buddhas in the Far East, while in the Tantra, the five eternal Buddhas as experienced in meditation had special significance.

These Buddhas reside in Buddha-fields (*kṣetra*) where men may find the ideal conditions for reaching a state of enlightenment and either go to nirvāṇa or become Bodhisattvas. The "fields" are not intended as the final goal, but only one more step along the path to enlightenment. Having accomplished that state, beings no longer have need for a paradise.

BUDDHA BODY

As speculation about the nature of the Buddha developed, attention was given to the body of the Buddha. In later Mahāyāna, the doctrine of the Three Bodies (*tri-kāya*) came into vogue among the *Yogācārins*. They taught that there was an apparition body (*Nirmāṇa-kāya*) which is the Form Body of the Buddha that appears before men and preaches the Dharma to them. When the Bodhisattvas view the body of the Buddha, they are able to see the Reward Body (*Saṃbhoga-kāya*) which has resulted from following the path of the Bodhisattva. The Transcendent Body of the Buddha (*Dharma-kāya*) can be perceived only by a Buddha.

This three-body doctrine was preceded in Mahāyāna by a twofold division of the Buddha body into the Form Body (*Rūpa-kāya*) and the Transcendent Body (*Dharma-kāya*). From basic formulations of these types, the elaborate systems of the *Mādhyamika*, *Yogācāra*, and *Tantra* have developed.

SUGGESTED READING

Conze, Edward. *Buddhism: Its Essence and Development*, pp. 119–60.

———. *Buddhist Thought in India*, pp. 195–237.

Dutt, Nalinaksha. *Aspects of Mahāyāna Buddhism and Its Relation to Hīnayāna.*

Renou, Louis, and Filliozat, Jean. *L'Inde Classique*. Tome 2, pp. 315–608.

Robinson, Richard H. *The Buddhist Religion*, pp. 49–70.

17

Major Schools of the Mahāyāna: Mādhyamika

Douglas D. Daye

I. INTRODUCTION

This essay is a philosophical, not a philological, introduction to *Mādhyamika*. Thus one will discover more questions than demonstrated answers. This essay exemplifies the necessary simplification and generalization (which lacks desirable documentation) required by the introductory nature of such an essay. Mādhyamika is a philosophically sophisticated, culturally complex subject and not easily simplified. Since this difficult essay will be read by individuals of greatly varying philosophical backgrounds, many of the following sections will possess an introductory section, (1), and a more inclusive but still introductory discussion, (2). It is my hope, of course, that the reader will construe the following hints and interpretations as merely "a ford and bridge for the intrepid" (Robinson, *Early Mādhyamika in India and China*, p. vii). As with Aristotle and Kant, "all things excellent are as difficult as they are rare" (Spinoza).

II. BACKGROUND SKETCH

In the Indian schema of orthodox (*āstika*, explicitly acknowledging allegiance to the authority of the *Vedas*) and unorthodox (*nāstika*) philosophical schools (*darśanas*), Mādhyamika belongs in the latter unorthodox category. Its early and middle developments occurred in the Indian context; however, it was also of tremendous influence in Tibet and in China. As with much of early Buddhist culture, it reflects an integration, assimilation, or reaction to the Indian cultural milieu. In the Buddhist schema it is one of the major schools of Buddhism, along with *Sarvāstivāda*, *Sautrāntika*, *Theravāda*, *Tantra*, and *Yogacāra*. The title, "Middle Position," refers to a philosophical position midway between the extreme metaphysical positions of postulating ontological ("existence," eternalism) categories of either (any) *X*, or its contradictory; i.e., that *X* does not exist, annihilation. One should note that the denial of a "known" thing is also a "position" (*dṛṣṭi*, i.e., a philosophical view). The Mādhyamikas deny *both* that other views are free from legitimate contradiction and that they possess a position (dṛṣṭi) to defend.

The Mādhyamika school was (probably) founded by *Nāgārjuna* during the second half of the third century A.D., in the developing Indian Mahāyāna complex. It purports to be and is a true and faithful development of the basic tenets of Buddhism. Its goal is ultimately soteriological (salvation-oriented), i.e., *nirvāṇa*.

Since the beginning of the last half of the nineteenth century when Mādhyamika first came to the notice of the modern scholarly tradition, it has remained one of the most fascinating, enigmatic religio-philosophic sets of concepts surfacing from Asia upon the international (and Western) consciousness.

A great variety of labels have been projected upon Nāgārjuna (A.D. 200–300), e.g., absolute monist, radical pluralist, nihilist, negativist, relativist, logician, and dialectician. It seems fair to say that the different labels, approaches, and descriptions of Nāgārjuna's writings found in the history of modern scholarship reflect almost as much about the viewpoints of the scholars involved as do they reflect the content of Nāgārjuna's concepts. (This essay is not an exception.) Representative samples of such scholarship may be found in the Suggested Reading at the conclusion of this lecture.

One popular biography of Nāgārjuna states that he was born in a South Indian brahman family, participated in a typical brāhmaṇical education in religious and nonreligious subjects, and acquired some fame for his wide learning while still a young man. He was also considered by later writers to have been a *Bodhisattva*. His Sanskrit style exemplifies his classical training and his interest in rather hard-nosed argumentation. He is a "rationalist" in the broad sense of the term; he argues systematically.

The two texts of Nāgārjuna in which his philosophical position is exemplified most clearly are the *Mūla-Mādhyamika Kārikās* (hereafter *MK*) and the *Vigraha-Vyāvartanī*. These are essentially polemic treatises which purport to refute the philosophical positions of both other Buddhist schools and other non-Buddhist darśanas. Those major schools to which the Mādhyamika polemics are directed are orthodox (āstika), *Saṃkhya*, *Nyāya-Vaiṣeśika*, *Mīmāṃsā*, and the other unorthodox (nāstika) Buddhist Abhidharma schools of the Sarvāstivāda and Sautrāntika. Mādhyamika exemplifies the growing methodological and stylistic influences of the epistemological (*pramāṇa-vāda*) inquiries of the early darśana systems. Nāgārjuna's assimilation and extensive use of rhetorical figures (e.g., reductio ad absurdum, *prasaṅga*) and the style and vigor of the early protologicians (see the lecture on Buddhist Logic) helped to tighten the rules of polemic debate among the later Indian schools. An example—a prasaṅga—may help to illustrate these qualities: "That existents (*bhāva*) are without own-being (*svabhāva*) is because their alter-being is seen; an existence without own-being does not exist; hence the emptiness (*śūnyatā*) of existents. If own-being does not occur, to whom might alter-being belong? If own-being does occur, to whom might alter-being belong?" (*MK*, 13:3–4, quoted from Robinson, *Early Mādhyamika in India and China*, p. 41). If one compares this style with a late *Upaniṣad*, one is struck by the obvious development of argumentation. By such formalistic emphasis, Nāgārjuna paved the way for a more systematic logical development of the later darśanas.

III. AN EPISTEMOLOGICAL AND METAPHYSICAL OVERVIEW

1. One crucial feature in contrasting the Buddhist philosophical assumptions with that of their Indian background is to note the fundamental and far-reaching change in Buddhist philosophy during the period from the late Upaniṣads to the explicit formulation of the early darśana systems (roughly 300 B.C. to A.D. 200). The change was essentially a metaphysical one. By a metaphysical position, I refer to the most fundamental conceptual elements and categories of description which represent the most basic ideas common to a particular cultural, philosophical, or religious world view. These ideas in this period in ancient India were in the process of gradual but significant change. Prior to the time of the Buddhists, the Indians of the late Upaniṣadic and very early classical period held that the question for metaphysical knowledge involved an examination of the most fundamental concepts, metaphysical elements, or reals which, because they were most fundamental, were seen as incompatible with the variety of *actual* change that we observe in our everyday lives. That is, the metaphysical axiom was that *basic* realities (e.g., *prakṛti* or nature, satya or realities, svabhāva or own-being) do not change. To *be* a "real *X*" means that such an *X* is not subject to causal conditioning. This quest for unchanging reals was essentially a quest for *stable* conceptual categories which describe things most fundamental in what appears (perhaps superficially) to be a very changing, fluxing world. It was a quest for elements different in *kind*, not merely in *degree*.

A significant feature of the Buddhist metaphysical position is that it contrasts strongly with its Indian predecessors. The Buddhists introduced a fundamental and radical change in the idea of the basic constituents of the Indian world view. This radical view is expressed in one of the oldest and most fundamental ideas of Buddhism: everything (involves) change (*sarvaṁ anityam*). Rather than looking for stable constituents of a description which reflected the way the world is, the Buddhist concluded that the described world was only superficially a set of stable projected relationships, however described in language; it is a world which, if examined minutely, could be seen to be a set of ever-changing, fluxing, moving, momentary "states of affairs." This is not to say that the early and the later Buddhists denied our everyday ordinary experience; on the contrary, they realized that language, the most widely used medium of human communication, expresses the commonalities shared in our public discussion of our individual experience first-person knowing relationships in third-person (publicly shared) language. What the Buddhists did hold is that the world is held together by a set of publicly agreed upon conceptual tools which "glues" the world together and renders it understandable in accordance with, and because of, our conceptual frameworks. In other words, they did not deny public reality; rather they held that it was simply not an accurate picture of the way the world really is (*yathābhūtam*). This shift from a quest for stable enduring realities to a viewpoint that the world consists of ever-changing, ever-shifting relationships, "mutually glued" together by language and public acceptance of conceptual categories upon which people then acted, represents a fundamental metaphysical shift in the history of early Indian philosophy.

2. Again to somewhat oversimplify, the metaphysical position of the Buddhist represents a fundamental change from a subject-attribute metaphysics (i.e., Sanskrit grammars of the world) to process metaphysics. The latter in turn may be likened to a reflexive flow chart concerned with the problems of language, metalanguage, reference, and reification. The Buddhists were concerned with the problem of dealing with the static components of language and experience in their philosophic descriptions. They were striving to bridge the gap between the perception of the ordinary individual and the supreme goal of perceiving the world process as it appears in itself. In the perception of things as they really are, one is freed from the projected conceptual and emotional distortions generated through our mutually conditioned worldly experience. One is also freed from our habitual, mutual and culturally generated epistemic (knowing) grids. The *relationship* between the knower and the background is also a product of these reified grids. There is no nongrided grid. The Buddhists suggest that language and the coordinated relationships presupposed by language and its constant cultural reinforcement through years of preadult development constitutes a framework or grid of reified static epistemic components projected (and reprojected) on both an ever-changing personal inner (first person) environment and a simultaneous outer (third person) environment. Of this total environment, it can be said (at best) that *it* is in a *continual* state of flux. The latter "it," of course, begs the epistemic question. Thus

they were led to conclude that if one assumes that the categories of language mirror reality as it really is, one commits the logical fallacy of circular reasoning. In a very restricted sense, their position is somewhat (but *only* somewhat) similar to Kant's. However, the Buddhists and Kant remain epistemological apples and oranges, not different types of apples.

To the question, "What are the most fundamental basic elements or categories of description in our collective perception of the world?," the Buddhist would answer that the question was a *logically complex* one and presupposes a metaphysical schema of ontological categories and epistemic elements (e.g., the object-attribute-dichotomy) which simply does not fit the case of experience as it really is.

The *general* Buddhist position seems to be that experience, either first person experience (one's own inner experience) and third person language customs of description *about* first person experience, consists of an infinite series of staccato-like unique moments (*kṣaṇa*). Unfortunately, that these moments are either unique *or* nonunique involves (at least the suspicion of) circularity. Without examining the long history of these related arguments, consider that to be able to answer the question of either the uniqueness or nonuniqueness of momentary experience presupposes first that there be a position independent of both the "world as it is" and our knowing of it, from which we might compare. This obviously seems impossible without further and equally weak appeals to assumptions which lead one to a circular argument. The "individual," in his selective awareness of his own personal field of epistemic relations, knows the "contents" of that experience by means of generic concepts and habitual correlations between the five senses plus various mental components which involve relationships of knowing and describing. These conceptual correlations are descriptive because they render the inner and outer worlds intelligible; also they are ostensibly descriptive rather than overtly prescriptive. Sometimes. however, these correlations are mixed together in such words as "love, hate"; i.e., they are both descriptive and carry an evaluative force. We strive to describe our inner world by means of such public words. We communicate to others by using these words, the meanings of which are held in common by various individuals. These meanings are verified by subsequent behavior patterns called conversations, communication, rapping, etc. However, those Buddhists who developed the Abhidharma literature devised a new set of first person epistemic descriptive categories modeled largely on experiences in meditation. These Abhidharma dharma analysis concepts were held to more accurately describe the way the inner world "really is" (see VII). These words and (thus) categories, and not *necessarily* the experiences, are held in common; therefore they constitute a third person public language *about* "private" experiences (see VI). One should note that there is nothing necessarily mysterious about the generation of such a technical, esoteric language. Musicians, race drivers, pimps, and others continually use such special languages. Ask yourself: What is the singular "it" in "He's got it all together"?

IV. CAUSATION AND LANGUAGE

1. One of the most fundamental ideas which puzzled all the early Indian philosophers, including the Buddhists and the Jains, was that of the problem of causation. All of us are familiar with the concept of change in causation. But have we stopped to consider the basic problems involved in identifying change? One may devise questions which seem trivial (and perhaps all too true) by asking: If there is something changing, then there is something which is different in each succeeding moment, different than "it" was in the preceding moment. Therefore one may ask: Why do we know that the "thing" which is *now* observed to be a changed "thing" is the *same* "thing" which we identified in the previous moment? This simple example exemplifies the relationship (and therefore the problem) between the identification of entities as the same (or as a different) entity in a state of continual change, the identity relationship between those changing entities, and the presupposed stable references common to such descriptors in a publicly operative language. Language consists of relatively stable units of description and prescription; the world, however, is changing from moment to moment, from day to day, and from lifetime to lifetime. How then may we justify the use of a stable system of conceptual referring units of language to describe something which is in a continual process of change?

2. The Buddhists also considered several answers to this problem. A great deal of philosophical discussion revolved around the two interrelated concepts of relational or dependent coorigination (*pratītya-samutpāda*) and the ontological status of certain words—in Mādhyamika, "own-being" (svabhāva) and language-constructs (*prajñapti*). The origins of this "causal" concept of the twelvefold prior conditions (*nidānas*) may be found in various of the earliest texts, such as the *Pāli Nikāyas* (e.g., *Majjhima Nikāya* II, 28). With such statements as "this thing being, that becomes; from the arising of this, that arises; this not becoming, that does not become," the concept of Buddhist causality seems to imply, in some scholars' eyes, a chain of physical and mental causality. However, if one combines the concept of sequential causality with the additional and equally fundamental tenet that everything is impermanent, that everything consists of a series of unique staccato-like moments, then the problem of "causation" does *not* become

one of sufficient and necessary causal conditions through succeeding public moments. The problem *does* become that of trying to distinguish the ontological criteria for distinguishing what constitutes an ontological category in one succeeding moment and its relationship, if any, with a specific "event" in a succeeding moment. In other words, "$\supset$" becomes "$\equiv$". Can this be done without blatant circular reasoning? Does the ordinary use of a general term (e.g., self, *ātman*, *pudgala*) *presuppose* that no legitimate (or possible) falsification can ever occur? In other words, do we beg the question in the language we use about what (basically) exists? Are we merely assuming the naive idea that if there is a descriptive word then there must be a distinct knowable entity to which the word supposedly refers? The Mādhyamikas suggest an affirmative answer to the latter two (rhetorical) questions. Consider then the following: What is the "it" in "it is raining"? Hence the problem of identifying entities through time about which there are sequential, causal relationships is a logically prior and soteriologically important question. The Mādhyamikas hold that although words and the world they map seem to be stable units in a changing world, identity and time are actually born fresh at every moment.

The general Mādhyamika problematic has been succinctly described by Professor Matilal in *Epistemology, Logic and Grammar in Indian Philosophical Analysis* (p. 148): "If we assume any object 'X' to be independently existent, then either we cannot give any consistent (rational) account of that object, by which we can avoid logical contradiction (cf. *na yujyate*), or our assumption of its independent existence will lead to some absurd consequence which will run counter to our experience (cf. *nopapadyate*)." We shall consider a part of this problematic.

V. METALANGUAGES AND LEVELS OF ABSTRACTION

1. Language is deceptively transparent in that we are so bombarded by it and immersed in it that we seldom take time to become aware of how complex and subtle many of our linguistic actions really are. We understandably perform these linguistic actions with a fantastic degree of *unawareness*; certainly we perform them every day. To understand some Mādhyamika problems, such as the use of different levels of language and their functions in the process of reification, we need to be more aware of the subtleties and bewitching aspects of language.

All of us have had occasions in which our grammar or word choice has been corrected (or at least criticized). At such times it is quite easy to distinguish what we said from what was said *about* what we said. In this context we may note that the former (i.e., what we said) is on a lower level of abstraction than the specific criticisms *of* what we said. The latter (i.e., talking *about* what we said) constitutes a metalanguage to the former object language. The writing you are now reading constitutes a meta-metalanguage to what was said in the preceding sentences; it is also a self-referring sentence much as is the Mādhyamika statement that "emptiness is empty too." This rational concept is important, for the Mādhyamikas (and most Indian and Western philosophers) were concerned with the problems of how we *must* talk about the world and, second, the characteristics of how the world *is* (or may be) apart from the ways in which we talk *about* it. If we assume (falsely, of course) that the categories of language always reflect the categories and distinctions of the way the world is apart from our talking about it, we are led to make judgments about the world which have a reality solely in pieces of language and not in pieces of the world. The structure of our descriptive language does not necessarily reflect or mirror the structure of the world; they do not stand in an isomorphic relationship. If we take a word which expresses a set of abstract relationships between aspects of the world, and if we presuppose that the reference of that relationship-word (e.g., self) is a thing, then we project this thing into our felt expectations of the world because of our language, and not in accordance with the particular reality of the world yathābhūtam (i.e., the way the world really is). The latter projective process is called reification.

An example of a category mistake may help. If I guided you around the campus and introduced you to the students, faculty, administrators, and passers-by, and showed you the buildings, the grounds, and maintenance vehicles, I would have showed you the university. However, after meeting all those people and seeing all those things, if you then asked me to point out the university, you would be making a category mistake. A category mistake is, in this context, a request for an ostensive, guided experience enabling one (falsely here) to couple a particular experience with a specific linguistic label; that is, to see the thing for which the word is merely a label. The university is a word which does not refer solely to the earth or the people on the campus. Rather it refers to a complex set of relationships *between* these peoples and certain portions of the earth. Therefore, to ask that the university be pointed out (as above) is to reify the word university as if it were a thing in ways in which trucks, pedants, and sidewalks are things. The Mādhyamikas attempted to show that the categories of description, the words used to describe the world in ordinary and philosophical language, of other schools was mistaken because it involved this fatal mistake of reification and the collapsing of levels of abstraction in the description of the way the world "really is"; thus they make a category mistake. The Mādhyamikas also held that they had no alternate position to defend.

Their position was purely metacritical and soteriologically therapeutic.

2. I have suggested that the central problem of Buddhist causation is one which concerns identity and difference, epistemic correlation and the relationship of language to the world; this in turn effects one's self-image, social role, actions, and values. Note that these are grounded in and *about* words and in words about other words; such words are the means of one's *understanding* of the world. We need now to distinguish levels of abstraction in the *Mūla-Mādhyamika Kārikās*. Words are the primary (but not the only) medium through which the world is both known individually and through which intrapersonal communication about it is achieved. We must therefore distinguish levels of reference and levels of abstraction to avoid reification and category mistakes.

There are at least four orders of description and abstraction operative in the *Mūla-Mādhyamika Kārikās*. First, there is the ordinary language abstraction level of "things" in the world, e.g., trees, stones, and properties of relationships such as hate, anger, and love. Second, there are rival metaphysical and epistemological theories which utilize such generic terms as Abhidharmic *dharmas*, prakṛti, etc., which the *Mūla-Mādhyamika Kārikās* holds are incorrect and inherently contradictory. The general word (in the text) for such generic terms is own-being (*svabhāva*). These rival metaphysical and epistemological theories are the objects of the polemics in the *Mūla-Mādhyamika Kārikās*. Third, there is the third-order capstone *reflexive* concept of emptiness (*śūnyatā*). Everything is empty, including "emptiness" itself. Fourth, there are certain implicit prescriptive relationships which involve a fourth order abstraction level, the concept of language-constructs (prajñapti; see VIII and IX).

VI. ABHIDHARMA DHARMA ANALYSIS

1. There is a special class of words which we use to describe experiences within the particular boundaries of our own consciousness, the contents of which are not open to public observation. We may call these words first person epistemic descriptive words. They are first person terms, on the analogy of the first person pronoun (e.g., I, *aham*). They refer not to publicly observable aspects of experience, but to the intimate known experiences within our *own* minds. They are epistemic because they are words which refer to categories of the different *functional* levels of mental (*citta*, *manas*) components of knowing. The most general Buddhist epistemological interpretation seems to be that the specific individual characteristics of any known entity is dependent upon the totality of causes and conditions (*hetu*, *pratyaya*) present in any given moment of its perception. Therefore the

relationship of subject-object and the epistemic discriminations present in the field of experience to one individual is a product of the effects of those forces in his experience over which he has ordinarily no conscious control. Second and simultaneously, the interrelated set of concepts by which he sorts out the known perception enables him thereby to *recognize* it as a meaningful set of relationships to him. All too simply put, everything is *what* it is because of what we habitually conclude it is not. From this position, the world consists (to the individual) of a series of interrelated projections and reactions. The reflexive nature of the problem of Mādhyamika epistemology revolves around the twin problems of generic concepts (e.g., own-being, svabhāva) and their reifications. The affective and emotive concomitants of believing that the categorized world as approved by and reinforced by one's own culture *is* really constituted in the manner in which we normally view it, is to generate ties of care and suffering (*duḥkha*). The word is not the thing, but the thing is known through word-relations; to know a thing is to know a word and its web-like context. The relationships between references to word (language constructs, prajñapti) and things (e.g., self) constitute a core problem in Mādhyamika.

Let us examine the concept of a dharma in Abhidharma dharma-analysis (*dharmavicaya*). Against this the Mādhyamikas reacted. A dharma is an epistemic and *descriptive component* (not a static entity) in a reductive (and phenomenological) analysis of first person epistemic relations. It is an alternate map of consciousness. The Abhidharmists held that third person epistemological situations commonly misdescribed in ordinary language (first order language) are better described by reference to their alternate epistemic second order relationships than by their opponents' metaphysical postulates and ordinary language epistemic categories. This better second order description (dharma-analysis, an alternate metalanguage) of reality is composed of a finite set (75 for the Sarvāstivādins) of mutually exclusive, totally exhaustive epistemic components of description, i.e., dharmas. By postulating these evaluative and epistemic categories these pre-Mādhyamika Buddhists offered an alternate descriptive world view, from a first person epistemological point of view, which contrasts markedly with ordinary (first person and third person) descriptive language. Dharma analysis is simply an alternative conceptual map. It is a map within which one must shift the gears of one's language categories and assume a *new* vocabulary and conceptual syntax. Terminology operative in one map may not be operative in the other. While becoming nimble in this new language-land, one notices that old, warm, familiar conceptual friends such as "the self" and "the will," strictly speaking, are no longer operative in the new epistemic landscape.

These Buddhist Abhidharmists postulated two kinds of reality or truth (Pāli: *sacca*, Sanskrit: *satya*) which correspond to two language frameworks—two coherent, consistent ways of talking. First, is the ultimate or highest reality (Pāli: *paramattha-sacca*, Sanskrit: *paramārtha-satya*), the highest level of philosophical insight and religious aspiration. The emphasis is epistemological, not ontological. Operationally, this is equivalent to both nirvāṇa and seeing things as they really are (yathābhūtam). Second, is conventional or mundane reality (Pāli: *sammuti-sacca*, Sanskrit: *samvṛti-satya*). This refers to the world of saṃsāra (birth and death), or the world as we usually know it. It is the world endowed by us as having coordinated objects in time and space. It is a flashing flux consisting of an almost infinite variety of things and their melting attributes. We shall see that the problem of these two truths will reoccur, in some cases, almost word for word within the Mādhyamika context. We shall also find that some of the same problems and terminology, found here in the earlier works of the Abhidharmists, will occur again in the Buddhist context of Nāgārjuna. Mādhyamika, like Zen, illustrates that although the vocabulary and expository structures may change through time, the basic Buddhist problematics continue to be developed.

2. What *is* a dharma? First, it is not a thing. Dharma analysis is a completely different and alternative conceptual language framework. When we refer to things we usually feel that there is some object out there to which the particular features (attributes) we know about the object somehow adheres or belongs to the object. There is no such terminological or ontological analogy in dharma analysis language. That is, a dharma is not an object which possesses attributes; a dharma is only the attribute, without an object. What we *do* know about an individual dharma is all we *can* know. There is nothing behind it which possesses or controls it. The Buddhists maintain that within the scope of this alternative epistemic language framework, there are only a finite number of these categories called dharmas. They are mutually exclusive, and in combination they are totally exhaustive. The various combinations of most (but not necessarily all) dharmas that constitute the concrete particulars of the first person experienced world at any given moment may more accurately and less misleadingly describe such first person experience by means of these dharmic categories than can ordinary language. Also we must note that there are *no* inferred causal relations between dharmas; dharmas simply arise, endure for a moment, and then go out of existence. They go to and come from nowhere. The rest is inference. As with the concept of karma, there is no agent, no overseer or administrator of dharmas (or karma) in their experienced combinations. Dharmas in combination at any given second constitute the world as

described by this alternative conceptual framework; within the descriptive confines of this framework the Abhidharmists hold that we can truthfully say that we *know* the world as it is.

Just as dharmas in their various, ever-changing combinations constitute an alternate description of the variety of the conventional world with which we are all too familiar, just so is the concept of a self (ātman, jīva, pudgala) merely another component in our familiar but alternative descriptive framework, ordinary language. However, within the dharma analysis framework there is neither need nor evidence for postulating the descriptive category of self (ātman); an accurate description of first person experience is possible solely by means of the categories of the dharma list.

In our everyday lives, we generally act as if there is an enduring personal entity which somehow is *there* "in the back of" or "possessing" the feelings and concepts we call our own. We easily, but inaccurately, utilize this assumption in ordinary first person language *about* our own experience. However, the self for the Buddhists is merely one more inaccurate component among many ordinary language components which do not accurately describe experience as it occurs within the first person context. Thus the particular and ever-changing combination of these dharmas allow one to pose (emphatically) the problem of the self in a familiar word; however, the word self represents merely a nominal but not an ultimate (ontological) reference.

The number of dharmic category elements operative varies from moment to moment; thus within the context of the various combinations of these epistemic categories the Abhidharmists suggest that there are value tendencies and specific reoccurring experiences which are important for the development of certain moral qualities within the context of religious language. Notice the shift in vocabulary.

There are multiple levels of reference *within* both the dharma list and in the implicit explanatory rules of its use, e.g., the class of the general functions contributing to wholesomeness (kuśalmahābhūmika) and one of its members, for example, the dharma energy (vīrya). These terms and levels represent (implicitly) descriptive differences and normative rules of conceptual syntax. These particular dharmas represent what we, in ordinary language, would call states of emotion and/or value references which even in the context of dharma analysis are said to be attributes that *should be* encouraged. One such dharma is that of insight or wisdom (Pāli: *paññā*, Sanskrit: *prajñā*). If such value dharmas, in combination with others, tend to predominate through the choice of the individual, then we may shift the gears of our language from the conceptual categories from dharma analysis language to that of the ordinary language framework. This enables one to refer to a development of wholesome qualities which lead "one" toward the "attainment" of nirvāṇa. Strictly speaking, there is no attainment and none to attain. In other words, we shift the vocabulary of our language to dharma analysis from the language of ordinary first person talk.

However, if there is no self, then who does the attaining? The simplified answer is: No one does. The world doesn't shift; only our conceptual language does. When the language shifts, it carries us "we's" along too.

One must remember that according to the Abhidharmists, the world as it is experienced *should* be analyzed according to this alternative dharma map of consciousness. Within this dharma context, there is simply no appropriate way to *speak* of such concepts as the self, of strictly anthropomorphic moral values without making category mistakes; nor is there an appropriate vocabulary to talk about the ontology of things which are said to exist or possess the attributes and qualities we see in the world *as described in* ordinary language. When we *talk* about moral development, we must shift the gears of our language so that we may then utilize ordinary language and thus use such anthropomorphic and ego-centered concepts as one's development toward religious and/or moral goals.

It is most important to note that certain terms or concepts which have a clear and unambiguous function within the operative framework of anthropomorphic religious language are not appropriate within the alternative language framework of dharmas analysis. Two examples of these inappropriate terms in the dharma language frameworks are "self" and the idea of an uncaused, unconditioned existing entity which "possesses" certain attributes. These two concepts are simply excluded from being operative in dharma analysis language. If such a concept is said not to be contextually applicable but is still used, we must then call the user's attention to the set of fallacious relationships called category mistakes.

Let us explicitly ask such an inappropriate question to illustrate the confusion of categories within these two epistemic and language frameworks, i.e., ordinary language descriptions and dharma analysis descriptions. First, if we were to say that we understood the concept of dharma analysis as an alternative map of consciousness and then, second, we were to go on to ask "to whom do these dharmas belong?," we would then be making a category mistake. We would be requesting an answer to a question wrongly put. The presupposition of the question is that there *is* someone or something which owns or possesses dharmas. It is a logically complex question. If we were to answer the question in the way in which it is posed to us, we would be implicitly agreeing to the underlying assumptions about the self and about such inaccurately described epistemic components, the inaccuracies of which dharma analysis was designed to clarify.

VII. "SELF" AND LINGUISTIC SURROGATES

We now turn to a linguistic surrogate of the "self" concept. To keep from making a category mistake such as the one concerning the self, the Buddhists devised this elaborate and technical dharma analysis vocabulary to prevent such category mistakes and to render a more accurate description of first person experience. In place of the concept of "self" they use the surrogate term "stream" or "current" (as in a stream), *santāna*. It is neither a dharma nor a replacement for "self." This word does *not* refer to a self or to any entity which either owns dharmas or appropriates the feelings of which we all are aware and do describe in ordinary language. The word santāna is a dharma analysis explicit *metaphor* which is a surrogate substitute for talk about "self." It refers to those specific and concrete concatenations of dharmas which are juxtaposed through the single dharma of memory (smṛti, and of course other dharmas too) which we habitually and inaccurately *wish* to call a "self." The generation of the metaphor santāna is an accommodation to the felt needs within ordinary language, about Abhidharma questions which cannot be answered conventionally concerning a *specific* concatenation of dharmas—the analogy of one's own dharmas. Speaking conventionally, questions about the features of my dharmas *are* important to me, but to speak in such a manner is inaccurate. Thus there is the need for a special term in the dharma analysis vocabulary which allows one provisionally to refer to the above concerns without totally violating the rules of (the conceptual syntax in the) dharma analysis language.

To summarize, in our first person ordinary language way of speaking these "self" feelings are connected or juxtaposed in our memory as belonging somehow to the stream about which we feel the need to make first person statements in ordinary language. Again, santāna is *not* a person; it *is* a descriptive metaphor which is an accommodation to nonenlightened, human ways of describing something which, until we come to know better through dharma analysis and samadhi, we shall continue to call first person experience and to which we then apply ordinary first person language words such as "self," "my," and "mine." To know the real difference of the two, "self" and "santāna," is to have insight or wisdom (prajñā, *vipaśyanā*).

VIII. THE ABHIDHARMIC BACKGROUND OF PRAJÑAPTI

We now turn to two Abhidharma schools concerned with ordinary first person experience as described in dharma analysis. They are the Sarvāstivādins and the Sautrāntikas. The Sarvāstivādins (all dharmas exist[through time]) postulated as an explanatory concept (somewhat similar to the early and rather naturalistic explanatory concept of karma as found in the speculative *Bṛhadāraṇyaka Upaniṣad*) a particular (and odd) meta-dharma called *prāpti* (adhesion). It was held to be a real agent which exists (*dravya-dharma*). To the extent to which one knows an individual stream (santāna), to that extent the adhesion dharma is operative; since without it there would be an absence of the coherence and consistency *presupposed* by the metaphor *santāna*. It was said to hold these dharmas in their specific experienced combinations. It is the agent which maintains the consistency and coherence one finds within the stream of one's single santāna (!). The other Abhidharma school, the Sautrāntikas, also reacted to the same problem of explaining the consistency and coherence we find in *both* ordinary language *and* dharma analysis descriptions. Both schools set out to answer the question of what gives consistency, nonrandomness, and coherence to first person experiences. The Sautrāntikas answered by saying that all dharmas are fruitful fictions, or language constructs (prajñapti). The Sautrāntikas criticized the Sarvāstivādin adhesion dharma by saying essentially that by appeal to dharmic experience, there would be no possible way to *explain* how this particular adhesion dharma could somehow glue together *experienced* dharma moments in the fairly consistent and coherent manner that they *are* experienced, that is, the dharmas which constitute one's individual momentary santāna. A metalanguage term is not necessarily operative at the object language level. By controlling other dharmas *prāpti* functions as a metaterm; but there is, by definition, nothing behind coordinated dharmas. So either prāpti, as an object language term, cannot adhere or grasp other dharmas and thereby bring about cohesion of dharmic experience, which violates both the reason for their postulation and definition; *or* prāpti, as a metalanguage term, can coordinate and group dharmas violating the implicit Abhidharmic definition which excludes the assumption that there is anything behind or in addition to the flashing staccato-like dharmas.

Another way to say the same thing is that no falsification of the dharma "adhesion" could ever occur in any possible (or theoretical) set of epistemic circumstances imagined by any individual whether he spoke *either* in the vocabulary of ordinary language or in the dharma analysis language framework. Therefore the Sautrāntikas held that the Sarvāstivādins were simply wrong. Furthermore, the Sautrāntikas held that *all* dharmas then were subject to the same criticism, i.e., that all dharmas were merely designations, pragmatic language constructs, conceptual concepts whether conditioned through ordinary language or ordinary Buddhist language. As this point was expanded by Mādhyamikas, the most important point is that the very *same word* fruitful fiction or language-construct (prajñapti) is used to describe emptiness (śūnyatā) in the *MK*. The passage in which it is so described constitutes the highest metalanguage level within the Mādhyamika system (24:18).

IX. LINGUISTIC RAFTS: UPĀYA AND PRAJÑAPTI

One may also note that there is an analogy between this use of the word language construct (prajñapti) and a word which has a more religious connotation, skillful means (upāya). The latter term is developed in the religious literature called Prajñāpāramitā ("Perfection of Wisdom") Sūtras. This literature contains many important Mādhyamika concepts such as emptiness (śūnyatā). (It is helpful to read it along with the *MK* to grasp the religious implications of Mādhyamika.) The Buddhist concept of karma implies (implicitly) that there must be some sort of accommodation by means of a variety of religious doctrines which are appropriate and suitable to the different karmic endowments of individuals; likewise there must be some metaconcept (upāya) which expresses the conclusion that all Buddhist religious doctrines are relative to and appropriate for the different levels of individual karmic capacities following the Buddhist path. In other words, religious doctrines are (ultimately) "pedagogical devices, fruitful fictions, gimmicks, teaching devices, or religious tricks." In a similar way, the concept of language constructs (prajñapti) is an accommodation to the Abhidharma Sautrāntika answer that all dharmas are *prajñaptis*, i.e., fruitful fictions, appropriate but unconfirmable outside the systemic context of dharma analysis language. As we shall see, there is also a Mādhyamika acknowledgment of this problematic. So, just as *prajñaptis* are fruitful fictions within the religious language frameworks, we find in a similar manner that the word emptiness (śūnyatā) is said also to be merely a prajñapti; it is a fruitful fiction which, if reified, leads to confusions which obviate the desirable religious ends for which both the concepts of emptiness and dharma analysis have been generated. Another way to say the same thing is that prajñapti(s), upāyas, and the "emptiness of emptiness" are reflexive metagrids which refer to relationships of epistemic evaluation but not to the ontological entities presupposed by the world's way of talking.

The Mādhyamikas strove to refute not only ordinary language concepts; in addition they strove to refute both the second order Abhidharma dharma analysis concepts and the rival second order concepts of own-being (svabhāva) held by members of opposing non-Buddhist schools. Such concepts of the rival schools are Sāṁkhya's nature (prakṛti) and Nyāya's ontological and epistemological map categories (*padārthas*, e.g., *pramāṇa*). Own-being is a Mādhyamika generic (cover term) for such general epistemic and metaphysical concepts. Therefore, to assume a similarity between the concepts and categories of description used in ordinary language and those of the words things, trees, stones, and love, and the second order concepts of dharmas, nature, and own-beings, is imply to collapse levels and to make category mistakes. The values and possible ontologies associated with each level are of different orders of abstraction and of different methods of verification and justification.

X. EMPTINESS

It is said about emptiness, the Mādhyamika third order concept, that "emptiness too is empty" (*MK*, 13:7–8). This reflexive third order concept of emptiness is derivative and logically dependent on the two concepts of dependent (or relational) origination and own-being. The *Mūla-Mādhyamika Kārikās* holds that emptiness is a reflexive designation (prajñapti); it is a descriptive device which has no ontological import. In fact to reify emptiness is again to make a category mistake. Emptiness is a third order context-restricted term; emptiness denotes or designates nothing. In a context it describes the relationship in which, combined with other correlated descriptions, it does indirectly refer to the epistemic "world" we know; it functions as a rule, a boundary or limitation of what we can know and what there is "out there."

To suggest an oversimplified analogy, with respect to orders of abstraction, emptiness is somewhat like the difference between a particular sound and the musical transformation rule that the sound of G flat is identical with F sharp in the European well-tempered diatonic scale. Ultimately they may refer to the same thing, but to describe one is not to describe the other. The former is a sound; the latter is a rule about the identification of a sound. So it is with own-being and emptiness; the former is a second order description. The latter belongs to the third order description of the ways in which first and second order concepts and terms are epistemically evaluated (i.e., a rule) and descriptively manipulated. That emptiness is empty means that the term emptiness has a restricted epistemic role but not an ontological descriptive role. It is not a "thing" word; rather it is a relation-word, the function of which is to evaluate and contrast the differences between what-is-happening and the methods and structures by which we recognize and communicate about what-is-happening. Emptiness is a nonreferring word *about* referring words; it has merely nine letters!

XI. LANGUAGE CONSTRUCT: PRAJÑAPTI

The implications (above) of the ontological status of language-descriptions and their correlations with publicly known objects in the furniture of the world lead one to the conclusion that all ontological descriptions are merely pragmatically useful but provisional fictions. They guarantee only that what is known is simply (and tautologically) consistent with what *is* known. That is, no conclusions about the transcendental or ultimate nature (yathābhūtam) are *authorized* by statements verified by public or private observation; rather, what can be known (explicitly) *is* to be known. Language and its correct, consistent use guarantees nothing except itself; it is empty. Words, then, are useful, pragmatic constructs constantly reinforced by personal, emotional, conceptual habits and general sociolinguistic cultural patterns. Nothing more is possible; nothing more can be described. However, a language which possesses a reflexive component can describe its own ontological *limitations*. The language of Mādhyamika does just this in the metaconcepts of emptiness (śūnyatā) and language constructs (prajñapti). Therefore the highest possible level of reflexive abstraction and description is that found in *Mūla-Mādhyamika Kārikā* 24:18. "It is dependent co-arising (pratītya-samutpāda) that we term emptiness; this is a designation (prajñapti, the fourth order) overlaid (on emptiness, the third order); it alone is the middle path." (This passage, from the *Prasannapadā*, is quoted from Robinson, *Early Mādhyamika in India and China*, p. 40. The parentheses have been added by the author of this lecture.)

XII. THE DOCTRINE OF TWO TRUTHS

Richard H. Robinson quotes (*Early Mādhyamika in India and China*, p. 48 ff., from *Mūla-Mādhyamika Kāraikā*, 24:8–10): "The Buddha's dharma-explanation relies on two truths: the worldly, conventional truth (*saṃvṛti-satya*), and the highest truth (*paramārtha-satya*). Those who do not know the distinction between these two truths do not know the deep reality in the Buddha's teaching. Without relying on the expressional (truth), the highest is not taught; without arriving at the highest, Nirvāṇa is not reached." (The parentheses have been added by the author of this lecture.) The *Mūla-Mādhyamika Kārikās*, firmly welded in conventional truth, possesses this important passage (24:14): "Everything is legitimately said for that of which emptiness is legitimately said; nothing is legitimately said for that of which emptiness is not legitimately said." Here is the familiar Indian idea first developed in the late Upaniṣads: there are different levels of "truth" (satya) for different levels of individuals who possess varied capacities and levels of understanding in accordance with their personal karmic endowments. (The question-begging nature of this also should not be overlooked.)

Conventional truth (samvṛti-satya) is the repository of the category mistakes and the projected conceptual distortions leading to suffering and existential illusion. However, the highest truth cannot be known except by *using* conventional truth as a ladder, each rung of which represents an epistemological metalanguage. Emptiness (śūnyatā, a term derived from early Indian mathematicians), like the zero, is a high-level descriptive word whose meaning is determined by its mutually defined/conditioned relations with the other conceptual components of the metalanguage grid, i.e., conventional truth. Emptiness is a reflexive term, a self-describer; thus it refers to *no* space-time empirical thing in our experience.

The doctrine of the two truths indicates there are progressively higher and higher levels of abstraction in which there is operative a sequence of metacritical points of view generated within each preceding metacritical position. It is within language that we talk about language. Since there can be statements about statements about language (ad infinitum), the postulation of an almost infinite series of metalanguages within which we refer to descriptions and capacities of language to describe the world is not an unfamiliar idea. For example, English grammar books about the German language are metalanguages to the German language. Book reviews in French about English grammars of German (language) are meta-metalanguages of German. One could extend this chain infinitely. The language you are reading now is a meta-meta-metalanguage concerning the preceding statements about German.

Although the doctrine of the two truths seems to be strange and potentially contradictory, I wish to suggest that there is nothing intrinsically unfamiliar about the explicit rational structure of this doctrine. It seems to maintain that one must progress to different levels of understanding, realizing that the word "level" is a metaphor (since we are not talking about spatial relationships), until one reaches a point in the process of articulation and metacriticism where one is able to realize that there is a *reflexive* metacriticism directed at our medium through which we speak and learn—language. The word emptiness refers to the nonontological, nonempirical, referential status of certain pieces of the object languages. It does *not* seem paradoxical to me to suggest that it is through language that we postulate that, except in epistemically restricted contexts, some language is ontologically empty.

There is nothing intrinsically or ultimately mysterious about the rational structure of the doctrine of two truths. I assume that there are parallels and isomorphic experiences common to us all within which we can understand the progressively sophisticated and ontologically restricting levels of metalanguage postulated in the *Mūla-Mādhyamika Kārikās* descriptions concerning language and the world.

Thus the Mādhyamikas are left with a set of distinctions and vocabulary about the relationship of language and the world in which it is soteriologically necessary to point out that there are subpockets of language within which the referents of such language are other pieces of language and not a postulated circular set of epistemic-linguistic behavior patterns. The doctrine of the two truths is the expression of a metaphorical ladder on which one progresses (up the ladder) by climbing different metalanguage levels until one realizes the reflexive turn at the top of the ladder. Hence one realizes that the ladder one has been climbing (metalinguistically) is itself as empty as the shadow it casts from the sun.

The doctrine of the two truths and emptiness are therapeutic in the sense that they diminish the magical attachments *to* and obscuration *of* our inner language. Also both diminish potential reificaions of language and its conceptual and value relationships. Abhidharma dharma-analysis theory is a way to unreify the world; it is a new epistemic map. Mādhyamika emptiness and the doctrine of two truths are additional Buddhist ways to unreify the world and its concomitant furniture and values by unreifying the Abhidharmist and non-Buddhist's metalanguage maps. It is a logician's joke; however, to get the joke, one must ask: Who's laughing?

XIII. VALUE IMPLICATIONS

In a world in which it is said that even the monks of the first century B.C. Mahāyāna countries were not free from avarice, arrogance, lust, and dissipation, reflection upon the reflexive concept of emptiness frees one from the reification of abstract terms, names, and the conventional human epistemic relationships which are mistakenly taken as real and soteriologically efficacious. The realization (or the potential realization) of the emptiness of all things is a therapeutic ploy by which one may realize the differences between languages and things (including the thing called "self"), by reflexively including one's own perception in that realization. After many years of assuming that Nirvāṇa is the goal and that saṁsāra is the starting point, the Mādhyamikas make the following startling claims:

> The own-being of the *Tathāgata* (i.e., the Buddha) is the own-being of this world; the Tathagata is without own-being, and this world is without own-being.(*MK*, 22:16)
>
> Saṃsāra has nothing that distinguishes it from nirvāṇa; nirvāṇa has nothing that distinguishes it from saṃsāra. The limit of nirvāṇa is the limit of saṃsāra; there is not even the subtlest something separating the two. (*MK*, 25:19–20)

The above suggests that such distinctions and limits are merely context-restricted but still seductive bits of language. One is also led to the suggestion that the distinctions of language (witness nirvāṇa and saṃsāra) are *merely* and *only* internally consistent and are only pragmatically correlated with our perceptions. This is quite enough and it is quite reasonable. However, such a view entails no noncircular conclusion about anything which is said to escape the warm boundaries of human care (duḥkha) and the bet-witching motherhood of talking (samvṛti-satya). As one modern philosopher has put it: "Whereof one cannot speak, therefore one must be silent."

Thus Mādhyamika tends to generate epistemic nimbleness, linguistic respect, a new sense of human wonder, and an alert suspicion of the conventional view of the world which we have projected through our linguistically and culturally colored glasses. Metaphorically, Mādhyamika is a system of implicit prescriptions which suggests that we remove our linguistically colored sunglasses and look at the warm sun as it is. Who *is* the warmness?

SUGGESTED READING

Bhattacharya, K., tr. "The Dialectical Method of Nāgārjuna, (Translation of the Vigrahavyāvartinī . . .)", in *Journal of Indian Philosophy*, 1 (1971): 217–61.

Conze, Edward. *Buddhist Thought In India.*

———. *Selected Sayings From the Perfection of Wisdom.*

Inada, Kenneth K., tr. *Nāgārjuna, A Translation of his Mūlamādhyamika-kārikā with an Introductory Essay.*

Murti, T.R.V. *The Central Philosophy of Buddhism.*

Robinson, Richard H. *Early Mādhyamika in India and China.*

Streng, Frederick J. *Emptiness: A Study in Religious Meaning.*

Sprung, Mervyn. *The Problem of Two Truths in Buddhism and Vedānta.*

18
Major Schools of the Mahāyāna: Yogācāra

Stefan Anacker

INTENTIONS

Yogācāra (literally, "practice of yoga," meaning here the entire path of practice of the *Bodhisattva*) is a Mahāyāna method for the alleviation of sufferings through the loosening and shedding of the mentally constructed. Its treatises include descriptions of progressive meditational practices as well as accumulations of various tentative theories, all of which serve as a temporary alleviating purpose before their implications lead to their own dissolutions. The meditational practices take one further and further in the realm of "signless cognition," and involve a complete revulsion, turning-over, revolution, of the entire basis of "one's" being (*āśrayaparāvṛtti*). In the central Yogācāra theory of the three kinds of reality, the mentally constructed (*parikalpita*) is what must be cleansed away from the inter-dependent (or relative, *paratantra*: the world of change) before there can be a fulfilled, or accomplished, state (*parinispanna*). Since all theories are mentally constructed, the best they can be is therapeutic aids to the dissolving of mental constructions.

BRIEF HISTORY OF THE SCHOOL IN INDIA

Yogācāra has found the attention of writers with the most diverse additional interests, and the specific expedients they have evolved have been markedly varied, which has also given the method an extraordinary all-inclusiveness.

THE SŪTRAS

The expedient of the three natures exists already in the *Pañcaviṃśati-sāhasrikā-prajñāpāramitā-sūtra*. Other sūtra influences on Yogācāra have come from the *Avataṃsaka*, with its statement that everything is *citta* only, and the *Tathāgatotpattiguṇakāraṇḍa*, with its mirror consciousness and Tathāgata's consciousness free from stains. The entire method, with its delineation of calm and insight meditations, its theory of an appropriating consciousness which carries karmic continuity and from which all developed consciousnesses evolve, the three natures leading to the realization of emptiness, the different stages in the realization of emptiness (including the discarding of notions of egolessness), apperception-only, fulfilled, etc., by the emptiness of ultimate truth, and finally, the abandonment of the idea of emptiness itself, through the emptiness of emptiness, is found in the *Saṃdhi-nirmocana-sūtra*. This realization may take eons, or it may take place in a moment, says the Saṃdhinirmocana.

It is the Saṃdhinirmocana which has been the most influential in shaping Yogācāra methods. Other Mahāyāna sūtras containing parts of the method are the *Laṅkāvatāra-sūtra* and the *Suvarṇaprabhāsa-sūtra*, but these may not antedate the great treatise writers of Yogācāra, as the Saṃdhinirmocana apparently does.

MAITREYANĀTHA, ASAṄGA, AND VASUBANDHU

Some time in the fourth century, a Gandhāran monk named *Asaṅga* in dissatisfaction left the *Mahīśāsaka* Hīnayānists under whom he had been trained, and went off to the forest to meditate. According to the traditional account, after twelve years Asaṅga received a vision of the future Buddha *Maitreya*, who dictated to him the Yogācāra works which go under the name of *Maitreya* (*nātha*): *Abhisamayālaṅkāra*, *Mahāyānasūtrālaṅkāra*, *Madhyāntavibhāga*, *Dharmadharmatāvibhāga*. Asaṅga himself then began writing a series of books further developing the method—*Mahāyāna-saṃgraha*, *Commentary on the Saṃdhinirmocana*, *Bodhisattvabhūmi* (?)—and succeeded in converting his brother, the great Abhidharmika *Vasubandhu*, to Mahāyāna. Vasubandhu subsequently produced prodigious amounts of treatises systematizing Yogācāra: commentaries on the works of Maitreyanātha and Asaṅga, *Karmasiddhiprakaraṇa*, *Vyākhyāyukti*, *Daśabhūmika-śāstra*, *Viṃśatikā*, *Triṃśikā*, *Trisvabhāvanirdeśa*, etc.

STHIRAMATI AND DHARMAPĀLA

In the sixth century the method finds two sharply differing interpretations at the hands of *Sthiramati* and *Dharmapāla*. The latter is the basis of *Hsüan-tsang's Vijñānavāda* and of its living descendant, the *Hossō* of Japan. All Tibetan schools have also been influenced by Yogācāra methods, and *rNying-ma-pa* and *dGe-lugs-pa* masters have written differing interpretations of key Yogācāra concepts.

PRACTICES

The meditational practices described in Yogācāra works usually begin with some form of the applications of mindfulness (*smṛtyupasthāna*), meditations on the flow of the body, feelings, consciousness-moments, and all moment-events. In Yogācāra they are not just to be done introspectively, but Mahāyānistically into the bodies of others, resulting in an extraordinary empathetic understanding and the annihilation of the boundary between self and others. They may be accompanied by special meditations called the aids to penetration (*nirvedhabhāgīya*), which shatter the holding fast to any mental cognition. This Path of Application is followed by insight meditations on the Four Noble Truths (this part of the practice is called the Path of Seeing), followed in turn by the calm meditation directed at the eradication of all afflictions, and which take one progressively through the ten Bodhisattva stages, each of which involves the complete carrying through of one of the *pāramitās* (perfections), which finally culminates in Buddhahood.

SAMPLE YOGĀCĀRA THEORIES

FROM MAITREYANĀTHA'S MADHYĀNTAVIBHĀGA

The capacity, or seeming necessity, for human beings to mentally construct is called the constructing-all-around of that which was not (*abhūta-parikalpa*). It exists (for otherwise there would be no problem), but it can be destroyed, and it is through its destruction that deliverance from sufferings is reached. For all constructions result in constrictions, and hence in sufferings. Mental constructions, however, have the reality of anything produced in a magical show: they exist as long as they exist, but only as apparitions, and they can be made to disappear entirely without a trace. The constructing-all-around of that which was not is the constructing apart (*vikalpa*, i.e., discrimination) of grasped and grasper, i.e., the split between object and subject. This is the basis of all further construction. An actual duality of any kind, however, is not found, finally, to exist (and there are meditations which can aid in shattering all these constructed walls making for dualities), and the absence of all dualities is emptiness. The nature of the universe had always been empty and unafflicted: all afflictions are adventitious and the result of constructions.

FROM ASAṄGA'S MAHĀYĀNASAṂGRAHA AND VASUBANDHU'S TRIṂŚIKĀ AND TRISVABHĀVANIRDEŚA

In addition to the six kinds of consciousness accepted by *Abhidharma*, there must be something additional to account for the sense of ego, psychic continuity, and the retribution of acts. The sense of ego comes from a special kind of consciousness called *manas*—like other Abhidharma concepts this is a cover term for an infinite number of broadly typified moment-events. Underlying the entire complex of consciousnesses is a series of subconscious or supraconscious psychic moments, called the store consciousness (*ālaya-vijñāna*), in which are deposited seeds (*bījas*, potential transformations of the series) from all the other consciousnesses, through a process called perfuming or penetrating (*vāsanā*). Each consciousness-moment deposits a seed in the store-consciousness, and these seeds in turn influence all future cognitions. If this is so, it follows that all of our normal ways of perceiving involve constructions (e.g., the construction of definite external objects) and that all definable natures and specifications assigned to things are constructions, including everything that has been hitherto or hereafter said. This realization is termed *vijñaptimātra*, apperception-only, is equivalent to emptiness, and, of course, negates the possibility of holding fast to apperception-only or any other theory.

LATER YOGĀCĀRINS

For Sthiramati, Dharmapāla, and later theorists following them, attention shifts from the three-nature method to the theory of consciousness. Asaṅga had assumed a three-part (*bhāga*) relation of the basic cognition capacity with an object part and subject part of consciousness. This division had been practically rejected by Vasubandhu, but was taken up again by his pupil *Dignāga* and forms one of the basic disagreements between Sthiramati and Dharmapāla. To Sthiramati, all parts of consciousness are constructed; to Dharmapāla, the three-part relation is of interdependent reality and dominated and fashioned by a consciousness which remains an absolute basis. It is Dharmapāla's view which can be called *Vijñānavāda*, and with some reservations, idealism, and it seems far away from the Yogācāra of Maitreyanātha or Vasubandhu, where all theories must be dissolved.

SUGGESTED READING

Conze, Edward, tr. *Abhisamayālaṅkāra, Introduction and Translation from original text, with Sanskrit-Tibetan Index.*

Lamotte, Étienne, tr. *La Somme du Grand Véhicule d'Asaṅga.* 2 vols.

———, ed. and tr. *Saṃdhinirmocana, L'explication des mystères, Texte tibetain édité et traduit.*

La Vallée Poussin, Louis de, tr. *Vijñaptimātratāsiddhi, La Siddhi de Hiuan-Tsang, traduite et annotée.* 2 vols.

Levi, Sylvain, ed. and tr. *Asaṅga, Mahāyānasūtrālaṅkāra, exposé de la doctrine du grand véhicule selon le système Yogācāra.* 2 vols.

Stcherbatsky, Th., tr. *Madhyāntavibhāga, Discourse on Discrimination*

between Middle and Extremes, ascribed to Maitreya and commented by Vasubandhu and Sthiramati.
Suzuki, Daisetz Teitarō, tr. *The Laṅkāvatāra Sūtra.*

19

The Saddharmapuṇḍarīka-Sūtra

Mark A. Ehman

INTRODUCTION

SOURCE AND CHARACTERISTICS

The *Saddharmapuṇḍarīka-sūtra* is a product of the Mahāyānists. The text of the sūtra reveals several stages of compilation. The poetic portions are composed in mixed Sanskrit, while the prose portions are composed in relatively correct Sanskrit. Some passages of the sūtra may antedate the Christian era, but the entire text could not have been completed much before A.D. 200. The sūtra reflects the growing conflict between the Mahāyānists and Hīnayānists. The designation *mahāvaipulya* (of great length) is ascribed to the sūtra, implying a process of adding to and embellishment of a few central themes.

THE NAME OF THE SŪTRA

Puṇḍarīka is a lotus: *sad* is from *sat* meaning true or real; *Dharma* is an untranslatable term (though most have chosen to translate it as Law or Doctrine) referring to the entire body of Buddhist teaching and expectation. Hence the compound *Saddharmapuṇḍarīka* means the Lotus of the True Dharma or simply the Lotus Sūtra. The implications of the name are that the lotus flower is the essence of all beauty and represents the fruition of the growth process. Similarly, the *Lotus Sūtra* is the essence of popular Mahāyānist teaching, and is the final manifestation of true Buddhism.

THEME OF THE SŪTRA

THERE IS ONLY ONE FORM OF BUDDHISM

The Buddha asserts: "By means of one sole vehicle, to wit, the Buddha-vehicle, Śāriputra, do I teach creatures the Law; there is no second vehicle, nor a third." This Buddha-vehicle or *Buddha-yāna* is characterized by a teaching which is beyond reasoning, a knowledge which is omniscient. It was customary to understand the variations of the religion according to a threefold division:

1. *Śrāvaka-yāna*—the vehicle of the hearers (or disciples). This is the vehicle of those who must follow authoritative teaching in order to reach *nirvāṇa*.
2. *Pratyekabuddha-yāna*—the vehicle of the private Buddha. This is the course of those who are their own teachers and who seek nirvāṇa only for themselves.
3. *Bodhisattva-yāna*—the vehicle of those who seek the salvation of all sentient being.

This threefold division, however, was only an expedient, a concession to the short-sightedness of man. In reality, there are no divisions.

SINGULARITY OF FORM INCLUDES SINGULARITY OF DHARMA

Although it may appear that there are many teachings of the Buddha which sometimes run contradictory to one another, there is in fact only one True Dharma.

SPECIAL TEACHINGS OF THE SŪTRA

ADHIMUKTATĀ—DISPOSITION

People are of varying dispositions or understandings. As a consequence, they conceive of their world and their spiritual attainments in limited terms. Their limited conception is due to varying degrees of ignorance. To overcome this ignorance and to insure the enlightenment of people with varying dispositions, the Buddha proclaims different teachings at different times. Hence any seeming contradictions which might appear in the teaching are not due to the paradoxical character of the religion; rather they are due to the deliberate efforts of the Buddha to accommodate himself to varieties of men. The forms of the Buddha's accommodating teaching assume a ninefold division:

1. *Sūtra*—discourse.
2. *Geya*—narrative and verse mixed.
3. *Vaiyākaraṇa*—prediction.
4. *Gāthā*—song.
5. *Udāna*—solemn utterance.
6. *Ityukta*—saying (literally, a pronouncement of the form "thus it was said").

7. *Jātaka*—story of previous births.
8. *Adbhutadharma*—miracle narrative.
9. *Vaipulya*—lengthy story.

UPĀYAKAUŚALYA—SKILL IN MEANS

Skill or skillfulness in this context refers to the Buddha's ability to know the dispositions of all beings, and to employ his own perfections and powers toward their salvation. The special techniques which the Buddha employs are *upāya* (means or expedients). These upāya are predicated upon the fact that ignorant beings cannot grasp the full truth of the Buddha directly. The sūtra asserts: " . . . all laws, Śāriputra, are taught by the Tathāgata, and by him alone; no one but he knows all laws, what they are, how they are . . . " If the truth is to be communicated at all, then it must be couched in parables, illustrations, stories, miracles, etc.; i.e., in the form of "means." The upāya, of necessity, distort the truth. Nevertheless, they are concessions to the various dispositions of people and are employed to *lure* men to the truth. In addition to being spiritual and educational techniques, the upāya are convenient justifications of sectarian Buddhism. The varieties of sects are merely means. As such, they are legitimized as way stations on the path to nirvāṇa. None of them, however, can be equated with a full embodiment of the truth.

TATHĀGATA

Meaning of the Term. The traditional interpretation suggests thus (*tathā*) come (*āgata*) or thus (*tathā*) gone (*gata*). Hence, the *Tathāgata* is one who is "thus come" into the world for the sake of sentient beings, or one who is "thus gone" to the farther shore of nirvāṇa. The term is employed as a designation for the Buddha. In the Lotus Sūtra the term refers to the being or beings who are fully enlightened and whose full knowledge is utilized for the salvation of all.

Characteristics of a Tathāgata. He is freedom. He is omniscience. He is everlasting. His abode is charity; i.e., he is present in the unselfish act of giving (*dāna*). His robe is forbearance (*kṣānti*). His pulpit is emptiness (*śūnyatā*).

Functions of the Tathāgata. It is the singular aim of the Tathāgata to appear in the world to manifest the Dharma. In order to do this he must know the dispositions of all so that he may choose the right means (upāya) for their spiritual benefit.

PARABLES

BACKGROUND

Illustrations of the various upāya are couched in parables, the pattern of which are:

1. Men are in a condition of ignorance.
2. A compassionate being appears on the scene to dispel the ignorance.
3. The compassionate being, sensitive to the needs of his followers (children), presents them with tangible objects or creations of fantasy (upāya).
4. As the followers mature, they come to understand the limitations (and unreality) of the objects and creations. Thus they are enlightened.

PROMINENT PARABLES

The Burning House. The children of a caring father are playing in a house which is being consumed by flames. The father lures the children out of the house by promising them finer toys than they have.

The Prodigal Son. A young man departs from his father's household and wanders for a long time. In the course of wandering ignorance beclouds the son's mind so that he does not know who he is or who his father is. He returns, unknowingly and quite by accident, to his father's country. The father recognizes his son and has him dragged to the house. The son, however, is frightened by the father's position and wealth. In the meantime the father determines to hire his son as a servant. The father himself assumes the guise of a servant in order to be with his son. Through these experiences the son becomes aware of his son-ship.

The Plants. The world possesses a variety of plants. The Tathāgata is like a huge rain cloud pouring down life-giving water upon the plants. Each plant absorbs the water according to its own capacity and thus comes to maturity.

The Blind Man. A man who is born blind is convinced that there are no shapes. A physician employs special medicines to restore the man's sight. Now the man born blind sees *things as they really are*.

The Magic City. A group of men are proceeding through a forest to an exalted goal. They, however, become weary and despair of ever reaching the goal. The leader of the group (the Tathāgata) creates a magic city in order to make it appear as if the goal has been achieved. After weariness and despair are overcome the magic city fades away and the group is ready to proceed onward toward the real goal.

ESCHATOLOGY

At the end of time the religion will be in a state of decay. The Tathāgata will have become extinct (or so it will seem). Men will have corrupted his true doctrine into a counterfeit one. This is the appropriate time for the "Lotus of the True Law" to be preached.

BODHISATTVAS

The preachers of the Lotus Sūtra in these last days will be the *Bodhisattvas*. Although it is true that the Bodhisattva-yāna is only an expedient, it does perform a vital function in the salvation process. If the Bodhisattva is to preach, his character must be firm in four things:

1. Morality—A Bodhisattva *Vinaya* emphasizes that he should not serve or wait upon kings, princes, or members of other sects, and that he should guard himself against all sensual involvements.
2. Emptiness—The Bodhisattva knows that the real character of all things is śūnyatā.
3. Avoidance of doctrinal disputes.
4. Compassion for all beings.

Prominent Bodhisattvas:

1. *Sadāparibhūta*—The suffering savior. Whenever this Bodhisattva approached others he would say "I do not condemn you." Such an action appeared ridiculous and earned him the wrath and insults of other people as well as the nickname Sadāparibhūta (Ever Not-Condemn). Finally, however, the people realized his superior wisdom and extensive compassion, and as a result, they became his disciples.
2. *Bhaiṣajyarāja*—The Bodhisattva who burns his body as an act of reverence to the Tathāgata.
3. *Gadgadasvara*—The Bodhisattva who assumes a variety of shapes (monk, nun, demon, serpent, layman, laywoman) in order to proclaim the True Dharma.
4. *Avalokiteśvara*—The Bodhisattva who saves from fire, flood, robbers, enemies, etc.
5. *Samantabhadra*—The Bodhisattva who protects the preachers of the Lotus Sūtra.

6. *Mañjuśrī* and *Maitreya* also appear at various points in the text.

CONCLUSION

There is a conflict between universalism and sectarianism in the sūtra. On the one hand, the sūtra wishes to be an all-inclusive and undogmatic statement, accepting all forms of Buddhism. On the other hand, it is driven to say that the gospel which the "Lotus of the True Dharma" proclaims is the *only* true Dharma. All others are false or counterfeit. This leads to Mahāyāna exclusivism. Because of the sūtra's duplicity and because of its simple dramatic form, it has found acceptance among a wide variety of Buddhists. Sectarian movements in China (*T'ien-t'ai*) and Japan (*Tendai*) were based on the study of it. Pietistic and evangelistic movements emphasized repetition of its title as a means of gaining enlightenment. The *Nichiren* sect of thirteenth-century Japan admonished its followers to utter *Nam Myōhō Renge Kyō* ("Hail to the Scripture of the Lotus of the True Teaching" or "Homage to the Lotus Sūtra"). Such an utterance was considered to be an act of faith. The *Sōkagakkai* sect of twentieth-century Japan continues this practice. Each man could find meaning in the Lotus Sūtra which correlated with his own disposition and needs.

SUGGESTED READING

Burnouf, Eugène, tr. *Le Lotus de la Bonne Loi.*
Kern, Jan Hendrik, tr. *The Saddharmapuṇḍarīka, or the Lotus of the True Law.*

20
The Vimalakīrti-Nirdeśa Sūtra

Stefan Anacker

INTRODUCTION

The *Vimalakīrti-nirdeśa-sūtra*, the "Sūtra of the Teachings of the Layman Vimalakīrti," is one of the most sublime of the Mahāyāna sūtras, showing early Mahāyāna anti-institutionalism at its highest. A sūtra of the extremely varied *Ratnakūṭa* collection, it has been of tremendous value in many aspects of Mahāyāna Buddhism. In Japan, for example, Prince Shotoku Taishi regarded Vimalakīrti as the second rebirth of the *Tathāgata Kenzoku*, and the sūtra later had a profound influence on Zen. The Sanskrit original is lost, but a Tibetan, a Sogdian, and three Chinese versions survive.

SYNOPSIS OF THE SŪTRA

The scene of the sūtra is set in *Vaiśālī*, where the Buddha *Śākyamuni* meets with 8,000 great *bhikṣus* and 32,000 *Bodhisattvas*. The latter are characterized as being fitted out with all the *pāramitās*, having gone to all parts of the world to all sentient beings in the hope of making them their friends and bringing them peace, as having peeled away all attachment to the ego and having reached the calm that comes in the cognizing of all *dharmas* as nonarising, as possessing great constancy, and with an intuitive insight into the dispositions of sentient beings, which allows them to always provide the right antidotes for all beings' sufferings. Upon being asked how one should attain the purity of the Buddha-realm, Śākyamuni replies that the Buddha-realm lies within each sentient being, that the Bodhisattva sets up a Buddha-realm according to the dispositions of beings (and this only to help them), and that the purity of the Buddha-realms consists of the pāramitās, the 37 limbs of enlightenment (*bodhipakṣya dharmas*), subjecting oneself to a moral code and yet never criticizing others, showing the way to others, and helping them in all ways. To *Śāriputra's* question on how this Buddha-realm can be called pure, Śākyamuni says, "Are sun and moon impure, because the blind man can't see them? The Buddha-realms are always pure—it's only you who can't see them in their fundamental purity."

The great layman Bodhisattva Vimalakīrti has taken on a sickness, to aid sentient beings. Śākyamuni sends various disciples to see him, but all refuse, finding themselves unworthy because Vimalakīrti has chided them on various occasions. For example, Śāriputra finds himself unworthy because once, when he was sitting in meditation, Vimalakīrti came up to him and told him that the way he was sitting was not necessarily the only way to meditate—that meditating means never leaving the way of emptiness and yet still acting like a normal being; not freeing oneself from all worldly passions and still going into *nirvāṇa*. The great Bodhisattvas also did not feel equal to Vimalakīrti. For example, the Bodhisattva *Prabhavyūha* feels himself unworthy because when he once asked Vimalakīrti where he came from, Vimalakīrti answered, "From the *bodhi-maṇḍala*." When Prabhavyūha asked where that was, Vimalakīrti said that it was in the body itself because one can see the irreality in it, and that all dharmas are the bodhi-maṇḍala because one recognizes the emptiness of all dharmas.

The Bodhisattva *Mañjuśrī* finally goes. Vimalakīrti tells him that he has become sick because all sentient beings are sick and afflicted, and because he has feelings of compassion for all sentient beings. When Mañjuśrī asks him why his room is empty, Vimalakīrti tells him that all Buddha-lands are empty. When Mañjuśrī asks why, Vimalakīrti says that emptiness is empty because there is no discrimination in emptiness. Discrimination is emptiness too, and emptiness can be found in the 62 heresies. Asked where these can be found, he says, "In the emancipation of all Buddhas." When Mañjuśrī asks him where this occurs, Vimalakīrti replies, "In the volitions and actions of all sentient beings."

Vimalakīrti further says that the body is a collection of dharmas that have haphazardly come together into a kind of unity. However, this thought of the reality of dharmas is also an error. To get rid of the notions of "I" and "mine" one must be totally unconcerned with the factors of the inner and outer world. One has to deal with everything without discrimination. In other words, "I" and nirvāṇa are identical. And why? Because both "I" and nirvāṇa are empty. In what way empty? Through provisional naming; both have no graspable nature.

The Bodhisattva should reject all compassion that is bound to attachment. A compassion with attachment brings fear of transitoriness, and besides, it is nonsense for someone who is himself bound to tell others to free themselves. Engaging in meditation because one has a desire to meditate is a form of bondage; having all necessary *upāyas* is liberation. Upāyas without *prajñā* are bondage; upāyas with prajñā are liberation. The Bodhisattva is neither constantly in the state of nonmastery, like a fool, nor constantly in the state of mastery, like a *śrāvaka*. The actions of a Bodhisattva are thus neither fully pure nor impure. He will strive for all-knowledge, but not crave it before he is ready. He will know dependent origination and yet enter into all sorts of false views; work for the good of all sentient beings and yet not be attached to it. He knows that there is no arising of anything in the world, and he will not stay on the threshhold of enlightenment. He will be free from all worldly concerns, and still not annihilate his own body. Truth is that central calm; it is nonattachment.

The Bodhisattva is to regard others as a magician does the phantoms he has created; as the wise man does the moon in the water or the reflection of his own face in a mirror; or as a blind man sees colors. When Mañjuśrī, at this point, asks Vimalakīrti how friendly love can be practiced, Vimalakīrti replies that after one has regarded all beings as phantoms (etc.), one should reflect that one has to teach such a teaching for the sake of delivering beings, and that this is true compassion. He should practice the compassion of absolute calm, the compassion of nonduality, the compassion of limitlessness, the compassion of openness. Two more of the unlimited are thus defined: sympathetic joy (*pramuditā*) is being happy at all joys of others, and equanimity (*upekṣā*) is remaining without desire for oneself.

Craving is traced to erroneous discrimination, and ultimately all discrimination rests in the impermanence of things. What conditions this impermanence? Nothing, for it is the beginning of all things.

At this point in Vimalakīrti's exegesis, a divine girl throws flowers all over the room. They stick fast to the robes of the śrāvakas, but glide off the robes of the Bodhisattvas. When Śāriputra tries to pluck off the flowers, because they are contrary to *Vinaya*, she says to him, "You shouldn't think that flowers are against the Dharma. This is all the result of discrimination. If one has gone to the extent of leaving one's home for the religion of the Buddha, and one is still stuck in discriminations, then *that* is against the Dharma." When Śāriputra later insists that emancipation is freedom from greed, hate, and delusion, she says that greed, hate, and delusion are themselves already enlightenment. Śāriputra is angry at this "mere woman," and asks her what she has attained, as well as what she has proved by being so talkative. She replies that she has attained nothing and proved nothing, and that is why she is so loquacious. She adds that if somebody is attaining something, or proving something, then he is a stubborn person, as far as the Dharma of the Buddha is concerned. Śāriputra says that if she is so smart, why doesn't she change herself into a man. Instead, she changes him into a woman.

Vimalakīrti and Mañjuśrī continue their discussions on the activities of the Bodhisattva. The Bodhisattva may appear to be angry, lazy, greedy, etc., but is really free from these afflictions. The seeds of Buddhahood are the afflictions, for it is only there that the thought of enlightenment (*bodhicitta*) can grow, just as a lotus grows from muck. When one sees that everything that has arisen by dependent origination is empty and without a self, then there is no difference between a Bodhisattva and a non-Bodhisattva because all dualities vanish. There is no duality even between being bound and being free, so there will be no joy in nirvāṇa or fear of saṃsāra. Mañjuśrī finally says that one cannot really validly say anything about anything, as emptiness lies apart from all discourse. Vimalakīrti seconds this by becoming silent. Stories on the innate purity of the Buddha Śākyamuni's realm, and admonitions on the superiority of understanding the Dharma over all external worship close the sūtra.

SUGGESTED READING

Lamotte, Étienne, tr. *L'Enseignement de Vimalakīrti.*
Robinson, Richard H., tr. *The Vimalakīrti Sūtra* (typescript).

21

The Laṅkāvatāra Sūtra

Mark A. Ehman

INTRODUCTORY CONSIDERATIONS

The *Laṅkāvatāra-sūtra* is a Mahāyāna text compiled ca. A.D. 300. It summarizes the major doctrinal tenets of the great vehicle—tenets such as *śūnyatā*, the *Bodhisattva*, Buddha-nature (*buddhatā*), transformations of the Buddha, the *Tathāgata*, etc. The occasion for the recital of the sūtra is the descent (*avatāra*) of the Blessed One to the mythical city of *Laṅkā*, hence the name Laṅkāvatāra. The sūtra purports to go beyond all previous teaching and practice. It singles out the philosophers for special castigation since they have been disposed to freeze reality into a categorical permanency and to discriminate between subject and object. Even the *śrāvakas* and *pratyekabuddhas* are regarded as inferior since they objectify their levels of attainment. *Truth is transcendence*; it is to be experienced in an inmost state of consciousness which far surpasses both analytical and experiential efforts at drawing distinctions. The sūtra represents a stage in the development of *Yogācāra* Buddhism. The text opens with the central theme of Yogācāra —that the objective world is but a manifestation of mind (*citta*)—and continues with a description of a theory of consciousness peculiar to the Yogācārins. Scholarship has generally located the sūtra at a point between *Mādhyamika* criticalism and the fully developed philosophies of *Asaṅga* and *Vasubandhu* (fourth to fifth century proponents of consciousness only). The Laṅkāvatāra agrees with Mādhyamika that everything is śūnyatā. However, it proceeds beyond Mādhyamika in its effort to establish some continuity between distinct perceptions.

THE STRUCTURE AND OPERATION OF CONSCIOUSNESS

The Laṅkāvatāra teaches a doctrine of eight consciousnesses (*vijñānas*).

1. Eye vijñāna for the perceiving of shapes.
2. Ear vijñāna for the perceiving of sounds.

3. Nose vijñāna for the perceiving of smells.
4. Tongue vijñāna for the perceiving of tastes.
5. Body vijñāna for the perceiving of tangibles.
6. Mental vijñāna for the perceiving of ideas.
7. *Manas*—a more subtle "mental" which has the function of reception and disposition of the data from the above six vijñānas. The manas is composed of two powers, *akliṣṭa* and *kliṣṭa* (nonpassionate and passionate). The nonpassionate power is the faculty which allows man to make correct judgments, to rise above the concerns of the senses, and to will what is good. The passionate power, on the other hand, is the faculty which fosters a false view of the self, egoism, attachment to self and ignorance. Indeed, kliṣṭamanas is the root cause of error, both in perception and in judgment. There is a reciprocal causal relation between manas and the vijñānas. The vijñānas deliver information gleaned from experience to the manas; manas, in turn, feeds back the categorical boundaries in which experience may occur.
8. *Ālaya-vijñāna* or storehouse consciousness. In actuality, the *ālaya* is not at all a separate and active consciousness—i.e., it is not conscious of anything. It is a receptacle for the various dispositions and habit-energies of the other consciousnesses. These dispositions and habit-energies are planted in ālaya as seeds (*bījas*). If these seeds are pollinated by existing constructs, they mature and serve to perpetuate the wrong-headed view of self and the world. It is a principle of continuity. Buddhism teaches that all *dharmas* are impermanent (*anitya*) and momentary (*kṣaṇika*); however, the momentariness of these dharmas does not allow for the phenomena of memory and predictability in the sphere of human knowledge. In order to provide some connection between experiences of the past, present, and future the Yogācārins posit the ālaya. It has a twofold character: *Vijñaptir ālaya*, the information containing ālaya which is comprised of objective images and mental representations; and *Pāramālaya*, the ālaya that is beyond subject-object dualism. In describing this twofold character the Laṅkāvatāra asserts that the ālaya is "like a great ocean in which the waves roll on permanently but the (deeps remain unmoved; that is, the ālaya) body itself subsists uninterruptedly, quite free from fault of impermanence, unconcerned with the doctrine of ego-substance, and thoroughly pure in its essential nature." Synonyms for the ālaya are *citta* (mind) and *Tathāgatagarbha* (womb of the Tathāgata).

Resultant upon the operation of the various consciousness faculties are *five dharmas* (knowledge-states).

1. *Nāma*—the state in which the ignorant mind freezes reality by naming it.
2. *Nimitta*—the state in which definite forms, shapes, colors, sounds are perceived.
3. *Saṃkalpa*—the state of discrimination in which it is noted that $A = A$ and $A \neq B$.
4. *Samyagjñāna*—the state of right knowledge in which the products of the six senses are seen as futile and the progress toward perfection is begun.
5. *Tathatā*—the state of Suchness in which the categories of being and non-being are transcended.

The specific character or self-nature of knowledge which ensues from these knowledge-states is designated under three aspects known as *svabhāvas*.

1. *Parikalpita*—imaginings. This is the type of knowledge which results from the ascription of reality to that which does not exist, e.g., claiming that a mirage is water.
2. *Paratantra*—relativity knowledge. This form of knowledge arises from perception of worldly phenomena. It represents an advance over parikalpita since it considers all things to be interdependent and since it has an objective (albeit impermanent) referent for its concepts. Paratantra, however, continues to distinguish between perceiver and perceived and thus falls short of ultimate wisdom.
3. *Pariniṣpanna*—perfected knowledge. This form of knowledge is the wisdom (*prajñā*) which supersedes all discrimination.

Realization of ultimate truth is equated with egolessness.

1. *Egolessness of persons* is the denial of being and having to the functioning subject. There are no states of consciousness, ideas, processes of thinking or categories of thought which a subject may *possess* since there is no permanent subject which may *possess* them.
2. *Egolessness of things* is the denial of substantiality to perceived objects. Although consciousness isolates objects for purposes of understanding, yet these objects are never in a state of fixity. Hence to isolate them is to focus upon them as they exist merely in a single moment, but to ignore their dynamic dimensions and their mutual interdependency. Since there is no substance to things, there can be no intrinsic or accidental properties related to them. As the sūtra notes: things are even "destitute of the marks of individuality and generality."

3. Question: If all subjects and all objects are devoid of ego and are merely imagistic representations, what do they represent? Answer: *Cittamātra.* Traditionally, this term has been translated as mind only or nothing but mind. However, this is misleading since it still conveys an idea of substance. A more proper translation would be intention only. Here the grosser forms of substantiality are given up and the representations which go to make up one's world are seen to be rooted in intentionality.

The twofold theme of the Laṅkāvatāra may be summarized:

1. The objective world is nothing more than the manifestation of one's own intentions.
2. To understand this fully one must understand thoroughly the eight consciousnesses, the five dharmas, the three svabhāvas, and the two egolessnesses.

ERROR AND TRUTH

Error arises when the lower consciousnesses (especially the manas) engage in representation and discrimination and when, as a result of discrimination, they become attached to the resultant phenomena, considering them to be real and permanent entities. Error itself has no substance; it is like *māyā* (an illusion). The most fundamental error is the failure to recognize phenomena are nothing but representations of citta.

Truth arises when discrimination ceases and when intentionality no longer seeks to construct a world external to itself. Steps in the process toward realization of this truth include a recognition of the mutual dependency of all things and a cessation of all the *āsravas* (outflows; i.e., constructs, beliefs, fancyings, etc., which flow out of citta and issue into an objective universe). Truth resulting from the former is designated as conventional or worldly truth (*saṃvṛti-satya*); truth from the latter is designated as ultimate truth (*paramārtha-satya*). This double-truth theory is an effort on the part of the Buddhists to note the functionality of perceptual knowledge, but also to note its limitations.

PROCESSES OF TRANSFORMATION

Nirvāṇa is realized only when there is a reversal in the activities of the various consciousnesses. The six sense consciousnesses must cease presenting information; the manas must cease discriminating; and the ālaya must cease carrying the reinforced habit-energies, memories, predispositions, etc.

The reversal is termed *āśraya-parāvṛtti*, turning back at the base. Preparatory stages to reversal include purification and insight. Purification entails both moral and meditational discipline in order to destroy the impurities (*kleśas*); insight is the recognition of the emptiness of all things. Reversal itself is the transcendental experience of consciousness in which there is no dependence on anything. The consequence of reversal is the production of a will-body (*manomayakāya*)—i.e., a stage in man's experience in which he is freed from the constrictions of his ordinary mind and body. One who possesses the will-body may travel unobstructed over mountains, walls, rivers, trees, etc., plus employ other suprahuman powers (e.g., clairvoyance and clairaudience) for the benefit of all sentient beings. The Laṅkāvatāra notes three types of will-body: 1. That obtained in the enjoyment of *samādhi* (trance)—i.e., the will-body which guarantees freedom from experiential limitations. 2. That obtained in the recognition of the true nature of Dharma—i.e., the will-body which guarantees freedom from conceptual limitations. 3. That obtained by the Bodhisattva for the purpose of saving a particular class of beings.

Reversal is an *inner-directed transformation*; its aim is the destruction of the objective accretions of experience and the realization of pure intention. There is also a willful *outer-directed transformation* taught by the sūtra, a transformation in which the Buddha takes upon himself specific objective form for the salvation of all. This latter transformation is represented by the *niṣyandanirmāṇa* Buddha, the Buddha who issues forth from a pure state (*dharmatā*) into specific incarnations (subhuman, human, suprahuman). The Laṅkāvatāra appears to speak of only two forms of Buddha, the eternal and the transforming. Later doctrine will institutionalize three: *Dharmakāya* (the eternal body of the Buddha), *Saṃbhogakāya* (the enjoyment body of the Buddha), and *Nirmāṇakāya* (the transformation body of the Buddha). Outer-directed transformation is simply the logical conclusion of the doctrine of compassion of the Buddha.

TATHĀGATAGARBHA

The transformation of the external consciousnesses into intention only is made possible by the *Tathāgatagarbha*. Robinson notes that this term has a twofold meaning: womb and the womb's contents. In the first definition it is equated with the ālaya-vijñāna and understood as the container and bearer of all latent influences which ultimately affect experience. In the second definition it signifies the presence of the *potentiality* for Buddhahood in all existence. The Tathāgata resides in all creatures *in utero*. The Laṅkāvatāra, however, denies that this bears any resemblance to the permanent soul of rival philosophies.

The sūtra notes that the Tathāgatagarbha is by nature bright and pure but that it is enveloped in a garment soiled with the dirt of greed, anger, folly, and false imagination. When this garment is removed, one is nothing other than Tathāgata. *Tathāgata in utero* has become *Tathāgata in res.*

CONCLUSION

Scholars have attempted to classify the doctrines of the Laṅkāvatāra under some sort of metaphysical system-idealism (similar to Bishop Berkeley), idealistic realism (Suzuki's assessment), etc. Each of these attempts fails to convey the persistent efforts of the Yogācārin monks to avoid all objectifying categories.

The sūtra is a compendium of sermons predicated upon Mahāyāna doctrine generally and a theory of depth-consciousness in particular. The sermons form no connected argument nor attempt a systematic defense of the religion. They merely answer specific questions concerning the Dharma and reiterate the general theme that all is cittamātra.

SUGGESTED READING

Suzuki, Daisetz Teitarō, tr. *The Laṅkāvatāra Sūtra.*
———. *Studies in the Laṅkāvatāra Sūtra.*

22

The Pure Land Sūtras

Mark A. Ehman

BACKGROUND

Three sūtras constitute this body of literature: *The Larger Sukhāvatīvyūha-sūtra*, *The Smaller Sukhāvatīvyūha-sūtra*, and *The Amitāyurdhyāna-sūtra*. These sūtras reflect the existence of a popular Buddhism developing in India. At the center of this popular religion is a Buddha known as *Amitābha* (Eternal Light) or *Amitāyus* (Eternal Life). This Buddha clearly stands in contradistinction to the historically conditioned Buddha. Although theoretically this Buddha is merely one among a pantheon of Buddhas arranged in *maṇḍala* fashion (i.e., one Buddha situated at each of the cardinal points of the compass, one situated at the nadir, and one at the zenith, all oriented toward *Śākyamuni* Buddha who sits in the center), the sūtras indicate that he is to be accorded special reverence. His nature is unique. He is possessed of light which knows no limit. This fact causes the narrator of the sūtra to confess: "There is not, O Ānanda, any case of likeness, by which the extent of the light of that *Tathāgata* Amitābha could be understood." No less than nineteen epithets relating to light are ascribed to him—e.g., *Amitaprabha* (possessed of infinite splendor), *Amitaprabhāsa* (possessed of infinite brilliancy), etc. The emphasis upon light has led scholars to suspect Iranian influence upon the formation of the Amitābha legend. His assembly of hearers is immeasurable, as opposed to the finite number of hearers in the assembly of *Gautama*. The length of his life is immeasurable, as opposed to the eighty-year life span of Gautama. The stress on the immeasurability of light, assembly, and life is a not too subtle effort to suggest the eternalness of *Dharma*, *Saṃgha*, and *Buddha*, respectively.

Amitābha presides over a special sphere known as *Sukhāvatī* or Land of Happiness or Pure Land. This sphere is located in the western region of the universe. Such a locale is mythological, not literal. It refers to the western sector of the maṇḍala. It is peopled with gods and men; no evil *gatis* (destinies) appear in it. It is the sphere into which every devotee should desire to be born.

This popular religion arose in Northwest India in the period between 100 B.C. and A.D. 100. Étienne Lamotte ascribes its appearance to the *Śaka-Pahlava* (*Scytho-Parthian*) era when Buddhism was particularly susceptible to the appeal of "savior beings" of non-Indic peoples. The language of the *Sukhāvatīvyūha-sūtra* is of northwestern origin. It is mixed Sanskrit, a form of the language corrupted by local dialects and foreign words.

The religion is characterized by mystical simplicity. None of the sūtras in the group bothers with an analytical description of reality. No elaborate discipline (*Vinaya*) is put forward as a prerequisite for salvation. The devotee is called upon to produce the desire for "complete perfect enlightenment" (or for birth in Sukhāvatī) to such a degree that all other desires will fade into insignificance and oblivion. Production of this desire is achieved by hearing the name of Amitābha. Fulfillment of the desire is accomplished by concentrating on (keeping the mind and/or repeating) the name of Amitābha. These acts are not to be construed as magical. Rather, they are to be understood as acts of reorientation. The mind of the devotee is turned from greed and suffering toward perfection, and the name Amitābha is the simplified symbol of perfection.

The religion became far more influential in China and Japan. It appealed to the laity who sought an "easy way" to salvation. At the hands of the Chinese and Japanese interpreters it became the basis for eschewing dogmatism and reforming national values. Sectarian movements of the religion were formed: *Ching-t'u* in China and *Jōdo* in Japan. In the practice of the religion emphasis shifts from concentration to faith.

THE SŪTRAS

THE LARGER SUKHĀVATĪVYŪHA-SŪTRA

The sūtra opens with Śākyamuni Buddha on *Gṛdhrakūṭa* (Vulture's Peak) surrounded by hosts of *śrāvakas* and *bodhisattvas*. All of the śrāvakas have acquired wisdom except *Ānanda*. Ānanda recognizes the omniscience and power; such recognition is due not to Ānanda's superior perceptiveness, but to the grace of the Buddha.

The Buddha proceeds to enlighten Ānanda. According to the story, many eons ago there lived a Buddha named *Lokeśvararāja* who proclaimed the Dharma. *Bhikṣu Dharmākara* heard this proclamation and desired perfect knowledge. Through the grace of Lokeśvararāja the excellences of all the Buddha countries were revealed. Dharmākara took these excellences and concentrated them on a single Buddha country, so that the latter was far superior to any other realm. Dharmākara then made a series of 46 vows (*praṇidhānas*). The aim of the praṇidhānas is perfection, while their accomplishment is dependent upon the purity of Dharmākara's intention and the efficacy of his stock of merit. The praṇidhānas thus become the spiritual declarations of bodhisattvas: they intend the welfare and spiritual fulfillment of all sentient beings. Dharmākara's own spiritual attainment is to be achieved only after the accomplishment of all vows for the sake of others. The most important praṇidhānas are:

1. That there should be no unfavorable births in the perfect Buddha country.
2. That no one should fall into lower births from the perfect Buddha country.
3. That all beings born in the perfect Buddha country should possess the divine eye, divine ear, etc.
4. That not evẹn the name of sin should exist in this perfect land.
5. That all beings who hear the name of Dharmākara should be born into this pure land and should be subject to no more births until they have achieved perfect wisdom.

Dharmākara then proceeds to perform the duties of a bodhisattva. These include:

1. The perfections (*pāramitās*): giving, morality, patience, heroism (or vigor), meditation, and wisdom.
2. Models of exertion: works, which should be performed by all who desire perfect knowledge.
3. Acts of grace: accomplishments through which sentient beings are benefited.

There is no radical distinction between works and grace in the Sukhāvatī-vyūha-sūtra.

This Dharmākara is none other than the Buddha Amitābha and his perfect Buddha country is none other than Sukhāvatī. The beauty of Sukhāvatī is unsurpassed: golden trees, huge lotuses, wide rivers, etc. The inhabitants of Sukhāvatī are constant in absolute truth. Birth into Sukhāvatī is achieved by those who make a vow to be born there, who employ their stock of merit (*kuśalamūla*) to that end, and who meditate on Amitābha (either continually or by means of a single thought only). Birth into Sukhāvatī is the last birth. No one will leave this existence until he has experienced perfect knowledge.

The sūtra ends with a vision of Amitābha. Light emanating from him illumines the entire Sukhāvatī. The light reveals the type of beings existing in Sukhāvatī: both those who are filled with faith and those who entertain some doubts. All are born there upon having heard the name of Amitābha or upon having obtained "one joyful thought" of him.

THE SMALLER SUKHĀVATĪVYŪHA-SŪTRA

Comparisons with the Larger Sūtra. The Buddha Amitābha or Amitāyus presides over Sukhāvatī. Hearing and keeping in mind his name insures birth in the Buddha country. Sukhāvatī is a land of splendor free from physical and mental suffering.

An Important Point of Contrast. Birth in Sukhāvatī *is not* the consequence of good works. The stock of merit, so strongly emphasized in the larger sūtra, is never mentioned. The key to the sūtra is found in the metaphor of sound. The variety of sounds in Sukhāvatī reminds man of the Buddha, the Dharma, and the Saṃgha. These sounds, especially the sound of Amitābha's name, are the prerequisites to meditation. Without them and their continued repetition, there would be no salvation.

THE AMITĀYURDHYĀNA-SŪTRA

Background. Far more mundane and technical than the other sūtras, it contains a series of sixteen meditations, explaining in detail the objects of meditation and the specific attainment resultant upon such mental effort. The aim of these meditations of to form a perception of the western quarter (i.e., Sukhāvatī).

Introductory Parable. A certain prince, *Ajātaśatru*, because of greed, imprisoned his father, King *Bimbisāra*. Queen *Vaidehī* remained faithful to her husband and brought him food in prison. Ajātaśatru, angered by the act, determines to kill Vaidehī. However, after contemplating the horrible consequences of matricide, he merely imprisons her. Vaidehī calls upon the Buddha to show her a place free from trouble, sorrow, imprisonment, etc. From among all the Buddha lands, she chooses Sukhāvatī as the realm for her new birth.

Prerequisites to New Birth. Cultivation of goodness (i.e., filial piety toward parents and respect toward all) is stressed, as is the practice of moral and ceremonial observances, and unwavering commitment toward the attainment of enlightenment. Specific meditations consist of focusing upon an object: sun, water, trees, land, etc. The most important meditation is the ninth: meditation on Amitāyus. In meditation upon any part of Amitāyus all other characteristics of him become evident. Indeed, correct meditation upon Amitāyus reveals all other Buddhas. The philosophical implication is that in any one part of reality all of reality is present.

CONCLUSION

The Pure Land Sūtras serve as manuals for those who desire to become nonreturners (*anāgāmins*) to this world, i.e., those whose next birth is the last before entering *nirvāṇa*. In accomplishing their task the sūtras seek to inspire the devotee with vision—vision of a Buddha and his realm. Meditation upon this vision results in the realization of Sukhāvatī at death.

SUGGESTED READING

Cowell, E.B., Müller, F. Max, and Takakusu, Junjiro, trs. *Buddhist Mahāyāna Texts: Part II* (The Larger Sukhāvatīvyūha-sūtra, pp. 1–85; The Smaller Sukhāvatīvyūha-sūtra, pp. 89–107; The Amitāyurdhyāna-sūtra, pp. 161–204).

Malalasekera, G.P., et al. "Amita," *Encylcopaedia of Buddhism*, vol. 1, fascicle 3 (1964): 434–63.

means world teachings or worldly designations. It refers to a portion of the *Abhidharma Piṭaka* which deals with the origins and destruction of the universe; it is essentially an early Buddhist polemic against rival views.

The Buddhists distinguished two worlds (*loka*): first, the receptacle world (*bhājanaloka*), and second, the world of beings (*sattvaloka*). The former is the abode of the gods. The existent texts deal with such questions as the length of their lives, the dimensions of their bodies, and the fact that their origins are nonphysiological. Along with such ideas, the sections also deal with, for example, the methods of generation of serpents, dragons, and the mythic bird Garuḍa. When we turn to the world of beings, we shall turn to the material beings whose existential needs are of a grosser scale (much in line with the readers of this article). Here in the realm of material beings we find that the sufficient condition for categorizing here is that all such beings are subject to sexual desire. Within this realm, beings are differentiated into the categories of their destinies (*gatis*) which are correlated with their operative karma. Concluding this line of thought, we might say (as La Vallée Poussin notes in the aforementioned article) that of the two Buddhist lokaprajñaptis, the first or receptacle world is precisely a cosmology while the second or world of beings is more accurately a zoology.

THE DESTINIES (GATIS) TO WHICH ONE MAY BE REBORN

GODS

Gods are of three kinds according to the constituent conditions of the plane of existence (*dhātu*) on which they live. An individual, according to his karma, may be reborn into this destiny. However, as he was able to be born into it, he is consequently doomed to exhaust the fruits of his good karma at some indefinite future time and so once again plunge back into the existential world of saṃsāra.

HUMAN BEINGS

Human beings are of four kinds who are allotted birth in the mythic regions of the early Indian concept of the physical world. Not unexpectedly, northern India was held to be the center of the then known universe.

THE REALM OF GHOSTS

The inclusion of the dead one or ghost (*preta*) or "things that just go bump in the night" is an intrusion from folk culture of many popular beliefs concerning the dead. These ghosts are said to co-inhabit the world of human individuals.

23
Cosmology

Douglas D. Daye

VALUE PRESUPPOSITIONS

In general the Buddhists have intended in theory (if not always in practic
to devalue speculation (*dṛṣṭi*) about the nature of the universe. Their rath
pragmatic soteriological approach to speculative questions is the result
a basic value presupposition that when an individual exists as a hum
being and therefore has existential needs and some degree of self-conscio
ness, his energies and religious motivation may be better devoted tow
questions which help him to escape the bondage of karma. To do so, he
adopts the Buddhist analyses of human experiences in order that he
see things as they really are (*yathābhūtam*). Speculative questions abo
nature of the universe and its relations (if any) with individuals and s
were devalued in light of this superior goal of enlightenment. The Bud
of the most ancient period (and sometimes later) were not interest
systemic inclusive explanation of the universe. Rather, they were con
deny piecemeal, for example, the reality of a supreme God (the Lord,
when debating with the orthodox (*āstika*) Brahmans. In their t
polemics against the Materialists and *Naiyāyikas* they denied th
independent production of entities (*svabhāva*). La Vallée Poussi
article in Hastings's *Encylcopedia of Religion and Ethics*, p. 130) q
following key phrase: "The diversity of the world comes from
This means that action and the fruit of action and its sequential
ical, social, and psychological concomitants are the result of su
This, in turn, is the manifestation of and the binding to one's o
Resolution of this problem, not philosophical speculation about t
was the key Buddhist problematic.

ON THE TERM COSMOLOGY

Perhaps the nearest term common to early Buddhism for wh
cosmology would be an accurate translation is *lokaprajñapti*,

ANIMALS

These living beings also exist in the world of men, but not (usually) in the world of the gods.

THE REALM OF THE DAMNED

A Dante-like description of the different tortures and situations individuals subject to karma may find can be gained by reading La Vallée Poussin's article referred to earlier. (Some Buddhist texts also posit a sixth gati, that of the *asuras* or demons.)

By reading the appropriate Buddhist texts, such as the *Abhidharmakośa* of *Vasubandhu* or the *Vimānavatthu* and *Petavatthu* of the *Pāli Canon*, it is possible to construct a map of the universe as it appeared to the early Buddhists. Such a map would necessarily include not only the earth proper, but also the waters, mountains, islands or continents, hells of various sorts, and the assorted heavens.

AGES OF THE WORLD-SYSTEM

The universe (by definition) and the species that exist in it are eternal. As Robinson notes (in "Classical Indian Philosophy"), ". . . there is no evolution of new species . . . certain species are vacant, but no species is ever filled which has not been occupied by beings in a previous cosmic cycle." The presupposition here is that there are cycles within an eternal process in which there are qualitative differences in the different cyclic ages (*kalpa*, *yuga*). A cycle of four was one common variation on this theme and there was usually a process of increasing corruption from a relatively nonmaterial, rather aesthetic and spiritual first age. As the beings in their various forms participated in the process from age to age—each age involving millions if not billions of years—there was a gradual lessening of the pure spiritual and aesthetic qualities associated with the early times. A gradual corruption and decay sets in culminating in the period disappearance of the world-system at the end of a particular cycle. Some speculation was concerned with the state of beings during the cosmic night that followed a world disillusionment. One Buddhist assumption is that the highest beings warn that destruction is immanent (100,000 years from the warning) so that others may achieve rebirth in higher realms not subject to the disillusionment of the universe. Generally speaking, the Hindus held that a beingless cosmic interlude was all pervading. This present age is that of the *kali yuga*, a destructive and evil time.

THE DECLINE OF THE DHARMA

Indian Buddhist texts suggest that there were three main periods in which there would be a gradual decline in both the quality of the teachings produced by the Buddhists and the karmic capacity of the individual to accept and practice these teachings. First, there is the period of the True Dharma (0–500 A.N., i.e., after nirvāṇa of the Buddha). The period of the Counterfeit Dharma follows with the period of the Latter-Day Dharma concluding. After great periods of time have passed from the end of the period of the Latter-Day Dharma, a new Buddha will appear in the world and a period of a True Dharma will start once again. The idea that the populace possesses little capacity to understand and practice such teachings, and are therefore thought to be progressively unworthy, has been appealed to by many Buddhists in different countries and at different times. This was done in order to both justify breaking some of the more rigid axioms of Buddhist social life and to inspire or motivate their followers to greater exertions on the road to enlightenment.

SUGGESTED READING

Lamotte, Étienne. *Histoire du Bouddhisme Indien des origines à l'ère Śaka*, pp. 34–36.

La Vallée Poussin, Louis de. "Cosmogony and Cosmology: Buddhist." In *Encylopedia of Religion and Ethics*. Edited by J. Hastings. Vol. 4, pp. 129–38.

———, tr. *L'Abhidharmakośa de Vasubandhu*, Vol. 2, chap. 3, pp. 1–217.

Robinson, Richard H., "Classical Indian Philosophy." In *Chapters in Indian Civilization*. Edited by Joseph W. Elder. Vol. 1, pp. 158–61.

24
Buddhist Logic

Douglas D. Daye

INTRODUCTION

Buddhist logic is that genre of literature in Sanskrit, Tibetan, Buddhist Chinese, and Japanese which is designated by the Sanskrit words *Nyāya*, *Hetu-vidyā*, *Pramāṇa-vāda*, and *Anumāṇa*; it remains a most important component of the systematic development of Indian and Tibetan Buddhist thought. The origins of logic in India are public debate and the exegesis of the Vedic texts. The early *Mīmāṃsā* exegetes (fourth century B.C.?) and the oral formulaic of early formal debate generated technical terminology and customs of argumentation which were later distilled into explicit patterns. These, in turn, became the basic problems on which the early Buddhist and non-Buddhist nyāya controversies turned. Although the Buddhist Pāli Canon exhibits a number of inferences and rules for argumentation (e.g., the *Kathāvatthu*, I, 1ff.), they remain only sketchy anticipations of the epistemological and metalogical concerns found in the later systematic *śāstra* literature. The main components and early developments of Buddhist nyāya were subsequently exported to and developed in Tibet; this remains relatively unexplored when compared with research in Indian logic. In China and Japan, early nyāya texts (A.D. 200–500) were received as an integral part of Buddhist doctrine, and although commentaries were written upon a few texts, no new developments of any note occurred. Within a few hundred years such interest had all but died out.

HISTORICAL PHASES AND MAJOR FIGURES

The complete historical scope of Indian Nyāya embraces a period from approximately A.D. 200 (perhaps the second century B.C.?) to the present century. By the eighteenth century it had lost most of its dynamism. By 1200 the Buddhist aspects had been exported or assimilated by the Hindu and Jain schools and it waned with the passing of Buddhism in India. However, as late as 1939, Buddhist logic (*yin ming*) was being studied in Shanghai by

Buddhist laymen, and until the Communist invasion, the long tradition of Buddhist Nyāya had been unbroken in Tibet.

Mature Buddhist Nyāya developed within the context of the Indian śāstra (or systematic treatise) tradition. The earliest works of Indian Nyāya indicate that they are summaries of lines of inquiry which had been in the process of development from perhaps the second century B.C.—as in the *Vaiśeṣika-sūtra* (first century A.D.) and the *Kathāvatthu* (of the Pāli Canon, ca. 150 B.C.). The general form and terminology of Buddhist logic may be viewed in three ways: it is a reaction to, an internal regeneration of, and (sometimes) an inclusion of the problematics and terminology from non-Buddhist sources. For example, topics in the *Nyāya-sūtra* (second century A.D.), the basic text of the *Nyāya Darśana* (philosophical school), and its terminology (*pratijñā, pramāṇa*) can be seen in the work of *Nāgārjuna*, for example in the *Vigrahavyāvartanī* (verses 29–31; for the reverse see Nyāya-sūtra, IV.i).

PROTO-LOGICAL PERIOD (200 B.C.–A.D. 300)

The general use of logical principles and explicit inference schemas, without the recognition of any metaconcepts *about* logic, can be found in a range of early texts from the Kathāvatthu to the *Mādhyamika-Kārikās*. There was, of course, influence from such non-Buddhist works as *Vātsyāyana's* fourth-century commentary (*Nyāya-sūtra Bhāṣya*) on the Nyāya-sūtra and the little explored works of the Jaina logicians (e.g., *Bhadrabāhu's Daśavaikālikanir-yukti*).

EARLY PROTO-METALOGICAL PERIOD WITH THE THREE-MEMBERED SCHEMA (A.D. 300–550)

Some scholars date this internal development from *Vasubandhu* (fourth century). The first chapter of *Dignāga's* (fourth to fifth century) *Pramāṇa-samuccaya* greatly influenced the Tibetan Mahāyāna tradition in epistemology and in logic. His *Nyāyamukha* (and perhaps the *Nyāyapraveśa*), two elementary manuals of logic widely circulated in India, are the sole sources of the short-lived tradition of logic in Buddhist China. Dignāga, in his *Hetucakra* ("Wheel of Justifications"), was also the first to construct a metalogical description of all the possible ways in which the property (*dharma*) of the justification (*hetu*) can be combined with the examples (*sapakṣa, vipakṣa*) in the exemplification (*dṛṣṭānta*) and the property of the thesis member (*sādhya*). Dignāga's list of fallacies (*ābhāsa*) was expanded by the Hindu logician *Praśatapāda* (fifth century) in his *Padārthadharma-saṃgraha*; the former's *Wheel* was greatly increased by *Uddyotakara* (seventh century) in his *Nyāya-vārttika*.

THE MATURE PERIOD (A.D. 550–1000)

Noteworthy figures and their texts are *Dharmakīrti's Nyāyabindu* (ca. 600), commented on by *Dharmottara* in his *Nyāyabindu-ṭīkā* (ca. 800). By the time of the latter commentator, many of the major metalogical developments of the *Yogācāra-Vijñānavāda* school had occurred (from Vasubandhu, fourth century onward). A host of brilliant scholastic commentators and astute logicians belong to the later centuries (750–1000); e.g., *Prajñākaragupta* (750), *Śāntirakṣita* (700), *Kamalaśīla* (725), *Karṇakagomin* (875). Some major opponents of Buddhism were *Vācaspatimiśra* (ca. 970) with his *Nyāyasūcinibandha* and his Tātparya, i.e., the *Nyāya-vārttika-tātparya-ṭīkā*; others are *Udayana* (1050), *Bhāsarvajña* and *Śivāditya* (both tenth century).

THE FINAL PERIOD (A.D. 1000–1100)

Here we find a subtle, intricate blending of epistemological, logical, and ontological inquiries with questions which today would be called philosophy of language. Two main figures are *Jñānaśrīmitra* (1025) and his pupil *Ratnakīrti* (1050), the latter being most widely known for his *Apohasiddhi* ("Treatise on the Differentiation Theory of Meaning").

A REPRESENTATIVE EXAMPLE OF BUDDHIST INFERENCE

From the *Nyāyapraveśa*, Taishō 1630 (Sanskrit equivalents of the Chinese are supplied by the author):

Thesis: (*pakṣa*)	SOUND (IS) IMPERMANENT (*śabdaś anityaḥ*)
Justification (*hetu*)	BECAUSE (IT POSSESSES THE PROPERTY OF) CREATEDNESS (*kṛtakatvāt*)
Exemplification (*dṛṣṭānta*)	WHATEVER (IS A) CREATED (THING), THAT (IS) WELL KNOWN (AS AN) IMPERMANENT (THING). (*yat kṛtakaṃ tad anityaṃ dṛṣṭam*)
Similar Example (*sapakṣa*)	. . . AS (IN THE) CASE OF A POT, ETC. (*yathā ghaṭā ādis*)
Dissimilar Example (*vipakṣa*)	. . . AS NOT IN THE CASE OF SPACE. (*yathā ākaśam*)

A COMPARATIVE SKETCH OF HETU-VIDYĀ INFERENCE THEORY AND CONTEMPORARY LOGIC

The Three Forms of the (relations of the) Justification member (*trairūpya-hetu*) is an example of an early explicit proto-metalogical evaluation rule.

The justification-property (*dharma*) must be concomitantly present with the thesis-property (*pakṣadharmatvam*), present in the similar example (*sapakṣe sattvam*), and absent in the dissimilar example (*vipakṣe cāsattvam*). Here modern logicians most familiar with the axiomatic mathematical logic developed in the last 100 years would expect to find, as a matter of course, the explicit use of variables. In addition, evaluation rules would be based upon the shape, pattern, or form (validity) of the argument rather than on the content or meaning of the inference schemas (*svārthānumāna*). Legitimate logical binary functors (e.g., "and or, if . . . then") would be defined in terms of truth-functional relationships. The truth or falsity of any complex statement joined together by one of the functors is a function of the truth or falsity of its component statements. The basic model for the description of such a system would be that of an axiomatic one. Compare the nyāya example in the previous section with the metalogical law, The Rule of Detachment ($[(p \supset q) \cdot p] \supset q$). This law can be abstracted from the following "ordinary language" discourse: "If p is true, then q is true, and p is evident, so q must follow, where $p =$ "traffic light is red," and $q =$ "I should stop." Roughly speaking $\supset =$ "if . . . then" and $\cdot =$ "and." Likewise one *might* paraphrase the nyāya example in two ways: first, as "WHATEVER IS A CREATED THING, IS WELL KNOWN AS AN IMPERMANENT THING AS IS A POT AND NOT SO OF SPACE, AND SOUND IS A CREATED THING. THEREFORE, SOUND IS AN IMPERMANENT THING." A second (incomplete and oversimplified) paraphrase might be "$(x)\ (y)\ ([Cx \supset Mx \cdot Cy] \supset My)$" where by definition y is a member of the class of x, C is a created thing, and M is an impermanent thing. However, this takes us quite some distance from the way Buddhist logicians conceived these relationships.

First, as noted in the trairūpyahetu above, they required the use of the empirical examples "pot" and "space" (omitted in the second formal paraphrase), a requirement abhorrent to modern logicians. Second, the use of the implication sign $\supset$ presupposes the truth-functionality of component statements; this is incompatible with the variety of metaphysical assumptions operative in "correct" svārthānumānas. Third, the locative case is used (although not here) many times to express the (linguistic) quantity (singular, dual, or plural) of the property possessor (*dharmin*), i.e., the locus of the property (*dharma*). Quantification is not explicit nor is explicit class membership an operative concept in this context.

It is obvious that these two paraphrases of the previous section *presuppose* implicit context-restricted transformation rules for such translation. Although such paraphrases are common in the scholarly literature, the *methodological* and *metalogical* assumptions have *seldom* been made explicit. To do so would be to engage in an analysis of the three interrelated fields of formal systems theory, natural languages, and the methodology of comparative logic. However, one can say that the two paraphrases above do seem to utilize something akin to the Rule of Detachment, the first implicitly, the second explicitly. The first paraphrase is a reassembling of the "content" in accordance with the innocuous metalogical tradition, starting with Aristotle, of stating the "premises" first and the conclusion last. It presupposes, for example, that the "therefore" and the "because" (the Sanskrit ablative case) are metalogically equivalent; this is not the case—hence the question of *implicit* context-restricted transformational rules. The second paraphrase presupposes, for example, that the universal quantification in "(x) (y) . . ." is metalogically equivalent to the property (dharma)—property-possessor (dharmin) relationship; J.F. Staal has suggested the "iota" quantifier (ix)—a restricted quantifier—but this leaves unsettled the relationship of property C in Cx and Cy without projecting (a questionable) extensional descriptive emphasis. Property C by definition is a nonparticular property. Therefore it stands in some opposition to the Yogācāra-Vijñānavāda denial of the ontological reality of general terms. They hold that there exist only unique staccato moments (*svalakṣaṇas*) upon which we project mutually intra-defined epistemic and linguistic symbol systems, one component of which is general terms such as the general property C. The degree of methodological explicitness and formal rigor in the relationships between the previous section and the two paraphrases exemplify some of the methodological controversies and scholarly trends in modern nyāya scholarship.

What we actually find here in the Sanskrit, Tibetan, and Chinese is a very mixed affair, e.g., equivocations (using the same term with two different sets of meaning) in use of the word justification: justification (hetu) as the *property* (dharma) "createdness" concomitant with the property "impermanence," and justification as the second member of the inference schema, namely the *whole* ascription: "BECAUSE (IT POSSESSES THE PROPERTY OF) CREATEDNESS." We find the systematic use of variable-like cliches rather than explicit variables, e.g., *sādhya* (property-to-be-demonstrated) which is a topic-neutral term but not an explicit variable. Evaluation rules were developed based on both darśana-restricted metaphysical presuppositions and an emerging awareness of the importance of the formal rather than the material relations of the inference schema. The source of the nyāya inference schema (like Aristotle) is oral public debate. In the sixth century the Indian logicians began to become more aware of the usefulness of these topic-neutral nonempty terms (cliches) for the structuring and evaluating of their schemas. With these terms it became easier to discern formal and material contradictions; incompatibilities are acknowledged more easily as are the judgments of the overall acceptability of any specific schema. With the introduction of topic-neutral terminology, although in the throes of historical development, the evaluation of inference schemas came to depend less and less on the content or meaning of the schema. This development acknowledges the importance of what the modern logician would recognize as the quest for completeness, formal brevity, and systemic elegance. However, metaphysical presuppositions still play an important part in the evaluation of the internal relations of the members of the inference schema; for example, the word *śabda* (word or sound) is held by the Indian (Hindu) *Mīmāṃsā Darśana* to be eternal and not created by causes and conditions. On the other hand, the Buddhists hold that everything is impermanent (*sarvaṃ anityam*) because everything for them is created (*kṛtakatvāt*) from causes and conditions. Therefore the evaluation of the inference schema above will be accomplished *partially* by appeal to both the concomitant properties shared by the similar and dissimilar examples and to the metaphysical presuppositions relevant to the thesis (pakṣa) and its properties. In other words, there are relationships within the schema which depend not on the internal metarules for evaluation (such as the trairūpyahetu above), but depend on the darśana-restricted rules of the game dictated by the metaphysical presuppositions of the darśana schools of traditional Indian philosophy. We have sketched the role of the Buddhists in the development of one stream in the long tradition of Indian logic in which there can be clearly seen a gradual development from the rudimentary argument by analogy to sophisticated metalogical evaluative concepts. Within the context of the developing metalogic of variable-like cliches, there emerges a slow but ever clearer attempt to generate inference schemas freer from metaphysical presuppositions, within which the legitimization of patterns of inference are less and less dependent on the content of the component parts and increasingly exhibit an expanding awareness of the purely formal relationships between pakṣa (thesis) and the two premises (hetu, dṛṣṭānta).

SUGGESTED READING

Barlingay, S.S. *A Modern Introduction to Indian Logic.*
Bochenski, I.M. *A History of Formal Logic*, pp. 416–46.
Chi, Richard S.Y. *Buddhist Formal Logic.*
Kajiyama, Yuichi. *An Introduction to Buddhist Philosophy.*
McDermott, A.C.S. *An Eleventh-Century Buddhist Logic of "Exists."*
Potter, Karl. *Presuppositions of India's Philosophies*, pp. 56–92.
Sharma, D. *The Differentiation Theory of Meaning in Indian Logic.*
Stcherbatsky, Th. *Buddhist Logic.* 2 vols.
Tucci, Giuseppe. *Pre-Dinnāga Buddhist Texts on Logic from Chinese Sources.*

25
Nirvāṇa

Francis H. Cook

INTRODUCTION

Nirvāṇa is the religious goal of Buddhism and equivalent in function to Christian salvation. As the religious goal of Buddhism, and that part of the system which gives meaning and focus to all practices and conceptual elements, it occupies the central position in any consideration of Buddhism. It has primarily two functions.

As mentioned, it is the object of all Buddhist practices, such as meditation. The philosophy or conceptual framework of Buddhism exists inasmuch as it supports the individual in his quest. As such, Buddhism is unthinkable without the guiding principle of nirvāṇa. If Buddhism is ideally the pursuit of this goal, then the vast and intricate systems of beliefs and practices have as their sole purpose the aiding of the attainment of nirvāṇa. In the *Cullavagga* (IX.1.14) of the *Pāli Vinaya*, the Buddha said, "As the vast ocean, O monks, is impregnated with one flavor, the flavor of salt, so also, O monks, is my teaching and discipline impregnated with just one flavor, the flavor of emancipation."

Another function of the experience of nirvāṇa is the validation of the teachings of Buddhism. Buddhism is not primarily a religion of faith or obedience to a superior being. It stresses the importance of personal experience of the goal. While in the earlier stages of the religious life the Buddhist must of necessity take the teachings of Buddhism on faith, it is agreed that finally these teachings must be validated through the experience of enlightenment and nirvāṇa.

DEFINITION OF THE TERM

The Western understanding of the nature of nirvāṇa has derived in part from etymological derivation of the word itself, and in part from the apparent direction of Buddhist thought. Nirvāṇa is commonly derived from the root $\surd$ *vā*, plus the prefix *nir*, which together carry the sense of the extinction of a flame. Some Western students of Buddhism have concluded from this that nirvāṇa entails self-extinction.

Buddhist canonical literature supports the interpretation of nirvāṇa as self-extinction in its rather negative view of phenomenal existence as experienced by common mortals (*saṃsāra*), and in its insistence that emancipation lies in an escape from the stresses, anxiety, and frustration, in fact from all that Buddhists mean by the term *duḥkha* (suffering), which is inherent in embodied existence. These two facts have led some Western scholars to conclude that nirvāṇa is a purely negative state, a kind of suicide, in which the individual ceases to exist in any sense.

INTERPRETATION

The above negative interpretation can be remedied if the following points are kept in mind.

Nirvāṇa in early canonical literature is described in three ways:

1. Negative. It is said to be extinction, cessation, the negation of the phenomenal world, and so on. One text says it is " . . . a realm where there is neither earth nor water, nor fire, nor wind . . . neither sun nor moon, neither coming nor going, neither lasting nor ceasing, nor rebirth . . . . "
2. Positive. A passage in the scriptures says it is " . . . the immortal, the pure, the refuge, the island, the ford, the support, protection, non-transmigrating, cool, non-impassioned, omnipresent, extremely pure, subtle, peaceful, without affliction, non-returning to existence, nirvāṇa."
3. These two conflicting testimonies are further complicated by several passages in which the Buddha refuses to say anything at all about nirvāṇa. It is so different from saṃsāric existence that words, which refer to things in the mundane realm, cannot describe the supramundane.

Nirvāṇa is a goal to be reached not only after death, but also, and perhaps primarily, in this very existence. There are two forms of the same state:

1. *Sa-upadhiśeṣa-nirvāṇa:* nirvāṇa with basis remaining, where basis means mind and body. This is nirvāṇa enjoyed in present existence. The Buddha is said to have dwelt in nirvāṇa during the last 45 years of his life.
2. *An-upadhiśeṣa-nirvāṇa:* nirvāṇa without basis. This is sometimes equated with *parinirvāṇa*, for it is nirvāṇa continuing after the destruction of the phychophysical being. It is not a new or separate nirvāṇa, but the one attained in life continuing after death.

The main point in this distinction is that nirvāṇa is a goal to be reached while one is still living.

A careful reading of canonical literature reveals nirvāṇa not as the extinction of the psychophysical being, but rather extinction of the factors which are conducive to suffering—greed, hatred, and ignorance. Nirvāṇa as cessation or extinction (*nirodha*) is better construed as the cessation of turmoil in one's life, rather than of life itself: "O monks, what is nirvāṇa? It is, monks, the cessation of desire, cessation of hatred, cessation of ignorance. This, monks, is called nirvāṇa."

The possibility of self-extinction makes no sense in a thought system which is in fact based on the teaching of the nonexistence of a self (*ātman*). It is readily accepted by all Buddhists that the being as a material-mental construct ceases to exist at death whether or not one has achieved nirvāṇa. But if there is no substantial, essential self to begin with, how can it become extinct?

To desire non-being or self-extinction would bind the seeker all the closer to saṃsāra, since, as the second of the Four Noble Truths says, the source of suffering in saṃsāra is in part a desire for either existence (*bhava-tṛṣṇā*) or nonexistence (*vibhava-tṛṣṇā*).

Negative interpretations of the Buddhist *summum bonum* frequently overlook the cognitive element in it. It is also wisdom and knowledge, the attainment of truth.

HĪNAYĀNA AND MAHĀYĀNA

Although the experience of nirvāṇa may be identical for all individuals (discounting the intensity of the experience), its conceptual formulation has varied. The so-called *Hīnayāna* and *Mahāyāna* forms of Buddhism discuss it in different ways.

Hīnayāna Buddhism considers nirvāṇa to be mainly an individual emancipation from existential turmoil and pain (duḥkha), conceived as a cooling of the passions (*kleśa*) which are responsible for duḥkha. It is a personal transcendence of pain and an end to rebirth.

Mahāyāna sources, such as the *Saddharmapuṇḍarīka-sūtra*, *Laṅkāvatāra-sūtra*, and *Daśabhūmika-sūtra*, reject the Hīnayāna nirvāṇa as selfish and incomplete. As part of the doctrines of the career of the *Bodhisattva* and the importance of compassion (*karuṇā*), nirvāṇa according to the Mahāyāna should not be a personal, selfish goal. This is rejected by the Bodhisattva, who deliberately remains within the cycle of saṃsāra in order to help other beings attain the goal. Paradoxically, this rejection of nirvāṇa for the good of living beings is considered to be the true nirvāṇa. If nirvāṇa is the elimination of desire, then one cannot attain nirvāṇa if one desires it. By rejecting this last fragment of attachment through the selfless devotion to the welfare of all living beings, the Bodhisattva wins the only nirvāṇa worth having. Also, whereas Hīnayāna generally felt that only the monk-professional was capable of emancipation, Mahāyāna insists that all can acquire it, including laymen. Mahāyāna Buddhism has many synonyms for nirvāṇa, including Buddhahood, Emptiness (*śūnyatā*), Limit of Reality (*bhūtakoṭi*), and Suchness (*tathatā*).

THE FAR EAST

The Far Eastern Buddhists interpret nirvāṇa (in this life) in a manner somewhat different from that of Indian Buddhists. The difference can be seen in their respective iconographies. Indian saintly figures, Buddhas and Bodhisattvas, are portrayed as superhuman, aloof, and regal. They wear the clothes and jewelry of princes and kings, the Buddhas usually sitting in cross-legged yogic fashion, the only expression on their faces a very slight smile, indicating their perpetual contemplation of the Absolute. Chinese figures, particularly those of the *Ch'an* school, rather exemplify the simple and ordinary, as can be seen in the figures of *Han-shan*, *Shih-tê*, *Pu-tai*, and the Ch'an patriarchs. Chinese and Japanese Buddhists tended to consider the religious goal a restoration of innate naturalness (*tzu-jan*) and simplicity, in which the individual comes to perceive the oneness of Being and his immersion in, and identity with, this oneness. A Ch'an saying illustrating this is "Chopping wood and carrying water, this is the wonderful Way."

SUGGESTED READING

Conze, Edward. *Buddhist Thought in India*. See nirvāṇa in index.

Dutt, Nalinaksha. *Aspects of Mahāyāna Buddhism and Its Relation to Hīnayāna*, pp. 129–204.

Johansson, Rune. *The Psychology of Nirvana*.

La Vallée Poussin, Louis de. *Nirvāṇa*.

———. *The Way to Nirvāṇa: Six Lectures on Ancient Buddhism*.

Rahula, Walpola. *What the Buddha Taught*, chap. 4, pp. 35–44.

Slater, Robert. *Paradox and Nirvana*.

Stcherbatsky, Th. *The Conception of Buddhist Nirvāṇa*.

Thomas, Edward J. *The History of Buddhist Thought*. See nirvāṇa in index.

Welbon, Guy Richard. *The Buddhist Nirvāṇa and Its Western Interpreters*.

26

The Doctrine of Meditation in the Hīnayāna*

Stephan V. Beyer

INTRODUCTION

The canonical collections of Buddhist scripture contain large numbers of texts devoted to meditation. It is clear that the Buddhists felt free to borrow contemplative techniques from other contemporary sects, and also that the early tradition would vary received techniques to suit the capacities of individual meditators. Thus the texts recount how the Buddha himself gave such-and-such a meditation to a particular monk, and an entirely different one to another monk, yet leading them both infallibly to the goal of liberation. Several of these techniques were enshrined in texts of their own, while others were mentioned only casually in the course of other discussions. Two of these techniques, however, became central to the entire contemplative path: the process of *withdrawal* from sensory input in progressive states of trance (*jhāna*), as set forth, for example, in the *Sāmaññaphala-sutta*, and the process of *observation* of senory input in progressive states of mindfulness (*sati*), as in the *Satipaṭṭhāna-sutta*.

The early and rather inchoate mass of material, often overlapping and occasionally contradictory, was given a semblance of order in the various *Abhidharma* schools and received its classical *Theravāda* formulation at the hands of *Buddhaghosa* in the fifth century A.D., in his compendious *Visuddhimagga*. By now the two opposite processes of sensory withdrawal and sensory observation had been coordinated as parts of a coherent whole, a standard structure of meditation that would persist in the Mahāyāna, and would be used in both the Chinese and Tibetan academies. Here the process of withdrawal, and the ascent to ever higher levels of abstract trance, was called *calming* (*samatha*), and was considered to be mental training prerequisite to the mindful observation of events. The mindful observation of events was called *insight* (*vipassanā*), leading recursively to the trances that finally freed the meditator from the ongoing world-process.

*Since this lecture is primarily an exposition of sources preserved in Pāli, technical meditational terminology in preserved in this language.

THE PRACTICE OF CALM

Buddhaghosa lists forty objects of contemplation that may be used in the process of calming the mind. These seem to fall into two classes: those that are involved directly in the induction of trance, and those that function to eliminate distractions and impediments in the contemplative process.

THE ANCILLARY TECHNIQUES

Meditators may generally be classed into three personality types, according to the predominance in them of lust, hatred, or delusion. These three defilements, when turned to the practice of religion, produce personalities based respectively on faith, intellectuality, or enthusiasm. It is the function of a meditation master to observe the way his disciple walks, stands, eats, and wears his robe, to determine from these clues his basic personality type, and prescribe for him those ancillary meditations that will either counteract his particular defilement or encourage the exercise of the corresponding religious virtue.

The Ten Uglinesses and Mindfulness of the Body. To counteract the defilement of lust, the master may prescribe a meditation on *ugliness*, here referring specifically to the ten stages of decomposition of a corpse, that the meditator may realize the loathesomeness of the body. He meditates upon the swollen purple rotting corpse, and he thinks: "This body of mine is the same as that one. It will become like that one, and it will not escape."

Again, the monk may perform *mindfulness of the body* with himself as the object, looking upon himself as a bag covered with skin and filled with all sorts of filth: "In this body there is hair, body-hair, nails, teeth, skin, flesh, sinews, bones, marrow, kidneys, heart, liver, membranes, spleen, lungs, stomach, bowels, intestines, feces, bile, phlegm, pus, blood, sweat, fat, tears, grease, saliva, mucus, fluids, and urine."

Neither of these meditations is designed to lead to the sensory withdrawal of the trance state; rather they function to eliminate the defilement of lust, so that the distractions of lust do not intrude upon the meditator when he turns to the inculcation of the trance. As such, they may be prescribed as preliminary to the trance meditations, or as specific antidotes to lustful distractions as they occur.

The Four Immeasurable Contemplations. To counteract the defilement of hatred, the master may prescribe the *immeasurable contemplations*, also called the *abodes of Brahma*, since they are held to lead to rebirth in the high heaven of the god. Here the meditator concentrates in turn upon love, compassion, sympathetic joy, and equanimity, diffusing these emotions throughout the four directions and toward all sentient beings.

Love is a feeling of friendship and brotherhood with all beings. But this emotion may easily degenerate into lust, so it is followed by *compassion*, an awareness of the pitiful state into which these beings have fallen through ignorance. But again this may lead to spiritual pride and a feeling of superiority, so the meditator trains himself in *sympathetic joy*, that he may share the happiness of others and rejoice in the merits they have accumulated. And finally he achieves a state of *equanimity* wherein he makes no distinction between friend or enemy, but is even-minded toward all creatures.

Although, technically speaking, these contemplations can lead into the trance states, they are in fact never so used, for the emotions aroused in them remain worldly qualities. They are prescribed to forestall the distractions of hatred in the course of meditation, or to counteract hateful feelings that may tumble into consciousness in the course of the trance itself.

Mindfulness of the Breath. For a meditator who suffers from the defilement of delusion—or enjoys the problematic virtue of enthusiasm—the master may prescribe a calming meditation called *mindfulness of the breath*. The meditator schools himself to be aware of the motion of his breath as it moves in and out of his body, gradually calming both his body and his mind with a one-pointed concentration upon its soothing motion, thinking: "Calming my body I shall breathe in . . . Calming my body I shall breathe out . . . ."

This meditation was something of a problem for the commentators on the early texts, for it is part of a larger technique called the *foundation of mindfulness*, which was held to be a path to *nirvāṇa* in and of itself. This technique began with mindfulness of breath, and proceeded to mindfulness of the body (as above), and then to mindfulness of the feelings, mindfulness of the thoughts, and finally mindfulness of events. It thus comprised both calm and insight, which the commentators were striving to maintain as separate processes within the structure.

In actual practice, then, the foundation of mindfulness has often been used alone as a special path for contemplatives of an active and imaginative disposition. But as incorporated into the standard structure it is used as an ancillary meditation for excitable individuals, as a preliminary to the trance itself, or as an antidote to the troubling delusions that may appear therein.

The Six Remembrances. A meditator whose lustful defilements have been transformed into the virtues of faith may be helped in his meditation by the practice of *remembrance*. Here he thinks repeatedly upon the virtues of the *Buddha*, the *Dharma*, and the *Saṃgha*, upon the rewards of *morality* and *charity*, and upon the *happy state of the gods*. Thus he increases his faith in the teachings, and in turn this increase of faith—although not directly leading to sensory withdrawal in the trance—provides him with the necessary motivation and reinforcement for his trance meditations.

The Mindfulness of Death, the Remembrance of Peace, the Loathesomeness of Food, and the Analysis of the Four Elements. Again, there are ancillary meditations that may be prescribed for one whose defilement of hatred has been transformed into the religious virtue of intellectuality. He may practice the *mindfulness of death*, wherein he analyzes intellectually the inevitability of his own passing away, or the *remembrance of peace*, wherein he reflects upon the safety of nirvāṇa amid the torments of this world. In both cases, he uses his intellect—as opposed to faith, as above—to motivate and reinforce his trance meditations. Or such a meditator may use similar intellectual means to counteract the distractions that may occur in his trance. He may contemplate the *loathesomeness of food*, reflecting upon the disgusting way in which food is prepared and ingested and eliminated, that he may turn away from greed and yearning for sensory pleasures; or he may perform the *analysis of the four elements*, examining the fact that his beloved body is nothing but an accidental concatenation of earth and water, fire and air.

This catalogue of ancillary techniques was a means for the commentators to deal with the mass of different meditations given in the canonical texts. We have noted that they had occasional difficulty in creating a workable scheme, especially where their sources specifically stated that an ancillary discipline in fact led to liberation. But the commentators also show that they possessed a keen insight into human nature, and into the efficacy of autotherapeutic techniques. Their scheme of ancillary meditations has continued in use to this day, and has been successful in training a wide variety of personalities to pursue the rigors of the trance.

THE TRANCE TECHNIQUES

Buddhaghosa has thus far dealt with twenty-six of his forty objects of contemplation (ten uglinesses, four immeasurables, and six remembrances, as well as mindfulness of the body, mindfulness of the breath, mindfulness of death, remembrance of peace, loathesomeness of food, and analysis of the four elements). The remaining fourteen objects of contemplation are all involved directly with the induction of the trance, proceeding to even higher levels of abstraction and withdrawal from sensory output.

THE TEN DEVICES

According to the standard scheme, all these trance states may be achieved through meditation upon a *device* (*kasiṇa*). Buddhaghosa lists ten of these: earth, water, fire, air, blue, yellow, red, white, light, and space. The *earth* device, for example, is a circle of earth of even color and texture. The *water* device may be a round vessel filled with rain water. Or the *blue* device may be a piece of blue cloth, or a blue painted disc, or a bunch of blue flowers arranged as a round dense mass. This device is then the basis or support for the meditation.

The Beginning Sign. The meditator erects his device in a quiet and secluded place, and seats himself in the cross-legged posture facing it, first reminding himself of the virtues of meditation and the fact that, in spite of all difficulties, holy men of the past have been able to achieve liberation thereby. He then proceeds to stare at the device, and his mental perception of the object is said to be the *beginning sign*. And he stares at it some more. And then he stares at it some more.

The Eidetic Sign. As he sits there staring at the device, he begins to memorize its form, and whether his eyes are open or shut, he clearly sees the object before him, with all its details, exactly as it appears. This memorized and totally accurate picture of the object is called the *eidetic sign*, and with this eidetic sign as his object he enters into *beginning meditation*. The meditator should immediately rise from his seat and leave the device, going into his dwelling and concentrating upon his eidetic sign rather than upon the beginning sign (his perception of the object itself). And should he be distracted from his concentration upon this memorized image (as he inevitably is), or should the image simply fade away (as it inevitably does), then he should arise once more, return to the device, and again establish the eidetic sign before returning to his dwelling.

The Representational Sign. In the course of this frustrating concentration upon the elusive eidetic image, *five hindrances* tend to arise in the meditator's mind:

1. *Lust:* images of desired objects appear before him, distracting him from his concentration, or he remembers sensory pleasures of the past.
2. *Hatred:* he begins to think of people and things he dislikes, and images of past injuries appear in his mind.
3. *Sloth and torpor:* he falls asleep (this is quite common), or becomes weary and depressed at the mental effort he is making.
4. *Remorse and distraction:* he becomes extremely sensitized to sensory input and is easily distracted, and becomes so frustrated that he is ready to abandon his attempts.

5. *Perplexity and doubt:* he is confused at his lack of success, and begins to doubt whether meditation actually works.

But as he focuses upon the eidetic sign, these five hindrances begin to fade. As he gets better and better at concentration, he enters into the *meditation of approach* for longer and longer periods of time. And in this meditation of approach the eidetic sign itself changes. It becomes the *representational sign*, a shining and glowing shape that appears before him, no longer a duplicate of the actual device but rather an abstract visual representation of its essence. Thus the earth device is no longer a particular piece of earth, with perhaps a twig here or a leaf there, but rather a shining disc like the rising moon. The representational sign of the water device appears like a mirror in the sky. The blue device is not seen as made of flowers and petals, but appears in its representational sign like a pure, clear, blue gem. And whereas the eidetic sign was fixed and unchanging, the representational sign is infinitely malleable, and may be contracted to a glowing dot or expanded to fill the entire universe. The meditator is thus in a state of approach with the representational sign as his object; the hindrances are suppressed, and he is approaching a state of trance. And as his meditation becomes more and more firm, he enters into the *meditation of attainment* with the representational sign as his object, and there he abides, for he has "attained" the first trance.

The Four Trances. In the first trance, the five hindrances are totally absent, for they have been replaced by the five factors of concentration:

1. Discursive thought: the meditator still engages in linear thinking, and is able to reflect upon his attainment of the trance.
2. Reasoning: he is aware of himself in his situation, and can consider its antecedents and consequences.
3. Enthusiasm: he enjoys the state of trance, is delighted at its attainment after all his struggles, and wishes to continue in such a state.
4. Pleasure: his body and senses are suffused with pleasant feelings.
5. One-pointedness: he is completely concentrated upon the object, and can no longer be distracted.

In the second trace the meditator realizes that discursive thought and reasoning are in themselves distracting, so he eliminates factors 1 and 2. He no longer thinks *about* his trance state, but simply *is* in trance, with inner tranquillity and concentration of mind, with the enthusiasm and pleasure that are born of his concentration.

Then the meditator realizes that his enthusiasm for this state is itself distracting, so he eliminates factor 3. He abides in a state of trance wherein there is nothing but pleasure and concentration, and this third trance is said to be the highest state of physical pleasure that can possibly be achieved.

Finally, the meditator realizes that pleasure is distracting, so he eliminates factor 4. He transcends both pleasure and pain, and can no longer be swayed by any worldly temptation. He abides in a state of pure and absolute concentration upon the representational sign, his mind pure and translucent, clear and undefiled, dextrous and supple, firm and unshakeable.

THE FOUR FORMLESS REALMS

Aside from the ten devices, there are now four objects of contemplation remaining in Buddhaghosa's list of forty, and these carry the meditator into even greater sensory withdrawal, into states further and further removed from the realms of form. These are the *formless attainments*, which render the mind of the meditator ever more pure and supple.

1. The Realm of Infinite Space: Here the meditator wearies of the material thing that is the object of his meditation, and wishes to transcend it. He sees that the fourth trance is full of danger, for it takes a material thing as its object. So he takes the representational sign and extends it to the very ends of the universe; and he eliminates the object itself, and concentrates exclusively upon the *infinite space* that remains.
2. The Realm of Infinite Perception: Then the meditator realizes that the trance of infinite space is full of danger, for it is not peaceful, and may slip back into the realm of material things. So he eliminates the infinite space that was the object of his trance, and concentrates exclusively upon the *infinite perception* that had pervaded it.
3. The Realm of Nothing-At-All: Then the meditator realizes that the trance of infinite perception is full of danger, for it is not peaceful, and may slip back into the realm of infinite space. So he eliminates his own infinite perception, and concentrates exclusively upon the *nothing-at-all* that remains.
4. The Realm of Neither Idea Nor Non-Idea: Finally the meditator realizes that the trance of nothing-at-all is full of danger, for it is not peaceful. He thinks, "It is ideas that are a disease, an abscess, a dagger in the heart." So he eliminates the idea even of nothing-at-all, and concentrates exclusively upon peace, and abides in the realm of *neither idea nor non-idea*.

We may note that the meditator ascended the four trances by eliminating one *factor* of concentration at a time, until only pure one-pointedness remained. Here the meditator has proceeded from one formless realm to the next by progressively eliminating the *object* of each formless trance, gaining states of abstraction ever further removed from the phenomenal world.

THE PRACTICE OF INSIGHT

Buddhaghosa's Visuddhimagga is based on a grand scheme of seven *purities*, of which the last five refer specifically to insight meditation. These seven purities are: purity of virtue, purity of mind, purity of view, purity of overcoming doubt, purity of knowledge and insight into right and wrong paths, purity of knowledge and insight into progress, and purity of knowledge and insight themselves.

PURITY OF VIRTUE

This purity refers to the prior moral training of the meditator, his gradual cutting off of impediments that bind him to the world, and the development of an attitude of moral detachment from worldly things.

PURITY OF MIND

The second purity is the state of mental suppleness and clarity, the purity of thought that is achieved through the development of the trance states. Except in special cases (the so-called dry arhants), one cannot gain true insight into reality while beset with the prejudices of desire. It is only through the trances and formless attainments that the meditator is able to gain the objectivity of desirelessness. With this objectivity he is ready to turn his mind to the practice of insight, and, no longer blinded by involvement, to see things as they really are.

PURITY OF VIEW

The meditator thus begins his training in insight by examining objectively the thirty-two constituents of his own body, or his senses and their objects, or his five aggregates. And with his now pure and supple mind he sees that there is no entity apart from name-and-form, and he realizes that there is neither *I* nor *mine* in this concatenation of mind and matter. He sees that sensory experience is as impermanent as the external objects that cause it, and he is freed of all attachment to a self.

PURITY OF OVERCOMING DOUBT

Then, like a doctor diagnosing the etiology of a disease, he turns his clear attention upon the source of his mind and body. He realizes that name-and-form come into being through a cause. He sees that his body is caused by ignorance and craving and grasping, projected from past into the present by the action of karma, and when this physical body exists, made up of the four elements, then mental events occur dependent upon the contact of a sensory organ with its corresponding object. Thus he realizes the twelvefold chain of dependent origination, and sees with insight that all things are impermanent, and suffering, and not the self. And thus he is cleansed of all his doubts about the past and present and future.

PURITY OF KNOWLEDGE AND INSIGHT INTO RIGHT AND WRONG PATHS

The meditator examines objectively the appearance and disappearance of all the things in the three realms of existence, and perceives their causal interrelatedness. Each event that passes before his eyes he sees as impermanent, and suffering, and not the self. He gains eighteen great insights, and permanently rejects any notion of finding permanence or happiness or self among conditioned things.

But herein lies danger, for with his budding insight he may be seized by the ten *defilements of insight*, and give way to excitement and the delusion of progress, thinking he has attained a fruition he has not yet gained. If a meditator has been properly trained by his master, however, he will not fall prey to the seductions of pleasure and magic power he gains here, and will be able to distinguish the right and wrong paths to liberation.

PURITY OF KNOWLEDGE AND INSIGHT INTO PROGRESS

Having freed himself from the dangers of wrong paths, the meditator continues his systematic and progressive development of insight. Gradually he gains nine knowledges, leading to a culmination of his understanding:

1. Knowledge gained by reflection upon the appearance and disappearance of conditioned things: He completely internalizes his realization of impermanence, and understands that the suffering is not the self, thus seeing everything as it truly is.
2. Knowledge gained by reflection upon the destruction of conditioned things: He sees that every conditioned thing decays and disappears, so he no longer craves for becoming.
3. Knowledge gained by becoming fearful of conditioned things: He sees all things as fearful and full of danger, a trap for the unwary, an empty mirage in the desert to lead him astray.
4. Knowledge gained by reflection upon the danger of conditioned things: He realizes that he is without protection in the midst of things, and turns toward nirvāṇa as safety amid afflictions.
5. Knowledge gained by reflection upon revulsion from conditioned things:

He turns his back upon this dangerous world, for he realizes that safety and happiness lie in detachment from things.

6. Knowledge gained by desire for liberation from conditioned things: He no longer clings to any form of worldly existence, and, like a man caught in a trap, seeks only to free himself.

7. Knowledge gained by reflection upon the analysis of conditioned things: With nothing but desire for freedom, he sees all things as calamity and destruction, and analyzes the true nature of things in order to escape from them.

8. Knowledge gained by indifference to conditioned things: As he thus analyzes, he realizes that he need neither fear nor desire any thing, for there is no *I* or *mine* anywhere, so he takes no thing as an object of his thought, but turns only to nirvāṇa.

9. Knowledge gained by following the Way: With the culmination of his insight into things, he sets forth to tread the path to nirvāṇa.

PURITY OF KNOWLEDGE AND INSIGHT THEMSELVES

Here the meditator gains knowledge of the four Noble Paths (of the stream-winner, once-returner, nonreturner, and arhant). He uses his insight to achieve two further contemplative attainments that bring him to the brink of nirvāṇa itself: the *attainment of his fruition* and the *attainment of the cessation of thought and feeling*.

The Attainment of Fruition. In this trance state, the meditator takes no thing as the object of his contemplation. He ceases to think upon any thing, and adverts only to nirvāṇa. This is known as *freedom of the mind*, for it has no "signs" at all. It is completely transcendent and divorced from the phenomenal. Thus the meditator goes through the series of knowledges gained in his insight meditation. As these knowledges arise in him, he realizes his rebirth as a holy person, with his mind totally fixed on nirvāṇa, and he emerges having gained the *fruition* of the appropriate Noble Path.

The Attainment of Cessation. In this trance state, the meditator takes the final leap from the world, thinking, "Let me be without thought, and dwell in bliss; here and now let me gain the cessation that is nirvāṇa." This is the ultimately transcendent experience, and is called *nirvāṇa in this very life*.

Thus the meditator ascends through all the formless realms, and emerges from each one to realize with his insight that all things therein were impermanent, and suffering, and not the self, and he enters the trance of neither idea nor non-idea, and when one or two moments of thought have passed, he becomes totally without either thought or feeling, and he gains *cessation.*

This personally experienced nirvāṇa is the final *extinction of all defilements.* All drunkenness with existence is destroyed, and when the arhant dies, he will further gain the final *extinction of the aggregates*, and never be born again.

The extinction of defilement is called *nirvāṇa with remainder*, for the arhant still has a portion of his life remaining to be lived. At the moment of his death he gains *nirvāṇa without remainder*, for with the dissolution of his body and the cessation of his last thought he totally transcends the phenomenal. His aggregates are extinct, and he passes into final nirvāṇa.

SUGGESTED READING

La Vallée Poussin, Louis de, tr. *L'Abhidharmakośa de Vasubandhu*, chap. 6.
Ñāṇamoli Thera, tr. *The Path of Purification* (Visuddhimagga).
Ñāṇaponika Thera. *The Heart of Buddhist Meditation.*
Swearer, Donald K., ed. *Secrets of the Lotus*, pp. 11–125 (Chao Khun Sobhana Dhammasudhi).
Vajirañāṇa Mahāthera. *Buddhist Meditation in Theory and Practice.*

27

The Doctrine of Meditation in the Mahāyāna

Stephan V. Beyer

INTRODUCTION

The Mahāyāna was a complex religious and social phenomenon. It was a religious revitalization movement and a reworking of metaphysics, a revival of archaic contemplative modes and a reordering of religious priorities. The very mood of meditation changed from peace and tranquillity to action and concern, from transcendence to immanence.

We find thus a complex array of meditative techniques generated within the movement, but these tend to fall into three major types: 1. The *standard meditative structure* inherited from the earlier attempts at systematizing the canonical materials, yet with the twofold process of calm and insight infused with a universalist fervor, making it the vehicle of the new metaphysics and the basis for moral action in the world; 2. The resurgence of older *visionary and ecstatic techniques* aimed at the construction of alternative realities and the gaining of magic power to control the world of experience; and 3. The development of new *techniques of spontaneity* to achieve a direct experience of freedom amid the events of public reality.

THE STANDARD STRUCTURE OF MEDITATION

There are many Mahāyāna texts dealing with the inherited contemplative structure, and setting forth the ordered sequence of meditative practice, composed not only in India but also in the academies of China and Tibet. Although the structure remains basically the same (whether in the Chinese *Mo-ho chih-kuan* of *Chih-i* or the Tibetan *Lam-rim chen-mo* of *Tsong-kha-pa*), there is considerable difference in the working out of details. Here we shall follow the path as it is given by the Indian scholar *Kamalaśīla* in his *Bhāvanākrama*, a text that has been used in Tibet since the ninth century as the model for all handbooks on meditation.

COMPASSION

Whereas earlier texts emphasized the moral training of the individual meditator as a means of inculcating detachment—as in the *purity of virtue* in the preceding chapter—the Mahāyāna demands specific training in compassion. The term has been taken from its context in the *four immeasurable contemplations* and has become not a prior antidote to hatred but rather the foundation of the entire contemplative path.

Thus the meditator begins by contemplating the sufferings of all sentient creatures: he realizes that the entire world is licked by the blazing flames of sorrow, and he meditates upon compassion for them, his enemies as well as those whom he loves. And finally he feels that all beings are as dear to him as his own suffering children, and he wishes to lead them out of pain. This is called the *great compassion*.

THE THOUGHT OF ENLIGHTENMENT

The Yearning for Buddhahood. It is through constant meditation upon compassion that there spontaneously arises the intention to achieve nothing less than Buddhahood itself for the sake of these suffering creatures. The meditator begins to yearn for the omniscience of Buddhahood, to think of it constantly: he hopes for supreme and perfect enlightenment, that he may save all beings from their sorrow.

The Vow of Buddhahood. This *thought of enlightenment* is held to be of two sorts: the *intention* and the *setting forth*. The intention is the yearning for Buddhahood in the heart of the meditator, while the setting forth is the actual vow that he will in fact tread the long and arduous path to enlightenment. This vow to become nothing less than a Buddha is a formal act, made in the presence of a master who himself holds the vow, and witnessed by all the Buddhas and celestial Bodhisattvas. By this act, the meditator himself becomes a *Bodhisattva*—a being destined for perfect Buddhahood—and as such he sets forth to strive in all the *six perfections*.

RELIGIOUS PRACTICE

Thus the new-made Bodhisattva must perform virtuous actions in the world: he must practice *charity*, *morality*, *forebearance*, *striving*, and *meditation*, all under the guiding power of his developing *wisdom*. For charity becomes *perfect* only when it is informed by a metaphysical understanding of the true nature of the giver, and the gift, and the one to whom it is given, while wisdom is sterile if it does not result in action. The meditator takes the past lives of the Buddha as the model for his action in the world, and he must be willing to sacrifice wealth as well as life itself in the name of virtue.

His *wisdom* and his *means* must reinforce each other; neither can be perfect without the other. And this then is the Middle Way. The meditator does not abide in nirvāṇa, for he works within the world, and he does not abide within the world, for he has cast aside all error. His wisdom shuns the extreme of affirmation, and his means shun the extreme of denial.

So the meditator begins to work within the world, giving charity, forgiving those who harm him, preaching the Law in spite of all obstacles, heroically coming to the aid of all suffering creatures. And he simultaneously cultivates his wisdom in three ways: 1. Through study and learning—he reads the scriptures and studies under a master who understands their meaning. 2. Through consideration—he himself ponders the scriptures and penetrates ever more deeply into their truth. 3. Through meditation—with logic and scripture as his guide, he meditates upon the true nature of reality.

MEDITATION

Meditation is the ultimate source of wisdom, and is thus central to the entire Bodhisattva path. The meditator is prepared by his study, so that his meditation will not be erroneous: the fruit of his true meditation will be a clear and manifest knowledge of reality.

The Practice of Calm. First the meditator must calm his mind, for he cannot know things as they really are with a mind unconcentrated. To this end he takes a contemplative object and focuses upon it one-pointedly, ascending through the four trances and the four formless realms.

The process of calm here given is exactly the same as that in the previous chapter. It is true that it is the ontology of the contemplative system that underlies its promise of universal salvation, that it is the wisdom of insight that feeds back into action in the world. But the system still takes as its basis the twofold process of calm as well as insight, for insight arises only in a meditator who has attained the objectivity of detachment, and this objectivity occurs only in a state of calm. This recursive relationship is called the *union of calm and insight*.

The Practice of Insight. Kamalaśīla quotes the following verse from the *Laṅkāvatāra-sūtra* as the basic outline for his process of insight: "He ascends to mind alone, and does not think that external objects really exist. But with reality before him, he transcends mind alone. He transcends non-appearance, and he abides in non-appearance, seeing the Mahāyāna. And in this effortless state, tranquil, made pure by his vows, where nothing appears, there he sees not-self, the highest knowledge."

The meditator first examines external events: are they really something external to their perception? or could they be simply the perception itself, as in a dream? He logically analyzes the concept of external things, and discovers that such a concept leads inevitably to ineluctable anomalies. Thus he realizes that there is no such thing as an external object. Every event is a mental event.

The meditator then considers that in the absence of an object there can be no such thing as a subject, and he realizes that reality must be nondual, with neither subject nor object. Thus, having transcended the notion of an object, he similarly transcends the notion of a subject, and abides in the knowledge of nonduality.

The meditator considers that no event can be caused by itself, nor can it be caused by something other than itself, and he realizes that both subject and object are falsehoods. But if they do not exist, then the knowledge of their nonduality cannot exist either. He transcends the notion that there is such a thing as the knowledge of nonduality, and he abides in the knowledge wherein there is no knowledge of nonduality.

The meditator thus abides in the realization that events neither exist nor nonexist. He enters into the highest reality, a state of meditation wherein he imposes no constructs at all upon experience: he sees all events with the eye of wisdom, and he knows that they have no essence at all.

Thus his calm firmly fixes his mind upon the object, and his insight sees it as it really is. Then the light of knowledge dawns to illuminate the darkness, for the *union of calm and insight* brings about true understanding, just as his eye sees with the aid of light. This state of meditation is effortless because there is nothing for him to see beyond it, and it is tranquil because he has calmed all the busy work of his mind, which imposed upon reality the constructs of existence and nonexistence.

THE RETURN TO THE WORLD

When the meditator wishes to arise from his contemplative state, he should not yet uncross his legs, but he should think: "All these events have no essence from the absolute point of view, yet they still exist in conventional reality." So he awakens his great compassion, and pities the sufferings of those who think that things are real, and thus experience all the sorrows of their delusion. He himself sees reality, and sets forth in great compassion to share his vision with all sentient beings.

Here his *means* have been made perfect by his *wisdom*, and all his action in the world is motivated solely by compassion, springing from his hope for the welfare and happiness of others. He realizes the emptiness of things, but he lives amid them for the sake of his suffering children. This is the ultimate religious practice, the *union of means and wisdom*. He seeks for nothing less than perfect Buddhahood for the sake of all beings, all the while knowing that there is no such thing as Buddhahood, and no such thing as a being.

THE STAGES ON THE PATH

As the Bodhisattva thus strives, his wisdom and his means growing gradually more perfect, he ascends through five paths to Buddhahood, and treads the ten stages of a Bodhisattva.

The Path of Accumulation. From the moment of his first thought to enlightenment, the Bodhisattva strives to accumulate a stock of merit and knowledge, acting in the world for the sake of others, and gaining enough skill in meditation that the light of knowledge begins to shine within him.

The Path of Preparation. Here the Bodhisattva practices, with firm conviction that events have no essence at all. And as conviction turns into realization, he passes through four modes of penetration into reality: 1. As the light of knowledge begins to shine, he attains to warmth, or the meditation of the kindling light. 2. As the light of knowledge shines more brightly, he attains to climax, or the meditation of the spreading light. 3. When the light of knowledge shines so brightly that external objects no longer appear and he realizes that nothing exists save mind alone, he gains acceptance, or the meditation of unity. 4. When he reaches the knowledge of nonduality, free of both subject and object, he gains the highest event in the world, the meditation of immediate succession, for he immediately passes into the path of vision and the first Bodhisattva stage.

The Path of Vision. Immediately after the highest event in the world there dawns in him a manifest and transcendent knowledge, and he sees directly the essencelessness of all events. As he ascends to this path of vision, he gains the first of the ten Bodhisattva stages:

1. *The Joyful Stage*: He rejoices in the realization of a truth he had not attained before, and his vision of reality arouses him to work for the welfare of others. Thus the *perfection of charity* predominates in all his deeds.

The Path of Development. As the meditator gradually develops the vision he has attained, he passes through the remaining nine Bodhisattva stages, gaining ever greater knowledge and power:

2. *The Stainless Stage*: He never slips into even the most subtle and inadvertent sin, and thus the *perfection of morality* predominates.

3. *The Luminous Stage*: He holds fast to all that he has learned, and enters into all the different meditations upon the world, enduring all sorts of suffering that he may do so, and thus the *perfection of forebearance* predominates.
4. *The Flaming Stage*: He abides every moment with all the qualities conducive to enlightenment, and thus the *perfection of striving* predominates.
5. *The Hard-To-Conquer Stage*: He continually contemplates all the aspects of the four noble truths, and thus the *perfection of meditation* predominates.
6. *The Face-To-Face Stage*: He abides in the contemplation of dependent origination, and thus the *perfection of wisdom* predominates.
7. *The Far-Going Stage*: He realizes that no labels really label anything, yet for the sake of others he does not turn away from labels, and thus the *perfection of means* predominates.
8. *The Immovable Stage*: He effortlessly embraces all that conduces to virtue, and thus the *perfection of the vow* predominates.
9. *The Good Stage*: He masters the content of the entire Law and is able to teach it to others, and thus the *perfection of power* predominates.
10. *The Cloud of the Law Stage*: He gains mastery over magical creations and can let fall a rain of the Law over all the worlds, and thus the *perfection of knowledge* predominates in all his deeds.

The Path Beyond Learning. And finally the meditator enters into the *diamond-like meditation*, and he emerges therefrom as a Buddha. He gains the knowledge that knows everything that can be known, unattached, unhindered, and omniscient. He fulfills all the proper aims of himself and others, and casts aside all the causes of suffering. With a host of magically created bodies he serves the aims of all suffering creatures for as long as the world shall last. He has reached supreme and perfect enlightenment.

VISIONARY AND ECSTATIC TECHNIQUES

The enlightenment of the Buddha was a visionary experience, with roots reaching back to the most ancient Vedic literature. There the vision and the word of the Vedic seer opened up the shining realm of the gods to his poetic—and therefore magical—control. Inspired by the drinking of *soma*, the priest homologized the cosmos to the sacred patterns of the sacrifice, and in his ecstasy coerced the gods and the universe itself.

There is considerable evidence that soma was in fact the psychotropic mushroom *Amanita muscaria*. Even after the secret of soma was lost, there remained a tradition of visionary techniques to produce the same glittering vision and the same magical power over the world thus seen. These techniques centered upon the process of *visualization*, wherein the meditator actually produced an alternative reality for himself: a reality as real (and as unreal) as the one we know, and a reality he could share with others.

THE PURE LAND TRADITION

Pure Land texts are often viewed as the products of a Buddhist devotionalism, but they fall also under the category of visionary exercises. This is seen quite clearly, for example, in the *Amitāyurdhyāna-sūtra*. Here is introduced not only the magical *mantra* whose recitation guarantees rebirth in the Western Land of Happiness, but also a series of meditations wherein the meditator in fact creates this paradise for himself. The vision is the magical evocation of the land and of the meditator's own rebirth therein; the word is *Namo Amita Buddha*, recited to this day by millions of the faithful.

The Vision. Thus the meditator sits down facing west, and first visualizes the setting sun, until he can see it with his eyes either open or closed. He gazes upon the water, and visualizes the water becoming ice, and the ice becoming crystal, and upon this crystal ground a tower of shining light. He visualizes the land as filled with gold and shining gems, every item so clear that it is ever before his eyes. He visualizes jeweled trees with glittering leaves and flowers, wherein are the mansions of the children of the gods. He visualizes crystal streams and lakes filled with lotus flowers, flowing over beds of gold and diamond sand. And he visualizes the entire Pure Land to be filled with five hundred million jeweled pavilions filled with gods playing heavenly music in praise of the Law.

Then he visualizes the lotus flower with eighty-four thousand petals whereon sits the *Buddha of Everlasting Life*. He visualizes the form of the Buddha seated upon his lotus throne, and he sees him surrounded by the waters and the trees, as clearly as he sees the palm of his hand. He visualizes every sign of greatness upon the body of the Buddha, shining with dazzling light. He visualizes the beautiful and glittering form of the Bodhisattva *Avalokiteśvara*, with his crown and halo and garlands of shining flowers, and the Bodhisattva *Mahāsthāmaprāpta*, shining with the light of wisdom and surrounded by multitudes of his retinue. Every single item must appear clearly before the meditator, so bright and detailed that it seems manifestly present to his vision.

And finally he visualizes himself being born in the *Western Land of Happiness*, seated within a lotus. The lotus had enclosed him, but now it opens up its petals. Rays of light shine upon his body as he opens his eyes and sees the Buddhas and Bodhisattvas filling the sky!

The Word. The second element in the meditation is the recitation of the word, the constant repetition of *Namo Amita Buddha*. At every recitation the meditator becomes exempt from the sins that lead to rebirth for eighty million eons. Whoever recites this mantra is a white lotus among men. When he dies he will be reborn in the Pure Land, and surely he will gain enlightenment.

THE TANTRIC TRADITION

The same visionary and ecstatic techniques are the basis of the complex contemplations of the *Tantras*. Here the meditator creates a world wherein he himself is the central Buddha, abiding within a divine mansion of knowledge called a *maṇḍala*. Within this new contemplative reality he magically manipulates the powerful sexual symbols of his own transformation, and coerces the attainment of Buddhahood itself.

The Process of Generation. Here the meditator first purifies himself of all past sins and erects about the place of contemplation a protective circle that delineates his new divine reality. He dissolves the world of experience into emptiness, and by the process of generation he emerges from the realm of emptiness in the body of the Buddha.

1. From the realm of emptiness, he appears upon the central throne of the maṇḍala in the symbolic form of the god, his many hands holding the weapons of power, and in sexual union with his consort. Into this *causal deity* enter all the Buddhas of the universe. They descend his central channel and emerge into the womb of the consort, whereupon they both melt into Great Bliss. This ball of Bliss is awakened by the song of the gods, and immediately becomes the *resultant deity*. The Buddhas radiate forth from the womb of the consort to take their places as his retinue in the divine mansion of the maṇḍala.
2. The meditator then empowers the senses of his new divine body by placing all the deities of the maṇḍala upon it, until his body becomes itself the abode of all the Buddhas, and his very senses are rendered divine.
3. The divine Buddha descends upon him from the realm of reality itself and he becomes inseparably united with Buddhahood, taking on the knowledge form of the god.
4. He visualizes that he is then *initiated* into his divine state by goddesses holding flasks filled with the nectar of the five knowledges, which fills his entire body. Upon the top of his head there appears the mantra OṂ, upon his throat ĀḤ, and upon his heart HŪṂ, and these mantras make his body, his speech, and his mind into an unshakeable diamond.

These four steps comprise the process by which he generates himself as the divine Buddha in actuality. Then, initiated as the god, he receives the offerings of a god, visualizing heavenly maidens descending and presenting him with all the worship due a Buddha. And finally he speaks with the divine speech, reciting the mantra of the deity, visualizing its syllables circling through his central channel into the womb of his consort, and upward from mouth to mouth, that he may accomplish the four divine functions: pacifying, increasing, subjugating, and destroying.

The Process of Perfection. In this visionary body he controls the power and enlightenment of the Buddha, and in the process of perfection he plunges himself into the divine understanding of emptiness. He dissolves his body into the Clear Light of emptiness. His *mantra body* disappears, and he emerges from his final contemplation possessed of the *knowledge body* of Buddhahood.

TECHNIQUES OF SPONTANEITY

Both the standard structure of meditation and the visionary techniques require great discipline and long training, and in the monastic universities of India they tended to ossify into intellectual rubrics divorced from both experience and action. The final flowering of the Indian Buddhist contemplative genius took place outside the academies, among the crazy long-haired wanderers of the Gupta dynasty and after. Here the search was for a technique that aimed directly at the problem of enlightenment in the world, a way to achieve a liberated mode of action amid the events of public reality, and the techniques are thus basically psychological in orientation. The aim was to achieve spontaneity and freedom, a genuineness of response rather than a controlled apprehension.

THE MAHĀMUDRĀ TRADITION

This search for spontaneity seems to have been closely associated in many ways with the Tantric tradition, and the term *Great Symbol* was used as a general term for an entire complex of contemplative techniques. Here the meditator concentrated not upon an external object but rather upon his own thoughts, the very source of his delusion. He watches his thoughts flash by, and he seeks neither to control them nor to fall under their spell. Gradually he learns to let his mind remain in its natural flow. He casts aside all labels, and abandons even the act of attention. His mind is left in its genuine state.

The meditator gains this freedom from his own mind by a number of different practices. He may cut off every thought that occurs, preventing every mental event from coming into manifestation. He may leave his thoughts to do whatever they want, but letting himself no longer be moved by them. Then he alternates these two practices, first cutting off each thought that occurs, then leaving every thought unformed. And finally he realizes that all his practices have themselves been thoughts, and he abandons even his mindfulness, keeping his mind free of all effort and letting it flow naturally and spontaneously in the stream of calm.

Thus he learns to recognize every mental event in its true nature, which is emptiness; by recognizing every thought he is spontaneously freed from every thought. He realizes that every event he experiences is innate and spontaneous, and that every event—being emptiness—is itself enlightenment. He no longer meditates, he no longer thinks, but in his natural and spontaneous flow he lives with his whole being in the magic show we call the world.

THE ZEN TRADITION

The same search for the natural and the spontaneous characterizes the Zen tradition as well. The early masters seem to have taught techniques very similar to those of the Great Symbol, but, even more important for their tradition as it developed in China, these masters acted out their spontaneity within the world. Tales of the strange and wonderful actions of the masters became first examples of genuineness to be emulated and then subjects of contemplation in themselves, for they were held to contain the key to truth.

The Zen tradition thus flows in two main streams, which we may label by their more familiar Japanese names. In the *Sōtō* tradition, the meditator practices just sitting, while in the *Rinzai* tradition he contemplates upon a *kōan*, a riddle setting forth the inexplicable and genuinely spontaneous deeds of the masters.

Here we find the search for spontaneity carried to its most extreme form. The master shouts at the meditator, beats him, and makes demands upon him that seem cruel and paradoxical. The aim is to break down, as directly as possible, the structures the meditator has erected upon his experience, to eliminate the constructs of existence and nonexistence that separate him from his true nature. The master woos and cajoles his students from their established responses, until in despair—in *Zen sickness*—the meditator suddenly abandons even his mindfulness. He suddenly understands the point, often in a great burst of laughter, and he sees reality.

CONCLUSION

There is one further point to be made concerning Buddhist contemplative traditions. If we take the process of sensory withdrawal in trance as the structural equivalent of alternative-reality creation, and the process of sensory observation as the structural equivalent of the techniques of spontaneity, we find that Buddhist cultures have almost always tended to erect a *tripartite structure* of contemplative techniques. Processes for the creation of *private realities* stand opposed to processes of enlightened participation in the given *public reality*, and this opposition is mediated in all cases by the *standard meditative structure*. There is every reason to believe that this tripartite structure in fact defines specifically Buddhist approaches to meditation.

SUGGESTED READING

Beyer, Stephan V. *The Cult of Tārā: Magic and Ritual in Tibet.*
Bharati, Agehananda. *The Tantric Tradition.*
Blofeld, John. *The Tantric Mysticism of Tibet.*
Chang, Garma Chen-chi. *The Practice of Zen.*
Guenther, Herbert, tr. *The Jewel Ornament of Liberation (sGam.po.pa).*
Suzuki, Shunryu. *Zen Mind, Beginner's Mind.*
Swearer, Donald K., ed. *Secrets of the Lotus*, pp. 127–211 (Reverend Eshin Nishimura).

PART II

Buddhism Outside India

28

Early History of Buddhism in Ceylon

Mark A. Ehman

PRE-BUDDHISTIC CULTURE

The island was inhabited by a number of tribal groups. Most prominent among these were the *Veḍḍas*, the *Yakkhas*, and the *Nāgas*. The Veḍḍas lived in the forest and hill districts and were huntsmen. The Yakkhas and Nāgas were worshippers of spirits (*yakkhas*) and snakes (*nāga*). The religion was animistic. The yakkhas were, in the main, tree spirits whose function it was to hover over and guard man from evil. They were to be distinguished from and ranked higher than the *petas* (hungry ghosts) or spirits who were being punished for their greed in previous lives. Trees became shrines around which worship was performed. Sometime between the fifth and third centuries B.C., the Sinhalese people (probably from Northwest India) settled in the coastal regions. These people seemed to possess a degree of civilization as evidenced from their practice of agriculture, their knowledge of iron, and their building of cities. In addition, they introduced Hindu deities (*Śakra*, *Viṣṇu*) and Hindu forms of worship into the island.

THE ESTABLISHMENT OF BUDDHISM

In the legends one tradition indicates that the Buddha himself visited the island and established the religion. The Buddha supposedly emits a heat ray from his body and destroys the yakkhas. He creates a darkness so that the nāgas will cease fighting. The nāgas are converted and offer Buddha a couch (symbolic of the seat of authority). Another tradition claims that Buddhism was introduced by the Indian monarch *Aśoka*. In about 247 B.C. *Devānaṃpiyatissa*, king of Ceylon, sent emissaries to Aśoka requesting friendship. In response Aśoka commissioned his son, the monk *Mahinda*, to proclaim the *Dhamma* to the island. Mahinda recited suttas containing the essential concepts of the religion: the three jewels, four noble truths, etc. Upon hearing the suttas, Devānaṃpiyatissa was converted and gave residence to the monks. This reciprocity in giving (Dhamma by the monk, residence by the layman) was the fundamental basis for the establishment of the religion. Additional elements necessary for the full establishment of the religion (noted in the *Dīpavaṃsa*) were:

1. Determination of *sīmā*, the boundary of the monastery's authority.
2. Consecration of the enclosure of the monastery.
3. Digging of the tank (for purification).
4. Planting of the tree (originally a branch of the *Bodhi Tree* from India).
5. Building of the *Uposatha* (Buddhist Sanskrit: *Poṣadha*) Hall for recitation of the *Pātimokkha* (Sanskrit: *Prātimokṣa*).
6. Recognition of the monastery as a treasury and a transmitter of merit.
7. Building of the refectory and the alms house.

Specific legends are mentioned centering around Devānaṃpiyatissa (250–210 B.C.). He converted the entire island to Buddhism during the first year of his reign and built scores of Buddhist monuments, many of them in proximity to his capital, *Anurādhapura*. He gave the park, *Mahāmeghavana*, to the monks for the establishment of the great monastery, *Mahāvihāra*. He constructed the *stūpa* (*Thūpārāma Dāgaba*) in which the relic of the Buddha's collar-bone resides, and he oversaw the planting of the branch of the Bodhi Tree in the precincts of the Mahāvihāra.

The implications of the above legends are that Buddhism confronted the indigenous cults, destroying the influence of some and incorporating the beliefs of others (both yakkhas and nāgas remain). The religion is sanctioned by and under the protection of the king. Monasticism is the basis of the religion, and the religion has a nationalistic character. It is not to be controlled from India. Aśokan pillars indicate contact between India and Ceylon during the third century B.C. However, there are no further factual data which might support or deny the legends.

DEVELOPMENT OF BUDDHISM

THREATS FROM WITHOUT

Because of its proximity to South India, Ceylon was always in danger of being controlled by outsiders.

The first of these outsiders came in the second century B.C. in the form of *Eḷāra* the *Coḷa*. He controlled the island for 44 years, being defeated by *Duṭṭhagāmaṇī Abhaya* (101–77 B.C.). Duṭṭhagāmaṇī's victory was "not for kingdom, but for Buddhism." The slogan indicates that Buddhism had cemented itself so firmly in the culture that the people considered it to be identical with everything Sinhalese. Duṭṭhagāmaṇī's victory indicates also the peculiar role of the king in relation to the religion. He was protector of the *sāsana* (religion).

A second invasion came in the first century B.C. at the hands of the *Tamils*. *Vaṭṭagāmaṇī* (29–17 B.C.) defeated the Tamils and restored Buddhism. In addition, Vaṭṭagāmaṇī founded a major monastery, *Abhayagiri*.

TENSIONS WITHIN

With the establishment of the Abhayagiri monastery, a continuing conflict developed between its monks and the monks of the Mahāvihāra. The dispute ostensibly centered around minor points of discipline discussed at the Council of *Vaiśālī* (whether or not a monk may receive gold or silver, etc.). The monks of the Mahāvihāra answered no. The monks of Abhayagiri answered yes. Actually the dispute was over the control of Buddhism. Monks of the Mahāvihāra believed that authority lay with an unbroken tradition. Monks of the Abhayagiri believed the tradition had become so corrupted that only a new beginning could reestablish the authority of the religion.

In the third century A.D. the sect of *Vetullavādins* (Sanskrit: *Vaitulya-vādins*) made inroads. This sect was a semi-Mahāyāna group which undercut the historical point of view of the Buddha (Buddha was nothing more than a phantasm) and the doctrine of merit. King *Vohārikatissa* (A.D. 269–291) suppressed this sect.

The full gospel of Mahāyāna swept the island in the fourth century A.D. King *Mahāsena* (334–362), supported by the Mahāyānist monk *Sanghamitta*, destroyed the buildings of the Mahāvihāra, turned out its monks, and plowed its fields. Moreover, the king forbade alms be given to Mahāvihāra monks. The monastery of *Jetavana* was built by the king and donated to the Mahāyāna monks. Favor toward the Mahāyānists was short lived. Mahāsena's son, *Sirimeghavaṇṇa*, reversed his father's policy. He rebuilt the Mahāvihāra, built a golden statue of Mahinda, and initiated the Mahinda Festival, symbolic of pure (as opposed to heretical) Buddhism.

In the ensuing three centuries the three monasteries (Mahāvihāra, Abhayagiri, Jetavana) vied for supremacy. In times of great national emergency (e.g., the Tamil invasion of the fifth century A.D.) the kings generally threw their support to the Mahāvihāra—bastion of conservatism and nationalism. King *Dhātusena* (460–478) threw off the Tamil yoke and patronized the Mahāvihāra. In times of relative peace, however, the kings endeavored to minimize strife among the monks by supporting all three monasteries.

LITERARY DEVELOPMENT

Dīpavaṃsa. A chronicle in verse form recounting the rise and development of Buddhism. It was composed in the fourth century A.D.

Mahāvaṃsa. A second chronicle composed in the fifth century A.D. by King *Mahānāma* (409–431). This second chronicle centers upon Duṭṭhagāmaṇī and his destruction of the Tamil invaders. Periodically, the chronicle has been updated by commentators so that the entire work is a running history of Buddhism from its inception to the nineteenth century. These additions have received the name *Cūlavaṃsa*.

Works of Buddhaghosa. Buddhaghosa was an Indian monk of the fifth century A.D. who settled in Ceylon and is credited as being one of the greatest Buddhist commentators. *Visuddhimagga* ("The Path of Purity") is a lengthy treatise in three parts (morality, concentration, wisdom) containing precepts, legends, miracle stories, etc., all of which glorify arhantship. *Samantapāsādikā* is a voluminous commentary on the Vinaya. He is said to have translated the greater portion of the Sinhalese commentary on the canonical literature into Pāli.

BHIKKHU AND UPĀSAKA—MONK AND LAYMAN

The *bhikkhu* (Sanskrit: *bhikṣu*) was primarily a teacher (in contradistinction to a meditator). In the first century A.D. the question arose as to the nature of the sāsana. Is it learning or practice? The answer given is learning. The bhikkhu is the promulgator of this learning. He is engaged in *Dhamma-dāna* (doctrine-giving) to the laity.

The *upāsaka* was a seeker after merit. He practiced *dāna*, giving of food, clothing, and money to the bhikkhus. He kept a detailed record of his accumulation of merit. This gave him an assurance of a favorable birth in the next existence. Indeed, the upāsaka did not look forward to *nibbāna* (Sanskrit: *nirvāṇa*). Rather, he employed the merit to win heaven in the next birth.

Special ceremonies in the lives of the bhikkhus and upāsakas are recorded:

1. *Vesākha*—The festival celebrating the Buddha's birth, enlightenment and nirvāṇa.
2. *Giribhaṇḍa-pūjā*—The festival in which the upāsakas offer goods to the bhikkhus.
3. *Gaṅgārohaṇa*—A ceremony (held as it was needed) to ward off famine and disease.
4. *Paritta*—A ceremony entreating protection from the evil spirits.
5. *Festival of the Tooth-Relic*—A ceremony reminding the people of the supremacy of the religion.
6. *Mahinda Festival*—A celebration of the purification of the sāsana from heresy.

CONCLUSION

The Sinhalese introduce very little that is new into the religion. They are content to rely upon Indian models in both doctrine and institutions. The significant contribution of the Sinhalese lay in preserving the literature and tradition of Theravāda Buddhism. In those areas in which innovation was made (e.g., the Mahinda Festival) a strong nationalistic mood is evident. Great ceremonial occasions are thus introduced to symbolize the resurgence of Sinhalese order and authority against threats of invasion, disasters of nature, and tendencies toward disunity.

SUGGESTED READING

Adikaram, E.W. *Early History of Buddhism in Ceylon.*
Geiger, Wilhelm, tr. *The Mahāvaṃsa or the Great Chronicle of Ceylon.*
Malalasekera, G.P. *The Pāli Literature of Ceylon.*
Oldenberg, Hermann, ed. and tr. *The Dīpavaṃsa.*
Rāhula, Walpola. *History of Buddhism in Ceylon.*

29

Monastic Life in Ceylon

Charles S. Prebish

INTRODUCTION

After its rather humble beginnings in the island, monastic life gradually developed into a well defined social institution, affording the monk a high level of respect and providing the laity with the proper context in which to pursue religious endeavors.

STRUCTURE OF THE MONASTERY

Monasteries in Ceylon, as in India, were usually called *vihāras*. Included within the confines of the vihāra were several structures, each with a varying degree of importance. The most important structure was the *caitya* in which relics of the Buddha or other famous saint were housed. Three circular terraces usually surrounded this structure with the dome of the caitya rising therefrom. In the case of small caityas the entire structure was enclosed in a house (*caityaghara*), protecting both the caitya and worshippers from the elements. Next in importance was the *paṭimāghara* or image house, containing an image of the Buddha. Almost all monasteries contained an *Uposatha* (Buddhist Sanskrit: Poṣadha) hall where the monks gathered on new and full moon days to renew their purity in accordance with the Vinaya and transact monastic business. A meditation hall was usually present in the monastery, but often this was used as the private apartment of the chief monk. Often too, there was a hall for preaching the Dharma to the laity.

The monasteries also had to provide ample living space for the individual monks, as well as a whole range of structures necessary for maintaining the monks: kitchen, bathing facilities, storeroom, courtyards, terraces, etc.

ADMINISTRATION OF THE MONASTERY

Each monastery was administered by a chief monk, usually having many years seniority, who was responsible for maintaining a high level of discipline and effecting the smooth running of the institution. As the monasteries grew, receiving both royal and private endowments, this became no small task. Departments were established to run the commissary, maintain the grounds, etc. Needless to say, as the monastery grew in size, an increasing labor force was needed. Consequently, the monasteries hired help, paying them out of monastic receipts. Records were kept by the monks in charge of revenues and balanced each year. In other words, a complete and developed monastic hierarchy emerged, not unlike that of a large corporation.

Many of the practices necessitated by the growth of the various monasteries seemed to run counter to the precepts of the Vinaya, and obviously, if the monastery was to survive, alternatives had to be found. Amendments to the stated rules were made under the heading *pālimuttakavinicchaya* or decisions not found in the Pāli texts. For example, since the extension of Saṃgha land was necessary for preservation of the monastery, monks had to discover alternatives to the land boundary-limit regulations of the Vinaya. This was done by recognizing that Saṃgha land was apportioned by the ruler, and since the Saṃgha owed him their allegiance, however much land was allotted was regarded as legal. In this way the monastery could prosper and expand, while still embodying its democratic method of self-government.

MONASTIC LIFE: THE MONK'S DAILY ROUTINE

After rising early, usually before sunrise, the monks performed a perfunctory meditation and then attended to their personal hygiene. After cleaning their quarters, as well as the communal monastic structures, the monks went to the refectory for the morning meal. Monks were then supposed to meditate until it was time to go on their alms-tour through the village. A second meal, consisting of food obtained through the alms-tour (*piṇḍapātra*), was eaten before noon. The rest of the afternoon was spent in performing monastic duties and personal study. By evening the laity would begin to frequent the monastery and each monk, when his turn came, was expected to preach to them. The rest of the evening was usually spent in meditation.

RITUAL

Apart from that ritual associated with compliance with the Vinaya, several other rituals were enacted by the monks. Several of these are worthy of note.

ARIYAVAṂSA

This festival surrounds the preaching of the *Ariyavaṃsa-sutta*. Essentially, the sermon has four parts. A monk is satisfied with 1. whatever robe he obtains, 2. the food he gets, 3. his lodgings, and 4. he delights in meditation. These four points highlight the life of a monk, and since the Saṃgha depends on the monk, they are stressed as integral to monastic life. It is not clear under what circumstances this text was preached, but it is clear that kings, ministers, and wealthy laymen contributed heavily to its regular performance.

VESĀKHA

Since Buddha was born in the month of *Vesākha* (full moon day of May), this festival is celebrated not only in Ceylon, but in all Buddhist countries. It is usually a glorious ceremony with magnificent floats, brightly colored traditional dress, and much rejoicing.

PARITTA

Paritta, which literally means extinction, is a ceremony performed at various occasions, both auspicious and inauspicious, such as moving into a new dwelling, curing disease, and exorcising spirits. In exorcising spirits it is allied with the *Āṭānāṭiya-sutta* and performed according to instructions carefully set out in the commentary to the *Dīgha Nikāya*.

FUNERAL CEREMONY

Funeral rites were most often associated with cremation. A funeral pyre was built, often outside of the limits of the vihāra, with the top lined with one or more fragrant woods (e.g., sandalwood). Steps to ascend the structure were built. After the body was carefully wrapped in cloth and placed on the funeral car, people gathered together presenting offerings of flowers and incense. Following this offering, the car was placed on top of the pyre and covered with oil. The flame was lit and while the body burned, the fire was strengthened by items thrown in by the onlookers. If the deceased was a famous person, the relics were gathered and a caitya constructed.

THE LAITY

For the ordinary layman, usually not philosophically sophisticated, and often believing in spirits, heavens, and the like, the monastery represented the stronghold of Buddhism where the religion was preserved in all its purity. Since there could be no monastic institution without the monks, monk and monastery alike became objects of veneration for the laity. Obviously, then, the laity was concerned with performing as much good work for the Saṃgha as possible, also accruing good karma in return. Some lay followers even carried a merit book which recorded all their good deeds and was read when the person was on his deathbed, so as to insure a favorable rebirth. This theme is highlighted by a consideration of the discourses most often preached to the laity: the *Dakkhiṇāvibhaṅga-sutta*, dealing with the various merits derived from giving gifts, and the *Devadūta-sutta*, clearly describing the agonies experienced by evil ones in hell.

Since the monk was both the most trusted teacher of the laity and a great aid to the individual lay follower in attaining a favorable rebirth, many pious laymen had favorite monks who they took special care to protect, provide with robes and alms, and, more generally, support. Thus this symbiotic relationship which existed between the Saṃgha and the laity strengthened and cemented Buddhist monasticism as a social institution in Ceylon.

SUGGESTED READING

Adikaram, E.W. *Early History of Buddhism in Ceylon.*
Malalasekera, G.P. *The Pāli Literature of Ceylon.*
Nārada, Thera. *The Buddha and His Teachings.*
Rāhula, Walpola. *History of Buddhism in Ceylon.*

30

Introduction of Buddhism to Southeast Asia and Subsequent History up to the Eleventh Century

Stefan Anacker

BURMA

ETHNOLOGICAL AND HISTORICAL BACKGROUND

In 500 B.C. the dominant people in Burma were the *Mon* (*Rmeñ*) or *Talaing* (*Tanluiṅḥ*), whose language belongs to the Mon-Khmer group of the Austro-Asiatic language family. In the second century A.D. the *Pyus*, speaking a Tibeto-Burmese language, wandered into northern Burma from the North. The Talaings remained predominant in Lower Burma and parts of present-day Thailand, with their centers at *Pegu* and *Thaton*. The Pyus in North Burma established their main center at *Prome*. The *Burmans* (*Mrammā* or *Mranmā*), linguistically related to the Pyus and said to have originated in an area of Northwest China, wandered into *Yünnan* and from there into North Burma in the eighth century. The first *Shan* and *Thai* migrations into Burma took place in the eighth and ninth centuries.

AŚOKA'S MISSION TO BURMA

There was contact both by land and sea with India by the time of the *Mauryan* Dynasty. According to traditional accounts, *Aśoka* sent *Soṇa* and *Uttara* as Buddhist missionaries to Burma, and they are the founders of the Theravāda Buddhist community at Thaton.

SUBSEQUENT MISSIONS

In the first century A.D. Theravāda missions, under the patronage of *Ikṣvāku Vīrapuruṣadatta*, again reached Thaton. Missions to Thaton from South India (particularly from *Nāgārjunikoṇḍa* and *Kāñcī*) in the succeeding centuries did much to revitalize Theravāda Buddhism among the Talaings. Brahmanism coexisted with Buddhism in the Talaing country as late as the eleventh century.

Missions from East India reached the Pyu country by land from the third to the fifth centuries. They included *Sarvāstivādins*, *Mahāyānists*, and representatives of Hindu theistic religions. Buddhist *stūpas*, brick buildings, and terracottas were fashioned in Prome in this period.

RELIGIOUS STUDIES UP TO THE ELEVENTH CENTURY

Native religion with a superstructure of Theravāda becomes dominant in the Talaing country, though evidences of struggles between Buddhism and Hinduism occur as late as the eleventh century. Thaton remained the main Buddhist center, and was known to *Buddhaghosa*. According to Burmese accounts, Buddhaghosa is even said to have visited Thaton.

By the fifth century, the native *Nat* religion has merged with Mahāyāna in the Pyu country, though Theravāda existed there too, as is evidenced by *Abhidhamma* fragments found in inscriptions. *Vaiṣṇavism* and *Śaivism* were also present, and Prome contains Vaiṣṇavaite and Śaivite sculpture, Buddhist *stūpas*, and statues of *Avalokiteśvara*. In Prome Mahāyāna cults evolved around Avalokiteśvara and *Maitreya*, as is evidenced by countless terracotta tablets. From the seventh century on, this Mahāyāna becomes more and more *Tantric*, with the continued contact of the Pyus with *Assam*. The priests of this Tantric Buddhism have the name *Samaṇakuṭṭaka* in later literature. When the Burmans enter North Burma, finally establishing their capital at *Pagan* (in 841), it is *Tantric* Buddhism that is dominant, and it becomes particularly patronized by a group of lords called the *Aris*. This form of Buddhism could readily adopt native Burman deities in its rites and festivals.

CAMBODIA

KOK-THLOK

The Cambodians or *Khmers* have had a continuous cultural history for at least two millenia, although at the moment of this writing their existence is being threatened by U.S. bombs. Their earliest known state, called *Kok-Thlok* in their own chronicles, is usually known to Westerners by its Chinese name, *Funan*.

Contacts between India and Cambodia were at first primarily of a mercantile nature. Indian adventurers and merchants, however, brought with them Brahmans, and during the first century A.D. these Brahmans began to affect the Royal Court. There are several different versions of the origin of this Brahmanical influence. Some say the Brahman *Kauṇḍinya*, who arrived with a group of merchants, married the Cambodian princess *Somā* and subsequently Brahmanized all court rituals. Others say a North Indian prince, called by the Khmers *Préah-Thông*, came to drive the *Chams* out of Cambodia, was recognized as king, and brought his Brahmans to attend him. Still others claim that the prince who introduced Brahmanism originally came from *Sumatra* and was among those converted by the *Chvéa-préahm*, descendents of those 20,000 Benares Brahmans that had settled in Indonesia. By the second century, Brahmans and honorary Brahmans of Khmer origin had hereditary functions at the Court, and Mahāyāna Buddhist communities had been founded in Cambodia.

MAHĀYĀNA BUDDHISM IN THE FIFTH AND SIXTH CENTURIES

The extent of Indian religious influence in Cambodia cannot be more exactly gauged until the fifth century. A body of *Karnatak* Indians, under the leadership of a Brahman named Kauṇḍinya, came to the north of *Malacca*, and by force of arms proclaimed their leader King of Kok-Thlok. Kauṇḍinya introduced Śaivism to Cambodia, and cast all laws on the model of laws in India. He was sympathetic to the Mahāyāna communities that were flourishing in his realm, and his embassy to China was headed by a Buddhist monk, *Śākya Nāgasena*. So learned were these Cambodian Mahāyāna communities that scholar-monks from Cambodia were sought after in China for translating texts from Sanskrit into Chinese. *Saṅghapāla* (*Saṅghavarman*) and *Mandrasena*, active in China as translators in the early sixth century, were both Cambodians.

Buddhist art was also much patronized at this time, with the superb Avalokiteśvara from *Rach Gia* being probably the most famous example of early Cambodian Buddhist sculpture. The standing Buddha figures from *Romlok* and *Ta Kèo* also belong to this period.

RELIGION OF THE PEOPLE

From Chinese travelers quite a bit can be gleaned about religious conditions in Cambodia at the time. In the towns people seem to have followed Brāhmaṇical as well as Buddhist customs. In their careful oblations before meals, their attention to ritual purity, and their cremation ceremonies, Brāhmaṇical influence can be seen. Yet many people went to hear recitations of Mahāyāna sūtras, and instead of cremation, there could be the practice of abandoning dead bodies for animals to eat, a conscious reflection of *Bodhisattvas* giving away their own flesh for other sentient beings. In roadside shrines and stations where travelers stopped, images of native spirits, Buddhas and Bodhisattvas, and Hindu deities could be seen side by side. The countryside, on the other hand, seems to have been far less affected by Indian religions at this time, and villagers seem to have continued unchanged their old religious practices.

THE SEVENTH CENTURY: CONFLICT BETWEEN RELIGIONS

It is during the reigns of *Īśānavarman*, *Bhavavarman II*, and *Jayavarman I* (611–681+) that there is the first evidence of the harmony of religions in Cambodia giving way to a spirit of competition and conflict. This may have been due to the new and militant cult of *Harihara* (Viṣṇu-Śiva in one), patronized by these monarchs. The Chinese pilgrim *I-tsing*, who visited Cambodia shortly after the reign of Jayavarman I, relates that Buddhism prospered in Cambodia until an evil king began a persecution which ended with the virtual (though temporary) destruction of Buddhism in Cambodia.

JAYAVARMAN II AND RENEWED RELIGIOUS SYNCRETISM

Jayavarman II (802–854), born in Java of a collateral line of the Cambodian royal house, and his religious preceptor *Śivakaivalya* (who was trained in India), were the founders of a new religious ideology which was to dominate Cambodian culture throughout its most brilliant period. In a complex ceremony, Śivakaivalya transformed the king into an incarnation of Śiva, and he was to be henceforth regarded as a living God-King. The center of the royal residence became a Śiva temple. But Mahāyāna reached a new importance with this development too, as a king could also be regarded as one of the great Bodhisattvas. In addition, there began the practice of deification of royal ancestors, identified after death with the deity of their choice under corresponding posthumous names.

MAHĀYĀNA UNDER THE SUCCESSORS OF JAYAVARMAN II

Though the posthumous name of *Jayavarman III* (869–877) is Vaiṣṇavaite, and those of *Indravarman I* (877–889) and *Yaśovarman* (889–900+) Śaivite, Buddhist communities were also patronized and new ones established during their reigns. It was at this time that Mahāyāna Buddhism was sweeping over the archipelago.

Rajendravarman II (944–968) made a deep study of Mahāyāna in his youth, but decided to remain a Śaivite. He remained attached to Buddhism, however, and one of his chief ministers, *Kavīndrārimathana*, was a Buddhist. This minister was responsible for many Buddhist foundations, including the *Bat Chum* shrines to the Buddha, *Vajrapāṇi*, and *Prajñāpāramitā*.

Jayavarman V (968–1001), builder of the temple of *Banteay Srei*, fostered Buddhism even more actively. His minister *Kīrtipaṇḍita* brought many Mahāyāna books from abroad, and in an inscription at *Srei Santhor*, directed that the court Brahman of the king should be versed in Mahāyāna.

VIETNAM

BUDDHISM IN THE TRAIN OF CHINESE IMPERIALISM?

The ancient Vietnamese Kingdom, which according to traditional history dates back to 2879 B.C., first succumbed to Chinese armies in 207 B.C. At that time the Chinese general *Chao T'o* (Vietnamese: *Triệu Dà*) established himself as an independent king. But in 111 B.C., Emperor *Wu-ti* sent Chinese troops to overthrow the Triệu and make Vietnam a Chinese province. This was the first Chinese domination of Vietnam which lasted until A.D. 39, when the heroic *Tru'ung Trắc*, outraged at the Chinese for the unjust execution of her husband, and her younger sister *Tru'un Nhị*, managed to free the land for a brief four years. Both of them were killed by Chinese armies, which again imposed the protectorate, destined this time to last for 500 years.

There is a source which claims that one of the earliest Buddhist monks to reach Vietnam, *Meu-Po*, came with the Chinese armies in 111 B.C. However, this is disputed, since other sources give a later time for this monk. At any rate, Chinese authorities were not at all interested in spreading Buddhism in Vietnam, and in their zeal to impose the entire Confucian system upon the land, probably actually discouraged too much Buddhism from entering.

BUDDHIST FUGITIVES

According to most accounts, Meu-Po came to Vietnam as a fugitive from China during the chaos of the Three Kingdoms, in about 189. He was one of the many former Taoists converted to Buddhism, and he worked for the propagation of Mahāyāna sūtras in Vietnam.

MISSIONS FROM THE SEA

Meu-Po's mission in Vietnam was succeeded by those of *Marijīvaka*, *Kalyāṇaruci*, and *Kang-seng-huei*, who arrived in Vietnam from the sea, or by way of China, in the third century A.D. Many of these missionaries were Indians, others Indo-Scythians and Sogdians. Some were Mahāyāna, some Hīnayāna, and for a time there seems to have been numerous followers of Hīnayāna in Vietnam.

THIEN AND AMIDISM

The two sects most prominent in Vietnam came to be the *A-Ham* (*Āgama* school) and *Thien* (*Ch'an*). A-Ham has its roots in the earliest conversions in the second century. Thien was founded by the great Indian *dhyāna* master *Vinītaruci* (ca. 580) at the *Phap-Vân Monastery* (*Bác-ninh* province, N. Vietnam). A second Thien school was founded much later (820) by *Vo-ngôn-Thông*. The country at that time had twenty stūpas to house relics sent by the Chinese emperors and many temples, including village pagodas (*chùa*) where incense to the Buddha was burned alongside the village common houses (*dinh*) which housed the native village gods. Thien being limited to certain specialist centers, village pagodas would be run on devotional lines, with offerings to the Buddha being presented on the first and fifteenth days of the lunar month. *Amidism*, or Pure Land Buddhism, gradually dominated these village pagodas.

PATRONAGE OF BUDDHISM IN THE TENTH CENTURY

Vietnam, independent again in 939, does not find its rulers actively patronizing Buddhism until the reign of *Dinh Bô-Linh* (968–980). The spread of Amidism among the common people was encouraged. Buddhist scholars of the period are all practitioners of Thien. Though Chinese characters had been taught in Vietnam since the first Chinese occupation, few people learned to read except Thien monks, who gained general respect among the populace. *Ngô Chân Luu*, a monk at *Phât-Da*, became famous as a scholar, poet, and Thien meditator. Dinh Bô-Linh invited him to court, appointed him head of the *Saṃgha* in Vietnam, and thereafter Imperial Councilor. Because of their literacy, Thien monks were often sought in advisory capacities, even on matters of purely political interest.

CHAMPA

The east coast of Vietnam was from the third to the fourteenth centuries under the control of the Hinduized *Chams* of *Malay* extraction, who maintained themselves with armies that were often mainly Vietnamese. Buddhism existed there already in the third century, as the sculpture of the Buddha at *Dong-duong* attests. The same kind of Mahāyāna-Śaiva syncretism that occurred in Cambodia took place also in Champa under *Bhadreśvaravarman*, whose great shrine at Dong-duong, in honor of *Lokeśvara*, is one of the few Buddhist sites in Champa (ca. 900).

INDONESIA

INDIAN INFLUENCE

Indian merchants reached Sumatra before the first century A.D. as Madagascar was colonized by Hinduized Sumatrans early in the Christian era. However, when *Fa-hien* visited Sumatra in 414, he found almost no Buddhists there.

INTRODUCTION OF BUDDHISM

Late in the fifth century, *Guṇavarman*, of the Kashmirian royal house, landed in Sumatra. He converted the reigning queen to Mahāyāna. She in turn converted her son, and Mahāyāna became the official cult of the *Śailendra* Dynasty of Sumatra and Java.

THE SEVENTH CENTURY

When I-tsing visited Sumatra in 690, Mahāyāna Buddhism was flourishing there. He studied Sanskrit as well as Malay in *Palembang*, and Buddhist texts in both languages. This indicates that Buddhist scholarship in Sumatra was of a high order, and that Malay was being employed in the composition of Buddhist texts.

THE EIGHTH CENTURY

Caṇḍi Kalasan, completed under the Śailendras in Middle Java in 778, is the first extant Buddhist monument in Indonesia. It is dedicated to *Tārā*, which shows that Buddhism in Indonesia at this time had become *Vajrayāna*.

The end of this century sees the completion of the most famous of all Śailendra monuments. *Caṇḍi Borobuḍur* is an enormous architectural structure supporting seventy complete stūpas. On its walls are reliefs of *Vajrasattvas* and Tārās, and of the life of the Buddha. It is a monument which contains in itself an entire cosmology.

THE NINTH CENTURY

Caṇḍi Sewu is the greatest Javanese Buddhist site of this century, with its large central temple with side chapels open to the outside air. All this artistic activity indicates that Mahāyāna, or more precisely, Vajrayāna Buddhism was by far the most heavily patronized religion in Sumatra and Java during this period. Both trade and political relations with India were maintained throughout this time.

THAIS, LAOS, SHANS

EARLIEST CONTACTS WITH BUDDHISM

The earliest homeland of the Laos, Thais, and Shans, to which there are clear references, is the area between the *Hwang-Ho* and *Yang-tse* rivers. When King *Khun Luang-Li-Maow* of *Nakorn Ngai-Lao* submitted to the suzerainty of the Chinese emperor *Ming-ti* in A.D. 69, he was also introduced to Mahāyāna, which had been made the Chinese state religion by that emperor. Luang-Li-Maow and his immediate circle seem to have practiced some form of Mahāyāna, but Buddhism does not seem to have penetrated to the Ngai-Lao people at large. With the further migrations of the Ngai-Lao southward, Buddhism seems to have become abandoned even by the kings.

THE KINGDOM OF NAN-CHAO AND VAJRAYĀNA

Pressed more and more southward, the Lao/Thai people finally established a kingdom to the east of the *Mekong River* in Yünnan. This kingdom is usually called *Nan-Chao*, though the ancient Lao name for it is *Nong-Sae*. By the ninth century, it had conquered parts of Burma and Tonking, and it is at this time that Lao/Thai contacts with the Indian cultural world are renewed, and, in particular, Vajrayāna seems to have had some following.

SUGGESTED READING

Briggs, Lawrence Palmer. *The Ancient Khmer Empire*.

Coedès, Georges. *The Making of South East Asia*. Translated by H.M. Wright, pp. 42–49, 50–70, 88–117.

Coomaraswamy, Ananda K. *History of Indian and Indonesian Art*, pp.169–215.

Nhat Nahn, Trich. *Vietnam: Lotus in a Sea of Fire*.

Ray, Niharranjan. *Theravāda Buddhism in Burma*, pp. 7–76, 160–67.

Viravong, Maha Sila. *History of Laos*, pp. 36 ff.

31
Medieval Buddhism in Southeast Asia

Stefan Anacker

BURMA

CONVERSION OF UPPER BURMA TO THERAVĀDA

King *Anawratā* of *Pagan* (1040–1077), a former strong patron of the *Samaṇakuṭṭakas*, became impressed by the simplicity of *Theravāda* doctrine as taught to him by a young *Talaing* monk from *Thaton*, *Shin Arahan*. Anawratā asked the Talaing king *Manuha* for Theravāda texts, and when Manuha refused, he invaded the Talaing country, which he conquered by 1057. Manuha and many Theravāda monks and texts were brought to Pagan. Anawratā converted to Theravāda, and put Shin Arahan in charge of the *Saṃgha* in unified Burma. Relations with other Theravāda countries, particularly Ceylon, were begun. Relics were obtained from Ceylon, and a great building activity for the new faith was begun in Pagan: the famous *Shwezigon*, with its glazed terracotta bricks representing *Jātaka* stories, the stone *Nanpaya*, the *Kondgawgyi*, with its mural paintings, and the *Bidagat Taik* for the housing of Theravāda manuscripts. Under Anawratā, Burma became the most prosperous Theravāda country, as Ceylon, under *Vijayabāhu*, was at the time struggling with the *Coḷas*. Vijayabāhu in fact begged for Pāli texts from Anawratā in return for relics.

INSTITUTIONS OF BURMESE THERAVĀDA

The process of conversion to Theravāda continued under kings *Kyanzittha* (1084–1112) and *Alaungsithu* (1112–1167), both fervent Theravādins. Building activity continued with the *Ānanda Temple*. In every village or village cluster, monastery schools (*phongyi kyaung*) were established. The monks were given the job of teaching children to read and write, and of introducing them to basic Theravāda doctrine. Each monastery was under a chief *thera* (elder), and each was an autonomous unit managing its own affairs. Sometimes federations of monasteries arose, with each member institution still autonomous, but sending their chief thera as a delegate whenever matters concerning the whole federation arose. Yet a central authority over all the monasteries existed in Burma in the person of the king's preceptor. Only in the fifteenth century is this head thera given the title *Saṃgharāja* (King of the Saṃgha), with the implication that he has the same kind of supreme authority over the monasteries as the king does over the realm. In major decisions the king's preceptor always seems to have consulted the leading theras of the kingdom. However, he was always appointed by the king himself, thus giving the king a certain control over activities of the Buddhist Saṃgha.

THE NATURE OF EARLY BURMESE THERAVĀDA

Though it is Theravāda Buddhism that is most patronized by the kings following Anawratā, *Tantric* influences continued to come in from Bihar, Bengal, Tibet, and Nepal. The ancient *Nat* worship continued too, and the new royal Theravāda accepted the Nats as temple guardians at Shwezigon. Purely *Mahāyāna* art continued. *Avalokiteśvara* and *Maitreya* were accepted into the Theravāda pantheon. Indian Brahmans still had many functions, and could take part in Buddhist *parītta* rites. All pious foundations were maintained by slaves, or rather, hereditary serfs of the Three Jewels. On some occasions donors would give themselves and their wives and children as slaves for the religious foundation.

In Buddhist scholarship much was accomplished by the Burmese at this time. *Aggavaṃsa's Saddanīti* (1154), a grammar of the *Tipiṭaka*, deeply impressed even Sinhalese scholars.

THE SINHALESE AND BURMESE LINEAGES

Shin Arahan's successor *Panthagu*, disgusted at the struggle between Alaungsithu's two sons for the throne, and at one of them, *Narathu*, for his treachery in gaining it, left Burma for Ceylon (which at this time was prosperous under *Parakkama Bāhu I*). He returned to Burma in the reign of *Narapatisithu* (1173–1210) with stories of the reform of the Sinhalese Saṃgha. The Talaing monk *Uttarajīva*, who succeeded Panthagu, went to Ceylon to investigate the reforms, bringing with him, among many others, a young novice named *Capaṭa*. Capaṭa became ordained in Ceylon and remained there for ten years to study the Tipiṭaka and *Buddhaghosa's* commentaries. After gaining the title *mahāthera*, he returned with four colleagues, severed all relations with the Burmese Saṃgha (which he considered to be improperly ordained), and began ordaining novices according to Sinhalese practice. Capaṭa was the author of a great many works in Pāli (*Vinaya*, *Vinaya-samuṭṭhānadīpanī; Abhidhamma*, *Saṅkhapavaṇṇana* on *Anuruddha's Abhidhammaṭṭhasaṅgaha*). After Capaṭa's death, struggles arose among his colleagues, until finally there were four mutually exclusive Saṃghas in Burma:

one, the *purimagaṇa*, going back to Shin Arahan and the other three going back to Capaṭa's colleagues *Sīvali*, *Tāmalinda*, and *Ānanda*. All kinds of controversies over Vinaya points arose.

The most famous Buddhist author of the time was *Saddhammasiri*, who wrote a version of *Varāhamihira's Bṛhajjātaka*, the *Bṛhaja* which is one of the earliest extant books in Burmese.

THE THIRTEENTH AND FOURTEENTH CENTURIES

The first half of the thirteenth century brings us such figures as the noble King *Kyaswa* (1234–1250)—called "*Dhammarāja*"—author of a text steeped in Theravāda sentiment, the *Paramatthavindu*. Under *Narathipate* (1254–1287), most serious Burmese Buddhist scholarship turned to Pāli grammar, whereas Vinaya squabbles were occupying the more politically-minded monks. Royal patronage was interrupted after Kublai Khan took Pagan, and the Shans swamped almost all of Burma. Within a generation, *Thihathu*, one of the Shan chiefs of Upper Burma, accepted Theravāda Buddhism, and subsequent Shan kings were responsible for building monasteries at *Myinsaing* and the *Nandawya Pagoda*. Thihathu's son *Sawlu* again gave the Tantric Aris patronage. At the beginning of the fourteenth century, the Talaing theras *Buddhavaṃsa* and *Mahānāga* founded a new division of the Saṃgha on strict Sinhalese lines in *Martaban*. In their immediate lineage is *Medhaṃkara*, author of the *Lokadīpasāra*, a compendium of various topics arranged in cosmological fashion and still famous in Burma today. King at the time was *Binnya U*, who heightened the Shwedagon spire at Rangoon. King *Razadarit* (1365–1423), the famous successor of Binnya U, erected the great *Shwemawdaw of Pegu*. Famous scholars under these two kings include *Ānanda Thera* (author of the *Abhidhammaṭīkāsaṃvaṇṇaṃ*) and *Saddhammālaṅkāra* (author of a commentary on the *Paṭṭhāna*).

Even with the unsettled state of affairs in the fourteenth century in Burma, the Saṃgha was not suffering, as it received support from all contending groups. Pilgrimages to Ceylon became a regular practice for important Burmese theras.

POETICAL ACTIVITIES OF BURMESE MONKS

Sīlavaṃsa wrote a life of the ascetic *Sumedha* (called the *Sumedhakathā*), and the *Buddhālaṅkāra* on the Buddha's life. *Shin Agyathamahdi* wrote a Burmese version of the *Jātakas*, and *Raṭṭhasāra* wrote poetic versions of individual Jātakas. Such poetical activity was condemned by the strict upholders of the Vinaya, who said that even poetical works of a religious nature were not to be written by Buddhist monks.

THE GREAT REFORM OF DHAMMACETI

Dhammaceti, who ascended the throne of Pegu in 1472, had originally been a monk. He was the builder of the *Shwegugyi* at Pegu, but his main efforts were directed toward reforming the Burmese Saṃgha. He eliminated all ordination groups except one, which was organized according to the Sinhalese *Mahāvihāra* tradition. Interpretation of Vinaya was also to follow Mahāvihāra lines. Though at first these reforms did not have a pan-Burmese character, in Pegu they were the law, and Upper Burma was soon affected.

CAMBODIA

INTERCHANGES OF MAHĀYĀNA AND ŚAIVISM

King *Sūryavarman I* (1001–1050) was a Mahāyānist, and given the posthumous name *Nirvāṇapāda*. Religious tolerance was a characteristic of the king, though the cult of God-King was somewhat deemphasized. The temples of his reign, *Phimeanakas*, *Takeo*, *Prasat Néak Buos*, *Vat Chisor*, *Préah Vihéar*, and *Vat Phu*, are all dedicated to *lingas*. The immediate successors of Sūryavarman I brought a certain amount of Śaivite reaction. The God-King cult was reinstituted, and these kings made only Śaivite donations. *Jayavarman* VI (1080–1107), however, was again absorbed in Mahāyāna and particularly interested in the cult of *Bhaiṣajyaguru*, the *Bodhisattva* of Medical Knowledge. He issued a proclamation by which both Buddhist and Brahmanical rites could be carried out by priests of the God-King. The great Mahāyāna temple and monastery at *Préah Khan* of *Kompong Svai* was flourishing at this time. *Sūryavarman II* (1113–1150+), the builder of *Angkor Wat*, was a Vaiṣṇavaite, and his reign sees a fusion of Śaivism and Vaiṣṇavism, as well as lessened Buddhist activity.

MAHĀYĀNA REVIVAL UNDER JAYAVARMAN VII (1181–1215+)

Prince Jayavarman, such a serious Buddhist that he twice hesitated to fight for the throne because of the bloodshed it would cause, in 1181 finally asserted himself, drove out the *Chams*, and became consecrated as King *Jayavarman VII*. His preceptor, *Maṅgalārthadeva*, substituted the cult of Buddha-King for that of God-King. Jayavarman VII's mother was deified as *Prajñāpāramitā*, and Jayavarman VII himself was given titles such as *Jayabuddha* and *Mahānātha* (Great Savior). His first queen, the devoted *Jayarājadevī*, had Jātakas performed as dramas, and *Indradevī*, his second wife, was famous as an accomplished instructress of the Buddhist doctrines of three schools.

Angkor Thoṁ, with its famous *Bayon* with its face towers, built under Jayavarman VII, housed statues of deified kings and queens, but also Śiva,

Viṣṇu, the Goddess in various forms, Buddhas, and Bodhisattvas. The faces on the tower represent Avalokiteśvara, and the Bayon as a whole is probably dedicated to him. Jayavarman VII was also a Mahāyānist on a practical plane, and built an extensive hospital system for his realm.

THE TRIUMPH OF THERAVĀDA IN CAMBODIA

Talaing monks propagated Theravāda among the Cambodian lower classes during the reign of Jayavarman VII. The common people, who stood in little relationship to the courtly Mahāyāna and Hinduism favored by the kings, found in Theravāda, with its undemanding monks and simple monasteries and doctrines accessible to all, a religion to which they could respond. The Thai invasions of the fourteenth century, which resulted finally in the abandonment of Angkor Thoṁ, also did much to spread Theravāda in Cambodia. Members of the royal family seem to have become Theravādins in the reign of *Indravarman III* (1296–1308).

By the middle of the fourteenth century, Cambodia is so thoroughly Theravāda that it is even converting its neighbors (refer to the section on Laos). Court rituals of the old state religion, however, continue to exist up to this day.

Several later Cambodian kings were most fervent in their Theravāda. King *Préah Thommo-réachéa* (1468–1514) knew the entire *Tipiṭaka* by heart and gave lectures on the First Sermon of the Buddha. His acts of charity were lavish. He constructed the great *caitya* at *Mount Santuk*. This and other religious institutions were maintained by serfs of the Three Jewels, called *pol-préah*. The sixteenth-century revolution of *sdach Kân*, himself a pol-préah, had as one of its aims the freeing of all these serfs of religious institutions. The revolt, after initial successes, failed.

VIETNAM

FAMOUS THIEN TEACHERS

The reign of *Ly-thaî-To* (1016–1028) sees great Buddhist activity in Vietnam, particularly in the field of *Thien*. The ruler himself was a pupil of the venerable *Van Hanh*, one of the greatest Thien teachers. Other Thien masters of the time included *Ba Dao* and *Sung-Pham*. Ly-thaî-To's successor, *Ly-thaî-ton* (1028–1034), a practicing layman of great fervor, obtained *satori* under his teacher *Thuyen-lao* of the *Von-ngôn-Thông* sect. He had 55 pagodas built, among them the famous one which rises from a lotus flower resting on a single column, the *Chúa Môṭ Côṭ*. *Ly-thânh-tôn* (1054–1071) instituted the practice of distributing food to the people in winter and reduced all prison terms. When invading Cham armies were defeated, among the prisoners was found the Thien master *Thao-Duong*. He was admitted to the Vietnamese Saṃgha by Ly-thânh-tôn, and began instruction at the *Khai-qûoc* pagoda. He founded a third Thien sect which the ruler joined and under which he gained satori. Under his successors, the famous Buddhist writers *Vien Chieu*, *Ngo-An*, and *Kho-dau* flourished.

AMIDISM

Recitation of the names of *Amida* and of the Goddess *Quan-Thê-Am* (Avalokiteśvara) constituted the Buddhism of the common people. The Buddhist shrines in the villages contained also the Ground God and Animal God of the old Vietnamese religion. Thien and Amidism came to be combined in most monasteries after the twelfth century, and this fusion is characteristic of Vietnamese Buddhism from then on.

INDONESIA

POSITION OF BUDDHISM IN THE ELEVENTH CENTURY

In the eleventh century the hegemony over the Indonesian coasts shifted from Sumatra to East Java (King *Airlangga*). Though the new rulers patronized both Vaiṣṇavism and Śaivism and stimulated the creation of old Javanese epics based on the *Mahābhārata*, Mahāyāna Buddhism was also flourishing. The communities that had been so patronized by the *Śailendras* continued to exist and were known for their all-encompassing Buddhist scholarship. Thus the famous *Atīśa* spent ten years in *Palembang* studying the *Sarvāstivāda* system.

ŚAIVA-BUDDHIST SYNCRETISM

The twelfth and thirteenth centuries, which see the rise of the empires of *Tumapel* and *Majapahit*, bring a fusion of Buddhism and Śaivism of a sort not seen even in Cambodia or Champa. The first king of Tumapel was called "Son of Śiva" and his wife is the model for the famous statue of Prajñāpāramitā now to be seen in Leiden, but the fullest extent of this Śaiva-Buddhist fusion can be seen in the reign of *Kertanagara* (1268–1292). The king himself is described by the poet *Prapañca* in his work *Nagarakertāgama* as a great saint of the Tantric type, who used palm wine in his secret ceremonies and who acquired great magical powers. In his Tantricism, Śaivism and Buddhism can no longer be distinguished. The *Caṇḍi Jawi*, built under this king, houses a Śiva and a Buddha above it. Even the king's own posthumous title, Śivabuddha, was a kind of combination never found in Cambodia or Champa.

THE TRIUMPH OF ISLAM

Gujerati merchants brought *Islam* to the coast of Sumatra at the end of the fourteenth century. Local princes adopted Islam often in a spirit of adding a new source of magic force to the ones they already knew. The people of coastal Sumatra, who were Hindus or Buddhists in a ritual sense but had never discontinued their indigenous religious practices, often adopted Islam in the same spirit, and one of the earliest Muslim graves bears Śaivite symbols as well as an Arabic inscription. At first there was no opposition from Brahmanical or Buddhist religious leaders, and it is only where religion becomes bound up with politics that it ever emerges at all. Thus certain nobles of the kingdom of Majapahit began to see in Islam a way of freeing themselves from the king's suzerainty. In 1478 the king of Majapahit, *Browijoyo* (*Bhravijaya*) *V*, attempted to discourage further conversion to Islam, and a revolution of his Moslem subjects followed, ending in his deposition. Those nobles and priests who refused to accept Islam retired to Bali. For some time they prevented the conversion of the East Javanese coast to Islam from this center, and, when this was no longer possible, successfully prevented the new religion from entering Bali itself.

LAOS

The Laos settled in the territories of the present-day Laos by the end of the thirteenth century. They had reverted completely to their ancestral worship by this time.

THE INTRODUCTION OF THERAVĀDA

Shortly after 1316, the Lao king, *Fah-Ngiao*, due to bad omens at the birth of his son, *Fah-ngum*, sent the infant boy away in a raft along the Mekong River, where he was found by a Cambodian monk, *Phra Maha Pa-sman*, who raised him and brought him to the Cambodian court. There he eventually married the daughter of the Cambodian king (Jayavarman IX?), called *Nang Keo Keng-Ya* by the Laos. She was a fervent Theravādin. When Fah-ngum returned to Laos to rule, his wife did her best to convert the people to Theravāda. She finally prevailed upon Fah-ngum himself, who was converted by his stepfather and *Phra Maha Thep-Lanka*. Twenty Buddhist monks were sent from Cambodia to Laos to propagate Theravāda among the people. With them came a Pāli Tipiṭaka and a golden Buddha statue (the *Prabang* after which *Luang Prabang* is named).

THAILAND

THE KINGDOM OF SUKHOTHAI

Through the pressures of the Mongol invasions, the Thais were pressed even further to the south, into the area of the present-day Thailand. Many of them recognized the suzerainty of Cambodia and came strongly under Cambodian cultural influence. But they were often restless under Cambodian rule and around 1238 two Thai chiefs defeated Cambodian armies and entered the town of *Sukhothai*, upon which one of them proclaimed himself King of Sukhothai as *Sri Intharathitya*.

RĀMA-KHAMHENG AND THE ADOPTION OF THERAVĀDA

Theravāda missionaries sent from Burma had been active in the Thai lands since the days of *Anawratā* and had a great measure of success. King *Rāma-Khamheng* (1275–1317), a great warrior and consolidator of the power of Sukhothai, converted to Theravāda and was instrumental in spreading the religion throughout his realm.

KING THAMMARAJA LÜTHAI

Successive kings of Sukhothai concentrated their efforts on religious matters. King *Lüthai* (1347–1370) was so concerned with religion that he received the name of *Thammaraja* or King of Dharma. In 1361, at the request of Lüthai, the head of the Saṃgha in Burma sent the monk *Sumana* to Thailand to initiate Sinhalese ordination rites there. In 1361 King Lüthai himself became consecrated as a Buddhist monk. He wrote a treatise on Buddhist cosmology, the *Traibhūmikathā*, and as king was most devoted to works of public utility: the digging of canals, the building of roads, etc. He also pardoned most criminals and freed all slaves within his realm.

THE KINGDOM OF AYUTHIA

It is the Kingdom of *Ayuthia* which is the basis of the Thai Kingdom of today. Its founder, *Rāmathibodi I*, was a Theravādin, though a less serious one than his erstwhile suzerain Lüthai. Characteristic of his and his successors' attitudes toward Theravāda is their wish to have some control over Buddhist activities through their preceptors, on the model of Burma.

SUGGESTED READING

Briggs, Lawrence Palmer. *The Ancient Khmer Empire*, pp. 144–261.

Coedès, Georges. *The Making of South East Asia*. Translated by H.M. Wright, pp. 121–144.

Leclère, Adhémard. *Histoire du Cambodge*, pp. 104–292.
Ray, Niharranjan. *Theravāda Buddhism in Burma*.
Viravong, Maha Sila. *History of Laos*, pp. 30–38.

32
The Spread of Buddhism into China

Roger J. Corless

PRE-BUDDHIST CHINA

CONFUCIANISM

According to the traditional account, *K'ung Fu-tzŭ* (Latinized as Confucius) lived from 551–497 B.C. He is said to have reformed the native religion, emphasizing a balanced and rational approach, and to have restored and edited the ancient texts. The *Lun-yü* ("Discussions and Sayings" or "Analects") contains what are said to be some of his apothegms. Much of his traditional biography is historically questionable. Confucianism, called *Ju-chao* or "The Teaching for Scholar-Gentlemen," stresses erudition and the social virtues. It understands the universe to be governed by a hierarchy of impersonal forces.

TAOISM

The foundation of Taoism is attributed to *Huang-lao*, a conflated deity formed from *Huang-ti* (Yellow Emperor), a mythical figure of Chinese prehistory, and *Lao-Tzŭ*, said to have been born in 604 B.C. and to have disappeared toward the west in 444 B.C. after composing the lapidary *Tao Tê Ching*—"Standard Work on Tao (Way) and Tê (Virtue, Power)." The existence of Lao tzŭ and the authorship of the book are much disputed. Taoism, called *Tao-chao* or "The Teaching about the Tao," comes to include everything in the native religion which is not labeled Confucian. It has a philosophical stream, stressing individualism and tending to skepticism, and a popular "religious" stream, with many personal gods and a complex technique for gaining corporeal immortality by meditation, diets, and alchemy.

ENTRY OF BUDDHISM

BUDDHISM IN CENTRAL ASIA

Central Asia in the second century B.C. (equivalent to modern Russian

Turkistān, and Sinkiang Uighur Autonomous Region) was composed of city-states that were Indian in literature and religion and Iranian in material things. It was more fertile then than now. Buddhism, mainly *Hīnayāna* (and especially *Sarvāstivāda*) in the north and *Mahāyāna* in the south, flourished. Between the eighth and thirteenth centuries A.D. it slowly became Muslim, but it remains a source of Buddhist archaeological artifacts.

ENTRY ROUTES

Buddhism traveled along the trade routes, leaving northwest India via Peshāwār, skirting the mountains via Bāmiyān and Balkh, and turning east to Kashgar, then going either north via Kuchā or south via Khotan and entering China at *Tun-huang*, which, having many cave-temples that largely escaped damage in the persecutions, is an extremely rich archaeological site. Legend says that *Emperor Ming* of *Han* (A.D. 58–75), after an auspicious dream, sent an embassy to import Buddhism along this route, ca. 61 or 64. It seems at least possible to date the entrance of Buddhism into China between the first half of the first century B.C. and the middle of the first century A.D. The first clearly historical mention of an emperor practicing Buddhism is A.D. 166 in a rescript of *Hsiang-K'ai* to *Emperor Huan* (A.D. 147–167) berating the emperor for hypocritically worshipping both Huang-lao and Buddha, without reforming his life.

EARLY BUDDHISM IN CHINA

GENERAL CHARACTERISTICS

Since Buddhism entered from the west (whither Lao-tzŭ had disappeared), was individualist, had many gods and paradises, taught meditation, and appeared to speak of immortality, it was mistaken for a form of Taoism, purer and simpler because it lacked alchemy and sacrifices. The Taoist *hua-hu* (conversion of the barbarians) theory claimed that Lao-tzŭ had instructed the westerners. The Buddhists indeed claimed the converse. An early interest in Hīnayāna gave way to a preference for Mahāyāna.

PERSONALITIES

An Shih-kao, a Parthian, settled at *Lo-yang* in A.D. 148 and headed a team of mainly Hīnayāna monks which translated works on meditation and breathing exercises. His countryman and disciple *An-hsüan* worked on *prajñāpāramitā* texts. An-hsüan converted *Yên Fo-t'iao*, the first Chinese Buddhist monk. *Lokakṣema*, an Indo-Scythian, arrived between 168 and 188 and represented Mahāyāna, producing, among other works, a partial translation of the *Aṣṭasāhasrikā-prajñāpāramitā-sūtra*. Translation at this period was precarious, no one member of the team being fluent in both the source and target languages. *Kumārajīva*, a Kuchanese who had lived in Kashmir, arrived in *Ch'ang-an* in 402 as the first scholar competent to oversee the whole process of translation, and his versions are generally preferred.

TEXTS

Sūtras translated during the Han Dynasty are mostly on meditation, morality, and the paradises (*ching-t'u* or pure lands) of *Amitābha* (*A-mi-t'o*) and *Bhaiṣajyaguru* (*Yao-shih*). The earliest text, said to have been imported by Emperor Ming, is the *Ssŭ-shih-êrh Chang Ching* or "Sūtra in 42 Chapters," putatively a translation but possibly an anthology. Cast in the style of the Lun-yü, it is Hīnayāna in its earliest recension, and pictures the holy persons (*ārya-pudgalas*), especially the *arhant* (Chinese: *Lo-han*), as *hsien* or Taoist immortals who levitate, etc. The *Ānāpānasmṛti-sūtra* or "Sūtra on Recollection of Breathing In-and-Out," translated by An Shih-kao (and called *An-pan shou-i Ching*), has a preface on breathing out-and-in (a Taoist practice). A native treatise, *Mou-tzŭ Li-huo Lun*, or "A Discussion of Doubtful Points by *Mou-tzŭ*" (late second century A.D., but possibly fifth century), is an apologia justifying certain Buddhist practices and beliefs that appeared strange or abhorrent to the Chinese.

SUGGESTED READING

Bassagli, Mario. *Painting of Central Asia*. Translated by Lothian Small.
Chan, Wing-tsit, tr. *The Way of Lao Tzu: Tao-te Ching*.
Ch'en, Kenneth K.S. *Buddhism in China*, chap. 2, pp. 21–53.
de Bary, William Theodore, ed. *The Buddhist Tradition*, pp. 132–38.
Gray, Basil, and Vincent, J.B. *Buddhist Cave Paintings at Tun-huang*.
Saha, Kshanika. *Buddhism and Buddhist Literature in Central Asia*.
Shaku, Soyen. *Sermons of a Buddhist Abbot*. Translated by D.T. Suzuki, pp. 3–21.

33
History of Buddhism in China

Roger J. Corless

CHRONOLOGY

INTRODUCTION (TO THE CLOSE OF HAN, A.D. 219)

Pioneer translations of miscellaneous texts appeared, with little or no indication of date or provenance.

ADAPTATION (THREE KINGDOMS AND TWO CHIN, 220–419)

Buddho-Taoism expressed Buddhist ideas in Taoist terminology. In the north, its ability to perform magic impressed the barbarian rulers, while in the south, its philosophical profundities attracted the Chinese intelligentsia.

DIFFERENTIATION (NORTHERN AND SOUTHERN DYNASTIES, 420–588)

Identifiable schools (*chung*) and sects (*tsung*) emerged.

Classical Schools. These schools represent modified forms of later Indian Buddhist doctrinal systems. They formed the basis of the sects, and gradually died out.

1. *Chü-shê:* Founded by *Paramārtha* (sixth century), organized by *Hsüan-tsang* (ca. 596–664). The name transliterates [*Abhidharma*]*kośa* in Sanskrit, and it corresponds to the Indian *Abhidharma* school.
2. *San-lun:* Founded by *Kumārajīva* (344–413), organized by *Tao-shêng* (ca. 360–434). The name means "Three Texts" and refers to the *Mādhyamika-śāstra* and *Dvadaśadvara* of *Nāgārjuna* and the *Śata-śāstra* of *Āryadeva*. It corresponds to the Indian *Mādhyamika* school.
3. *Fa-hsiang:* Organized by Hsüan-tsang and his disciple *K'uei-chi* (632–682) out of Shê-lun, begun by Paramārtha. The name translates the Sanskrit *Dharma-lakṣaṇa* ("the specific marks of the dharmas") and the school corresponds to the Indian *Yogācāra* school.

Scholastic Sects.

1. *T'ien-t'ai:* Founded by *Hui-ssŭ* (515–576), organized by *Chih-i* (538–597). The name is derived from *T'ien-t'ai Shan*, the mountain on which Chih-i exercised.
2. *Hua-yen:* Founded by *Tu-shun* (557–640), organized by *Fa-tsang* (643–712). The name translates the Sanskrit *Avataṃsaka*, from the sūtra on which it is based.

Both, in different ways, constructed comprehensive systematizations of all Buddhist doctrines and practices then known.

Popular Sects.

1. *Ch'an:* Founded by *Bodhidharma* (fifth century?). The name transliterates the Sanskrit *dhyā[na]*, meditation, which it emphasizes.
2. *Ching-t'u:* Founded (?) by *Hui-yüan* (334–416), organized by *T'an-luan* (476–542). The name translates the Sanskrit *pariśodhana-kṣetra* (the field which purifies, pure land), meaning the Western Paradise to which its adherents go after death.

Both of the above had a more direct appeal to the common people.

CONSOLIDATION (SUI, 589–617)

Hsüan-i (the hidden significance) commentaries were written to reveal the essential characteristics of a Sect or a text, and lists of Sect Patriarchs were drawn up to establish authentic lineages.

DOMINANCE AND DECLINE (T'ANG, 618–906)

Rising to its apex of power, Buddhism was vigorously put down in 845 by the Taoist emperor *Wu-tsung*. The Scholastic Sects, heavily dependent on the specialists at the elaborate monastic institutions, disappeared. The Popular Sects, being less encumbered, revived after Wu-tsung's death and the lifting of the persecution. *Chên-yen* (corresponding to Buddhist *Tantra*) was introduced in the eighth century by *Śubhakarasiṃha*. Its name, meaning efficient (true) word, which translates the Sanskrit *mantra*, indicates its emphasis. It had no great influence.

PERSISTENCE (907 TO PRESENT)

Ch'an and Ching-t'u endured quietly as features of the general religious scene. A brief revival in the nineteenth century (especially promoted by

T'ai-hsü, 1890–1947) was followed by the suppression or manipulation of Buddhism by the Communists after 1949.

PROBLEMS OF SINICIZATION

BUDDHISM AND TAOISM

Buddhism was at first regarded as a form of Taoism. It expressed its thought in Taoist terms by *ko-i* or "stretching the meaning" (e.g., *tao* was used for *bodhi*). This was condemned as compromising by *Tao-an* (312–385), and a distinctively Buddhist terminology evolved, although it adapted, rather than entirely abandoned, many Taoist ideas (this being especially true for Ch'an). A point of special controversy was between the Buddhist *anātman* doctrine and the Taoist doctrine of a composite soul based on the *yin-yang* interaction, implying (for the Buddhist) an immortality in a transcendental, incorporeal sense, rather than the corporeal immortality sought by the Taoists. When Buddhism became a successful religion in its own right, Taoism reacted by forming a canon, pantheon, and ecclesiastical structure on a quasi-Buddhist model.

BUDDHISM AND CONFUCIANISM

Other-worldly and non-Chinese, Buddhism was always in danger of criticism from the practical and patriotic Confucian literati. Points of special controversy were its refusal to worship the emperor, claiming that it was superior to all earthly kingdoms, and celibacy, which struck at family unity and ancestor-worship. However, Chinese monastic customs gradually took on many of the features of Confucian family etiquette (worshipping deceased abbots as ancestors, etc.).

INTERNAL CONTROVERSIES

SUBITISM AND GRADUALISM

Beginning with the controversy between *Tao-shêng* and his contemporary *Hui-kuan*, it was debated whether enlightenment was obtained completely at one time (subitism) or in stages (gradualism). The controversy influenced Ch'an during the T'ang period.

SELF-HELP AND OUTSIDE-HELP

The extent to which enlightenment may be obtained by one's own power (*tzŭ-li*) or by relying on the power of another (*t'o-li*) (i.e., the Buddha), divides Ch'an from Ching-t'u.

LINEAGE

There were continual squabbles between similar branches of a sect over proper text or patriarchal lineage.

SUGGESTED READING

Ch'en, Kenneth K.S. *Buddhism in China.*

Reischauer, Edwin O., tr. *Ennin's Diary.* (See also Reischauer's *Ennin's Travels in T'ang China.*)

Robinson, Richard H. *The Buddhist Religion*, pp. 79–99.

Takakusu, Junjiro. *The Essentials of Buddhist Philosophy.*

Welch, Holmes. *The Buddhist Revival in China*, Chap. 4–12.

Wright, Arthur F. *Buddhism in Chinese History.*

34
Ch'an

Roger J. Corless

HISTORY

INTRODUCTION

Brought to China by the semi-legendary *Bodhidharma* (Chinese: *P'u-t'i-ta-mo*) who was possibly Indian and may have worked between A.D. 470 and 520, the lineage is said to go back via a series of direct mind-to-mind transmissions of the "lamp" of inner enlightenment to *Mahākāśyapa*, a disciple of *Śākyamuni*, who is stated to have wordlessly comprehended the Dharma when Śākyamuni silently held up a flower. Mahākāśyapa thus became the first to receive the "seal of the Dharma" (*fa-yin*) with authority to pass it on in an appropriate manner. Bodhidharma is variously said to be the eighth, twenty-eighth, twenty-ninth, or thirty-fifth in line from Mahākāśyapa, but is universally regarded as the first Chinese Patriarch.

THE SIXTH PATRIARCH

The identification of the Sixth Chinese Patriarch occasioned severe controversy. First identified as *Shên-hsiu* (600–706) of Northern Ch'an, an imperial decision of 796 confirmed his rival, *Hui-nêng* (638–713) of Southern Ch'an. The *Liu-tzŭ T'an-ching* ("Platform Sūtra of the Sixth Patriarch," ca. 820) claims that *Hung-jên* (601–674), the Fifth Patriarch, had given the *fa-yin* to Hui-nêng after judging him the winner in a mnemonic-verse contest, but secretly, and Hui-nêng had fled to escape the jealousies of Shên-hsiu's party.

T'ANG DYNASTY

T'ang Dynasty Ch'an was divided into five houses, of which only two have survived:

1. *Lin-chi* (Japanese: *Rinzai*), founded by *Lin-chi I-hsüan* (d. 867), taken to Japan by *Eisai* (1141–1215). Emphasizes *kung-an* and Subitism.
2. *Ts'ao-tung* (Japanese: *Sōtō*), founded jointly by *Tung-shan Liang-*

chieh (807–869) and *Ts'ao-shan Pên-chi* (840–901), taken to Japan by *Dōgen* (1200–1253). Emphasizes *chih-kuan-ta-tso* and Gradualism.

Rinzai and Sōtō remained separate, but Lin-chi and Ts'ao-tung merged during the Ming Dynasty.

THE RULE

Po-chang Huai-hai (720–814) drew up a Monastic Constitution for Ch'an monks which was more detailed than, and in some respects contrary to, the *Vinaya*. For example, the Vinaya prohibits agriculture for fear of harming organisms, while Po-chang (colloquial pronunciation, Pai-chang) prescribes daily manual labor under pain of excommunication from the Refectory.

DOCTRINE

SŪTRAS

1. Mainly the *Prajñāpāramitā* group, especially the *Vajracchedikā* and *Mahāprajñāpāramitā-hṛdaya-sūtra*.
2. Also important are *Kuan-yin Ching* ("Sūtra on Avalokiteśvara" which is chapter 24 of the *Saddharmapuṇḍarīka-sūtra*, circulating independently), *Laṅkāvatāra-sūtra*, *Śūraṅgama-sūtra* (*Yogācāra* viewpoint; synopsis in Suzuki, *Manual of Zen Buddhism*, pp. 64–72), *Vimalakīrtinirdeśa*, and *Yüan-chüeh Ching* ("Sūtra on Complete Enlightenment," *Vaipulya* group, Yogācāra viewpoint).

DIRECT TRANSMISSION

Ch'an emphasizes individual enlightenment or *wu* (Japanese: *satori*) as the one essential. Study, worship, etc., are normally necessary but, should they become obstacles, they must be abandoned. Thus the Patriarchs resorted to apparent sacrilege, e.g., tearing up the sūtras. *Wu* is caught, not taught.

YOGĀCĀRA AND MĀDHYAMIKA

Ch'an is doctrinally conservative within the Mahāyāna tradition; development and innovation occur in the practice. From Yogācāra it takes the Idealist world-view of mentation-only (*citta-mātra*) and the necessity of transforming (*parāvṛtti*) the eight ways of mediate knowing (*vijñāna*) into immediate knowing (*jñāna*), after which there is no projection (*pravṛtti*) of a personal universe. From Mādhyamika it takes a pedagogy of rapid multi-level negative dialectic. Both elements can be seen in the exchange between Shên-hsiu and Hui-nêng in Liu-tzŭ T'an-ching 9.

PRACTICE

Ch'an practices the *triśikṣā* of general Buddhism, with special modifications.

SITTING

Aiming at nothing except sitting or *chih-kuan-ta-tso* (Japanese: *shikantaza*, *shikandaza*) is used to stop the mind in the present moment (*nien*). It must be goalless and objectless. Breath-observation (*ānāpānasmṛti*) is often practiced, but a concrete symbol (*kṛtsna*) is seldom employed. Eventually, one strives to retain goallessness and objectlessness of nien within any activity. Dōgen said shikantaza recreates (sacramentally) the sitting of Śākyamuni under the Bodhi Tree.

DIALOGUE

Most Ch'an instruction is according to everyday logic (*samvṛtitas*), but occasionally the Master will engage the pupil in question-and-answer at the level of ultimate truth (*paramārtha satya*), in which all viewpoints (*dṛṣṭi*) are negated. The dialogue is intelligible only in the context of Mādhyamika dialectic. At first spontaneous, some of these dialogues were collected into anthologies with commentaries, of which the most famous are:

1. *Pi-yên Lu* or "Blue Cliff Records" (Japanese: *Hekigan Roku*): 100 dialogues compiled in 1125 by *Yüan-wu* (1063–1135), each with a mnemonic verse of *Hsüeh-tou* (988–1052) and comment by Yüan-wu. It is named for a painting in Yüan-wu's room.
2. *Wu-mên Kuan* or "The Gateless Barrier" (Japanese: *Mumonkan*): 48 dialogues compiled in 1228 by *Hui-k'ai* (1184–1260; later known as Wu-mên), with his comments. A book of riddles, with the title itself a riddle.

The dialogues are known as *kung-an* (Japanese: *kōan*), literally, public records meaning authenticated cases of dialogue which have led to enlightenment, and are objects of study during monastic formation. When assigned by a Master to a particular student, a kung-an is called *hua-t'ou* (Japanese: *watō*), literally, the head of the saying meaning the one word which forms the nub of the question. The right answer is the one that arises naturally from the wu of that student at that moment. The dialogue is salvific, not descriptive.

INVOCATION

Nien-fo (Invocation of Buddha) was advocated by early Ch'an, but dropped as incompatible with *tzŭ-li* (one's own power). Revived during the Ming

Dynasty, it is advocated as a supplementary practice by Korean Chen. Japanese Zen rejected it, but *Hakuin* (1685–1768) strongly recommends the *Emmei Jukku Kannon Gyō* ("Text in Ten Phases to Avalokiteśvara for Prolonging Life"), based on the ideas of the Kuan-yin Ching (Japanese: *Kwannon Gyō*). *Dhāraṇīs* are commonly used during worship, at meals, etc.

SUGGESTED READING

Books listed here include writings on both Ch'an and Zen.

Chang, Garma Chen-chi. *The Practice of Zen.*

Ch'en, Kenneth K.S. *Buddhism in China*, pp. 350–64.

de Bary, William Theodore, ed. *The Buddhist Tradition*, pp. 211–40, 363–93.

Dumoulin, Heinrich. *A History of Zen Buddhism.* Translated by Paul Peachey.

Kapleau, Philip. *The Three Pillars of Zen.*

Kennett, Jiyu. *Selling Water by the River: A Manual of Zen Training.*

Masunaga, Reihō. *A Primer of Sōtō Zen.*

Sekiguchi, Shindai. *Zen: A Manual for Westerners.*

Suzuki, Daisetz Teitarō. *Essays in Zen Buddhism*, series 1, 2, 3.

Welch, Holmes. *The Practice of Chinese Buddhism 1900–1950.*

Yampolsky, Philip B., tr. *The Platform Sūtra of the Sixth Patriarch.*

35
Ching-t'u

Roger J. Corless

HISTORY

FOUNDER

Devotion to *Amitābha Buddha*, who rules over the western, and best, *ching-t'u*, began as an optional practice within any sect. *Hui-yüan* (334–416) was perhaps the first to give the practice autonomy, forming the *White Lotus Society*, an aristocratic sodality for meditating upon the Ching-t'u in 402.

ORGANIZER

T'an-luan (476–542) is reckoned as the first Chinese Patriarch of Ching-t'u. Wandering through China searching for corporeal immortality from Taoist Masters, he met the Indian missionary *Bodhiruci* (who had arrived at *Lo-yang* in 508), who convinced him that true immortality lay in devotion to *Amitābha* (Immeasurable Light), alias *Amitāyus* (Immeasurable Life). T'an-luan's commentaries form the theoretical basis of all later Ching-t'u. He advocated *Nien-fo*, which has become one of the most popular practices of Far Eastern Buddhists.

TRANSMISSION

The movement passed to Japan, again as an option within other sects, then as an independent sect under *Hōnen* (1133–1212), founder of *Jōdo Shū* (Pure Land School), and *Shinran* (1173–1262), founder of *Jōdo Shinshū* (True Pure Land School), the latter of which commands very wide allegiance among lay people. A list of Patriarchs was drawn up, each of whom set forward the doctrine and practice in a special way.

DOCTRINE AND PRACTICE

SŪTRAS

Devotion to the person of Śākyamuni Buddha is as old as our earliest records about him. By faith or trust (*śraddhā*) one assayed and observed the preliminary efficacy of the Eightfold Path, etc., and believed it valid to extrapolate this to final nirvāṇa. Formal *buddha-bhakti* appears with the *Sukhāvatī-vyūha* texts and the *Amitāyurdhyāna-sūtra*, in which Śākyamuni points to *Amitābha* (abbreviated to *Amita* and transliterated as *A-mi-t'o* in Chinese and *Amida* in Japanese) as the most glorious, wise, and long-lived of all Buddhas, ruling over *Sukhāvatī* (Chinese: *Chi-lo Kuo*; Japanese: *Gokuraku-koku*), the most blissful of all paradises, far to the west, which Amitābha has obtained consequent upon his 48 Great Resolutions (*mahāpraṇidhāna*), made long ago. If one here devotedly contemplates Sukhāvatī and Amitābha, the power (*adhiṣṭhāna*) of Amitābha will cause one to go to him after death.

PATRIARCHS

The following is the list accepted by Jōdo Shinshū.

Nāgārjuna. "The Chapter on the Easy and Difficult Paths," section 5 of the *Daśabhūmikavibhāṣā* ("Explanation of the Ten [Bodhisattva] Stages") is attributed (uncertainly) to Nāgārjuna. The Difficult Path is that of self-help or *tzŭ-li* (Japanese: *jiriki*) by meditation, morality, etc., while the Easy Path is that of outside help or *t'o-li* (Japanese: *tariki*) by trusting in Buddha.

Vasubandhu. The *Amitāyuḥsūtrānyupadeśapratyājātipraṇidhānagāthā* ("Verses on the Resolution to be Re-born [in Sukhāvatī] with an Exposition of the Sūtras of Limitless Life") is attributed (again uncertainly) to Vasubandhu. The Chinese translation was made by Bodhiruci during the Former Wei Dynasty (386–534). It summarizes and harmonizes the three Pure Land Sūtras.

T'an-luan. His major work is an extended commentary on the above text, called (for short) the *Wang-shêng-lun Chu* ("Commentary on the Essay on Re-birth"). Its doctrine is a combination of *Yogācāra* and *Mādhyamika*. Sukhāvatī is transcendental, outside of saṃsāra, therefore birth there is no-birth, and on entering it one becomes a nonlapsing Mahābodhisattva. Practice is fivefold: bodily worship (bowing, etc.), vocal praise, especially the *Nien-fo* (Japanese: *Nembutsu*)—"Hail! Amita Buddha" (Chinese: *Nan-mo A-mi-t'o Fo*; Japanese: *Namu Amida Butsu*), resolution (to be born in Sukhāvatī), contemplation (of Sukhāvatī, Amitābha, and the Mahābodhisattvas), and dispersing merit (*pariṇāmaṇā*), especially by, after having been perfected in Sukhāvatī, manifesting changed-forms (*nirmāṇa-kāya*) in saṃsāra for the universal good.

Tao-ch'o (562–645). Tao-ch'o's major work, *An-lo Chi* ("Compendium on Sukhāvatī"), recommends Ching-t'u practice as most suitable for the period of the Latter-Day Dharma or *mo-fa* (Japanese: *mappō*), then thought to be operative. A rosary or *nien-chu*, literally recollection beads, for counting off the Nien-fo is advocated, and herculean feats of recitation are recorded.

Shan-tao (613–681). His *Kuan-ching Chu* ("Commentary on the Amitāyur-dhyāna-sūtra") advocates one primary practice (the Nien-fo) and four secondary practices (chanting, contemplation, worship, and hymn singing).

Other Chinese Masters. *Tz'u-min* (680–748) attempted to harmonize Ching-t'u and Ch'an. *Fa-chao* (ca. 800) received the "Nien-fo on Five Notes" by revelation. Neither is accounted a Patriarch, but modern Ch'an chants the Nien-fo, and the *Reihai Seiten* ("Service Book") of Jōdo Shinshū contains Fa-chao's melody.

Japanese Patriarchs. Pure Land doctrine evolves to term in Japan. *Genshin* (942–1017) wrote *Ōjōyōshū* ("Compendium on the Essence of Re-birth"), vividly contrasting the miseries of the hells with the joys of Sukhāvatī. Hōnen stressed the necessity of selecting (senchaku) the Nembutsu above all other practices, to increase faith, while Shinran identified the moment of faith with the essence of Nembutsu, henceforth recited minimally (the rosary being wrapped around the hands but neither counted nor rubbed), solely out of gratitude (*hō-on*).

SUGGESTED READING

Books listed here contain writings on Chinese and Japanese Pure Land.

Bloom, Alfred. *Shinran's Gospel of Pure Grace.*
Ch'en. Kenneth K.S. *Buddhism in China*, pp. 338–50.
Coates, H.H., and Ryugaku Ishizuka. *Hōnen, the Buddhist Saint.*
Corless, Roger J. *T'an-luan's Commentary on the Pure Land Discourse.*
de Bary, William Theodore, ed. *The Buddhist Tradition*, pp. 197–207, 314–44.
Hsiao, Ching-fên. *The Life and Teachings of T'an-luan.*
Suzuki, Daisetz Teitarō. *Shin Buddhism.*

36

Chinese Academic Schools and Doctrinal Innovations

Francis H. Cook

INTRODUCTION

Chinese academic schools of Buddhism consisted of groups of monks devoted to the study, exegesis, and propagation of certain philosophical trends within Buddhism. They were not sects in the Western sense of the word. A member of the *Hua-yen* tradition, for example, might observe the monastic disciplinary code of the *Lu School*, meditate in the *Ch'an* tradition, and accept the teachings on emptiness which were the special province of the *San-lun School*. He would be considered a follower of Hua-yen because he thought that school taught a more perfect form of the truth, and he would be interested in studying its philosophy. Most likely, he would write essays dealing with Hua-yen philosophy.

REASONS FOR THE EMERGENCE OF ACADEMIC SCHOOLS

Chinese Buddhists were bewildered by the conflicting, or apparently conflicting testimonies of scriptural works coming from India. Differences particularly between Mahāyāna and Hīnayāna doctrines led the Chinese to believe that either the Buddha had lied at times, which was impossible, or that there must be a good reason why the scriptures contradict each other.

In attempting to make some sensible order out of these conflicting testimonies, the Chinese imposed their own rationale. Their method was dividing the teaching (*p'an chiao*). This was a system of dividing the whole corpus of Buddhist teaching in parts according to some criterion. Each part was represented by a text or group of cognate texts.

As a result of p'an chiao activity, a monk-scholar would often determine that one text, or a group of texts, was more important than all others and would concentrate his energies on studying and teaching that particular text. He in turn would attract other monks who would pursue the same study, and a school would result.

CHINESE ACADEMIC SCHOOLS, THEIR TEXTS, AND THEIR PHILOSOPHIES (OR OBJECTS OF CONCERN)

TI-LUN SCHOOL

The *Ti-lun School* or School of the Treatise on Stages arose in the *Liang Dynasty* through the work of the Vinaya Master *Kuang*, *Hui-shun*, *Tao-shen*, and others, and is based on the *Commentary on the Sūtra on the Ten Stages*, by the Indian monk *Vasubandhu*.

The *Sūtra on the Ten Stages* (*Daśabhūmika-sūtra*) is basically a scripture which describes the progress of a *Bodhisattva* through ten phases in his career. The commentary by Vasubandhu discusses the complete harmony and interfusion of the six characteristics of universality and particularity, identity and indifference, and integration and disintegration. In trying to establish the identity of all things temporal and spatial, this philosophy foreshadowed the Hua-yen school, into which it was absorbed.

SHÊ-LUN SCHOOL

The *Shê-lun School* was based on the *Compendium of Mahāyāna* (*Mahāyānasaṃgraha-śāstra*), which was translated from Sanskrit by *Paramārtha*, who came to China from India during the Liang Dynasty. This school ceased as an independent entity when it was absorbed by the Hua-yen in *T'ang* times.

The Mahāyānasaṃgraha-śāstra, ascribed to Vasubandhu (or Asaṅga), attempts to draw together all major philosophical trends in Mahāyāna. One of its central doctrines centers around the philosophical debate over whether the absolute remains forever transcendent, apart from the impure, mundane world of conditionality, or is found immanent in the mundane, mixed with it as pure water with dirt. The treatise affirmed the latter position, allying itself with other texts such as the *Awakening of Faith in the Mahāyāna* (Chinese: *Ta-ch'eng ch'i-hsin lun; Sanskrit: Mahāyānaśraddhotpāda*), but setting itself against the *Fa-hsiang School* and its interpretation. The Chinese were apparently very receptive to the idea that things are a mixture of the relative and absolute.

SAN-LUN SCHOOL

The *San-lun School* or "Three Treatise School" is the Chinese version of Indian *Mādhyamika*, originating with the translations and scholarship of the great *Kumārajīva* (344–413), a native of Central Asia living in China. Among his many important translations were those of the *Middle Stanzas* (*Mādhyamika-kārikās*), *Twelve Topics* (*Dvādaśanikāya-śāstra*), and the *Hundred Treatise* (*Śata-śāstra*), all important Mādhyamika treatises dealing with the doctrine of emptiness (*śūnyatā*). The school was instituted by later students such as *Chia-hsiang* and *Chi-tsang*, and lasted until late in the T'ang Dynasty.

This school was important because it was one of the main avenues by which the Chinese came to approach the extremely important Indian Buddhist concept of emptiness. It can be said that the emptiness doctrine is the philosophical and religious base of all forms of Mahāyāna Buddhism, and therefore indispensible for the correct understanding of Buddhism. However, the San-lun School studied and taught a pure, theoretical form of emptiness which was indigestible for the average Buddhist, and so the school had no lasting vitality as an independent entity. The emptiness doctrine could only be assimilated when it came to serve as the tacit background of Ch'an and Pure Land Buddhism, like salt flavoring a soup.

LU SCHOOL

Lu (Sanskrit: *Vinaya*) refers to the code of monastic discipline, which constitutes one of the three parts of Buddhist sacred literature. Although Vinaya study and observance was of concern to all Buddhists, a separate academic tradition arose under *Tao-hsüan* in the T'ang Dynasty, which had as its main concern the study and teaching of Vinaya texts.

Vinaya texts cover such matters as procedures for ordination, lists of offenses and punishments, rules of seniority, and, in general, rules which, when observed by the monastic community, ensure the orderly functioning of the monastery. Buddhists have always felt that the Dharma could only exist and prosper when based on a strict observance of the Vinaya code.

A-PI-TA-MO SCHOOL

A-pi-ta-mo is the Chinese transliteration of the Sanskrit *Abhidharma*, which refers to a type of Buddhist literature and its subject matter. Abhidharma texts were translated and studied before the arising of an independent school, but a renewed interest in Abhidharma studies was stimulated when the Chinese pilgrim *Hsüan-tsang* returned from India in 645 with a copy of the *Abhidharmakośa*, one of the most important texts of this nature.

Abhidharma texts are scholastic treatises which exploit topics in the sūtras. They discuss in minute detail such matters as cosmology, meditation devices and techniques, stages of spiritual development, moral and intellectual faults (*kleśa*), the nature of the Buddha, etc. While not very inspiring or edifying, they clarify concepts which are not discussed clearly or in detail in the sūtras, which are dogmatic and undemonstrative.

CH'ENG-SHIH SCHOOL

The *Ch'eng-shih School* is based on the *Satyasiddhi-śāstra* (Chinese: *Ch'eng-shih lun*) by the Indian *Harivarman*, and translated into Chinese by Kumārajīva. Although a Hīnayāna text, its ideas on the emptiness of the *dharmas* so closely approximated Mahāyāna ideas on emptiness that it was included as a part of San-lun studies and closely tied as a school with San-lun. The name of the text is derived from the claim that it divulges the true meaning of the sūtras.

T'IEN-T'AI SCHOOL

T'ien-t'ai, although eclectic in its approach to Buddhist teachings, is based primarily on the *Lotus Sūtra* (*Saddharmapuṇḍarīka-sūtra*). The school is considered to have been started by *Chih-i*, in the latter part of the sixth century. As a result of his *p'an chiao* work, Chih-i came to feel that this scripture embodied the mature, final teaching of the Buddha.

While claiming the Lotus Sūtra as the apex of Buddhist teaching, T'ien-t'ai was nevertheless eclectic in trying to include all periods and schools of Buddhism within one all-comprehensive system. Doctrinally and practically, the following are considered to be characteristic teachings of T'ien-t'ai.

1. A system of meditation, propounded in Chih-i's voluminous *Mo-ho chih kuan* ("Tranquillity and Insight According to Mahāyāna").
2. The threefold truth of empty, temporary, and middle. Empty means that things are empty of the subjective reality we superimpose on them. Temporary refers to the fact that things do have an empirical, concrete existence. Middle means that things are both empty and existent, intersections of the particular and universal, at the same moment. While particular things remain distinct, they are identical on the basis of their common emptiness, and thus all things are part of one organic unity.
3. The above idea is elaborated in the doctrine of *i nien san ch'ien* (3,000 realms in an instant of consciousness). Ten realms—Buddhas, Bodhisattvas, Pratyekabuddhas, Disciples, divine beings, demons, human beings, hungry ghosts, animals, beings in purgatories—interpenetrate each other, giving rise to a hundred realms. Each of these has ten features such as form, nature, and force, thus making a thousand realms, and these thousand each is further divided into living beings, the five groups (*skandhas*), and space, making three thousand. The system thus tries to signify the interpenetration of all existent things, and then claims that these are all contained as an organic unity within the reality which is called, for want of a better word, mind. It is the goal of the meditant to discover this himself.

FA-HSIANG SCHOOL

This school was created by *Hsüan-tsang* and his disciple *K'uei-chi* after Hsüan-tsang returned from India in 645 with the textual materials which form the basis of the school: the *Thirty Verses* (*Triṃśikā*) of *Vasubandhu*, along with commentaries on it by ten scholars, notably *Dharmapāla* and *Sthiramati*.

The *Fa-hsiang School* is also called the Mind-Only School because its teaching is that nothing exists external to consciousness. What we mistakenly believe is a world out there consists only of ideas, images, concepts, words, etc., existing in the mind. The mind is a complex interacting of eight mental functions, which, in collaboration with innate, archetypal potentialities called seeds, give rise to an illusory external world. When the mind is cleansed, the illusion disappears, resulting in enlightenment. The school arose in response to the question of the nature of the mechanism whereby human beings dwelt in illusion.

HUA-YEN SCHOOL

The *Hua-yen* or Flower Ornament School was the creation of *Fa-tsang*, who was active in the latter part of the seventh century and first decade of the eighth (d. 712). This school was based on the *Avataṃsaka-sūtra* (Chinese: *Hua-yen Ching*), from which it takes its name. Like T'ien-t'ai, it was eclectic and syncretic, attempting to formulate a doctrine which would embrace all aspects of Buddhist teaching.

The complicated Hua-yen philosophy is impossible to summarize in a few words. Basically, the school teaches the mutual indentity and interdependence of all phenomena. All things are interrelated. In their emptiness, they are essentially identical; in their empirical, concrete existence, they are mutually dependent for their existence. Identity and interdependence are simply two expressions for emptiness, and the view of existence as one organic whole of interrelated and interdependent parts is called *fa-chiai yüan-ch'i*, the interdependent existence of the universe, or interdependent existence which is the universe. All things are empty, and this emptiness is the body of *Vairocana*, the cosmic Buddha. Hua-yen is thus a cosmic ecology, which views existence as one organic unity, in which all things are identical, and in which each part is dependent on the whole, and simultaneously contributes to the whole.

CHINESE INNOVATIONS

Of the above philosophical schools, T'ien-t'ai and Hua-yen are Chinese innovations, having no corresponding Indian antecedent. Their innovations consist of the following points.

1. Both schools used Indian Buddhist philosophical formants as a basis for constructing distinctly Chinese views of reality. The Indian Buddhist concept of emptiness (śūnyatā) was the most fruitful source of new ideas.
2. Both schools, but particularly Hua-yen, either consciously or unconsciously were influenced by indigenous Chinese presuppositions, chiefly those identified as Taoist, in interpreting Indian Buddhist ideas.
3. A doctrinal innovation which apparently appealed to the Chinese sensibility was the idea that the Absolute (Buddha, emptiness, etc.), while retaining its absolute nature, nevertheless became subject to conditions and devolved into the form of the conditioned, impure, mundane world. Either absent from, or merely germinal in, Indian Buddhism, this idea was probably due to Taoist influence. It is expressed in various Chinese pseudo-epigraphs such as the *Ta-ch'eng ch'i-hsin lun* ("Awakening of Faith in the Mahāyāna") and the chapter in the Hua-yen Ching (Avataṃsaka-sūtra) called "The Arising of the Tathāgata from Essential Nature."
4. Whereas the Indian doctrine of the interdependent origination of phenomena (*pratītya-samutpāda*) seems to have had as its function the devaluation of things by virtue of their emptiness, the Chinese interpreted the doctrine in a more positive manner, stressing the interdependence of things per se. Thus things in concrete nature assumed a positive value *when rightly viewed* as empty of independent existence and existent purely by virtue of their intercausality or interdependence.
5. There is a tendency in Chinese Buddhism to misconstrue the nature and function of the Indian doctrine of emptiness. Indians employed the concept as a device for destroying the conceptual approach to concrete existence, and thus emptiness referred to human *ideas* about existence and did not refer to concrete existence itself. The Chinese habitually spoke of emptiness as the true mode of existence of phenomenal reality.
6. In summary, it may be said that the preceding innovations had the general effect of sacralizing mundane things and experiences, with the proviso that things must be seen as they really are, in their "suchness."

SUGGESTED READING

Chan, Wing-tsit. *A Sourcebook in Chinese Philosophy*, pp. 336–424.
Chang, Garma Chen-Chi. *The Buddhist Teaching of Totality: The Philosophy of Hwa-yen Buddhism.*

Ch'en, Kenneth. *Buddhism in China*, pp. 297–364.
Hurvitz, Leon. "Chih-i." *Mélanges Chinois et Bouddhiques*, 12 (1962).
Robinson, Richard H. *Early Mādhyamika in India and China*, pp. 3–173.
Wright, Arthur F. *Buddhism in Chinese History*, pp. 20–85.

37

Chinese Buddhism and the Communist Regime

Roger J. Corless

IDEOLOGY

THE MARXIST-LENINIST-MAOIST POSITION

Theory. Religion is a symptom of a sick society: heal the society and its religion will vanish. Religion began as a nonrational response to natural calamities, which were assigned to gods or fate. With the evolution of social differentiation, religion was artificially perpetuated by the rulers/executioners/priests, who used superstitious fear to cow the masses. Marxism-Leninism removes the ruler class, and religion, exposed as a fraud and serving no further purpose, will then starve to death. Buddhism was used in China as an instrument of oppression. *Wei-shih* (Sanskrit: *Yogācāra*) is especially pernicious, since it locates suffering only in the mind, not in society, encouraging a resigned and passive peasantry. Ch'an was at first a popular, revolutionary movement, but it became corrupted by official patronage.

Practice. Initiate Class Struggle, guaranteeing freedom of religious *belief or disbelief* (not of *action*), and the masses will see how they have been duped. Accelerate the process by Party indoctrination and destruction of the religious institution (closing/destroying temples, etc., laicizing religion). Preserve/restore significant artifacts, e.g., Tun-huang and Kumbum, as inspiring examples of folk-creativity under ancient oppression.

BUDDHIST ADAPTATION

Theory. The Venerable *T'ai-hsü* (1890–1947) opposed Communism (*kung-ch'an* or common property), saying that only the realization of *anātman* would eliminate private property. Conversely, some contemporary Chinese Buddhists say Communism leads to a realization of anātman. *Po-chang* (720–814) had prescribed manual labor within the cloister: this is now extended to mean work for the benefit of the masses, fulfilling the Resolutions of *Samantabhadra* by returning to saṃsāra to construct *Sukhāvatī* in this world-realm. *Ahiṃsā* means harmlessness to good people, i.e., Party supporters.

Practice. The *Saṃgha* shifts from the contemplative to the active life, evolving a *vita mixta* of cottage industries or farm work by day, meditation/liturgy/study by night. (Information on lay practice is unavailable or unreliable; it may be a work ethic based on the Resolutions of Samantabhadra.)

CHRONOLOGY

MAINLAND CHINA

Since the reforms of *Ou-yang Ching-wu* (1871–1943; China Buddhist Association, 1912) and the Venerable T'ai-hsü (Chinese Buddhist Society, 1929), there has been a search for a viable contemporary Buddhism, especially vis-à-vis Marxism, emerging in the 1920s. A shift to this-worldly practice under lay leadership seems observable. This was accelerated after Communist control of the Mainland began (1929). The Land Reform Act of 1950 confiscated the glebe and reapportioned it to religious estates on the same basis as secular estates reapportioned to peasants (abbots were regarded as landlords). This resulted in extensive (?) laicization and, among the remaining religious groups, mutual aid teams (1954), cooperatives (1956), and communes (1958), and some monastic cottage industry, e.g., dyeing and weaving. The Chinese Buddhist Association was formed in 1953 to unite Buddhists under Party control and develop friendly relations with Buddhists overseas. It is apparently now defunct. The official periodical, *Hsien-tai Fo-hsüeh* (*Modern Buddhism*), was last issued in December 1964. A prohibition of stipends for liturgies was made in 1958, and political self-molding was encouraged and enforced. The New Constitution (1965) moved sharply against Buddhism, which was not withering fast enough. In August-September 1966, Red Guards destroyed the Four Olds, attacking many temples. There were reports of street processions of deposed Buddhist images, similar to the Festivals of the Burial of the Catholic Faith in France in the 1790s. Buddhism based on the city temples appears dead, but there are reports of functioning rural monasteries. The present extent of lay belief is indeterminable.

TIBET

In 1948 the *Dalai Lama* opposed the Communists. They marched on Tibet in 1950, and he fled to *Yatung* (i.e., *Sikkim* and *Bhutan*). After the Agreement of 1951, in which Peking guaranteed Tibet's autonomy but pledged to exterminate imperialism, he returned and visited Peking in 1952. Heavier taxes and land redistribution was imposed in 1955–56. The Tibetans rebelled in 1959 and were quickly crushed, with the destruction of monasteries and the killing or dispersing of monks, but the Dalai Lama and others escaped to India. Tibet was then vigorously sinicized. The 1959 report of the International Commission of Jurists called this genocide. The *Panchen Lama*, at first used by Peking as a substitute puppet, then denounced (1968), disappeared in 1969.

INTERPRETATION

Analyzing the condition of Buddhism under the Chinese Communist Regime is like forecasting the weather; the data are incomplete and of doubtful significance. The physical plant seems to have been destroyed more effectively than under Emperor *Wu-tsung* in 845. Some scholars (e.g., Holmes Welch, Arthur Wright) see this as the end, or nearly so, of Buddhism in China. Other scholars (e.g., David Yu) foresee a diffused Buddhism (of the Bonhoeffer religionless Christianity type?) with no formal *Bhikṣu-bhikṣuṇī-saṃgha*. Since Buddhism is basically the flavor of mokṣa added to different sociocultural mixtures, coexistence of some sort with Marxism-Leninism-Maoism may not be impossible. Holmes Welch, adopting a Jungian standpoint, wonders if present suppression may not lead to future explosion in a violent but unforeseeable form.

SUGGESTED READING

Bush, Richard C. *Religion in Communist China*, chaps. 1 and 9.

Chan, Wing-tsit. *Religious Trends in Modern China*, chaps. 2 and 3.

Ch'en, Kenneth K.S. *Buddhism in China*, pp. 460–70.

China Quarterly. This periodical has published a series of reports which are valuable: No. 6 (April-June 1961), pp. 1–14 (Holmes Welch); No. 22 (April-June 1965), pp. 14–30 (Kenneth Ch'en), pp. 143–53 (Holmes Welch); No. 40 (October-December 1969), pp. 127–36 (Holmes Welch).

Ling, Trevor. *Buddha, Marx and God*, pp. 154–61.

Ngag-dbang Blo-bzang Ye-shes bsTan-'dzin rGya-mtsho (His Holiness the 14th Dalai Lama). *My Land and My People*.

Thubten, Jigme Norbu. *Tibet is my Country*.

Trungpa, Chögyam. *Born in Tibet*.

Welch, Holmes. *The Buddhist Revival in China*.

———. *Buddhism under Mao*.

Wright, Arthur F. "Buddhism in Modern and Contemporary China." In *Religion and Change in Contemporary Asia*. Edited by Robert F. Spencer.

Yang, C.K. *Religion in Chinese Society*, chap. 14.
Yu, David C. "Buddhism in Communist China: Demise or Co-existence?" *Journal of the American Academy of Religion*, 39 (March 1971): pp. 48–61.

38

Introduction of Buddhism to Korea and Subsequent Development

Lewis R. Lancaster

INTRODUCTION

The earliest known religion in Korea is *Shamanism*, which came into the peninsula by way of Manchuria, spread southward by the Tungusic tribes. Even today Shamanism is widespread with a belief that ancient trees, bodies of water, unusual rock formations, house sites, the fertility of harvests, and human health are guarded or governed by spirits. The intermediary for humans and these spirits are priestesses known as *Mudang*, who are called upon to heal the sick and control the spirits or communicate with them.

Interwoven with the Shamanism was the Tun-gun myth, based on the idea that the son of the Creator had fallen in love with a maiden who had been transformed from her original form as a bear. She bore him a son, the semidivine Tun-gun, who was both the founder of the Korean nation and the son of the Creator.

THREE KINGDOM PERIOD

Into this tradition of Shamanism and the belief in Tun-gun came the Chinese traditions, particularly those of Confucianism and Buddhism. In the first century B.C. Chinese colonies had been set up in Korea and from them had spread many of the ideas of the mainland peoples.

Buddhism, according to traditional sources, was introduced into Koguryŏ when the monk *Shun-tao* (Korean: *Sundo*) came from China in A.D. 372, directed there from the court of *Fu Chien*, ruler of the Ch'in Dynasty. *Ibullan* was built for him, the first monastery for the Buddhists in Korea. Later, another monk came to Korea, *Mālānanda*, a Serindian, who is said to have spread the teaching to Paekche in 384.

The third kingdom of Silla put up more resistance to the new religion and clung more firmly than the other two to the older religious traditions. The first record of Buddhist activity there is the information that a Buddhist monk was sent from Koguryŏ in the middle of the fifth century. However, the problems faced by the monks must have been formidable, for the official date of introduction was not until 528, when the monk *Ichadon* was martyred.

During this period, Buddhism moved out of Korea to Japan when the king of Paekche sent texts and statues to the Japanese court.

During the sixth and seventh centuries, the process of sending Korean monks to China to study became widespread and they brought back the teachings and literatures of the various schools which were part of Chinese Buddhism: *T'ien-t'ai*, *Vinaya*, *San-lun*, *Satyasiddhi*, *Nirvāṇa*, and *Hua-yen*.

UNIFIED SILLA (688–935)

When the Silla Kingdom became powerful enough, it dominated the whole country and while Buddhism had found difficulty in being accepted there, it was during the period of Silla rule, a major institution.

It was at this time that the famous and later to be dominant teachings of the *Ch'an* school came to Korea. In 820 *Toui* went to China and studied with a third generation descendent of *Hui-nêng*, the Sixth Patriarch of the school. In Korea the Ch'an group known as *Sŏn* broke into nine branches, known as the nine "mountains" in monasteries scattered throughout the country.

KORYO PERIOD (935–1392)

During the Koryo period, Buddhism reached the height of its importance. The government sponsored projects such as monastery construction and art works.

Events on the continent impinged on Korea and the Mongols of Genghis Khan invaded. The government in an attempt to stop the attacks on the nation had carved on wooden blocks the Buddhist canon in Chinese translation. This set was destroyed when the Mongols arrived. Later *King Kojong* was exiled to Kanghwa Island, and there he initiated a new project to recarve the blocks. After nearly sixteen years, a second set was completed in the thirteenth century. It survives today in the mountain monastery of *Hae-in*, where the 81,258 panels are preserved as one of the national treasures of Korea.

YI DYNASTY

The Yi Dynasty adopted the Confucian teachings from China as the national norm. At first there was tolerance toward Buddhism, especially since the new dynasty needed support and Buddhism was a major social institution in the life of the people. However, by the reign of the third king, *Chungjong*, at the end of the fourteenth century, repressive measures against the powerful Buddhist community became evident. The number of sects was reduced to seven and the monasteries to a total of 242. This policy was continued under

Sejong, the fourth king, who reduced the number of sects from seven down to two. The *Sŏnjong* Meditation school was composed of the *Vinaya* school, the *T'ien-t'ai*, and *Ch'an*. The *Kyojong* or Textual school was a union of *Hua-yen*, *Yogācāra* (Chinese: *Fa-hsiang*), *Mādhyamika* (Chinese: *San-lun*), and a minor branch of the *T'ien-t'ai*. These two remained the official sectarian divisions until 1935.

Not every king of the Yi was hostile to the Buddhists. *Sejo*, for example, was a devout Buddhist, but his support was short-lived and his successor, *Sungjong*, a supporter of the Confucians, abolished the state-supported ceremonies of the Buddhists.

As the government stepped up its anti-Buddhist policies, monks began to move into mountain monasteries in order to practice undisturbed by political pressures. They were not out of touch with the problems of the nation, and when the Japanese warlord *Hideyoshi* invaded in 1592, some 5,000 soldier monks were in the field. The voluntary Buddhist militia was also active when the Manchus invaded in 1627 and 1637.

But while the Buddhists were willing to participate in the defense of the nation, the proscriptions against them became more severe, and in 1623 monks were barred from living in the capital or building monasteries there. Under *Hyojong* there was an edict barring the sons of daughters of the important families from seeking a career in the Saṃgha and those who were already in monasteries were urged to return to secular life.

Beset with such problems, it is not surprising to find the Buddhist reaching a low ebb of influence in Korea by the nineteenth century. However, through all the troubles there were from time to time great monks, learned and devout, who appeared in the Saṃgha and continued to inspire confidence and support from the believers.

SUGGESTED READING

It must be noted that much of the western literature about Korean Buddhism is limited and often out of date.

Clark, Charles Allen. *Religions of Old Korea.*

Lee, Peter H. *Lives of Eminent Korean Monks.*

Seo, Kyun-bo. *A Study of Korean Zen Buddhism Approached Through the Chodangjip.*

Starr, Frederick. *Korean Buddhism.*

39

Buddhism in Korea Survives Suppression and Change

Lewis R. Lancaster

INTRODUCTION

The Buddhism which emerged from the Yi Dynasty in Korea was dominated by the *Sŏnjong* or Meditation school. The practices of this form of Buddhism followed the most ancient pattern of Korean and Chinese monastic practice and represented a preservation of *Ch'an* which was not to be found in China in the present century or among the Zen sects of Japan. The task of preserving and indeed of even keeping alive the tradition of Buddhism had been a most difficult one in Korea. Under severe restrictions by the government, monks were even denied access to the capital and the religion had declined to only a fragment of its former influence.

When the proscription banning monks from the capital was lifted in 1895, a conference of all Japanese and Korean Buddhists was called in Seoul to discuss cooperation. This conference was followed by the establishment of the first headquarters and general business office in 1899.

JAPANESE CONTROL

When the Japanese assumed more control of Korean life, they began to import and encourage their own forms of Buddhism. One of the main differences between the Japanese and Korean clergy was the long tradition of married priests in Japan. It was inevitable that this issue would cause trouble in Korea where the strict celibacy of the *Vinaya* was observed. In 1908 the Japanese Resident-General was petitioned to give his permission for monks to be married, and the granting of that petition caused a division in the Korean Saṃgha between married and celibate monks which is still an issue of debate.

CONTACT OF JAPANESE AND KOREAN BUDDHISTS

The organization of the Buddhist Saṃgha was a victim of the international turmoil of those days. *Yi Hwae-kwang*, the leader of the Buddhist Sŏnjong national organization went to Japan in 1910 and consulted secretly with the *Sōtō* leaders regarding cooperation of Japanese and Korean Buddhists. When he returned to Korea, a group of monks with more nationalistic sentiments broke away from the group and set up their own headquarters in Pusan. The Japanese exerted their control in 1911 and closed the Pusan headquarters.

REORGANIZATION OF THE SAṂGHA

In 1922 a group of monks met and began to reorganize Buddhism. The sectarian divisions officially recognized by the government at that time were the *Sŏnjong* and *Kyojong* sects. Out of this meeting grew a serious movement to unite all Korean Buddhists into one body. This was finally achieved in 1935 and the *Chogye* sect was formed.

WAR YEARS AND AFTER

The Japanese control of Korea came to an end only after the Second World War. In 1949 the land reform movement took place and income-producing land was taken from the monasteries. In the South the repayment came in the form of government bonds, but for a period of time the monasteries were left with hardly any money for the support of resident monks. The situation was so critical that the government set aside arable farmland and woodland for their support. Today the money from the bonds has been invested and the Buddhists of South Korea once again have a financial base from which to operate.

In the North the government land reform was very difficult for the monasteries and from the limited information available it appears that Buddhism is no longer a viable social institution there.

SOUTH KOREAN BUDDHISM

Internal dissension rocked the Saṃgha, stemming from the edict of 1908 which had permitted married monks. The government gave its support to the celibates in 1954 and ordered all married abbots to leave the monasteries. The case was taken to court and a long battle raged until in 1962 an uneasy reconciliation took place and married monks were permitted to remain and hold every office in the national organization but the highest.

ADMINISTRATIVE ORGANIZATION

Although the deep division over the married monks was a handicap in the recovery of Buddhism in South Korea, some advances were made in the

1960s. The national organization continued to develop headed by a leader who holds the position for five-year terms. Under his direction are two councils, one composed of elder monks who are appointed for life. The real administrative power lies in the Central Council, which is made up of fifty monks and nuns.

ACTIVITIES

The Buddhists of South Korea have become active in education with Dongguk University in Seoul as their most important institution. In addition, they have set up schools for all ages across the country. One of the important new efforts has been in the area of youth groups and lay organizations, both of which have thrived in recent years.

Due to the government suppressions of Buddhism, they had never been able to make a complete translation of the canon. The famed blocks in *Hae-in Sa* are in Chinese and thus not available to the general population. In 1964 Dongguk University set in motion the project to translate the canon into modern Korean.

Today, Korean Buddhism has a following that may reach six million. The educational programs and the fact that its monasteries are the center of Korean cultural preservation from the past have given it a new lease on life. Monasteries are being built and the ancient ones are slowly being repaired. Thus there are some signs that Korean Buddhism may come out of its long period of decline and once again be an important part of Korean life.

SUGGESTED READING

It must be noted that much of the western literature about Korean Buddhism is limited and often out of date.

Clark, Charles Allen. *Religions of Old Korea.*
Lee, Peter H. *Lives of Eminent Korean Monks.*
Seo, Kyun-bo. *A Study of Korean Zen Buddhism Approached Through the Chodangjip.*
Starr, Frederick. *Korean Buddhism.*

40

Introduction of Buddhism to Japan and Its Development During the Nara Period

Francis H. Cook

INTRODUCTION

Though known by the Japanese earlier, Buddhism is given an official date of A.D. 538 (sometimes 552) for its introduction. At that time, Korea, anxious for political stability with Japan, sent emissaries laden with Buddha images and copies of several scriptures.

CONDITIONS SURROUNDING THE RECEPTION OF BUDDHISM

Independent warring clans (*uji*) had been subdued and brought under control by one dominant clan, which now acted as the one central authority for all. This ruling faction was in search of principles which would strengthen unification. The indigenous religion, *Shintō*, could not perform this function, because it had a weak ethic which did not emphasize unity and cooperation; moreover, the great diversity of Shintō *kami* afforded no single unifying factor.

The newly established government was aware of the cultural poverty of the country and felt a need to improve its status in the eyes of its Chinese neighbor. Buddhism was seen as a source of instant culture.

In the latter part of the sixth century, China became unified for the first time in centuries, and as its political and cultural brilliance spread centrifugally outward, Japan was one of the countries which felt this strong influence.

Korea, desiring political peace with Japan, began sending envoys, who frequently came laden with Buddhist materials. The Korean ruler recommended these Buddhist things as having a potential for bringing great benefit to the Japanese.

BUDDHISM: TANGIBLE AND INTANGIBLE ASSETS

It brought the Chinese fine arts and architecture, transforming the Nara Plain into a splendid panorama of Buddhist temples filled with images of Buddhas, Bodhisattvas, and celestial beings. It brought the Chinese writing system and the tradition of recording important events. This made the Japanese literate, with access to Chinese poetry, history, philosophy, science, and medicine.

In the growing stream of Buddhist scriptures which entered Japan, the Japanese found an ethic of tolerance, compassion, and nonviolence, which eliminated much of the cruelty and harshness of the people. This ethic did tend to mitigate some of the interclan rivalry and foster domestic peace and tranquillity.

In the minds of the Japanese rulers, the Buddha was seen as a super-kami, the source of a magical power even greater than that of the Shintō kami, to be used to ensure political tranquillity, health and prosperity, protection in battle, and protection from natural calamities.

With Buddhism came knowledge of the Chinese model of governmental administration, important to a country still experimenting with centralized authority.

MODE OF IMPORTATION AND UTILIZATION OF BUDDHISM: CONSEQUENCES FOR FUTURE DEVELOPMENT

From earliest times, when Buddhism was protected and nourished by the *Soga* clan, Buddhism came to be allied with the secular needs of powerful ruling factions. The early advocates of Buddhism were largely ignorant of the religious mission of Buddhism, and the cult centering around the Buddha image had as its sole end the magical protection of the ruler.

A close symbiotic relationship developed between the Buddhist *saṃgha* and secular authority. Buddhism depended on the court for protection and support, while the court looked to Buddhism for magic. In time, however, Buddhism came to be strongly controlled by the secular authorities, who feared its growing power, feeling an increasing threat from the saṃgha, which had designs on the throne.

In its close ties with the court, serving its needs in primarily magical ways, Buddhism became strongly formalistic and liturgical. The three legs of Buddhism—morality, meditation, and wisdom—were replaced with an empty formalism, devoid of religious concerns, the sole end of which was to entertain the nobility with extravagant and colorful ceremonies and to ensure the political, physical, and social health of the ruler and his court.

DEVELOPMENT

Probably the early course of the development of Buddhism was determined by the character and actions of *Shōtoku*, the prince regent (died 621). He is spoken of as the Japanese counterpart of the third century B.C. Indian emperor *Aśoka*, who was responsible for the early growth and expansion of Buddhism. Shōtoku is still revered by Japanese for his piety and wisdom.

Through his alleged commentaries on three important Buddhist scriptures—*Vimalakīrti-sūtra* (Japanese: *Yuima-kyō*), *Śrīmālādevī-sūtra* (Japanese: *Shōman-gyō*), and *Saddharmapuṇḍarīka-sūtra* (Japanese: *Hokke-kyō*)—he stressed a catholic form of Buddhism which transcended differences of class, sex, or religious status and affiliation. By stressing the universality of Buddha nature and the idea that all beings without exception are embraced by the Buddha's truth, he tried to eliminate the divisive forces in society which would weaken Japan.

His "Seventeen-Article Constitution," a mixture of Confucian and Buddhist moral and social ideals, enjoined subjects to deal with each other honestly and humanely, demanded of his court administrators that they deal with the people fairly and humanely, encouraged harmony as being beneficial to all, and recommended the Buddhist Three Treasures (Buddha, Dharma, and Saṃgha) as being the best of religions. In effect, he established Buddhism as the state religion through his support.

His real devotion, and the corollary royal support, led to the creation of many Buddhist temples and works of art, such as *Hōryū-ji* temple. Students and monks were sent to China, and Japanese monks were encouraged to study the scriptures.

THE NARA PERIOD

In 710, a permanent capitol was established at *Nara*, thus inaugurating a new phase in the development of Buddhism which was to last until 794, when the capitol was moved to the site of the present-day *Kyoto*. For Buddhism, it was a time of consolidation of its growing power and magnificence, of increasing corruption, and the establishment of the characteristic Nara form of Buddhism.

What we call Nara Buddhism consisted of six academic traditions which had been imported without modification from China at various times. These were the *Jōjitsu*, *Kusha*, *Sanron*, *Hossō*, *Ritsu*, and *Kegon* traditions. They were academic traditions or schools, rather than sects, being primarily concerned with the study, exegesis, and propagation of certain aspects of Buddhist philosophy. They did not proselytize and had little intercourse with the common people. The Hossō school was probably the most powerful politically, while the Kegon philosophy was influential in the realm of political and social theory.

Buddhism continued to grow in the number of monks and temples, and with this growth there occurred a growth in the purely secular concerns of the saṃgha, resulting in political intrigue and corruption.

GROWTH

Much of the growth can be attributed to the Emporer *Shōmu*, perhaps the most devout and energetic of all Japanese sovereigns, under whom many new temples and works of art were created. Most notable was the erection of *Tōdai-ji*, the headquarters temple of the Kegon School, which was dedicated in 752. It houses the immense 53-foot sitting bronze image of the Buddha *Vairocana*.

Shōmu's daughter, Empress *Shōtoku*, like her father was energetic in furthering the interests of Buddhism, issuing many royal edicts fostering Buddhist ideals. In an edict of 765, she stated her duties as first to Buddhism, second to Shintō, and third to the people.

The Hossō monk *Gyōgi* is an example of the type of monk who did much to increase the prestige of the saṃgha. He performed many acts of charity for the common people, came to be a trusted advisor of the Emperor Shōmu, and was instrumental in the erection of Tōdai-ji. He was called *Gyōgi Bosatsu* (Sanskrit: Bodhisattva) in recognition of his superior qualities.

INTRIGUE AND CORRUPTION

Temples and land were donated by the court, thus encouraging saṃgha efforts to form close connections with the court. The custom of commanding a number of men each year to become monks in order to gain merit for the ruler had the effect not only of swelling the ranks of the priesthood, but of filling the ranks with men who had no real religious vocation as well. As connections with the court increased the wealth and power of the saṃgha, more and more men became monks with the sole object of gaining rank, power, and wealth.

Court fears of the power of Buddhism were not unjustified. The devout Empress Shōtoku fell under the magnetic influence of the Hossō monk *Dōkyō*, who apparently was ambitious enough to aspire to ruling Japan. Since ecclesiastical titles were awarded by the court, monks who aspired to high rank tended to be conformist and at the same time to enter into intrigues with members of the court.

Overly close connections between the court and saṃgha were encouraged by the bureaucratic structure of the government. Under the *Taihō* reforms of

702, the saṃgha was administratively set down as a department of government. Buddhism from the beginning saw its mission as being coterminous with state needs. It therefore felt satisfied to do the bidding of the court, but with the proviso that it would be suitably rewarded.

CONCLUSION

In conclusion, it may be said that the course of Buddhism during its first 250 years in Japan was both inspiring and disheartening. It gave much of beauty and usefulness to the few who could enjoy it, and though restricted to a fortunate few, it began to exert its spiritual and ethical influence on them, softening their hearts and raising their minds to something beyond material things. At the same time, we witness a Buddhism firmly under the royal thumb, subservient, conformist, and opportunistic. While there were a few saints like Gyōgi, there were far more men to whom the saṃgha was a steppingstone to a life of luxury and privilege. In all this, the common people were left outside the temple doors, so to speak. It was, by and large, a condition that would persist until the social and religious upheavals of the *Kamakura Period*.

SUGGESTED READING:

de Visser, M.W. *Ancient Buddhism in Japan*. 2 vols.
Eliot, Sir Charles. *Japanese Buddhism*, pp. 179–232.
Kitagawa, Joseph. *Religion in Japanese History*, pp. 3–45.
Watanabe, Shoku. *Japanese Buddhism: A Critical Appraisal*, pp. 8–110.

41

Heian, Kamakura, and Tokugawa Periods in Japan

Francis H. Cook

HEIAN PERIOD

The *Heian Period* began in 794 when the Emperor *Kammu* moved his court to the site of modern-day *Kyoto* (then called Heian), probably to separate himself from the power of the Nara Buddhists and the intrigue of powerful families. In terms of power, prestige, and magnificence, the Heian Period was probably the high-water mark for Japanese Buddhism. Several important events and tendencies of the period were to have far-reaching consequences for later Japanese Buddhism.

IMPORTATION OF TWO MORE SCHOOLS OF BUDDHISM FROM CHINA

Tendai (Chinese: *T'ien-t'ai*) Buddhism was brought to Japan from China by *Saichō* (*Dengyō Daishi*) early in the ninth century. It quickly became almost a state religion, assuming great power with the court. While granting primary importance to the *Lotus Sūtra*, it was avowedly eclectic and syncretic, a prime example of one-vehicle Buddhism (*ichijō Bukkyō*), which aimed at embracing all forms of Buddhism within one comprehensive scheme of religious emancipation. (See the information on Chinese T'ien-t'ai in the lecture on Chinese Academic Schools and Doctrinal Innovations.)

Shingon (Chinese: *Chen-yen*) was introduced to Japan by *Kūkai* (*Kōbō Daishi*) upon his return from China in the first decade of the ninth century. Japanese Shingon is a form of the *Tantric* Buddhism which also entered Tibet, Nepal, and other countries. It is characterized by a belief in *Vairocana* as the cosmic Buddha. It was very popular with the court and nobility because of the grandeur and color of its rituals, and came to supplant Tendai as the favorite of the capitol. Kūkai was a great favorite with the court.

SETTING UP AN ORDINATION PLATFORM ON MT. HIEI

In doing this Saichō accomplished two important goals. He demonstrated the independence of the Tendai sect from the Nara schools. And he instituted a new ordination of monks more in keeping with Mahāyāna principles, which was to be fruitful in *Kamakura* times.

APPEARANCE OF HOLY MEN (HIJIRI) IN INCREASING NUMBERS

Critical of established schools, the hijiri worked independently of institutionalized forms. They were eclectic, using many different, often unorthodox, methods to reach the common people. They tended to disregard traditional regulations for monks—meat-eating, wearing distinctive robes, etc.—thus setting the stage for later secularizing and popularizing developments, and frequently taught a simple means of salvation—the invocation of a Buddha's name, usually that of *Amida*. There was also growing contact with common people and an increasing influence among sophisticated nobles.

DEVELOPMENT OF KNOWLEDGE OF BUDDHIST THEORY OF MAPPŌ AND A CORRESPONDING PESSIMISM

Many believed that the period of the decay of Buddha's teaching, and the corollary inability of men to achieve emancipation, would arrive in the middle of the eleventh century. This was predicted in Buddhist scriptures. The social, political, and religious chaos of the late Heian Period led many to see these as a corroboration of the theory of *mappō*.

STEADY GROWTH IN THE AMIDA CULT

Though the invocation of *Amida's* name as a means of salvation was used in the Tendai school, and before that, the cult began to grow on an extra-institutionalized level in mid-Heian times. While the earlier cult had consisted of the invocation of Amida's name as a means of aiding the spirits of the dead, the new cult grew out of the fears of a leisured, wealthy aristocracy for the "next world." The new cult was aided and abetted by the hijiri, who utilized it as a simple means of salvation available to all, and grew out of the personal charisma of men like *Kūya* (903–972) and *Genshin* (942–1017), rather than out of the charisma of institutional Buddhism.

While the Heian Period was marked by cultural brilliance and the appearance of sincere, concerned monks, such as Saichō, Kūkai, Kūya, Genshin, and many others, the general state of Buddhism was one of continued corruption, ambition, and cynicism. Increasing rivalry between schools of Buddhism, which by now had their own armies of monk-soldiers, led to bloody fights, burning of temples, and perpetual intrigue.

The power of the huge Tendai monastic complex on Mt. Hiei led to clashes between monks and court guards. The *inke* system, started during the Nara Period, whereby wealthy nobles "donated" their lands to monasteries and temples, thereby avoiding taxation but still receiving the financial benefits, led to an increasingly wealthy saṃgha, eager to cooperate with powerful factions. And the system whereby emperors retired from office to become monks, often retaining real power, led to a corrupt relationship between government and saṃgha.

KAMAKURA PERIOD

The *Kamakura Period* began in 1192 with a shift in real ruling power from the Heian court to a group of *samurai* who established headquarters at Kamakura. Civil power was to remain in the hands of the military until the *Meiji Restoration* in 1867. With the political revolution, there also occurred during the Kamakura Period a religious revolution, characterized by the emergence of distinctly Japanese, popular forms of Buddhism.

Pure Land Buddhism (*Jōdo*) was started by *Hōnen* (1133–1212), who based his new religion on the teachings of *Genshin* (particularly his "Essentials for Rebirth in the Pure Land") and those of the Chinese Pure Land teacher *Shan-tao*. Dissatisfied with traditional Buddhist means of emancipation, and a victim of *mappō* pessimism, he taught that the only way for wicked people in mappō to be saved is to recite the name of *Amida* (*Namu Amida Butsu*) with faith that Amida would ensure their rebirth in his paradise in the Western region after their death.

The *True Teaching of the Pure Land* (*Jōdo Shinshū*) was the creation of *Shinran* (1173–1263), a disciple of Hōnen. On the basis of his own reading of Buddhist literature and his own religious nature, he taught that one need not, and should not, try to earn one's way into the Pure Land of Amida by reciting Amida's name or by performing other meritorious acts. One need only have faith that Amida, in accordance with his vows, has already assured all rebirth in his paradise. Rebirth in the Pure Land results from an act of compassion and love on the part of Amida, not from our own efforts.

Nichiren Buddhism is the only sect of Buddhism named after its founder, *Nichiren* (1222–1282). Like Hōnen and Shinran, he studied at the Tendai monastery on Mt. Hiei, but was not satisfied with traditional Buddhist methods. He came to feel that the truth of Buddhism was embodied in the *Lotus Sūtra* (*Saddharmapuṇḍarīka-sūtra*) and that all other teachings such as Zen and Pure Land were wrong. He taught that salvation could be attained by reciting the name of the Lotus Sūtra with the words "*Nam Myōhō Renge Kyō*" ("Hail to the Scripture of the Lotus of the True Teaching") and gazing at a diagram (*daimoku*) with the faith that the Buddha, the scripture which embodies the truth, and living beings, are all one. He had a strongly nationalistic streak in his nature and was intolerant of other forms of Buddhism, and his life was marked by conflict with civil authorities and other Buddhists.

Eisai (1141–1215) introduced *Rinzai Zen* (Chinese: *Lin-ch'i*) to Japan upon returning from a trip to China. Whereas meditation had been an integral part of many of the former schools, under Eisai it became the central purpose of his school. The primary method of achieving enlightenment (*satori*) lay in the use of the *kōan*, enigmatic words or phrases of earlier Zen masters which, when meditated upon, have the effect of thwarting the conceptualizing faculty of the mind. The individual, freed of concepts, is thus brought into contact with the real world of "suchness."

Dōgen (1200–1253) studied Zen in China and brought back to Japan the tradition later to be identified with the Chinese *Ts'ao-tung* (Japanese: *Sōtō*) form of Zen. Under Dōgen, a form of Zen was taught in which the individual does nothing but sit (*zazen*) in the faith that he is already a Buddha, and that the zazen is an organic unfolding of Buddha nature. Since one *is* a Buddha, zazen is not practiced in order to *become* a Buddha. When all selfish graspings after such things as enlightenment are abandoned, and he can sit in zazen with no desire, his true nature will begin to reveal itself.

Characteristics of Kamakura Buddhism included distinctive forms of the teachings, which grew out of the personal experiences of the founders. Followers of the new schools tended to be attracted to the personalities of the founders. There was a heavy emphasis on the element of faith in all forms of the new schools, even in Zen, which was perhaps a reflection of the spirit of the times. All Kamakura schools taught simple methods which could be utilized regardless of level of intelligence or learning, occupation, sex, or class. Dōgen's Zen was called farmer's Zen because it could be practiced even by a farmer. Due to the directness, simplicity, and promise of salvation of their teachings, the new schools were popular and had mass appeal. In contradistinction to the older schools, these schools emphasized religious concern and practice, and offered means of salvation in a time of social and political chaos.

Kamakura Buddhism gave a strong impetus to the development of the arts. The tea ceremony, black-ink paintings (*sumi-e*), *Noh* theater, and *haiku* poems, for instance, were directly influenced by Zen, and often the foremost masters were associated with Zen. The simplicity of Zen life was attractive to the samurai rulers of Kamakura Japan, and as fighters, they were attracted to a discipline which would help them function more effectively in combat.

Whereas many of the military rulers of Kamakura Japan were devotees of the newer religions, there was often much friction between religious and civil groups, occasioned by the fear of the power of religious groups by civil authority and the frequent uncooperativeness of religious groups. This friction reached a peak when *Oda Nobunaga* destroyed the huge Tendai monastic complex on Mt. Hiei in 1571, and later, the Shingon stronghold of Negoro and the Jōdo Shinshū stronghold in Osaka were destroyed. Part of the reason Christian missionaries were welcomed at this time was that it was felt that Christianity would detract from some of the Buddhist power and influence. When the missionaries in turn became involved politically, they were expelled from Japan.

TOKUGAWA PERIOD

Nearly 400 years of warfare and destruction ended in the establishment of the *Tokugawa* regime in 1603, when *Iyeyasu Tokugawa* seized control and set up a military dictatorship lasting until 1867. During these centuries, Japan was completely isolated from the outside world, and Buddhism, as well as all areas of life, was strictly controlled by the military *shoguns*. For Buddhism, even in its Kamakura forms, it was a time of stagnation and degeneration.

New schools which had evolved in part as reactions to the corruption and inertia of institutionalized religion became themselves tightly organized institutions. These schools which in the beginning had appealed to all people in a spirit of egalitarianism became narrow and exclusive. The destruction of Mt. Hiei, Negoro, and Osaka had destroyed Buddhist centers of power, and strict regulation by the shoguns precluded any future concentration of power. The Tokugawa policy of forcing all Japanese to register as members of some (any) sect created mostly a nominal adherence to Buddhism. But new forms of Buddhism were just as eager as the Nara and Heian schools to accommodate themselves to secular power in return for privileges.

Despite the fossilization of the Buddhist saṃgha during Tokugawa rule, many monks continued to exemplify the very finest ideals of compassion. Among those who devoted their lives to helping people in need, often at the expense of personal sacrifice, the names of *Bassui*, *Shōsan Suzuki*, *Takuan*, *Tetsugen*, and *Hakuin* should be mentioned.

SUGGESTED READING

Anesaki, Masaharu. *Nichiren, the Buddhist Prophet.*

Bellah, Robert. *Tokugawa Religion.*

Bloom, Alfred. *Shinran's Gospel of Pure Grace.*

Coates, H.H., and Ishizuka, Ryagaku. *Hōnen, the Buddhist Saint: His Life and Teachings.*

Dumoulin, Heinrich. *History of Zen Buddhism* (particularly the chapter on Dōgen).

Eliot, Sir Charles. *Japanese Buddhism*, pp. 233–431.
Kitagawa, Joseph. *Religion in Japanese History*, pp. 46–130.
Masunaga, Reihō. *A Primer of Sōtō Zen.*
Sansom, Sir George. *Japan, A Short Cultural History* (revised), pp. 222–30, 244–46, 327–39, 368–400.
Suzuki, Daisetz Teitarō. *Introduction to Zen Buddhism.*
———. *Shin Buddhism.*
———. *Zen and Japanese Culture.*
Watanabe, Shoku. *Japanese Buddhism: A Critical Appraisal*, pp. 8–161.
Yamamoto, Kosho. *An Introduction to Shin Buddhism.*
Yampolsky, Philip B. *The Zen Master Hakuin.*

42

Japanese Innovations in Buddhism

Francis H. Cook

INNOVATIONS COMMON TO MOST OR ALL FORMS OF JAPANESE BUDDHISM

Nonadherence to traditional Buddhist codes of conduct (*śīla* and *Vinaya*).

1. The śīla code prohibited any sexual activity for monks, but Japanese monks for centuries have married at their option, after completion of training. The custom is ascribed to the example of *Shinran*, founder of *Jōdo Shinshū*.
2. Both monks and laymen commonly eat meat, which is prohibited under the śīla injunction against killing.
3. The śīla prohibition against consuming alcoholic drinks is broken by both monks and laymen.
4. Indian Buddhist monks could own only two robes, made of reclaimed rags, but Japanese monks, particularly high-ranking priests, wear elaborate robes of brocaded silk.

Japanese Buddhism is characterized by a tendency toward a "dechurched" form of religious activity. Devotional acts are commonly performed in the home, before a family altar, rather than at a temple.

Since the *Kamakura Period*, there has been a breakdown of the traditional distinction between the monk and the layman. The office of the monk is distinguished by function, rather than by a belief that he possesses any special power, is more religiously oriented, has a special charisma, or lives a different kind of life. He is the caretaker of temples, knows Buddhist liturgy, and officiates at funerals. Whereas ecclesiastical office, the position of spiritual preceptor, management of temples, or other positions of authority traditionally were gained by seniority or special talent, in Japan, temples are transferred from priest-father to priest-son, as is ecclesiastical authority. Priests frequently are sons of priests in a family tradition of the priesthood.

There is, in Japanese Buddhism of the Kamakura type, a tendency to reduce the many traditional types of devotional practice to a single practice, on the theory that a certain practice is the only right one, or that all other practices are included in the one.

1. In *Hōnen's Jōdo Buddhism*, it is felt that the *nembutsu* (recitation of *Amida's* name) is the only efficient means of being reborn in the Pure Land of Amida. His disciple, Shinran, reduced all practices to the matter of faith, rejecting all other methods such as meditation as ineffectual. Both Jōdo and Jōdo Shinshū base their position on the notion that in the period of *mappō* (the decline of religion), beings are too wicked and stupid to perform difficult practices.
2. *Dōgen*, founder of Japanese *Sōtō Zen*, felt that all practices were included in the simple act of doing *zazen*. While other practices were not forbidden, he felt that sitting in meditation was enough.
3. *Nichiren Buddhism* places complete emphasis on reciting the *daimoku* ("*Nam Myōhō Renge Kyō*"; i.e., "Homage to the Sūtra of the Lotus of the True Law") in the belief that all beings are consubstantial with the Buddha, who in turn is nothing but the truth as embodied in the title of the scripture.

Characteristic of Kamakura forms of Buddhism is a strong, even dominant, emphasis on the importance of faith. Although faith is not entirely absent from older and non-Japanese forms of Buddhism, Zen, Pure Land, and Nichiren are remarkable for the centrality of this aspect to their systems. This is probably due in part to the personalities of the founder of these religions, and in part to the search by each founder for a religious practice which all people could practice.

Japanese Buddhism is perhaps unique in the extent to which it is expressed in artistic or esthetic modes. Buddhism may be the actual source of the art, as in the tea ceremony, it may supply the ideological foundation for the art, or it may be practiced using an art form or esthetic expression as a vehicle.

1. Esthetic elements such as simplicity, directness, *sabi*, and *wabi*, are basically elements of Buddhist religious consciousness.
2. *Haiku* (seventeen-syllable poems) at their best are literary remains of a fleeting glimpse of existence just as it really is (*sono mama*).
3. Traditional martial arts such as swordsmanship and archery can serve as disciplines which develop the no-mind (*mu-shin*) state of Zen consciousness.
4. Buddhist temple ritual attempts to appeal not only to the mind, but

to the whole body of the worshipper, through the careful utilization of fragrance (incense), the visually beautiful (flowers), light (candles), and sound (chant).

5. The tea ceremony, properly conducted, attempts to give the participants a taste of Zen consciousness by means of the actual taste of the tea, the architecture of the tea house, the simplicity and elegance of the utensils, and the spirit with which the ceremony is conducted.

Many of the above examples are expressions of a loss in Japanese Buddhism of a sense of the distinction between the purely sacred and the profane. In its most extreme form, this results in the attitude that "ordinary everyday life is the life of the Buddha." One need not enter a monastery, practice meditation, follow any special code of conduct, or in fact do anything extraordinary. *Shōsan Suzuki*, a sixteenth-century Zen monk, said, "Farming is nothing but a Buddhist exercise. If your intention is bad, farming is a lowly work; but if you are deeply religious, it is the saintly work of a Bodhisattva."

INNOVATIONS OF PARTICULAR SECTS

Besides the foregoing innovations, which are common to many or all forms of Japanese Buddhism, several sects founded during the Kamakura Period are either unique to Japan or have developed in ways different from their Chinese antecedents.

Nichiren's Buddhism has no Chinese or Indian antecedents, being evolved from his own personality and his understanding of the Buddhist scriptures. His search for truth led him to believe that the *Lotus Sūtra* (*Saddharma-puṇḍarīka-sūtra*) contained the final and complete teaching of the Buddha, all other scriptures being incomplete or purely provisional. He felt that he alone possessed the truth, other sects such as Zen and Pure Land being in error, pernicious, and destructive to national welfare. He thought he was the incarnation of the Bodhisattva *Viśiṣṭacārita* who, in the Lotus Sūtra, was predicted to return in the period of the *decline of the Dharma* (*mappō*). He taught that beings, the truth, and the Buddha are all one, embodied in the title of the Lotus Sūtra, and that one may identify himself with this truth by gazing at a picture of the name of the sūtra along with names of the Buddha and other Bodhisattvas (the *honzon*) and reciting the name of the sūtra with the formula *Nam Myōhō Renge Kyō* (the *daimoku*) with faith in the truth of this teaching. Nichiren Buddhism is thus innovative in stressing faith and having as its object of worship the title of a scripture.

Shinran inherited the Pure Land tradition from the Chinese via *Genshin* and *Hōnen*, but the sect which he founded differs from all predecessors.

Based on three sūtras which tell of a Buddha named *Amida* (Infinite Light) and his paradise or Pure Land in the Western region, Chinese Pure Land Buddhism was a simple matter of reciting the name of Amida with faith that Amida would ensure one's rebirth in his Pure Land after death. Thus the recitation (Japanese: *nembutsu*) and the element of faith were central to the practice. This was also the teaching of Genshin and Hōnen. Shinran's innovation lay in rejecting any other practice but faith itself, even the recitation of the nembutsu. His understanding of the scriptures led to the positions that beings in the time of mappō are too wicked and corrupt to engage in meditation, austerities, etc., and Amida, who alone is capable of good, has transferred his merit to beings and thereby ensured our rebirth in the Pure Land. Thus the source of rebirth is not our own efforts (*jiriki*), but the power and goodness of Amida (*tariki*). To try to earn the right to be reborn in the Pure Land is, in effect, a denial of the truth which is that Amida has already done it for us. We therefore need only have faith in the vows which Amida has made ensuring this rebirth. Even this faith is a gift of Amida through his boundless grace, and hence we neither need to, nor must try to, earn the right of rebirth. Pure Land Buddhism, in effect, is a rejection of the traditional seeking of *nirvāṇa* in favor of a heaven-like paradise, and it is, likewise, a nontraditional belief that another being can save us.

Present-day Japanese *Sōtō Zen* is traced to the efforts of *Dōgen*, who, unable to satisfy his spiritual yearnings at home, journeyed to China in search of the truth. His method, called *zazen* (sitting Zen), was taught as a method accessible to everyone, regardless of social rank, sex, or occupation, for all one needs to do is sit in the cross-legged full lotus position and empty the mind of discursive thought. The technique is aided by breath control, counting of breaths, etc. In *shikantaza*, the perfection of this technique, one just sits, unaided by any other device. Dōgen believed that all things are Buddhas just as they are, and to perform any religious act as a means of becoming a Buddha was a denial of this truth. Therefore we must just sit, in the faith that we are already Buddhas, and that this sitting is, in fact, an outward expression of our true Buddha nature. We must learn to do zazen with no thought of attaining anything, for the moment a selfish thought arises, our true Buddha nature becomes obscured. For Dōgen, desireless, purposeless sitting and faith in our intrinsic Buddhahood are the keys to realizing our true being in everyday life.

SUGGESTED READING

Anesaki, Masaharu. *Nichiren, the Buddhist Prophet.*

Bloom, Alfred. *Shinran's Gospel of Pure Grace.*
Dumoulin, Heinrich. *History of Zen Buddhism* (particularly the chapter on Dōgen).
Eliot, Sir Charles. *Japanese Buddhism*, pp. 179–431.
Herrigel, Eugen. *Zen in the Art of Archery.*
Kapleau, Philip. *The Three Pillars of Zen.*
Masunaga, Reihō. *A Primer of Sōtō Zen.*
Suzuki, Daisetz Teitarō. *Zen and Japanese Culture.*

43

Japanese Buddhism and the New Religions

Francis H. Cook

INTRODUCTION

The most remarkable aspect of contemporary Japanese Buddhism is the appearance and considerable growth of the new religions (*shinkō shūkyō*). By new religions is meant those forms of contemporary, popular Buddhism which grew out of older, established forms, but which in some respects diverge in doctrine, practice, and goal from the parent religions. The following characteristics indicate the nature of the new religions.

All are new both in the sense that they diverge in many ways from the older religions and in the sense that all have arisen in the last hundred years. In fact, most began in the present century, and most of them after the Second World War. Since 1945, over 170 new sects have been recorded. They are not the religions of monk-professionals, but rather of laymen, particularly of the economically and socially frustrated groups in Japanese society. Put in another way, the new religions seem to have no appeal to people who are well educated, fairly affluent, or occupied with satisfying and meaningful occupations.

The goals of these new groups are not, in practice, other-worldly—occupied with emancipation or salvation in the Buddhist sense, which is merely incidental in these religions. Rather, members seem to be overwhelmingly concerned with materialistic goals, such as financial success, good health, power. Faith healing, for instance, is often the most obvious factor in attracting dedicated members.

Part of the appeal of these groups lies in a psychology of revolution (in the spiritual sense), individual and group achievement of immediate goals considered important to the group, struggle, and purpose. Publications of these groups are filled with words such as struggle, advance, overcoming obstacles, progress, challenge, and success. Another appeal of these groups lies in their ability to organize adherents in such a manner that the individual simultaneously finds satisfaction in identifying with a small, like-minded group, and with a larger, successful organization which is self-defined as being the wave of the future, the hope of mankind, etc. The smaller organizational unit furnishes the individual with friends, social gatherings, and a general sense of belonging, while the larger unit satisfies the individual's need for self-importance and participation in great events transcending the individual, neighborhood, or community.

FOUNDATIONS

Various reasons have been given for the phenomenon of the new religions. The new religions fill a void in the social and religious spheres of life created with the defeat of Japan in 1945. Defeat brought with it the collapse of older values and institutions, and the new religions function as a means of restoring confidence, giving a sense of purpose and destiny, and giving a sense of identity.

Urban Japan, as a good example of mass society with its concomitant problems, creates feelings of frustration, boredom, and insignificance on the part of the poor and the working class. The new religions offer these anonymous people a sense of importance and achievement in their achievement of rank and recognition in the organization's hierarchy, and in leadership roles and efforts to enlist new members. The older established religions seem to have been incapable of helping a nation of people who, since the Meiji Restoration, and particularly since 1945, have witnessed vast changes in society. Social unrest frequently is accompanied by religious experimentation and innovation. It must be said that the new religions have succeeded in giving the Japanese new perspectives on life where the more conservative older religions have been impotent.

The amazing growth of new religious sects since 1945 probably is due in part to the lifting of prewar and wartime bans on these religions. When the occupation authorities insisted in making religious freedom a part of Japan's new constitution, they created a climate favorable to the emergence of formerly repressed groups as well as the arising of entirely new groups.

AN EXEMPLARY MODEL: SŌKAGAKKAI

Some indication of the nature of the new religions can be seen in the example of *Sōkagakkai*. It is the largest and most active of the new religions, and it is of consuming interest to students of Japanese culture.

The origin of Sōkagakkai (Society for the Creation of Value) lies in the amalgamation by *Tsunesaburō Makiguchi*, during the early part of the present century, of the thirteenth-century Buddhism of *Nichiren* (1222–1282) with his own secular theory of value creation. The teaching was further refined by *Jōsei Toda* and is now in the process of further modification under the leadership of *Daisaku Ikeda*, the third president of the organization.

Objects of worship consist of the *daimoku*, or magic formula, which is *Nam Myōhō Renge Kyō* (Homage to the Scripture of the Lotus of the True Law), chanted by the devotee, the *gohonzon*, a picture containing the above formula along with the names of various Buddhas and Bodhisattvas which the devotee gazes at as he chants, and the *kaidan*, the religious center and future world center of religion and government. Religious practices consist of daily services before the family altar, which contains the gohonzon, along with numerous repetitions of the formula.

In practice, Sōkagakkai, which in theory considers traditional Buddhist goals to be the ultimate value, is a mechanism for material advancement among the socially and economically frustrated segments of the society. By sincerely chanting the daimoku, the practitioneer is promised such things as job promotion, financial success, family harmony, the ability to give up smoking or drinking, alleviation of physical ills, and greater confidence and poise.

Sōkagakkai has been very active in proselytizing since the end of the war. In fact, the goal of Sōkagakkai is no less than the ultimate conversion of everyone to its faith, and in recent years it has gone abroad to other Asian countries, Africa, the Americas, and Europe in its effort to convert the world. It is notorious for its conversion tactics, best known of which is *shakubuku* (Smash and Flatten), an aggressive, persistent, often violent attempt to wear down the resistence of the victim by means of threats, destruction of rival altars and religious objects, economic sanctions, and mass assaults on the home of the victim. Perhaps the major obligation of each member is to convert his family and friends to Sōkagakkai.

While many of the new religions are tolerant and inclusive, Sōkagakkai is well known for its extreme intolerance of any other religion. It is felt that any recognition of the rights or truth of another religious group is an admission of something less than total faith in one's own group. Since Sōkagakkai is the true religion and the hope of mankind, it is felt that it is an exercise in compassion to make members of other religions see the error of their ways. Although many religious groups no doubt would like to exert political influence, Sōkagakkai alone has been able to do so, because of its vast membership. Under the leadership of Ikeda, it has managed to make its desires known, and with the election of its own representatives to the Japanese Diet, it has become a political force to be reckoned with. This political power combined with the self-admitted intolerance of the society have led some observers to fear for the future freedom of religion in Japan.

IMPACT

The new religions have made a considerable impact on the religious and social life of Japan, and whatever they may offer their followers, they have also had the effect of making the established sects take a few faltering steps in the direction of accommodation with the twentieth century. Conservative as all religious establishments are, their efforts have been hesitant and reluctant, but a few developments indicate their felt need to infuse new vitality into their systems.

Perhaps one of the most encouraging signs is the great amount of excellent basic research into the historical and doctrinal roots of Buddhism, in an attempt to learn more about the religion. Part of the purpose of this vast flood of research is to be able to objectively distinguish between what is authentically Buddhist and what is not.

Some sects, such as *Jōdo Shinshū*, have in recent years begun to try to update their teachings through a criticism and reinterpretation of basic tenets of their faith. Through a process of demythologization they have sought to explain in more meaningful terms such matters as the nature and locus of the Buddha, the real locus of the Pure Land, and the nature of emancipation. This activity is being carried on by a few within Shinshū, while it is probably safe to say that the power hierarchy has been reactionary.

The Zen sect has, in the persons of a few individuals, tried to break away from sectarian differences. Some Zen masters have willingly chosen the best elements from both the *Rinzai* and *Sōtō*, and even from non-Zen sects, and combined these into effective methods of Zen enlightenment, rather than to insist that the individual restrict himself to the practices of one sect. It is felt that if Buddhism is to remain a viable religion in the twentieth century, sectarian distinctions must be eliminated.

CONCLUSION

In the last hundred years, with Japan's increasing intercourse with the West and with its own modernization and corollary changes in its basic attitudes and behavioral patterns, Buddhism has been faced with the same crisis it was faced with when the reins of power changed from the hands of the aristocrats to those of the samurai commoners at the end of the Heian Period. Important changes within Buddhism at that time saved it from complete stagnation and irrelevance. With an equally great social change now occurring in Japan, it remains to be seen if established Buddhism can once again accommodate itself to change. So far, this accommodation has taken place in the new religions, outside the structure of the Nara and Kamakura sects.

SUGGESTED READING

Earhart, H. Byron. *Japanese Religion: Unity and Diversity*, pp. 82–98.
Kitagawa, Joseph. *Religion in Japanese History*, pp. 262–340.
McFarland, H. Neill. *The Rush Hour of the Gods.*
Schecter, Jerrold. *The New Face of the Buddha*, pp. 253–73.
Thomsen, Harry. *The New Religions of Japan.*
White, James W. *The Sokagakkai and Mass Society.*

44
Buddhism in Tibet

Stephan V. Beyer

INTRODUCTION

The unique character of Tibetan Buddhism derives primarily from two sources: Indian Buddhism, as it developed during and after the Gupta Dynasty, and the native religious traditions of Tibet. Later Indian Buddhism was transmitted to Tibet through two separate but complementary institutional channels: the scholars and academicians of the great monastic universities, and the wandering saints of the Tantric tradition.

THE MONASTIC UNIVERSITY

The great monastic universities founded during the Gupta Dynasty were the central institutions of learning for the entire Buddhist world. The governance of the Tibetan monastery was based almost entirely upon this Indian prototype, and even Tibetan monastic costume is modeled on the academic robes of the Indian university.

Curricular Buddhism. But perhaps more important is the fact that these universities developed the concept of a logical and universal Buddhist philosophy, which would incorporate all that had gone before, and synthesize on appropriate levels what had at one time seemed profound doctrinal differences. Metaphysical disagreement was thus subordinated to the concept of a scholastic curriculum, embracing all the arts and sciences of the time, and where differences remained, they were seen simply as devices for leading the student gradually into a deeper understanding of the truth. The creative work had been done; all that was left was to work out the details.

Thus the university scholars who brought Buddhism to Tibet had been trained not to explore new problems but rather to lay out the parameters of the old. Yet the university system produced many brilliant thinkers, with encyclopedic breadth and a talent for systematization. Such scholars have remained the ideal type in Tibetan Buddhism, just as curricular training has remained the basic program of the academic life.

The Standard Contemplative Structure. These academic institutions, too, concentrated on the classic structures of meditation, even formulating the processes of insight as inescapable logical syllogisms. This ordered program of meditation, proceeding carefully from level to level under the guidance of a trained and systematic intellectual apprehension, was formally declared the official Tibetan doctrine in the eighth century A.D., when the Indian academician *Kamalaśīla* successfully defended it against the new Chinese heresy of instantaneous enlightenment.

The Academic Heritage. The Indian monastic university was thus the source for several cultural features of Tibetan Buddhism: the concept of ordered and sequential contemplative training, the love of subtlety and universality in metaphysics, an ideal of broad yet careful scholarship, and a structure of discipline and training within a monastic setting.

THE TANTRIC TRADITION

These same ideals, however, were not themselves unchallanged in India. The Chinese heresy of instantaneous enlightenment was itself an Indian idea, where genuine spontaneity was seen as the goal of meditation, and the enlightened person acted out his freedom in the world.

The Wandering Saints. During and after the Gupta Dynasty, a new type of contemplative appeared in Buddhism: long-haired, mad wanderers who sought an enlightenment they called the Whore, for she opened herself to all who came to her. These wandering saints mocked the established traditions of the monastic institutions, and sang their mystic songs and riddles in the language of the marketplace. Their enthusiasm could infect even the academicians themselves. The story is told, for example, of how the sober scholar *Nāropa* gave up his academic career to wander the roads seeking the half-clad and crazy *Tilopa* as his guru.

Visionary and Spontaneous Techniques. These saints saw the bliss of Buddhahood as residing unseen within the human body, and they transformed the earlier cults of physical immortality and sexual magic into a means to attain Buddhahood itself. Using their visionary and spontaneous techniques, they directed their meditation to the creation of alternative and divine realities on the one hand, and toward active participation in public reality on the other.

Not only did they seek to penetrate directly into the empty dream of this world, and walk through it as a magic show put on for their enjoyment, but they also sought to gain magical control of the dream itself—to become magical master of the universe, fly through space to magical Buddha heavens, and create an infinite variety of realities through which they could wander, controlling and enjoying.

The Tantric Heritage. These crazy saints quickly became part of Tibetan Buddhism, and provided a niche in the monastic ecology for both individuality and dissent. Their visionary and spontaneous techniques found fertile ground in the native religious traditions of Tibet, where they were quickly amalgamated with the ecstatic flight of the Tibetan shaman and the potent magic of the native sorcerer.

THE NATIVE TRADITION

The success of Buddhism in Tibet can thus be seen as due to the ability of these Indian institutions to utilize preexisting Tibetan political structures and belief systems. These may be divided into two major segments: the sacral kingship as the model for monastic power, and the shamanist heritage as the model for the social integration of Buddhist practice.

THE SACRAL KINGSHIP

The Symbol of the Spirit Rope. The ancient Tibetan kingdom was in fact a confederation of tribes bound together by the sacred power of the *Yar-lung* Dynasty of kings. The mythic ancestors of these kings had descended upon a sacred mountain by means of a spirit rope which bound earth to the heavens. The first king and his six descendants ascended at death to the heavens whence they had come, and thus had no tombs upon the earth. The eighth king in the lineage was slain by an evil and crafty minister, and the spirit rope was cut forever.

The Royal Tombs. Yet the kings continued to occupy a special place at the intersection of heaven and earth. The tombs of some of the later kings have been found in the old Yar-lung burial grounds, and the cosmological structure of the monuments emphasizes the sacral power of the Tibetan kingship. There was even the practice of human sacrifice when a dead king was entombed. The king himself was the spirit rope, connecting the sacred and the profane worlds, and it was this divine power that enabled him to bind together the bickering nobility that formed the confederacy. Yet the frequency of assassination reported in the chronicles is evidence of the tension inherent in the relation between the royal center and the nobility of the tribes.

The Introduction of Buddhist Institutions. It was in A.D. 754 that Buddhism became an active factor in this struggle. What had once been a religion of foreign queens was espoused by the king himself. He founded the first Tibetan monastery, and under his reign Tibetans became Buddhist monks for the first time. He invited Indian scholars to his court, but the powerful native deities of the Tibetan soil greeted them with thunder and hailstorms, until the king summoned an Indian Tantric magician to conquer them with his more potent Buddhist spells.

Buddhism and its institutional structure was thus embroiled in the internal politics of the court, and the native deities represented the conservative nobility in their struggle for continued decentralization of power. The king clearly saw in Buddhism a means for the consolidation of his rule, placing the throne upon a new and more powerful sacred basis, while the nobility relied upon the ancient gods to preserve their traditional rights under the confederacy.

This was the archtypical Tibetan confrontation, a battle of the gods for political supremacy. The king stood at the intersection of the sacred and the profane; political power and religious power were synonymous. Such confrontations would be the pattern of Tibetan history.

The Heritage of Kingship. The sacral kingship was finally destroyed in 836, when the court was torn completely apart by fresh assassinations and usurpations, centering on this new confrontation with Buddhist institutions. But as the powerful families themselves gradually learned to utilize the new sacred power of the Buddhist monasteries for political ends, the sacral kingship was translated into its final Tibetan form; the monastery itself became the focus of both political and sacred power.

THE SHAMANIST TRADITION

The Religion of the Bon. The ancient Tibetan religion seems to have preserved many features of an Asian proto-shamanic tradition that spread as far as the Americas over the frozen Bering Sea. The central figure was the *bon*—he who cries out or he who evokes the gods. Dressed in his black hat and beating his sacred drum, the bon-shaman fought the battle against the demons of hailstorm and disease, slaying them with his magic weapons and binding them with the magic knots of his cobweb thread-cross. He mounted into the air, or as psychopomp guided it at death to its ultimate destination. He intervened with the unpredictable gods who dwelt on the snowy mountains, burning fragrant evergreen boughs before them, and was himself possessed by the spirits, to give oracles to his people.

The Shamanist Heritage. It is clear that many of these shamanist elements entered into Tibetan Buddhism. The Black-Hat Dancer still slays demons, and the monks read the so-called *Book of the Dead* to guide the spirit of the departed. The *maṇḍala* is laid out on a ground protected by magic daggers, and the *Gnas-chung Oracle* spoke with the voice of the god *Pe-har* to guide the policies of the central government of the Dalai Lama.

Institutionally, the functional relationship between the shaman and his clients was utilized by the new Buddhist ecclesia. The monasteries became pools of ritual talent, and the monks, either collectively or individually, took over the shaman's role as professional technician of the sacred. An Indian merit relationship between householder and renunciant became in Tibet a ritual relationship between expert and client. It has been this ritual bond perhaps more than anything else that has bound together the Tibetan people and their monasteries.

TIBETAN BUDDHISM

THE LINES OF TRANSMISSION

There are generally said to be four "sects" in Tibetan Buddhism, but the situation was far more complex than the simple separatism implied by the English term. These sects were more than anything else lineages of transmission from great masters to their chief disciples, and the greatest masters have often been those who most consciously accumulated the teachings of many such lineages. There have indeed been real partisan tendencies in Tibetan Buddhism, but these have often been ameliorated by a syncretistic and tolerant tradition inherited from the Indian university.

There has thus been considerable cross-fertilization between the sects, as each Tibetan master sought to acquire the whole of the Law for his posterity. On the other hand, the sects have traditionally regarded themselves as the special guardians of specific revelations passed down from India, and as devotees of particular deities or of special forms of a common god.

The rNying-ma Sect. The *rNying-ma* sect—the ancient ones—may with some justice be considered separate from the so-called new sects that were founded during the eleventh-century Buddhist renaissance. The rNying-ma trace their lineage back to the very foundation of Buddhism in the seventh and eighth centuries, and there can be little doubt that they in fact possess authentic Indian teachings lost among the other sects.

The rNying-ma have tended to be the least political and least centralized of the Tibetan sects, and have remained closest to the old shamanist traditions. It is through them that Buddhism has managed to keep its roots deepest in the Tibetan soil, and to renew itself periodically by a revitalization of the Tibetan past.

The New Sects. With the destruction of the central power that held the ancient confederacy together, the delicate balance of Tibetan sovereignty was thrown into confusion. Small Tibetan groups in the east continued to survive, and even carve out kingdoms for themselves from the still breathing corpse of the Chinese T'ang Dynasty. The descendents of the royal house moved west to reestablish their line in the border lands and continue their support of institutional Buddhism. Small kingdoms rose and fell in the old royal center, but without the power of the throne, Buddhist institutions gradually withered.

The Renaissance in the West and East. In western Tibet, the old royal lineage continued to support the old tradition of scholarship and translation. *Rin-chen bzang-po* (A.D. 958–1055) was sponsored in his travels back and forth from India in search of authentic scripture, and he founded temples and monasteries that still survive. He brought back many texts from Kashmir, chiefly of the *yoga tantras*, and he covered his temples too with murals of the shining Buddha *Vairocana* and his retinue.

In the far east of Tibet as well events were shaping themselves toward a renaissance of Buddhism. An Indian scholar named *Smṛti* wandered into Tibet, working as a lowly shepherd for several years before he was recognized and honored. The knowledge of Tibetan he had thus acquired made him a uniquely competent missionary and translator. Indeed, Tibetan tradition takes his date as the dividing line between the old translations of the rNying-ma sect and the new translations of the others.

But the renaissance finally crystallized around the charismatic figure of the Indian scholar *Atīśa* (982–1054), who arrived in western Tibet in 1042. There he met Rin-chen bzang-po, and was so impressed with his learning that he said: "If there are such men as you in Tibet, then there was no need of my coming here." Atīśa was clearly a most gracious person, for he is also famed for his praise of Tibetan tea, a beverage that other travelers have often found vile.

The Renaissance in the Center. Atīśa's chief disciple *'Brom-ston* (1008–1064) persuaded the master to travel to central Tibet, which was finally recovering from the chaos of the past centuries. There Atīśa, already an old man, continued to teach until his death, and based upon his teachings 'Brom-ston founded the *bKa-gdams* sect.

Other lineages were simultaneously being founded in the center, as Tibetans there too began to travel back to India to regain the old traditions. These Tibetan masters brought back from Bengal texts of the *anuttarayoga tantras*, whose fierce and potent sexual symbolism was angrily denounced by the rather straitlaced 'Brom-ston, who did not want master Atīśa to preach such things.

Thus *'Brog-mi* (992–1072) studied under the Indian Tantric *Ratnākara-śānti* and received from him the cycle of the *Hevajra Tantra* and from *Ḍombi-Heruka* the teachings of the "Path and its Fruit." *Mar-pa* (1012–1096) studied under the scholar-turned-yogin *Nāropa* and was taught the cycle of the *Cakrasamvara Tantra* and its attendant mystic practices. It was from these travelers that there descended the *Sa-skya* and *bKa-rgyud* sects, respectively, whose political power was based as much upon the sacred power of their teachings as upon the political astuteness of their leaders.

POLITICS AND POWER

The chief monasteries of these three new sects quickly took upon themselves the fragmented mantle of the old sacral kingship. Mar-pa was a powerful landholder in the Lho-brag Valley, but the early death of his son prevented him from passing his spiritual and temporal power to one of his own family. It was the beloved poet-saint *Mi-la ras-pa* (1040–1123) who finally received the secret teachings, but he had no ambitions save to wander upon the snowy mountains that he loved so much. He passed the bKa-brgyud lineage on to *sGam-po-pa* (1079–1153), and after him the sect split into four branches, each establishing temporal authority over the lands about the chief monastery and sometimes, with the tides of fortune, over vast territories.

The Sa-skya sect quickly passed into the hands of the *'Khon* family, just as, for example, the *'Brug-pa* branch of the bKa-brgyud lineage was passed down in the *Rgya* family. Political and spiritual power tended to remain within the family, and lordship of the monastery passed from father to son or from uncle to nephew. All these sects and subsects, and their ruling families and patrons, jostled each other in their search for temporal power, and they all sought to legitimate their claims by an appeal to the Mongols, the new overlords of Asia.

The dGe-lugs Sect. One more actor was yet to make an appearance on this complex political stage, and when the *dGe-lugs* sect arose, it proved to know its lines better than anyone else. *Tsong-kha-pa* (1357–1419) took as his own the lineage of Atīśa's bKa-gdams sect and founded three great monasteries in the old royal capital of *Lhasa*. He himself was a brilliant scholar and something of a fundamentalist, purging his sect of practices for which he could find no explicit warrant in the Indian texts. We may note, however, that his successor was eventually his own nephew *dGe-'dun-grub*. Tsong-kha-pa refused to allow succession from father to son, and enforced strict celibacy, but the tradition of familial claims to religious prestige and wealth was still strong.

Reincarnation. These familial claims during the fifteenth and sixteenth centuries were gradually taking new forms. To reinforce the holiness of their descent, the powerful families adopted the idea of reincarnation, setting up the lords of their monasteries as embodiments of the great celestial *Bodhisattvas*. This idea was remarkably viable in the political arena, for as the various families suffered political and military defeats, or when no male child was forthcoming, the now powerful monasteries themselves could find their lords in other families of wealth and prestige.

The dGe-lugs sect actually came fairly late to the uses of reincarnation. *bSod-nams-rgya-mtsho* (1543–1588) was recognized as the incarnation of Tsong-kha-pa's nephew, as well as of the Bodhisattva *Avalokiteśvara*, and was given the title of *Dalai Lama* by the Mongols, over whom he wielded considerable personal influence. It was remarkably fortunate that he then chose to be reborn as the grandson of the Mongol chief, and then once again as the shrewd and able *bLo-bzang rgya-mtsho* (1617–1682). With the help of the Mongol armies he crushed the opposition of the other sects, took over the bKa-rgyud holdings in the province of *Gtsang*, and established the dGe-lugs sect as the temporal lords of the center.

This political scuffling should not blind us to the tremendous vitality of all the Tibetan sects. Although the new Manchu emperors of China confirmed the temporal powers of the Dalai Lama, the other sects continued to flourish in their own monasteries. Reincarnation proved to be more than a political device; it became a vast resource for renewal and innovation within the tradition, as the authority of the past was vested in the voices of the present. The rNying-ma sect was a constant source of revitalization, as it was a link to the practices of the people and the deep roots of the shamanist heritage. Political struggles came and went, but even into the twentieth century new religious movements turned both to the past and to the future.

The Tibetans were one of the last of the proud free peoples of the world who did not so much taint their religion with politics as make even their politics religious. Theirs was not a stagnant culture. Politics and religion, the past and the present, the great monasteries and the lonely wanderers—

all these were creative tensions that expressed themselves in vitality and renewal.

SUGGESTED READING

Beyer, Stephan V. *The Cult of Tārā: Magic and Ritual in Tibet.*
Blofeld, John. *The Tantric Mysticism of Tibet.*
Eliade, Mircea. *Shamanism: Archaic Techniques of Ecstasy.* Translated by Willard R. Trask.
Hoffmann, Helmut. *The Religions of Tibet.*
Snellgrove, David, and Richardson, Hugh. *A Cultural History of Tibet.*

45

Buddhism and the West

Roger J. Corless

HELLENISTIC AND MEDIEVAL PERIODS

HELLENISTIC EXPANSION

The Indian Expedition of Alexander the Great (327–325 B.C.) opened up the "land of the philosophers" to the West, which then, as now in some circles, competed with Ancient Egypt as a source of Gnosis. Contact is presumed to have occurred along the trade routes, but its extent is uncertain. Aretalogical literature (tales of Hellenistic heroes) and Bodhisattva legends have much in common and there are scattered references to *Boutta* in Greek texts.

CHRISTENDOM

Opposition to Islam. Jerusalem, captured by Arabic Muslims in A.D. 637, fell to the fiercer Seljuk Muslims in 1071, rendering Christian pilgrimage there impossible, and threatening the Eastern border of Christendom. This led to the eight Crusades (1096–1270) of varying success. Simultaneously, expeditions were dispatched to treat with Prester (i.e., priest) John, presumed to be a king and priest ruling over a Christian State in India, in order to engineer an East-West pincer movement against the Muslims. (The legend of Prester John may be based on certain Biblical and Patristic passages, plus the observed similarity of Tibetan and Catholic ceremonial.) Hence we have the factual accounts—e.g., *The Journey of William of Rubruck* (1220–1293), who visited the Khan—and the legends—e.g., *The Book of the Infante don Pedro of Portugal* (early sixteenth century, based on much earlier sources), which records a meeting with Prester John.

Islamic Influence. Islamic, especially Persian, literature channeled Indian legends into Christendom. Many European tales can be traced through, e.g., the *Kitāb Kalīlah wa-Dimna* to the *Pañcatantra.* The legend of Saints Barlaam and Josaphat (commemorated on 27 November in the Catholic calendar) is derived from the legend of Śākyamuni (Josaphat being a corruption of Bodhisattva).

RENAISSANCE AND MODERN PERIODS

EXPLORATION

Secular journeys are contemporaneous with the search for Prester John, e.g., Marco Polo (1271–1295), but were insignificant until the fifteenth and sixteenth centuries, e.g., Vasco de Gama (ca. 1460–1524). The accumulating data were made available in such works as Richard Hakluyt, *The Principall Navigations* (1589).

CATHOLIC MISSIONS

Realizing now that the East was heathen, the Catholic Church, especially the Society of Jesus, attempted to convert it. Thus we find the journeys of St. Francis Xavier (1506–1552) to India and Japan, Fr. Matteo Ricci (1552–1610) to China, and Fr. Ippolito Desideri (1684–1733) to Tibet. The influence was mutual; e.g., Japanese aristocrats affected Portuguese dress and the Chinese calendar was revised under Jesuit influence, while the West gained grammars and dictionaries of Eastern languages and Latin versions of Buddhist texts. After initial success, the missions were suppressed.

BUDDHOLOGY

Academic study of Buddhism was stimulated by material brought back from the Colonies during the age of Western Imperialism (e.g., the Sanskrit and Tibetan manuscripts collected by *Brian Houghton Hodgson*, 1800–1894, while British resident in Nepal) and was influenced both by the Buddhist denominational allegiance of the Colonies held, and by the Christian denominational allegiance of the Colonial Power. Thus Protestant Britain, holding Ceylon, looked for the pure Gospel of Buddha and found the Pāli Tipiṭaka, while Catholic France, holding Indo-China, looked for scholastic *Summae* and found the great Sanskrit commentaries.

France. *Eugène Burnouf* (1801–1852) worked on Hodgson's manuscripts, tackled Buddhist philosophy, and published *Le Lotus de la bonne loi* (a translation of the *Saddharmapuṇḍarīka-sūtra*, published posthumously in 1852). *Paul Pelliot* (1878–1945) of the *École Française D'Extrême-Orient*, Hanoi (later Saigon, then Paris), collected manuscripts from Central Asia and published *La Mission Pelliot en Asie Centrale* in 1924. *Louis de La Vallée Poussin* (1869–1938) worked on Abhidharma and Mahāyāna, publishing *L'Abhidharmakośa de Vasubandhu* (1923–1931) and *La Siddhi de Hiuen-tsang* (Vijñaptimātratāsiddhi) (1928–1948).

United Kingdom. The Right Honorable *Friedrich Max Müller* (1823–1900), German/British, edited the *Sacred Books of the East* translations (1880–1910), among which are many Buddhist works. *Thomas William Rhys Davids* (1843–1922), after Foreign Service in Ceylon, founded the *Pali Text Society* in 1881, overseeing the editing (in Roman characters) and translating of the Tipiṭaka, and the compilation of the *Pali-English Dictionary* (1921–1924, completed by William Stede). His wife, *Caroline Augusta Foley Rhys Davids* (1858–1942) succeeded her husband as head of the Pali Text Society, continuing to oversee the *Sacred Books of the Buddhists* series (begun in 1895) and arguing for a "positive" original Buddhism antedating the "negative" accretions of Abhidhamma. Sir *Mark Aurel Stein* (1862–1943), Hungarian/British, followed the route of Alexander the Great and published *Serindia* (1921) and *Innermost Asia* (1928). To him and Pelliot we owe the rediscovery of Tun-huang.

Germany. German interest was centered on Indology and linguistics, but *Hermann Oldenberg* (1854–1920) produced important studies of "Urbuddhismus" in *Buddha: Sein Leben, seine Lehre, seine Gemeinde* (1881) and *Die Lehre der Upanischaden und die Anfänge des Buddhismus* (1915).

Other Countries. *Körösi Csoma Sándor* (1784–1842) of Transylvania made colorful expeditions to Tibet in search of the original Hungarians, producing a *Tibetan-English Dictionary* and *Grammar* (1834). *Henry Clarke Warren* (1854–1899) of Cambridge, Massachusetts, overcame a fearsome physical deformity to produce *Buddhism in Translations* (1896), a still unsurpassed anthology from the Pāli sources. *Fedor Ippolitovich Shcherbatskoĭ* (Th. Stcherbatsky) (1866–1942), an awesome Russian aristocrat, worked on epistemology and logic, and produced *Buddhist Logic* (1930).

Buddhology Today. Buddhism is an accepted feature of many university curricula in America, Europe, and Asia, though usually as a branch of "Comparative Religion." Some excellent independent work is produced in various places, e.g., by *Étienne Lamotte* (1903–   ) at Louvain. Integrated Buddhist Studies programs are now beginning to develop, e.g., at the University of Wisconsin (1961) under *Richard Hugh Robinson* (1926–1970). The growing practice of Buddhism in the West, the greater number of émigrés and improved communications, has increased the accessibility not only of the texts but also of the living commentatorial tradition.

BUDDHIST INFLUENCE ON WESTERN CULTURE

The non-Buddhological Westerner had, and has, difficulty distinguishing

Buddhism from other Oriental systems. In this adulterated form, certain Buddhist ideas have influenced certain Western intellectuals and truth-seekers.

Influence on Intellectuals. *Arthur Schopenhauer* (1788–1860) espoused some Buddhist ideas in *Die Welt als Wille und Vorstellung* (1818). He in turn influenced *Richard Wagner* (1813–1883) in the composition of the opera *Tristan und Isolde* (1865). Both of them influenced *Friedrich Wilhelm Nietzsche* (1844–1900), who developed the Übermensch theory. *Ralph Waldo Emerson* (1803–1882) and *Henry David Thoreau* (1817–1862), American Transcendentalists, incorporated elements of Buddhism into their theory and practice. The novels of *Hermann Hesse* (1877–1962), especially *Siddhartha* (1922), have a Buddhist flavor, and remain popular. *Oswald Spengler* (1880–1936) recounts *Der Untergang des Abendlandes* (1918) in a Buddhist manner.

Influence on "Truth-Seekers." Many explicitly soteriological organizations have been influenced by Buddhist ideas, especially the *Theosophical Society*, and new groups and communes of this sort are increasingly numerous, especially in California.

BUDDHISTS IN THE WEST

Societies established for the actual practice of Buddhism in the West were often independent of the academic societies and without frequent contact with Asia. Thus early Western Buddhism displays many idiosyncracies, especially the view that there is a pan-Buddhism behind traditional sectarian Buddhism. Many articles in the Societies' journals explicitly state that they are thus avoiding the errors of traditional sectarian Christianity. They may be implicitly influenced by the Christian Ecumenical Movement (begun around 1900). Buddhism in present-day America is the least cut off from Buddhologists and traditional practitioners.

France. Les Amis du Bouddhisme was founded in Paris, 1929, by the Venerable *T'ai-hsü* and *G. Constant Lounsberry*. *La pensée bouddhique* was begun in 1939 with some contacts with Tibet, Cambodia, Thailand, and Viet-Nam.

United Kingdom. The Buddhist Society of Great Britain and Ireland was founded in London, 1907, under *T.W. Rhys Davids*. *The Buddhist Review* was published from 1909–1922. It collapsed around 1924. The Buddhist Lodge of the Theosophical Society was formed in 1924 by *Travers Christmas Humphreys* (1901–   ) and published *Buddhism in England*, 1926–1943;

in 1943 the organization was renamed The Buddhist Society and the periodical *The Middle Way*. A Siṅhalese Vihāra opened in 1954. Tibet Society, formed in London in 1959, moved to Dumfriesshire under Venerable *Chög-yam Trungpa*, Rinpoche, who himself moved to the United States. An English Saṃgha was formed in 1962, and a Thai Vihāra opened in 1966. There are occasional visits by Zen masters.

Germany. Altbuddhistische Gemeinde was founded in Utting-am-Ammersee, Upper Bavaria, in 1921 by *Georg Grimm* (1867–1945) and *Karl Seidenstücker* (1876–1936). The first issue of the periodical *Yāna* was in 1949. Various other groups emerged, centralized in 1955 at Frankfurt-am-Main as Deutsche Buddhistische Gesellschaft. A component group was *rNying-ma-pa*, under *Lama Anagarika Govinda* (now in the United States), *Westlicher Orden des Arya Maitreya Mandala.*

United States. (See the appendix for a partial listing of representative Buddhist groups in the United States.) Asians who emigrated to the land of opportunity brought their religion with them, but they did not proselytize at first. The most active group was *Western Branch Jōdo Shinshū*, organized in 1899 (or possibly 1898) in San Francisco as Buddhist Mission of North America, incorporated in 1942 as Buddhist Churches of America. Temples of *Eastern Branch Jōdo Shinshū*, *Jōdo Shū*, *Shingon Shū*, and *Ching-t'u Tsung* were also founded. When Hawaii became a state in 1959, it contained Buddhist communities dating from the importation of Japanese laborers for the sugar plantations in 1868.

The World's Parliament of Religions, held in Chicago in 1893, aroused a keen but passing interest in Buddhism. The lecture tour of Right Reverend *Soyen Shaku*, Abbot of Engakuji (Kamakura), a *Rinzai Zen* monk, in 1905–06, had more effect, and the Buddhist Society of America, founded in New York City in 1930 by the Venerable *Sōkei-an* (1882–1945), is Rinzai. It is now called The First Zen Institute of America. *Sōtō Zen*, popular in Hawaii, is now represented in the continental United States, as is *Ch'an* (San Francisco) and *Chen* (founded near Easton, Pennsylvania, in 1971). Since 1959, Tibetan émigrés have formed *rNying-ma-pa*, *bKa-rgyud-pa*, and *dGe-lugs-pa* temples. There is a Siṅhalese Vihāra, serving Embassy personnel with some community outreach, in Washington, D.C. In 1960, the American General Chapter of *Nichiren Shōshū* was formed in Los Angeles. Indigenous groups were founded by *Dwight Goddard* (1869–1939), The Followers of Buddha: An American Brotherhood, and *Robert Clifton*, The Western Buddhist Order (a Jōdo Shinshū group).

THE WEST IN THE EAST

Reverse Missions. Some Western converts of Buddhism, returning to the East, contributed to an indigenous Buddhist Renaissance. Foremost were disciples of *Helena Petrovna Blavatsky* (1831–1891) who, claiming to be under the instruction of two Masters, wrote *The Secret Doctrine* (1888), which argued for a common divine wisdom or *theosophy* behind all actual religions. She and Colonel *Henry Steel Olcott* (1832–1907) of Orange, New Jersey, had founded The Theosophical Society in New York City in 1875. It moved to Adyar, Madras (India), in 1882. The Adyar Library series of Sanskrit texts and translations is a valuable tool for Indologists East and West. Believing in the essential unity of all religions, but the superiority of Indian forms, *Alfred Percy Sinnett* (1840–1921) wrote *Esoteric Buddhism* (1883) in which Buddha meant A Wise One in a theosophical sense. *Annie Besant* (1847–1933) attempted to revive Gnosticism within Anglo-Catholicism in *Esoteric Christianity* (1902) (with Christ also meaning A Wise One), which influenced the Liberal Catholic Church (reorganized in 1915–16), and founded a girls' school in Benares in 1904, which became Benares Hindu University. She was active for Indian Home Rule, 1916–1919, and in 1909 claimed *Jiddu Krishnamurti* (1895–   ; whose writings remain popular) as her adopted son and Messiah. Krishnamurti renounced the title in 1932. Colonel Olcott directly encouraged the return of education in Ceylon from Christian to Buddhist hands, and inspired *David Hewavitarane* (1864–1933) to enter the Saṃgha when, as *Anagarika Dharmapala*, he founded the Maha Bodhi Society in Colombo in 1891. It moved to Calcutta in 1892, and its journal, *The Maha Bodhi* (1892–   ), is a major organ of East-West contact. There are branches in London, Budapest, New York, and Chicago. Official Buddhist groups in the United Kingdom and the Netherlands are still influenced by Theosophy.

Buddhology. Western critical analysis of Buddhist texts and doctrines stimulated Easterners to rework their traditional commentatorial approach. In India, *Dharmananda Kosambi* (1871–1947) worked on the Tripiṭaka and completed editing the *Visuddhimagga* (1932, published 1950) begun by Henry Clarke Warren. In Japan, *Bunyiu Nanjio* (1849–1927), a student of F. Max Müller, drew up *A Catalogue of the Chinese Translation of the Buddhist Tripiṭaka* (1883).

SUGGESTED READING

Bapat, P.V., ed. *2500 Years of Buddhism*, pp. 380–94.

Ellwood, Robert S., Jr. *Religious and Spiritual Groups in Modern America*, pp. 74–79, 98–103, 125–30, 255–75.

Humphreys, Christmas. *Sixty Years of Buddhism in England (1907–1967).*
Hunter, Louise H. *Buddhism in Hawaii.*
Lubac, Henri de. *La Rencontre du Bouddhisme et de l'Occident.*
Needleman, Jacob. *The New Religious*, especially chaps. 2 and 7.
Riepe, Dale. *The Philosophy of India and its Impact on American Thought.* See references to Buddhism, etc., in index.
Welbon, Guy Richard. *The Buddhist Nirvāṇa and Its Western Interpreters.*

Appendix: Partial Listing of Representative Buddhist Groups in the United States

Roger J. Corless and Charles S. Prebish

Note: Although we believe this list is accurate, it cannot be regarded as definitive or complete. It is merely a preliminary guide. Inquiry should always be made of groups before attempting to visit them, as some are quite small and unable to accommodate more than a few persons. Occasionally, due to the ecumenical views noted in the preceding lecture, the denominational allegiance of a group is doubtful.

SIṄHALESE TRADITION

THERAVĀDA

The Buddhist Vihāra Society, Inc.
5017 16th Street, N.W.
Washington, D.C. 20011
Teacher: Venerable Henepola Gunaratana Mahāthera
Newsletter: *Washington Buddhist*

BURMESE TRADITION

THERAVĀDA

The Buddhist Society
Monastery and Nunnery
Meditation Center
Denver, Colo.
Teacher: Venerable Anagarika Sujata

TIBETAN TRADITION

RNYING-MA-PA

Tibetan Nyingmapa Meditation Center
2425 Hillside
Berkeley, Ca. 94705
Teacher: Tarthang Tulku, Rinpoche
An institute, offering a wide variety of courses, is now in progress, under the auspices of the Center.

BKA-RGYUD-PA (*Centers of Chögyam Trungpa, Rinpoche*)

Vajradhatu (Religious Unit)
1111 Pearl Street
Boulder, Colorado 80302

Divisions

Dorje Khyung Dzong
Huerfano County, Colo.
(Retreat Center)

Karma Dzong Meditation Center
1111 Pearl Street
Boulder, Colo. 80302

Rocky Mountain Dharma Center
Livermore, Colo.

Karmê Chöling
(Formerly Tail of the Tiger Meditation Center)
Star Route
Barnet, Vt. 05821

City Centers known as Dharmadhatus are located in major American and Canadian cities.

NALANDA FOUNDATION (*Secular Unit*)
1111 Pearl Street

Boulder, Colo. 80302

Divisions
Maitri
Old Forge Road
Wingdale, N.Y. 12594
(Therapeutic Community for Disturbed People

Naropa Institute
1441 Broadway
Boulder, Colo. 80302

Padma Jong
Dos Rios, Ca. 95429
Coordinating Office: 802 Camelia Street
Berkeley, Ca. 94710
(A Community for the Creative and Expressive Arts)

Periodical: *Garuda*

DGE-LUGS-PA

Lamaist Buddhist Monastery
Box 69–C, Freedom Acres
R.D. 3
Farmingdale, N. J. 07727

SA-SKYA-PA

Evam Choden Tibetan Buddhist Center
254 Cambridge
Kensington, Ca. 94708
Teacher: Lama Kunga Thartse Tulku

CHINESE TRADITION

CH'AN

Sino-American Buddhist Association
Gold Mountain Monastery
1731 15th Street
San Francisco, Ca.
Teacher: Hsuan Hua
Periodical: *Vajra Bodhi Sea*

CHING-T'U

Eastern States Buddhist Temple of America, Inc.
64 Mott Street
New York, N.Y. 10013
Similar temples in "Chinatown" sections of many cities.

KOREAN TRADITION

CHOGYE CHEN

Hui-nêng Zen Temple
P.O. Box 18361
Philadelphia, Pa. 19120
Teacher: Venerable Il-kwon Shin, abbot
Newsletter: *Sangha Life*

JAPANESE TRADITION

PURE LAND—JŌDO SHŪ

Jōdo Shū Temple
2003 West Jefferson Boulevard
Los Angeles, Ca. 90018
Teacher: Bishop Raikai Nozaki

PURE LAND—JŌDO SHINSHŪ

Western Branch (Nishi Honganji Ha)
Buddhist Churches of America
National Headquarters
1710 Octavia Street
San Francisco, Ca. 94109

Periodicals: *Buddhist Churches of America Newsletter*
American Buddhist
Horin (Japanese)

Educational Centers:

Institute of Buddhist Studies
2717 Haste Street
Berkeley, Ca. 94704

American Buddhist Academy
332 Riverside Drive
New York, N.Y. 10025

Branches: 60 independent churches and 40 branches

Eastern Branch (Higashi Hongangi Ha)
Higashi Hongwanji Buddhist Church
118 North Mott Street
Los Angeles, Ca. 90033

SHINGON SHŪ

Kōyasan Buddhist Temple
342 East First Street
Los Angeles, Ca. 90012
Teacher: Bishop Seytsū Takahashi

NICHIREN

Nichiren Shū
Nichiren Buddhist Church
Nichirenshū Betsuin
2800 East Third Street
Los Angeles, Ca. 90013

Nichiren Shōshū (known as Sōkagakkai until 25 September 1966)
Nichiren Shōshū of America
America Headquarters
1351 Ocean Front
Santa Monica, Ca. 90401

Periodicals: *Seikyo Times*
World Tribune

Major Centers: Santa Monica, San Diego, Culver City, San Francisco, Montebello (Ca.), Honolulu, Denver, Boston, Seattle, Phoenix, New York, Dallas, Chicago, Washington, D.C.

Other small centers in numerous American cities.

ZEN

Rinzai—California Bosatsukai ("Flower Sangha")

California Bosatsukai (main group)
5632 Greek Oak Drive
Los Angeles, Ca. 90028
Teacher: Nakagawa Soen, Roshi

Los Gatos Zen Group
16200 Matilya Drive
Los Gatos, Ca. 95030

San Diego Zen Group
Box 74
Del Mar, Ca. 92014

Rinzai—Centers of Joshu Sasaki, Roshi

Cimarron Zen Center
Rinzai-Ji, Inc.
2505 Cimarron Street
Los Angeles, Ca. 90018

Mt. Baldy Zen Center
Rinzai-Ji, Inc.
P.O. Box 526
Mt. Baldy, Ca. 91759

Redondo Beach Zen Center
2305 Harriman Lane
Redondo Beach, Ca. 90278

Stony Brook Zendo
State University of New York
Stony Brook, N.Y.

Zen Center of Vancouver
139 Water Street
Vancouver 3, British Columbia
Canada

Rinzai—Diamond Sangha

Koko An of the Diamond Sangha
2119 Kaloa Way
Honolulu, Hawaii 96822
Teacher: Nakagawa Soen, Roshi

Maui Zendo of the Diamond Sangha
R.R. 1, Box 220
Haiku, Maui
Hawaii 96708

Other Rinzai Groups

Yellow Springs Zen Group
Route 1, Box 257
Yellow Springs, Ohio 45387

First Zen Institute of America, Inc.
113 East 30th Street
New York, N.Y. 10016

New York Zendo
The Zen Studies Society, Inc.
223 East 67th Street
New York, N.Y. 10021
Teacher: Eido Tai Shimano, Roshi

Affiliate: International Daibosatsu Zendo
Star Route (Beecher Lake)
Livingston Manor, N.Y. 12758

Periodical: *Dharma Seasons*

Rinzai Zen Temple
P.O. Box 1467 FDR Station
New York, N.Y. 10022
Teacher: Isshu Miura, Roshi

Washington, D.C., Zen Group
c/o Strauss
Route 1, Box 604
Accokeek, Md. 20607

SŌTŌ

San Francisco Zen Center
300 Page Street
San Francisco, Ca. 94102

Teacher: Richard Baker, Roshi
Formerly led by Shunryo Suzuki, Roshi (now deceased)

Affiliates: Berkeley Zendo
1670 Dwight Way
Berkeley, Ca. 94703
Teacher: Richard Baker, Roshi

Los Altos Zendo
746 University Avenue
Los Altos, Ca. 94022
Teacher: Kobun Chino-sensei

Mill Valley Zendo
Wistaria Way—Altomonte Boulevard
Mill Valley, Ca. 94941
Teacher: Richard Baker, Roshi

Monterey Zen Group
638 Oak Street
Monterey, Ca.
Teacher: Dainin Katagiri, Roshi

Monterey Zen Group
638 Oak Street
Monterey, Ca.
Teacher: Dainin Katagiri, Roshi

Monterey Soto Zen Temple
456 Casanova Avenue
Monterey, Ca.
Teacher: Kisan Ueno (Osho)

Zen Center of Los Angeles
927 S. Normandie Avenue
Los Angeles, Ca. 90006
Teacher: Hakuyu Maezumi, Roshi

Zen Mission Society
Shasta Abbey
R.R. 1, Box 577
Mount Shasta, Ca. 96067
Teacher: Jiyu Kennett, Roshi

Chicago Zen Buddhist Church
2230 N. Halsted Street
Chicago, Illinois 60694
Teacher: Reverend Soyu Matsuoka

Cambridge Buddhist Association
126 Brattle Street
Cambridge, Mass. 02138

Zen Center
19 High Street
Haydenville, Mass.
Teacher: Shojo Sensei

Twin Cities Zendo
136 Amherst Street
St. Paul, Minn. 55105

Miscellaneous Zen Group (No Listed Sectarian Affiliation)

The Zen Meditation Center of Rochester
7 Arnold Park
Rochester, N.Y. 14607
Teacher: Philip Kapleau, Roshi

Affiliate: The Zen Centre
54 McGee Street
Toronto, Ontario
Canada

Periodical: *Zen Bow*

Glossary

Abhayagiri—A major monastery in Ceylon, founded by Vaṭṭagāmaṇī.

Abhidhammaṭṭhasaṅgaha—A later Theravādin Abhidhamma work written by Anuruddha (11th century).

Abhidharma (P. Abhidhamma)—"That which is above Dharma," or "That which represents superior Dharma." That portion of Buddhist literature dealing with abstruse philosophy or psychological matters.

Abhidharmakośa—A philosophical treatise written by Vasubandhu, covering almost all the philosophical topics espoused in the Sarvāstivādin Abhidharma and offering many refutations of Vaibhāṣika viewpoints.

Abhidharma Piṭaka (P. Abhidhamma Piṭaka)—The third basket of the Buddhist canon.

Abhidharmavibhāṣā-śāstra—An extensive commentary on the Abhidharma of the Sarvāstivādins.

Abhiniṣkramaṇa-sūtra—The "Discourse of the Great Renunciation," a noncanonical legend of the life of the Buddha, attributed to the Dharmaguptaka school.

Abhisamayālaṅkāra—A Yogācāra commentary by Maitreyanātha that sums up the contents of the Large Sūtra on Perfect Wisdom.

Abhisamayālaṅkārāloka—A commentary, by Haribhadra, on the Aṣṭasāhasrikā-prajñāpāramitā-sūtra.

adbhutadharma—"Miracle Narratives"; a means by which the Buddha taught the Dharma to people of varying dispositions.

adhimuktatā—"Disposition"; Buddha taught according to people's dispositions, utilizing his skill in means (upāyakauśalya) in order for them to understand.

Āgama—A traditional or canonical text, corresponding to the Nikāyas of the Pāli Sutta Piṭaka. They include the Dīrghāgama, Madhyamāgama, Ekottarāgama, Saṃyuktāgama, and Kṣudrakāgama.

Ajātaśatru—Bimbisāra's son who imprisoned his father as a result of his (i.e., Ajātaśatru's) involvement with Devadatta. Later he relented and expressed faith in Buddha (after one of Devadatta's unsuccessful attempts to murder Buddha).

Ājñāta Kauṇḍinya—One of the five ascetics who practiced austerities with Siddhārtha Gautama. Upon hearing Buddha's first sermon, Kauṇḍinya became enlightened, and accordingly received ordination as the first monk (bhikṣu).

Akṣobhya—The first celestial Buddha to be mentioned in the Aṣṭa-sāhasrikā-prajñāpāramitā-sūtra.

ālaya-vijñāna—"Storehouse consciousness"; receptacle for the various dispositions and habit-energies of the other consciousnesses. The "seeds" planted here, according to the Yogācārins, provide some connection between past, present, and future experiences.

Amita (J. Amida; C. A-mi-t'o)—The abbreviation of Amitābha, the Buddha of the Western Paradise, and the object of devotion in Pure Land Buddhism.

Amitābha—The Buddha of "Eternal Light"; presiding over the Western Paradise. See Amita.

Amitāyurdhyāna-sūtra—"Sūtra of the Meditation on Limitless Life"; a Pure Land text which contains a series of sixteen meditations necessary to form a perception of the Pure Land (Sukhāvatī).

Amitāyus—The Buddha of "Eternal Life"; another name for the celestial Buddha presiding over the Western Paradise.

anāgāmin—Literally, a "nonreturner," or that stage of sanctification in which the adept is assured of attaining enlightenment during his current lifetime. This is predominantly a Hīnayānist notion.

Ānanda—Siddhārtha Gautama's cousin who became his favorite disciple and personal attendant. He is said to have recited all Buddha's sermons for the First Council (held at Rājagṛha) and was instrumental in establishing the order of nuns (bhikṣuṇīs).

Anāthapiṇḍika—A wealthy banker of Śrāvastī in Kośala who, as a lay disciple (upāsaka), built and donated Jetavana monastery to the saṃgha. It was here that Buddha spent many rainy seasons.

Anātmalakṣaṇa-sūtra—The "Discourse on the Marks of Not-Self"; Buddha's second sermon to the five ascetics near Benares, discussing the self, impermanence, and suffering.

anātman—"Not-self"; that doctrine of the Buddha which contradicts the Hindu notion of a pure, eternal, subtle self (ātman). The doctrine, intended to eliminate attachment, later became problematic in terms of Buddhist explanations of rebirth.

Anawratā—King of Pagan (1040–1077) who converted to Theravāda and put Shin Arahan in charge of the saṃgha in unified Burma.

Aṅga—A region in the eastern part of India which was strongly influenced by Buddha's teachings, even during his lifetime.

Aṅguttara Nikāya (S. Ekottarāgama)—"Collection of Discourses Treating Enumerations Classed in Ascending Order"; the fourth section in the Sutta Piṭaka of the Pāli Canon.

An-hsüan—A disciple of An Shih-kao who converted Yên Fo-tiao, the first Chinese Buddhist monk.

anitya—"Impermanence"; that Buddhist doctrine which states that all things originate, have duration, and decay. This notion of constant flux or impermanence forms the second of Buddha's "three marks of existence" (tri-lakṣaṇa).

An-lo Chi—"Compendium on Sukhāvatī," written by Tao-ch'o; it recommends Ching-t'u (Pure Land) practice as the most suitable for the period of the decline of the Dharma (mo-fa).

An Shih-kao—A Parthian who settled at Lo-yang in A.D. 148 and headed a team of mainly Hīnayāna monks which translated works on meditation and breathing exercises.

antarābhava—"Intermediate existence"; according to the Theravādins rebirth occurs in a fluid, continuous stream with no antarābhava.

Anumāṇa—A designatory Sanskrit word denoting Buddhist Logic in general. More precisely in Buddhist Logic, it refers to the science of inference.

Anurādhapura—The capital of King Devānaṃpiyatissa of Ceylon (250–210 B.C.).

Anuruddha—A later Theravādin Abhidhamma commentator, said to have written the Abhidhammaṭṭhasaṅgaha.

Apadāna—"Verse Accounts of the Lives of Certain Monks and Nuns"; traditionally the thirteenth book contained in the Khuddaka Nikāya of the Sutta Piṭaka of the Pāli Canon.

Apohasiddhi—"Treatise on the Differentiation Theory of Meaning"; a Buddhist logic text composed by Ratnakīrti (A.D. 1050).

Ārāḍā Kālāma—The first teacher under whom Siddhārtha Gautama studied in his quest for enlightenment. He taught the experience of the state of the "sphere of nothingness." Buddha found the experience lacking, turned down his offer of co-teachership, and searched for another teacher.

ārāma—A park which was donated to the saṃgha and maintained by the wealthy donor, designated for use by the monks (bhikṣus) during the rainy season retreat.

Āraṇyaka—Literally "Forest Treatise"; sacred Hindu texts whose speculative philosophy was created and studied in the solitude of the forests and which served as a precursor to the Upaniṣads.

arhant—Either "Worthy One" or "Slayer of the Foe," depending on the applied etymology; the final stage in the Hīnayāna stages of sanctification: one who has gained enlightenment.

Aris—A group of lords patronizing Tantric Buddhism shortly after the establishment of the Burmese capital at Pagan in 841.

Ariyavaṃsa—A festival surrounding the preaching of the Ariyavaṃsa-sutta. The sutta highlights the life of the monk, and while it is not clear under what circumstances the text was preached, it is clear that it was highly patronized.

Āryadeva—Nāgārjuna's closest pupil whose work supplemented that of his master. He wrote the Śata-śāstra, a Mādhyamika work.

ārya pudgala—Literally "Noble Persons"; a class name which denotes those who have gained entry into the ārya saṃgha or group of "spiritually elect" persons.

ārya satyas—The "Four Noble Truths"; the basic doctrine of Buddha's teaching. At the very heart of his teaching, this doctrine states that (1) all life is suffering (duḥkha), (2) there is a cause to the suffering (samudaya), (3) there is a cessation of suffering (nirodha), and (4) there is a path to the cessation of suffering (aṣṭāṅgika mārga). This teaching formed the core of Buddha's first sermon, the Dharmacakrapravartana-sūtra.

Āryaśūra—Author of the Jātaka-mālā, or "Garland of Birth Stories," containing stories of Buddha's former lives.

asaṃskṛta—"Unconditioned"; a term used often to describe dharmas in Hīnayāna Abhidharma. The number of asaṃskṛta dharmas in the various Hīnayāna schools varies with the Theravādins positing one, while the Sarvāstivādins note three. The Yogācārins, a Mahāyānist school, expand the list even further.

Asaṅga—Originally trained as a Hīnayānist (Mahīśāsaka school), Asaṅga left this tradition (and his brother Vasubandhu as well) and was the major creative force in the establishment of the Yogācāra school of Buddhism. In addition to supposedly receiving a vision of the future Buddha Maitreya, in which several Yogācāra texts were dictated to him, Asaṅga wrote several books in his own right, and finally converted his brother Vasubandhu.

Aśoka—The third emperor of the Mauryan Dynasty in India, he brought India together under his rule around 260 B.C. According to Buddhist legends, he became a lay disciple (upāsaka) and took up a policy of Dharma-conquest. Author of an extensive missionary movement, it is also said that the Third Council of Buddhism was held during his reign.

Aśoka became the model for many other rulers who sought to govern in accordance with the Dharma.

Aśokāvadāna—Written around the third century A.D. (?), this text is perhaps the main source for many of the stories surrounding Aśoka.

āsravas—Literally "outflows"; these impurities, consisting of sensual desire, desire for continued existence, false views, and ignorance, must be destroyed to experience enlightenment. Much of Buddhist practice aims at totally uprooting them.

āśraya-parāvṛtti—Literally "turning back at the base"; essentially a complete reversal in the activities of the various consciousnesses. This is the result of the arduous meditational practices. The doctrine is found in Yogācāra literature.

Aṣṭadaśasāhasrikā-prajñāpāramitā-sūtra—"The 18,000 Line Sūtra on the Perfection of Wisdom"; one of the most important texts in the "large" group of Prajñāpāramitā Sūtras.

aṣṭāṅgika mārga—"Eightfold Path"; the fourth of the Noble Truths, being an eight-membered guide to practice culminating in the realization of enlightenment. It is organized around the triple training (tri-śikṣā) of Morality (śīla), Concentration (samādhi), and Wisdom (prajñā).

Aṣṭasāhasrikā-prajñāpāramitā-sūtra—"The 8,000 Line Sūtra on the Perfection of Wisdom"; the earliest, and perhaps basic, Mahāyāna text. It was translated into Chinese in 179 A.D. as the Tao-hsing Ching ("Practice of the Way Sūtra").

Aśvaghoṣa—A Buddhist poet, probably contemporary to King Kaniṣka, who composed the Buddhacarita or "Acts of the Buddha."

Atharva-veda—The fourth of the Hindu Vedas, dealing with magic, witchcraft, spells, and the like.

Atīśa—An Indian scholar (982–1054) who arrived in Tibet in 1042. He was a critical factor in the renaissance of Buddhism in Tibet, with his chief disciple, 'Brom-ston, founding the bKa-gdams sect.

ātman—In Hinduism, the "self," that which is pure, subtle, and eternal, which transmigrates from life to life, carries karmic residues, and is of like essence with the absolute.

Aṭṭhakathā—In the tradition of Theravāda, these texts represented commentaries on the seven Pāli Abhidhamma books.

Aṭṭhasālinī—Buddhaghosa's commentary on the Dhammasaṅgaṇi of the Abhidhamma Piṭaka of the Pāli Canon.

Avadānaśataka—A Sarvāstivādin collection of avadānas (or legendary stories) probably composed around the time of King Kaniṣka.

Avalokiteśvara (C. Kuan-yin; J. Kwannon)—A Bodhisattva who gradually assumed greater importance in Buddhism, finally arriving at a position in which his image was to be found along with Buddha's, or even standing alone as the sole recipient of reverence. Referred to frequently in Mahāyāna texts, he is one of the most important of the celestial Bodhisattvas.

āvāsa—Dwelling places, staked out, constructed, and kept up by the monks for use during rainy season retreat.

Avataṃsaka-sūtra (C. Hua-yen Ching)—The "Flower Ornament Sūtra"; a Mahāyāna text which gave an extensive portrayal of the Bodhisattva's search for enlightenment, and offered a view of existence as one of complete identity and interdependence.

āyatana—Literally "sense-field"; an Abhidharma category, including the six sense-fields (eye, ear, etc.) and their objects (visibles, sounds, etc.).

Bahuśrutīya—A sect of Hīnayāna Buddhism which broke from the Mahāsāṃghika sect. One of their chief doctrines held Buddha's teaching to be twofold: transcendent, on the one hand, and mundane, on the other.

bhaiṣajya—That which deals with curing, medicine. One entire Karmavācanā procedure in the Vinaya is devoted to this issue.

Bhaiṣajyarāja—A Bodhisattva in the Saddharmapuṇḍarīka-sūtra who burns his body as an act of reverence to the Buddha.

bhājanaloka—In Buddhist cosmology, the "receptacle world," or world of the gods.

Bhāvanākrama—A textbook on meditation, written by the Indian scholar Kamalaśīla, and which has been used as a model for all meditation books in Tibet since the ninth century.

Bhavya—Another name for Bhāvaviveka, a Mādhyamika adherent who lived around A.D. 400. His text, the Nikāyabhedavibhaṅgavyākhyāna, provides information on the early sectarian movement in Buddhism.

bhikṣu—This is the word in the Buddhist's technical vocabulary to denote the monk or religious professional, as opposed to the layman. In addition to taking a more severe vow with regard to practice, the monk usually lived in the confines of a monastery, having devoted his life to the practice of Buddhism.

bhikṣuṇī—This is the female counterpart to the monk. See bhikṣu.

bhūmi—Literally "earth," but usually meaning "stage" in Buddhist usage. The ten stages on the path of the Bodhisattva are referred to as bhūmis, and are the subject of separate discourses: the Bodhisattvabhūmi and Daśabhūmika.

bhūtakoṭi—The "limit of reality," a synonym for nirvāṇa in Mahāyāna Buddhism.

bīja—Literally "seeds" which, according to Yogācāra, are planted in the ālaya-vijñāna. They carry the various dispositions and habit-energies and, if "pollinated," give rise to a wrong view of the world.

Bimbisāra—A king, contemporary with Buddha, who ruled Magadha from his capital of Rājagṛha. He donated the first monastery to the saṃgha, Veṇuvana ārāma, and was somewhat responsible for the Buddhists' adoption of the Poṣadha ceremony.

bKa-gdam-pa—Tibetan Buddhist sect founded by 'Brom-ston, based on the teachings of his teacher Atīśa.

bKa-rgyud-pa—Tibetan Buddhist sect tracing its origins to Mar-pa (1012–1096), who studied under Nāropa and learned the cycle of the Cakrasamvara Tantra.

Blavatsky, Helena Petrova—Co-founder of the Theosophical Society. Her writings include *The Secret Doctrine* (1888).

Bodh-gayā—The traditional birthplace of Buddhism, marking the spot at which Buddha attained enlightenment.

bodhi—"Enlightenment," or that complete and perfect state experienced by the Buddha.

bodhicitta—The "thought of enlightenment." It is with this initial step that the Bodhisattva begins his path to complete, perfect enlightenment.

Bodhidharma (C. P'u-t'i-ta-mo)—The first patriarch of Chinese Ch'an Buddhism. Said to have come to China from India around A.D. 520, it is from Bodhidharma that the Ch'an lineage begins with his transmission of the Laṅkāvatāra-sūtra.

bodhi-maṇḍala—The "seat of enlightenment," traditionally thought to be the spot under the bodhi-tree on which Buddha attained enlightenment.

bodhipakṣya dharmas—The thirty-seven "factors of enlightenment" which Buddha declares, in the Mahāparinibbāna-sutta of the Dīgha Nikāya, to be a summary of his teaching. They are grouped in seven categories.

Bodhiruci—An Indian Buddhist missionary in China who convinced T'an-luan (of the Ching-t'u sect) that true immortality lay in devotion to Amitābha.

Bodhisattva—"Buddha to Be" or "Enlightenment Being." Before becoming a Buddha, Siddhārtha Gautama was held to be a Bodhisattva, generally taken to mean a future Buddha. Whereas the Hīnayānists hold there to be but one Bodhisattva, Siddhārtha, the Mahāyānists adopt this concept as the ideal type around which to model religious practice. In Mahāyāna the Bodhisattva (who now can be virtually any person) holds off becoming enlightened out of compassion, and attempts to lead all sentient beings to complete, perfect enlightenment.

Bodhisattvabhūmi—A text outlining the ten stages (bhūmis) to be practiced by the Bodhisattva.

Bodhisattva-yāna—The "Bodhisattva Vehicle," or vehicle of those who seek the salvation of all sentient beings. This concept is found, for example, in the Saddharmapuṇḍarīka-sūtra.

Bodhi Tree—The "Tree of Awakening"; that tree under which Siddhārtha Gautama resolved to sit until he attained complete, perfect enlightenment. Branches of this tree were sent to various parts of the Buddhist world after Buddha's death.

bon—An ancient Tibetan religion (embodying much that is shamanistic) antedating Buddhism in which the central figure was the bon, "he who cries out" or "he who evokes the gods."

Brahman—The priestly class in Hinduism.

'Brog-mi—Founder of the monastery of Sa-skya in Tibet, and consequently, the Sa-skya sect of Tibetan Buddhism. From Ratnākaraśānti he received the cycle of the Hevajra Tantra and from Ḍombi-Heruka the teachings of the "Path and Its Fruit."

'Brom-ston—Atīśa's chief disciple, who founded the bKa-gdams sect of Tibetan Buddhism on his teacher's doctrine.

'Brug-pa—A branch of the bKa-rgyud-pa lineage which was passed down in the Rgya family in Tibet.

Buddha—The "Awakened One"; title given to Siddhārtha Gautama after he achieved complete, perfect enlightenment under the Bodhi Tree.

buddha-bhakti—The practice of paying devotion to the Buddha, particularly with regard to the Buddha Amitābha.

Buddhacarita—Literally "Acts of the Buddha"; a noncanonical legend of the life of the Buddha, a portion of which remains in Sanskrit and is attributed to the poet Aśvaghoṣa.

Buddhaghosa—Probably the greatest of all Theravāda exegetical writers. Coming from South India to Ceylon in the fourth or fifth century A.D., his classic Visuddhimagga or "Path of Purity" and his numerous commentaries establish him as expert in virtually all aspects of Buddhism.

buddhatā—Literally "the state of being a Buddha," Buddha-nature.

Buddhavaṃsa—"The Lineage of the Buddha"; the fourteenth book contained in the Khuddaka Nikāya of the Sutta Piṭaka of the Pāli Canon.

Buddha-yāna—"Buddha-vehicle"; the one sole vehicle by which the Buddha teaches the Law. The concept may be found in the Saddharmapuṇḍarīka-sūtra.

Burnouf, Eugène—French scholar who worked on the manuscripts collected by Brian Houghton Hodgson. His translation of the Lotus Sūtra (*Le Lotus de la bonne loi*) was published posthumously in 1852.

Bu-ston—Tibetan Historian living from 1290–1364 who collected and edited the Tibetan scriptures.

caitasika—Literally "mental constituent" or that which is derived from mind (citta). In the various early Buddhist schools we find no agreement on the number of caitasikas with the Theravādins noting 52, while the Sarvāstivādins posit 46.

Caitīyas—A sect of Hīnayāna Buddhism which broke from the Mahāsāṃghika sect. They held that the Buddha's discourse was transcendent, his enlightenment was already determined when he was born, that he could violate the natural laws, and he could, in his previous lives as a Bodhisattva, be reborn wherever he wished.

caitya—A religious monument or stūpa in which the relics of the Buddha or another famous saint are housed.

caityaghara—"Caitya-Hall"; that structure erected to house caityas.

Cakrasamvara Tantra—One of the most important texts of Tantric Buddhism, transmitted from Nāropa to Mar-pa.

cakravartin—Literally "turner of the wheel (of the law)." It was predicted that Siddhārtha Gautama would become a cakravartin, either in the political or religious sense. It may mean he who dwells or abides in the cakra (i.e., the maṇḍala or land), equally applying to Buddha.

Cariyā-piṭaka—"Collection Concerning Conduct"; the fifteenth book contained in the Khuddaka Nikāya of the Sutta Piṭaka of the Pāli Canon.

carman—Literally "leather"; it is mentioned as one of the traditional topics of the Karmavācanā.

cetanā—"Volition"; the notion that all acts may be volitional or willful, thus increasing the scope of potential karmic responsibility.

Ch'an—Ch'an is a Chinese transliteration of the Sanskrit term dhyā[na]. It is a Mahāyāna Buddhist school said to have been brought to China by Bodhidharma (usually regarded as the twenty-eighth Indian Patriarch) around A.D. 520. It emphasizes rigorous meditation and a disdain for the "trappings" of religion, and gave rise to Zen in Japan.

Ch'ang-an—An early center of Buddhist importance in China, and the major locale of Kumārajīva's translation enterprises.

Ch'eng-shih Lun—Kumārajīva's Chinese translation of the Satyasiddhiśāstra. The text formed the basis of the Ch'eng-shih School of Buddhism in China.

Chên-yên—The "efficient (or true) word." It corresponds to the Buddhist Tantra and was introduced into China in the eighth century A.D. by Śubhakarasiṃha. Chên-yên transliterates to mantra in Sanskrit.

Chia-hsiang—Chinese Buddhist instrumental in instituting the San-lun School of Buddhism in China.

Chih-i—Chinese Buddhist (538–597) who served as the major systematizer of T'ien-t'ai Buddhism in China.

chih-kuan-ta-tso (J. shikantaza)—Practice employed in the Ts'ao-tung School of Ch'an (and Sōtō Zen) which means "aiming at nothing except sitting." It aims at "stopping the mind" in the present moment by merely sitting.

Chi-lo Kuo—The "Land of Happiness" or "Pure Land"; that special sphere known as the Western Paradise, presided over by A-mi-t'o (in Chinese Buddhism).

Ching-t'u—"The field which purifies" or "Pure Land"; the Pure Land School of Buddhism in China, founded by Hui-yüan and organized by T'an-luan, and emphasizing faith and devotion as the way to salvation.

Chi-tsang—Chinese Buddhist instrumental in instituting the San-lun School of Buddhism in China.

Chogye—Buddhist sect in Korea (formed in 1935), established by uniting the Sŏnjong and Kyojong sects.

Chungjong—King of Korea during the fourteenth century whose reign marked repressive measures against the Buddhist community.

Chü-shê—School of Buddhism in China founded by Paramārtha (sixth century A.D.) and organized by Hsüan-tsang (ca. 596–664). It corresponds to the Indian Abhidharma School.

citta—"Mind"; one of many words used by Buddhists to denote the mental sphere. Due to its variable character and the general inconsistency in the use of the term, it became a prime target for Abhidharma analysis.

citta-mātra—Literally "mind-only"; this concept appears in several Buddhist texts, among them the Laṅkāvatāra-sūtra, and represents a response to the problem of what exists if all subjects and objects are devoid of ego and are only imagined. It has frequently been used as a synonym for Yogācāra or Vijñānavāda.

cittasaṃprayukta-saṃskāras—Literally "factors associated with mind (or consciousness)"; in a sense this term is a synonym for caitasika (at least in the Sarvāstivādin Abhidharma).

cittaviprayukta-saṃskāras—Literally "factors not associated with mind (or consciousness)"; these dharmas can be included neither among the material or mental elements. In the Sarvāstivādin Abhidharma they are fourteen in number, and include such nebulous entries as nāma-kāya or that force which gives significance to individual words.

Cūlavaṃsa—A collection of material added to the Mahāvaṃsa (the Great Chronicle of Ceylon), periodically, to bring it up to date.

daimoku—A formula used by Nichiren Buddhists to attain salvation with the words Nam Myōhō Renge Kyō ("Hail to the Scripture of the Lotus of the True Teaching").

Daisaku Ikeda—The third and present leader of the Sōkagakkai sect of Buddhism in Japan.

Dalai Lama—The official political head of Tibetan Buddhism. The title, coined by the Mongols, is bestowed on that person thought to be the incarnation of the Bodhisattva Avalokiteśvara.

dāna—Literally "charity" or "giving"; one of the six perfections (pāramitās). For the layman it includes the giving of food, clothing, etc., to the monk. For the monk, it includes giving advice, teaching, etc., to the layman.

darśana—Derived from the Sanskrit verb meaning "to see," it is a technical term in Indian Philosophy applied to a school of philosophical thought such as Nyāya.

Daśabhūmika-sūtra—A Mahāyāna text that sets out, in detail, the ten stages of the Bodhisattva path.

Daśādhyāya Vinaya—Literally the "Vinaya in Ten Recitations," a name applied to the Vinaya of the Sarvāstivādins.

Dengyō Daishi—A posthumous title given to Saichō, the Japanese Buddhist responsible for establishing Tendai Buddhism in the ninth century.

deva—Divine, heavenly; a god.

Devadatta—Buddha's cousin who tried to usurp leadership of the saṃgha by murdering Buddha. After several unsuccessful attempts, he founds his own order, but when his followers return to Buddha, he spits blood and dies.

Devānaṃpiyatissa—King who ruled Ceylon from 250 to 210 B.C. It is said that in 247 B.C. he sent emissaries to Aśoka requesting friendship.

Devaśarman—A Sarvāstivādin monk who is the reputed author of the Vijñānakāya, one of the texts in the Abhidharma Piṭaka of this school.

dGe-'dun-grub—The nephew of Tsong-kha-pa, and successor in the lineage of dGe-lugs-pa Buddhism in Tibet.

dGe-lugs-pa—Sect of Tibetan Buddhism founded by Tsong-kha-pa (1357–1419), based on the lineage of Atīśa's bKa-gdams sect.

Dhamma-dāna—Literally "doctrine-giving," or the main role of the monk for the layman.

Dhammapada—"Stanzas on the Teaching"; second book in the Khuddaka Nikāya of the Sutta Piṭaka of the Pāli Canon.

Dhammasaṅgaṇi—One of the books in the Abhidhamma Piṭaka of the Theravāda School. The title literally means "Explication of Mental States." The factors considered are categorized with regard to the ethical domain.

Dharma—The Teaching or Doctrine of the Buddha. Dharma is said to include all Buddha's sermons and doctrinal pronouncements. It is sometimes called "The Law" (P. Dhamma).

dharma—We make the distinction between Dharma and dharma primarily because the word came to be used as a technical term, usually in Abhidharma, to denote experiential moments, i.e., the building blocks of existence. Thus to analyze existence one must simply break it down into its experiential elements. Of course various Buddhist schools posited differing numbers of dharmas. It is also used in the psychological sense to signify mental states.

Dharmacakrapravartana-sūtra—"Discourse on the Turning of the Wheel of the Law"; Buddha's first sermon to the five ascetics at Benares. Here he preached the futility of the extremes of luxury seeking and asceticism, and outlined the Four Noble Truths.

Dharmaguptaka—A sect of Hīnayāna Buddhism whose name means "those who protect (or preserve) the Law." They most likely separated from the Mahīśāsakas and were located in northwest India and Central Asia. They were instrumental in forming the cult of the stūpa, and were expert in incantation.

Dharmākara—In the Larger Sukhāvatīvyūha-sūtra, a monk who hears the Dharma from the Buddha Lokeśvararāja. He takes a series of 46 vows aimed at establishing a pure land. Ultimately Dharmākara reveals himself to be Amitābha, and the sūtra ends with a magnificent vision of this Buddha.

Dharmakāya—Literally the "Body of Dharma." In earliest Buddhism this was likely to mean the body of doctrine. After Buddha's death it was given a metaphysical interpretation by the Sarvāstivādins. When incorporated into the Mahāyānist doctrine of the Three Bodies of Buddha (trikāya), Dharmakāya is elevated to the "Body of Essence" or Buddhahood itself. It is that ultimate reality which can only be perceived by a Buddha.

Dharmakīrti—A great Buddhist logician of the seventh century whose major writings include the Nyāyabindu, the Pramāṇaviniścaya, and the Pramāṇavārttika.

dharma-mahāmātra—Literally "superintendents of Dharma"; that title given to Aśoka's officers. They engaged in activities such as propagating the religion.

Dharmapāla—An Indian Buddhist scholar whose commentary on Vasubandhu's Triṃśikā is one of the bases of the Fa-hsiang School of Chinese Buddhism.

Dharmaskandha—One of the books in the Abhidharma Piṭaka of the Sarvāstivādins. Its author is reputed to be either Śāriputra or Maudgalyāyana. It discusses practices preparatory for sainthood, major and minor defilements, the 22 faculties, the sense-fields, and the skandhas.

dharmatā—Literally "nature"; it is used in the Laṅkāvatāra-sūtra as the pure state from which Buddha issues. It is often used in Yogācāra texts.

Dharmottara—Buddhist logician writing an important commentary, called the Nyāyabindu-ṭīkā, on Dharmakīrti's Nyāyabindu.

dhātu—Used in two primary contexts, dhātu refers to the Abhidharma classification of existence in 18 "realms" (i.e., the āyatanas or sense-fields plus their corresponding consciousnesses), or, in the cosmological sense, to a plane of existence inhabited usually by one consonant with the plane. The three usual cosmological realms are the "realm of desire" (kāma-dhātu), "form realm" (rūpa-dhātu), and the "formless realm" (ārupya-dhātu).

Dhātukathā—The "Discourse on the Elements"; one of the books in the Abhidhamma Piṭaka of the Pāli Canon.

Dhātukāya—One of the books in the Abhidharma Piṭaka of the Sarvāstivādins. Its author is reputed to be either Pūrṇa or Vasumitra. It discusses the complex mahābhūmika-dharmas (psychological events occurring in each consciousness-moment), klesá-mahābhūmikas (major factors causing defilement), and parīttakleśa-bhūmikas (minor factors causing defilement).

Dhātusena—King who ruled in Ceylon from 460–478, and who threw off the Tamils after their fifth-century invasion.

dhyāna—Technical term used to denote the states experienced in meditation. In traditional Hīnayāna, as outlined in many sources, these are held to be fourfold.

Diamond Sūtra—English translation for the Vajracchedikā-prajñāpāramitā-sūtra.

Dīgha Nikāya (S. Dīrghāgama)—"Collection of Long Discourses"; the first section in the Sutta Piṭaka of the Pāli Canon.

Dignāga—Famous Buddhist logician of the fourth to fifth century A.D. whose writings include the Pramāṇasamuccaya, Nyāyamukha, and Hetucakra.

Dīpavaṃsa—Literally, the "Island Chronicle"; with the Mahāvaṃsa, it provides much information on the history of Buddhism in Ceylon.

Divyāvadāna—Sarvāstivādin text containing much material aimed at popularizing Buddhism, and also containing much Vinaya material.

Dōgen—Japanese Buddhist (1200–1253) who went to China to study and was responsible for establishing Sōtō Zen (based on the Ts'ao-tung branch of Ch'an).

Ḍombi-Heruka—A contemporary of Padmasambhava who taught the "Path and its Fruit" to 'Brog-mi.

dṛṣṭi—Technically speaking, the term means "views," but this was usually interpreted in Buddhism to mean "false views," namely those that maintained positions heretical to Buddhism.

duḥkha (P. dukkha)—Literally "suffering"; the first of the Four Noble

Truths points out the transciency of all mental and physical pleasures. Thus we find the statement that all life is characterized by suffering.

durbhāṣita—In the Sūtravibhaṅga of the Vinaya Piṭaka, a technical term meaning "offense of improper speech."

duṣkṛta—In the Sūtravibhaṅga of the Vinaya Piṭaka, a technical term meaning "light offense."

Duṭṭhagāmiṇī Abhaya—King of Ceylon during the first century B.C. After driving out the invasion of Eḷāra the Coḷa, he claimed his victory was not for the kingdom but for Buddhism.

Eisai—Japanese Buddhist (1141–1215) who went to China to study and who was responsible for establishing Rinzai Zen (based on the Lin-chi branch of Ch'an).

Ekavyāvahārika—A sect of Hīnayāna Buddhism which broke from the Mahāsāṃghikas. They held that the mind is by its nature pure and radiant, inaccessible to defilement.

Ekottarāgama—"Increased by One Discourses"; the counterpart, in the Sanskrit Buddhist Canon, of the Aṅguttara Nikāya of the Pāli Canon.

Emmei Jukku Kwannon Gyō—"Text in Ten Phases to Avalokiteśvara for Prolonging Life"; text recommended by Hakuin for Zen Buddhists.

Emperor Huan—Chinese ruler (A.D. 147–167) who worshipped both Huang-lao and Buddha.

evam mayā śrutam ekasmin samaye—Literally "Thus have I heard. At one time . . . " The beginning words in Buddhist sūtras.

Fa-hien—Chinese pilgrim who traveled to India (A.D. 399–414). Upon returning to China, he translated many Buddhist texts into Chinese.

Fa-hsiang—School of Buddhism in China organized by Hsüan-tsang (ca. 596–664) and his disciple K'uei-chi (632–682) out of Shê-lun. It corresponds to the Indian Yogācāra.

Fa-tsang—Chinese Buddhist (643–712) who organized the Hua-yen School of Buddhism on the basis of Tu-shun's (557–640) teachings.

fa-yin—The "seal of the Dharma"; seal which denotes that a person has comprehended the Dharma. It is used by Chinese Buddhist patriarchs to denote their successor.

Fu Chien—Chinese ruler of the Ch'in Dynasty who directed Buddhism into Korea.

Gadgadasvara—A Bodhisattva in the Saddharmapuṇḍarīka-sūtra who assumes a variety of shapes (monk, nun, demon, serpent, layman, laywoman) in order to proclaim the "True Dharma."

Gandhāra—An early locale of the Sarvāstivādin School of Buddhism. Later it is known for its beautiful art work.

Gaṅgārohaṇa—A ceremony in Ceylon aimed at warding off famine and disease.

gathā—"Song"; one of the nine traditional ways Buddha taught the Dharma to people of varying dispositions.

gati—"Destiny"; in cosmology, one of the six realms or destinies into which one may be reborn.

Gautama—Formal name of the clan into which Siddhārtha, later to become the Buddha, was born.

Genshin—Japanese Pure Land Buddhist (942–1017) who wrote Ōjōyōshū. Due to his personal charisma, he played a major role in the growth of the Amida cult of Buddhism in Japan.

Giribhaṇḍa-pūja—A festival in Ceylon in which the laymen offered goods to the monks.

gohonzon—In Nichiren Buddhism and Sōkagakkai, a picture containing the formula Nam Myōhō Renge Kyō, along with the names of various Buddhas and Bodhisattvas. The devotee gazes at the gohonzon as he chants.

Gokulika—A Sect of Hīnayāna Buddhism which broke from the Mahāsāṃghikas. They held that there is no happiness whatsoever in the world, just suffering.

Gyōgi—A Hossō Buddhist monk who did much to increase the prestige of the Japanese saṃgha by performing many acts of charity for the common people. He was a trusted advisor to Emperor Shōmu, and was later called Gyōgi Bosatsu (Bodhisattva).

Hakuin—Japanese Zen Buddhist monk (1685–1768) who strongly recommended the Emmei Jukku Kwannon Gyō for Zen Buddhists. He helped to exemplify the very finest ideals of compassion during the stagnant and degenerate Tokugawa Period.

Han-shan—A great Ch'an master who lived from 1546 to 1623.

Haribhadra—Buddhist commentator of the eighth century whose chief work was the Abhisamayālaṅkārāloka (on the 8,000-line prajñāpāramitā text).

Harivarman—Indian Buddhist who wrote the Satyasiddhi-śāstra.

Heart Sūtra—English equivalent for the Hṛdaya-prajñāpāramitā-sūtra.

Heian Period—Period in Japanese history (794–1192) which was probably the high-water mark for Japanese Buddhism.

Hekigan Roku—The "Blue Cliff Records"; Japanese translation of the Pi-yên Lu.

hetu—Literally "cause"; in Buddhist logic, the second member of the syllogism (referred to as the "justification").

Hetucakra—Buddhist logic text written by Dignāga. It literally means the "Wheel of Justifications."

Hetu-vidyā—A generic term used to signify Buddhist logic.

Hevajra Tantra—One of the most important of all the Buddhist Tantric texts. The Indian Tantric master Ratnākaraśānti taught it to the Tibetan 'Brog-mi.

Hīnayāna—Literally "Smaller (or Lesser) Vehicle"; a name given to the early (and conservative) schools of Buddhism by the newly emergent Mahāyāna ("Great Vehicle"). It designates the traditional eighteen schools that arose between the first and fourth centuries following the parinirvāṇa. It was clearly a pejorative term in this use.

Hodgson, Brian Houghton—Early British resident in Nepal largely responsible for gathering many Buddhist texts.

Hokke-kyō—Japanese translation of the Saddharmapuṇḍarīka-sūtra.

Hōnen—Japanese Buddhist (1133–1212) who was responsible for founding the Jōdo Shū or Pure Land School of Buddhism in Japan.

Hossō—One of the six academic traditions of Japanese "Nara" Buddhism which had been imported, without substantial modification, from China. It corresponds to the Indian Yogācāra.

Hṛdaya-prajñāpāramitā-sūtra—Literally the "Heart Sūtra"; an extremely short Mahāyāna text which is said to contain, in summary form, the essence of the prajñāpāramitā (and consequently, Mahāyāna) teaching.

Hsien-tai Fo-hsüeh—*Modern Buddhism*; the official periodical of the Chinese Buddhist Association. It was last issued in December 1964.

Hsüan-i—The "hidden significance" commentaries which were written to reveal the essential characteristics of a sect or text.

Hsüan-tsang—Chinese pilgrim who traveled to India and back between 629 and 645 to study the language and bring back Buddhist texts for translation into Chinese. He lived from 596 to 664 and played an instrumental role in organizing the Chü-shê or Abhidharma School of Buddhism from Paramārtha's teaching and the Fa-hsiang School of Buddhism, modeled on Yogācāra viewpoints.

Hsüeh-tou—Chinese Ch'an Buddhist monk whose mnemonic verses are contained in the Pi-yên Lu.

hua-t'ou—"The head of the saying"; a hua-t'ou is that which exists in the moment before a thought arises. Not unlike the famous kung-an (J. kōan) or "public case," it aims at bringing the student to a realization of what is. An example of a hua-t'ou is "Before you were born, what was your real face?"

Hua-yen—School of Buddhism in China, based on the Hua-yen Ching (S. Avataṃsaka-sūtra) or "Flower Ornament Sūtra." It was founded by Tu-shun (557–640) and organized by Fa-tsang (643–712).

Hui-k'ai—Chinese Ch'an Buddhist, later known as Wu-mên, who composed the Wu-mên Kuan (J. Mumonkan).

Hui-kuan—Buddhist monk who debated with Tao-shêng on the controversy of whether enlightenment was obtained gradually or immediately.

Hui-nêng—Chinese Buddhist monk of the Southern Ch'an School who became the Sixth Patriarch after a long and bitter controversy with his rival Shên-hsiu of Northern Ch'an. The Platform Sūtra of the Sixth Patriarch is attributed to Hui-nêng.

Hui-shun—Chinese Buddhist who was instrumental in forming the Ti-lun School of Buddhism in China.

Hui-ssŭ—Chinese Buddhist (515–576) who founded the T'ien-t'ai School of Buddhism in China. Later this school was organized by Chih-i.

Hui-yüan—Chinese Buddhist (334–416) who founded the Ching-t'u (Pure Land) School of Buddhism in China. This was later organized by T'an-luan (476–542).

Hung-jên—Chinese Buddhist (601–674) who was the Fifth Patriarch of Ch'an Buddhism.

Hyojong—Korean king during the Yi Dynasty who delivered an edict barring the sons or daughters of important families from seeking a career in the saṃgha, and those who were already in monasteries were urged to return to lay life.

ichijō Bukkyō—"One Vehicle Buddhism"; a concept which aimed at embracing all forms of Buddhism within one comprehensive scheme of religious emancipation.

i nien san ch'ien—"3,000 realms in an instant of consciousness"; a doctrine which tries to signify the interpretation of all existent things, and then claims that these are all contained as an organic unity within the reality called "mind."

Itivuttaka (S. Ityukta)—"Thus it is said"; The 4th book in the Khuddaka Nikāya of the Sutta Piṭaka of the Pāli Canon.

I-tsing—Chinese pilgrim who traveled to India and back between 671 and 695. He returned to China to translate the Buddhist texts he brought back.

Jātaka—Literally "Birth Story"; a collection of 550 tales which tell of Buddha's previous lives as a Bodhisattva. It forms the tenth book of the Khuddaka Nikāya of the Sutta Piṭaka of the Pāli Canon. Most of the stories are in fact extracanonical.

Jātaka-mālā—Literally "Garland of Birth Stories"; a collection of Jātakas attributed to Āryaśūra.

jaṭila—"Matted-hair ascetic"; a rival group in the wanderers' community. 1000 of these are converted by Buddha at one time.

Jetavana—"Grove of Prince Jeta," a monastery built for the Buddha by Anāthapiṇḍika and located in Śrāvastī. In the fourth century A.D., a monastery in Ceylon was built which carried the same name.

jhāna—The Pāli counterpart of the Sanskrit technical term dhyāna; see dhyāna.

Jina—Literally "Conqueror"; a title applied to Siddhārtha Gautama after he achieved complete, perfect enlightenment. It is said that he conquered the āsravas or "outflows."

jñāna—Knowledge, in an intuitive sense. It is the tenth perfection (pāramitā) and arises in the tenth Bodhisattva stage, that of Dharmamegha or "The Cloud of Dharma." Jñāna is a direct knowing of things as they really are.

Jñānaprasthāna—One of the books in the Abhidharma Piṭaka of the Sarvāstivādins, attributed to Kātyāyanīputra. It is perhaps the basic Abhidharma text of the school.

jñapti—Literally a "motion," used by assembled Buddhist monks in their transaction of monastic business.

Jōdo Shinshū—The "True Pure Land" School of Buddhism in Japan, founded by Shinran. In some respects it is based on both Chinese Ching-t'u and Hōnen's Jōdo Shū. It emphasizes, in radical fashion, the saving grace of Amida.

Jōdo Shū—The "Pure Land" School of Buddhism in Japan, founded by Hōnen. Based on Chinese Ching-t'u, it emphasizes faith and devotion to Amida, as well as the repetition of Amida's name in the formula Namu Amida Butsu.

Jōjitsu—One of the six academic traditions of Japanese "Nara" Buddhism which had been imported, without substantial modification, from China.

Kaidan—In Nichiren and Sōkagakkai Buddhism in Japan, the religious center and future world center of religion and government.

Kamakura Period—Period in Japan which began in 1192 with a shift of the ruling power from the Heian court to a group of samurai. Civil power was to remain in the hands of the military until the Meiji Restoration in 1867.

Kamalaśīla—Indian Buddhist of the eighth century who wrote the Bhāvanā-krama, was a great scholar, and defended the official Tibetan doctrine against the Chinese notion of instant enlightenment.

kami—Deities in Japanese Shintō.

Kammu—Japanese emperor who began the Heian Period in 794 by moving his capital from Nara to Heian, the modern-day Kyoto.

Kaniṣka—Kushan emperor who reunified India around the turn of the Christian Era and was sympathetic to Buddhism. Much Buddhist learning went on during his reign, one which he perhaps fancied as modeled after Aśoka.

Kanjur—Literally "Translation of Buddha-Word"; that portion of the

Tibetan Buddhist Canon containing what is thought to be Buddha's authoritative teaching.

karma—"Action" or "deed" in Sanskrit. The moral law of causality which states that what a person does in this life will have an effect in his later rebirths. In Buddhism, it has also been interpreted to represent volition.

Karmasiddhiprakaraṇa—Yogācāra text written by Vasubandhu.

Karmavācanā—The functional, legalistic device by which the communal life of the saṃgha is regulated. With the Prātimokṣa, it forms the basis of what later emerged as the Vinaya Piṭaka.

karuṇā—Literally "compassion"; the primary force behind the action of the Bodhisattva. It was this compassion which led him to make vows to save all sentient beings before entering nirvāṇa.

kasiṇa (S. kṛtsna)—A technical meditational term meaning "entire," but referring to a series of ten devices used as meditational objects by the meditator.

Kāśyapa—A leading disciple of the Buddha. He is said to have presided over the first Buddhist council at Rājagṛha. Ch'an also refers to a Mahā-kāśyapa as the second Patriarch in India (Buddha being the first).

Kathāvatthu—"Subjects of Discussion"; one of the Abhidhamma books in the Abhidhamma Piṭaka of the Pāli Canon. These "subjects" were apparently discussed in the Third Council, held at Pāṭaliputra during Aśoka's reign.

kaṭhina—The preparation and distribution of robes. Eventually this became a distinct ceremony in Buddhism, regulated by a Karmavācanā.

Kātyāyanīputra—A Sarvāstivādin Buddhist monk who lived around 200 B.C., and is reputed to be the author of the Jñānaprasthāna.

Kauśāmbī—Early Indian city, in an eastern direction, which was influenced by Buddha's teaching. Also the site of an Aśokan edict.

Kegon—One of the six academic traditions of Japanese "Nara" Buddhism which had been imported, without substantial modification, from China. It corresponds to the Indian Avataṃsaka and the Chinese Hua-yen.

Khmer—A name representing the Cambodians.

Khuddaka Nikāya—The fifth section of the Sutta Piṭaka of the Pāli Canon, containing fifteen miscellaneous or "minor" texts.

Khuddaka-pātha—"The Reading of Short Passages"; the first book in the Khuddaka Nikāya of the Sutta Piṭaka of the Pāli Canon.

kleśa—Defilement, both moral and intellectual, which must be overcome in order to attain enlightenment.

kōan (C. kung-an)—Literally "public records" or authenticated cases of dialogue of Zen masters. These seemingly insoluble and confusing statements, sometimes resembling riddles, were aimed at bringing the student to full realization of enlightenment.

Kōbō Daishi—A posthumous title given to Kūkai, the Japanese Buddhist responsible for establishing Shingon Buddhism in the ninth century.

ko-i—A translation device of "stretching the meaning" by which it was possible to express Indian Buddhist concepts in light of Taoist terminology in China.

Kojong—Korean king during the end of the Koryo Period (935–1392) who was exiled by the Mongols to Kanghwa Island.

Koliya—Kingdom to the east of Kośala and north of Magadha in India which, although being a Brāhmaṇical stronghold, was influenced by Buddha's teachings.

Körosi, Csoma Sandor—A Transylvanian who lived from 1784 to 1842 and made colorful expeditions to Tibet while searching for the original Hungarians. We owe much of our early knowledge of Tibetan Buddhism to his work.

Koryo Period—Period in Korea (935–1392) in which Buddhism in Korea reached the height of its importance.

Kośala—A kingdom in the northeastern part of India, strongly influenced by Buddha's teaching.

kṣaṇa—Literally "moment"; that concept in Buddhism that states all things to be of momentary duration. In the formalized doctrine of "momentariness" (kṣaṇikatva), we find things to have an origin (utpatti), duration (sthiti), and decay (vināśa).

kśānti—Literally "patience" or "forbearance"; the third of the perfections (pāramitās) practiced by the Bodhisattva.

Kuang—The Vinaya master who helped found the Ti-lun School of Buddhism in China.

Kuan-yin Ching (J. Kwannon-Gyō)—"Sūtra on Avalokiteśvara"; the twenty-fourth chapter of the Saddharmapuṇḍarīka-sūtra, circulating independently, and dealing with this celestial Bodhisattva.

K'uei-chi—Disciple of Hsüan-tsang who lived from 632 to 682 and helped his master organize the Fa-hsiang School of Chinese Buddhism.

Kūkai—Chinese Buddhist who went to China to study and returned to introduce Chinese Chên-yên or Tantra into Japan under the name of Shingon. This esoteric school of Buddhism emphasized mantras, maṇḍalas, etc. From its introduction in the ninth century, it was very popular. Kūkai was posthumously named Kōbō Daishi.

Kumārajīva—Great Buddhist translator, from Kucha, who lived from 344 to 413. With the aid of royal patronage, he made much headway translating Indian Buddhist texts into Chinese (from the time of his arrival in Ch'ang-an in 401). He is said to have founded the San-lun

School of Chinese Buddhism, based on Nāgārjuna's teachings.

kung-an (J. kōan)—Literally "public records" or authenticated cases of dialogue of Zen masters. These seemingly insoluble and confusing statements, sometimes resembling riddles, were aimed at bringing the student to full realization of enlightenment.

kung-ch'an—"Common property," a Chinese term for communism.

kuśalamūla—"Stock of good merit"; that stock of positive karmic seeds which have been gathered over a period of time and which aid one in progressing toward enlightenment (or, in the case of the Pure Land Sūtras, toward rebirth in the Western Paradise of Amitābha).

Kuśinagara—The place where Buddha entered parinirvāṇa.

Kusha—One of the six academic traditions of Japanese "Nara" Buddhism which had been imported, without substantial modification, from China.

Kyojong—A Buddhist textual school in Korea which was a union of the Hua-yen, Fa-hsiang, and San-lun Schools of Chinese Buddhism, as well as a minor branch of Chinese T'ien-t'ai.

Kūya—Japanese Buddhist (903–972) who, through personal charisma, fostered the growth of the Amida cult in Japan.

Kyoto—The capital of Japan immediately after the Nara Period. It was formerly called Heian.

lakṣaṇa—Literally "mark"; the doctrine of the three marks of existence, anātman (no-self), anitya (impermanence), and duḥkha (suffering), is said to have been set forth by Buddha as one of his cardinal teachings.

Lalitavistara—The "Detailed Account of the Sports [of the Buddha]"; a noncanonical legend of the life of the Buddha, usually associated with the Sarvāstivādin School.

Lamotte, Étienne—Modern Buddhologist working in Louvain, and author of the classic *Histoire du Bouddhisme Indien des origines à l'ère Śaka*, as well as translator of many important Buddhist texts.

Lam-rim chen-mo—Tibetan text on meditation, written by Tsong-kha-pa.

Laṅkā—Ceylon, now called Śrī Laṅkā, an island off the southern tip of the Indian subcontinent.

Laṅkāvatāra-sūtra—"Sūtra on the Descent into Laṅkā"; a Mahāyānist text emphasizing the doctrines of mind-only (citta-mātra), the three svabhāvas, and the ālaya-vijñāna. Although problematic to classify, it does have many Yogācāra affinities.

Lao-tzŭ—Born in 604 B.C., he is regarded to be the founder of Taoism in China, and is said to have disappeared towards the West in 444 B.C. after composing the Tao Tê Ching.

La Vallée Poussin, Louis de—Great Buddhologist of the early twentieth century, offering translations of many critical Buddhist texts (e.g.,

Vasubandhu's Abhidharmakośa) and many books and articles on various Buddhist subjects. He is regarded as one of the "superstars" of modern Buddhology.

Lhasa—City in Tibet where Atīśa spent most of his time. It remained of primary importance to Tibetan Buddhists up to the time of the takeover by the Communist Chinese.

Liang Dynasty—Dynasty in China, A.D. 502–557.

Licchavi—Kingdom to the east of Kośala and north of Magadha in India which, in spite of being a Brāhmaṇical stronghold, was influenced by Buddha's teaching.

Lin-chi—One of two "houses" of T'ang Dynasty Ch'an which survived until modern times (three other "houses" did not). It emphasizes kung-an and hua-tou, as well as subitism. It was founded by Lin-chi I-hsüan.

Lin-chi I-hsüan—Founder (d. 867) of the Lin-chi "house" of Chinese Ch'an Buddhism.

Liu-tzŭ T'an-Ching—"Platform Sūtra of the Sixth Patriarch"; Chinese Ch'an text which outlines the controversy regarding Hui-nêng, the Sixth Patriarch.

loka—Literally "world." In Buddhist cosmology one of two usual distinctions: the receptacle world (bhājanaloka) and the world of beings (sattvaloka).

Lokakṣema—An Indo-Scythian who arrived in China between 168 and 188 and represented Mahāyānist viewpoints. He produced a partial translation of the Aṣṭasāhasrikā-prajñāpāramitā-sūtra.

lokaprajñapti—This term, literally meaning "world teachings" or "worldly designations" is the nearest equivalent to the English word cosmology.

Lokeśvararāja—A Buddha who lived eons before Siddhārtha Gautama. In the Larger Sukhāvatīvyūha-sūtra it is Lokeśvararāja that preaches to Dharmākara.

Lokottaravāda—"Holders of the Doctrine of the Other-Worldliness [of the Buddha]"; a sect of Hīnayāna Buddhism which broke off from the Mahāsāṃghikas. They maintained that the body of the Buddha was transcendental from the time of his birth to the time of his death. Consequently, his behavior as a human was merely a convention.

Lotus Sūtra—English equivalent for the Saddharmapuṇḍarīka-sūtra.

Lo-yang—Capital of the Northern Wei Dynasty in China, and an important Buddhist center.

Lu—Chinese word for Vinaya. A school emerged in China whose primary concern was the study and teaching of the Vinaya texts.

Mādhyamika—A Mahāyāna Buddhist school, founded by Nāgārjuna which purported to be (as the title indicates) "the middle way." A clever dialectician, Nāgārjuna was able to defeat many opponents of Buddhism in debate. He was careful not to establish a position of his own, which also could be defeated. In his classic Mūlamādhyamika-kārikās, as well as his Vigrahavyāvartanī, Nāgārjuna discusses and utilizes such basic concepts as śūnyatā (emptiness), pratītya-samutpāda (dependent origination), and prajñapti (language constructs) in establishing a forceful Buddhist school.

Madhyāntika—In Sarvāstivādin legends it is stated that Madhyāntika converted the city of Kaśmīr, establishing a home for this newly emergent school, around 250 B.C.

Madhyāntavibhāga-śāstra—Yogācāra text attributed to Maitreyanātha.

Magadha—Kingdom in India ruled by Bimbisāra (and his descendents) from its capital of Rājagṛha. It was a most forceful and viable kingdom during Buddha's lifetime.

mahābheda—Literally "great schism"; this refers to the first split in Buddhism, resulting of the separation of the Sthaviras and Mahāsāṃghikas.

Mahābodhivaṃsa—Noncanonical Pāli text providing information on Aśoka's council at Pāṭaliputra.

Mahādeva—Buddhist monk in the second century following Buddha's parinirvāṇa who raised the notorious "five theses" concerning the status of the arhant. These five theses may have played a part in the mahābheda.

Mahākāśyapa—Disciple of Śākyamuni regarded by Chinese Ch'an as the second Indian Patriarch (Buddha being the first).

Mahākauṣṭhila—In some circles thought to be the author of the Saṅgītiparyāya, one of the books in the Abhidharma Piṭaka of the Sarvāstivādins.

Mahāmeghavana—Park in Ceylon given to the Buddhists by Devānaṃpiyatissa, where they established the great monastery Mahāvihāra.

Mahāmudrā—Literally "Great Symbol"; general term for a complex system of Tibetan meditative techniques aimed at spontaneity.

Mahānāma—King of Ceylon who ruled from 409 to 431. It is said he composed the Mahāvaṃsa.

Mahāpadma Nanda—King whose capital was located in Pāṭaliputra, probably the site of the council at which the mahābheda occurred.

Mahāprajāpatī—The sister of Queen Māyā who married King Śuddhodana after her sister's death and served as foster mother to Siddhārtha Gautama. She later became the first Buddhist nun.

Mahāprajñāpāramitā-śāstra—A commentary, attributed to Nāgārjuna (perhaps incorrectly).

Mahāsāṃghika—Literally "Great Assembly"; one of the two schools resulting from the mahābheda. At the time of the schism they were considered liberal and progressive. In many senses, they contributed much to the rise of the Mahāyāna. Although officially being classed as

Hīnayānists, we might call them Mahāyāna precursors.

Mahāsattva—Literally "Great Being"; another descriptive applied to those on the Bodhisattva path.

Mahāsena—King of Ceylon who reigned from 334 to 362 and supported Mahāyāna Buddhism in Ceylon.

Mahāvaṃsa—The "Great Chronicle" of Ceylon, written by King Mahānāma in the fifth century A.D. It contains much information on the history of Buddhism in Ceylon, as well as providing some information on Indian Buddhism. It is available in Pāli.

Mahāvastu—The "Great Account"; a noncanonical legend of the life of the Buddha, written in Buddhist Sanskrit, belonging to the Lokottaravādin school.

Mahāvibhāṣā—A later Sarvāstivādin Abhidharma text whose title literally means "the Great [Book of] Options." It apparently emerged out of a huge gathering of monks, assembled by Kaniṣka, in which all the opinions on doctrinal points were recorded and many conclusions arrived at.

Mahāvihāra—Great monastic institution in Ceylon, built during the reign of Devānaṃpiyatissa (250–210 B.C.) in Mahāmeghavana park, and housing a branch of the Bodhi Tree.

Mahāyāna—Literally "Great Vehicle"; a school of Buddhism which arose gradually several hundred years after Buddha's parinirvāṇa. More liberal socially and more speculative philosophically than the traditional, orthodox Buddhists of the time, this new group emphasized the Bodhisattva path, the concepts of śūnyatā (emptiness), trikāya (three bodies of Buddha), and tathatā (suchness), as well as sparking a new creative drive in the production of Buddhist sūtras and śāstras (many of these written in the author's own name).

Mahāyānasaṃgraha-śāstra—Yogācāra discourse ascribed to either Asaṅga or Vasubandhu, and literally meaning the "Compendium of Mahāyāna." It was later translated in Chinese by Paramārtha, and formed the basis of the Shê-lun School of Chinese Buddhism.

Mahāyānaśraddhotpāda—Literally the "Awakening of Faith in the Mahāyāna"; a Yogācāra oriented discourse. Translated into Chinese as the Ta-ch'eng Ch'i-hsin Lun, it was important in the Shê-lun School of Chinese Buddhism.

Mahāyānasūtrālaṅkāra—Yogācāra text attributed to Maitreyanātha.

Mahinda—Son of King Aśoka who led a mission to Ceylon, thus establishing Buddhism in the island kingdom. He is celebrated in Ceylon with the Mahinda Festival, aiming at purifying the religion (sāsana) from heresy.

Mahīśāsaka—Hīnayāna Buddhist school which may have broken from the

Vibhajyavādins. They have some similarities to the Theravādins and may be "continental" brothers to this latter group. They do, however, hold that enlightenment comes suddenly rather than gradually.

Maitreya—The future Buddha. Legend has it that he dictated many of the Yogācāra texts to Asaṅga, and they are listed under the name of Maitreya-nātha.

Maitreyanātha—Yogācāra has many texts ascribed to this figure who may be, as noted in the previous entry, simply a rubric to represent the future Buddha Maitreya. Texts ascribed to him include the Abhisamayālaṅkāra, Mahāyānasūtrālaṅkāra, Madhyāntavibhāga, and Dharmadharmatā-vibhāga.

Majjhantika—Leader of an Aśokan mission to Gandhāra. Because of the similarity in the name of this person mentioned in the Pāli records, and his Sanskrit counterpart Madhyāntika (said in one legend to be responsible for the Sarvāstivādin sect in Gandhāra), some scholars have concluded that they are the same person. The above statement would make Aśoka responsible for the rise of the Sarvāstivādin School of Buddhism.

Majjhima Nikāya—"Collection of Middle Length Sayings"; the second section in the Sutta Piṭaka of the Pāli Canon.

Makiguchi, Tsuneburō—Founder of the Sōkagakkai sect of Buddhism in Japan.

Mālānanda—Buddhist monk who helped spread Buddhism in Korea in A.D. 384.

manas—One of the many terms in Buddhist vocabulary used to represent mind, and consequently, of prime interest for Abhidharma. In the Laṅkāvatāra-sūtra manas represents a more subtle "mental" which receives input from the other consciousnesses and processes it. It is in Yogācāra that we see an attempt to differentiate between citta, manas, and vijñāna (often used synonymously in other Buddhist schools).

maṇḍala—In Tantric Buddhism, a diagram or symbolic representation, in which the meditator creates a world wherein he is the central Buddha. Thus the maṇḍala becomes the entire universe, replete with Buddhas, deities, etc.

Mañjuśrī—A Bodhisattva, gradually gaining importance in Buddhism, to the point where his image was often found along with that of Buddha, or in some cases, stood alone as the sole recipient of reverence. He is one of the prime interlocutors in the Vimalakīrti-nirdeśa-sūtra.

manomayakāya—That which results as a consequence of āśraya-parāvṛtti or "turning back at the base." It is a will-body in which man is free from mundane contradictions.

mantra—In Tantric Buddhism a "tool for thinking" (in Lama Anagarika

Govinda's words) which utilizes the symbolic power in sounds as a means for directly experiencing things as they really are. It is of such importance that this remarkably complex system became known as Mantrayāna or the "Mantra Vehicle." One of the most famous mantras is the oft quoted Oṃ Maṇi Padme Hūṃ.

mappō (C. mo-fa)—"Latter-Day Dharma"; that period of time (which we are now experiencing) in which Buddha's teaching has fallen into decay.

Māra—Derived from the verb which means "to die," this is the name of a Demon who tempted Buddha with his three daughters (Discontent, Delight, and Desire). He also suggested to Buddha at the end of the latter's life, that he enter parinirvāṇa.

mārga—The "path" leading to the cessation of suffering. The fourth Noble Truth is often referred to as the mārga.

Mar-pa—Tibetan Buddhist who was the father of the bKa-rgyud-pa lineage. He went to India, studied with Nāropa, and returned to Tibet where he eventually passed on the lineage to Milarepa.

Maudgalyāyana—One of Buddha's chief early disciples. Converted to Buddhism shortly after his friend Śāriputra, he was reputed to be very adept in magical powers. Several Sarvāstivādin sources mention a figure named Maudgalyāyana as the author of the Prajñaptiśāstra, an Abhidharma text.

Mauryan Dynasty—That dynasty in India, beginning with Candragupta Maurya (around 320 B.C.), and which continued with his son Bindusāra and grandson Asoka. In Indian history it represents one of the most forceful and important dynasties recorded.

Māyā—The wife of King Śuddhodana and mother of Siddhārtha Gautama. She dies seven days after the birth of her son.

Meiji Restoration—That movement (1867) which marked the end of the military control of Japan by the samurai.

Menander—Bactrian king who was apparently converted to Buddhism by the learned monk Nāgasena. Their conversations are recorded in the very valuable Pāli text Milindapañha ("The Questions of King Milinda").

Mi-la ras-pa—The chief disciple of Mar-pa. After much trial and tribulation, he received the "Teaching" from Mar-pa and became one of the most revered persons in the history of Tibetan Buddhism. Much of his life is revealed in the textual story of Milarepa's (as he is often called) life.

Milindapañha—"The Questions of King Milinda"; a noncanonical Pāli text recording the conversations of the Bactrian king Menander and the Buddhist monk Nāgasena. The text is most valuable as it serves as a compendium of Theravāda doctrine.

Ming—An Emperor in the Han Dynasty in China who is said to have had a dream which caused him to send an embassy to India to import Buddhism to China (around A.D. 61 or 64).

Mo-fa (J. mappō)—"Latter-Day Dharma"; that period of time (which we are now experiencing) in which Buddha's teaching has fallen into decay.

Moggaliputta Tissa—Buddhist monk chosen to preside over Aśoka's council at Pāṭaliputra.

Mo-ho chih-kuan—"Tranquillity and Insight According to Mahāyāna"; a work by the T'ien-t'ai Buddhist Chih-i which propounds a system of meditation.

Mou-tzŭ—Chinese figure sympathetic to Buddhism during its early history in China.

Mou-tzŭ Li-huo Lun—"A Discussion of Doubtful Points"; a native Chinese treatise which falls into "apologetic" literature, justifying Buddhist practice and doctrine initially found to be abhorrent to the Chinese.

Mudang—A priestess in Korean Shamanism who functions as an intermediary between humans and spirits.

Mūlamādhyamika-kārikās—The "Middle Stanzas" of Nāgārjuna, representing his chief work and which reflects his doctrinal position. It is perhaps one of the greatest of all Buddhist documents being perplexing, complicated, and remarkably insightful, clearly demonstrating the genius of this brilliant Buddhist thinker.

Mūlasarvāstivāda—The name, meaning "Root Sarvāstivādins," indicates that this Hīnayāna school either envisioned themselves as the original Sarvāstivādins or the preservers of its orthodoxy. They probably broke from the Sarvāstivādins around the fourth or fifth century A.D., and their name is not mentioned in the records until around the seventh century. They produced an elaborate Tripiṭaka and a complete biography of the Buddha.

Müller, Friedrich Max—German philologist (1823–1900) who was a pioneer in bringing Indian religious texts to the attention of Europeans. He edited the fifty volume Sacred Books of the East Series.

Mumonkan—"The Gateless Barrier," a Japanese translation of the Chinese text Wu-mên Kuan.

mu-shin—"No-mind," a state of consciousness in Zen Buddhism.

nāga—Literally "serpent"; in Buddhism they, for example, represent snakes worshipped by early tribal groups in Ceylon.

Nāgārjuna—Buddhist philosopher who probably lived in the second or third century A.D. and founded the Mādhyamika School of Buddhism. A clever dialectician, as evidenced in his Mūlamādhyamika-kārikās and Vigrahavyāvartanī, he excelled at debate, was a mystic of high attainment, and ranks among the very greatest of Buddhist thinkers. To this day his writings are still being puzzled over by Buddhologists.

Nāgasena—Learned Buddhist monk, whose conversations with the Bactrian king Menander are recorded in the Milindapaña ("The Questions of King Milinda"). He excelled in debate, was a master of Buddhist doctrine, and is said to have converted the erudite king to Buddhism.

Nālandā—City on the outskirts of Rājagṛha which became the seat of one of the most important Buddhist universities.

Nam Myōhō Renge Kyō—Literally "Hail to the Scripture of the Lotus of the True Teaching" or simply "Homage to the Lotus Sūtra." Nichiren Buddhists repeat this formula in the hopes of high attainment.

Namo Amita Buddha (C. Nan-mo A-mi-t'o Fo; J. Namu Amida Butsu)—Literally "Homage to Amida Buddha"; a formula used by Pure Land Buddhists as a means of offering devotion to Amita, thus hoping to gain rebirth in his Western Paradise. In Chinese, this practice is called nien-fo; in Japanese, nembutsu.

Nara—Period in Japanese history so named because the capital was Nara. Established in 710, it survived until 794 when the capital was moved to Heian (modern-day Kyoto).

Nāropa—An Indian scholar who turned yogin. He received the "Teaching" from Tilopa after much difficulty. Nāropa later served as Mar-pa's guru.

Nat—The native, indigenous religion in Burma. It later takes on strong Buddhist influences.

nembutsu (C. nian-fo)—"Invocation of Buddha"; vocal praise of the Buddha by the repetition of Amida's name. In Japanese Buddhism this practice is followed by both Pure Land Schools (Jōdo Shū and Jōdo Shinshū).

nian chu—"Recollection beads"; a rosary for counting off the nian-fo.

nibbāna—The Pāli equivalent of nirvāṇa. For the definition, see the entry for nirvāṇa.

Nichiren—Japanese Buddhist and founder of a sect bearing his name. After originally studying Tendai, he was not satisfied with Buddhist methods, but was convinced of the efficacy of the Lotus Sūtra. He was so convinced that he believed enlightenment to be the result of chanting Nam Myōhō Renge Kyō (see above) while gazing at a diagram or daimoku. He lived from 1222 to 1282.

nidāna—This word has two usages in Buddhist vocabulary. First, it means introduction and is used as such at the beginnings of texts. Secondly, it means link and is used to identify specific elements in the chain of causation (pratītya-samutpāda).

Nidānakathā—"Connected Story"; a noncanonical story of the life of the Buddha, sometimes attributed to the great Theravādin exegete Buddhaghosa and forming the introduction to the Pāli Jātakas.

Niddesa—"Exposition"; the eleventh book in the Khuddaka Nikāya of the Sutta Piṭaka of the Pāli Canon.

nien-fo (J. nembutsu)—"Invocation of Buddha"; vocal praise of the Buddha by the repetition of A-mi-t'o's name. The practice was of primary importance to Chinese Pure Land (Ching-t'u). It was also advocated by early Ch'an, but later dropped as imcompatible with tzŭ-li or one's own power to gain enlightenment.

Nikāya—"Collection"; that title applied to the various parts of the Sutta Piṭaka of the Pāli Canon, so named because they are collections of various kinds of sermons.

Nikāyabhedavibhaṅgavyākhyāna—Buddhist text written by Bhavya and containing much information on the early Buddhist sectarian movement.

Nirmāṇakāya—Literally "Magical (or Apparitional) Body"; that term used by Mahāyānists in the trikāya (Three Bodies of Buddha) doctrine to signify the historical Buddha. The Nirmāṇakāya is reputed to have been the preacher of the Hīnayāna discourses, and apparently represents a refinement, on the part of the Mahāyānists, of the notion that Buddha was merely a man.

nirodha—Literally "cessation"; the third Noble Truth, stating that there is a cessation to suffering. As a religious attainment, often used synonymously with nirvāṇa, two forms are noted: sa-upādiśeṣa nirodha (nirodḥa with a "remnant") and an-upādiśeṣa nirodha (nirodha without a "remnant"). Of course it has been debated whether "remnant" was moral or physical.

nirvāṇa—Literally "blowing out"; in Buddhism the goal of religious practice. The texts are very enigmatic on the subject of nirvāṇa, and, of course, Buddha refused to offer speculations when questioned about its nature. Clearly, it is that which is to be experienced. According to Hīnayānists it is release from the suffering of saṃsāra; for the Mahāyānists it is the experience that saṃsāra and nirvāṇa are not different.

niṣyandanirmāṇa Buddha—The Buddha who issues forth from a pure state into specific incarnations, be they subhuman, human, or suprahuman.

Nobunaga, Oda—He destroyed the huge Tendai monastic complex on Mt. Hiei in 1571 in Japan.

Nyāya—Literally, "model," "axiom," or "system"; in philosophy it refers to the science of logic. In Hinduism, one of the classical six darśanas is Nyāya. It also refers to the study of logic in Buddhism.

Nyāyabindu—Buddhist logic text written by Dharmakīrti.

Nyāyabindu-ṭīkā—Dharmottara's commentary on the Nyāyabindu.

Nyāya Darśana—The School of Logic in Indian philosophy.

Nyāyamukha—Buddhist logic text written by Dignāga.

Nyāyapraveśa—Buddhist logic text written by Dignāga.

Nyāya-sūtra—Basic text of the Nyāya Darśana in Indian philosophy, ascribed to the Hindu (not Buddhist) sage Gautama.

Ōjōyōshū—"Compendium on the Essence of Rebirth," written by Genshin; it vividly contrasts the miseries of hell with the joys of the Pure Land.

Olcott, Henry Steel—Co-founder, with Madame Blavatsky, of The Theosophical Society. He lived from 1832 to 1907.

Oldenberg, Hermann—Great German Buddhologist (and Indologist) (1854–1920) who translated many Buddhist texts, edited the Pāli Vinaya Piṭaka, and wrote the classic *Buddha: Sein Leben, seine Lehre, seine Gemeinde.*

Pagan—Established as the capital of Burma in A.D. 841.

Pāli Canon—The Tripiṭaka of the Theravāda School of Buddhism.

pālimuttakavinicchaya—"Decisions not found in the Pāli texts"; the heading under which exceptions to the stated rules of Vinaya could be made.

pañcaśīla—The five vows which Buddhist lay disciples observe. They include not to kill, lie, steal, take intoxicants, and engage in unlawful sexual intercourse.

Pañcaviṃśatisāhasrikā-prajñāpāramitā-sūtra—The "25,000 Line Perfection of Wisdom Sūtra"; one of the most important texts in the "large group"

p'an chiao—"Dividing the Teaching"; a system of dividing the whole corpus of Buddha's teaching into parts according to some established criterion. of prajñāpāramitā sūtras.

Paramārtha—Buddhist translator and commentator of the sixth century A.D. who helped introduce Yogācāra to China.

paramārtha satya—"Ultimate truth," as contrasted with worldly truth, (loka) saṃvṛti-satya, in Mādhyamika thought particularly.

pāramitā—"Perfection"; the traditional six (sometimes ten) practices engaged in by the Bodhisattva on his path to complete, perfect enlightenment. They include dāna (giving, charity), śīla (morality), kṣānti (patience), vīrya (vigor, energy), samādhi (meditation), and prajñā (wisdom).

paratantra-svabhāva—Relative knowledge, according to Yogācāra; that which arises from the perception of worldly phenomena. While an advance over imagined phenomena (parikalpita), it still maintains the duality of perceiver and thing perceived.

parikalpita-svabhāva—In Yogācāra, that which is imagined or mentally contructed. It is the sort of reality emerging from mistaking the unreal for the real.

parinirvāṇa—The final "blowing out," or that which describes Buddha's experience at the moment of his death.

pariniṣpanna-svabhāva—Perfect knowledge, according to Yogācāra; it is seeing things as they really are, having gone beyond all discrimination.

Paritta—Literally "extinction"; a ceremony performed on various occasions, both auspicious and unfortunate, such as moving into a new dwelling or exorcising spirits.

parivrājaka—A generic term identifying the general wanderers' community of religious mendicants in ancient India. Buddha's followers represented only one of these groups.

Pārśva—Sarvāstivādin Buddhist monk who issued invitations to all those who were to be considered initially for inclusion in Kaniṣka's council. 499 were finally selected and Vasumitra presided over the council.

Pāṭaliputra—Capital of Magadha during the reign of King Aśoka. It was the scene of Aśoka's council, as well as probably being the site of an earlier council held during the reigin of Mahāpadma Nanda.

paṭimāghara—Literally "image house"; place where, in the Pāli records, we are informed that Buddha images were placed.

Paṭisambhidā-magga—"The Way of Analysis"; the twelfth book in the Khuddaka Nikāya of the Sutta Piṭaka of the Pāli Canon.

Paṭṭhāna—Literally "Causal Relations"; one of the books in the Abhidhamma Piṭaka of the Pāli Canon. It contains a thorough discussion of dependent origination.

Pegu—Prominent center of the Talaings in Lower Burma.

Pelliot, Paul—Member of the École Française D'Extrême-Orient in Hanoi who collected manuscripts from Central Asia and published *La Mission Pelliot en Asie Centrale* in 1924.

Petavatthu—"Stories About Hungry Ghosts"; the seventh book in the Khuddaka Nikāya of the Sutta Piṭaka of the Pāli Canon.

Pi-yên Lu—The "Blue Cliff Records"; 100 dialogues compiled in 1125 by Yüan-wu, each with a mnemonic verse of Hsüeh-tou and comment by Yüan-wu (who was a Chinese Buddhist monk).

Po-chang Huai-hai—Chinese Ch'an monk (720–814) who drew up a monastic constitution which was more detailed and, in some respects, contrary to the Vinaya.

poṣadha—The Buddhist Sanskrit form of the Sanskrit upavasatha (fast day) and the Pāli uposatha. It is a twice monthly meeting where the monks read the Prātimokṣa (confessing any offenses) and transact monastic business (according to Karmavācanā). It was instituted at King Bimbisāra's suggestion.

prajñā—Literally "wisdom"; it is the sixth of the perfections (pāramitās) and is applied to the first two steps on the eightfold path (right understanding and right thought). The Bodhisattva who attains wisdom may be said to be "face to face" with ultimate reality as the title of the sixth Bodhisattva stage (bhūmi) indicates.

Prajñākaragupta—Well known Buddhist logician who lived in the eighth century A.D.

Prajñāpāramitā-sūtras—Literally "Perfection of Wisdom Sūtras"; that class of Buddhist scriptures which marks the rise of Mahāyāna Buddhism. The sūtras often feature Buddha's famous disciples as interlocutors (such as Śāriputra), but we find a less well known person, Subhūti, as perhaps most important. These texts frequently contrast mundane and ultimate reality, using śūnyatā (emptiness) as a striking epistemological tool. It is said that originally a prajñāpāramitā sūtra existed in Prakrit, but perhaps the earliest text is the Sanskrit Aṣṭasāhasrikā-prajñāpāramitā-sūtra.

prajñapti—Literally "designations" or "language constructs"; the superimposition of "concepts" onto bare experience.

Prajñaptiśāstra—One of the books in the Abhidharma Piṭaka of the Sarvāstivādin School of Buddhism. It is attributed to Maudgalyāyana, and contains the cosmological notions of the school, as well as a study of volition and a section on the nature of Buddha.

Prajñaptivāda—A sect of Hīnayāna Buddhism which broke off from the Mahāsāṃghikas. They held that there was a distinction between real entities (referred to in Buddha's teaching) and mere concepts.

Prakaraṇapāda—One of the books in the Abhidharma Piṭaka of the Sarvāstivādin School of Buddhism. It is attributed to Vasumitra, and contains two ways of ordering events: an older one, organized around the skandhas, and a newer one, organized around form (rūpa), mind or consciousness (citta), factors associated with mind (cittasaṃprayukta-saṃskāras, caitasikas), factors not associated with mind (cittaviprayukta-saṃskāras), and unconditioned elements (asaṃskṛta dharmas).

pramāṇa—Right, measure, standard, or authority. In Logic, the various sources of knowledge (i.e., authority).

Pramāṇasamuccaya—Buddhist text by the logician Dignāga, the first chapter of which had much influence on the epistemology and logic of Tibetan Mahāyāna.

Pramāṇa-vāda—Sanskrit term often used to indicate the science of logic (in general terms).

praṇidhāna—Literally "vow"; taken by the Buddha (and all Bodhisattvas), the vow emphasizes saving all sentient beings by leading them to complete, perfect enlightenment.

prasaṅga—The Sanskrit term for the reductio ad absurdum argumentation used by Nāgārjuna in debating his opponents. A branch of Mādhyamika later takes the name prasaṅgika indicating the orientation of their emphasis.

Prasenajit—The Indian king of Kośala who, during Buddha's lifetime, made gifts to the saṃgha.

Prātimokṣa—A paracanonical code of monastic offenses which is recited twice monthly at the Poṣadha ceremony and represents the primary tool for the enforcement of monastic discipline.

pratītya-samutpāda—Literally "dependent origination"; the Buddhist chain of causation emphasizing the relational aspect of all elements of existence. It is depicted as a twelve spoked wheel, operating on the formula "because of this, that becomes; because of that, something else becomes."

Pratyekabuddha—Literally "private" or "solitary" Buddha; the term applies to those attaining enlightenment on their own and not going into the world to preach the path. Of the three vehicles mentioned most often by the Mahāyānists, this is the second (the other two being the Śrāvaka and Bodhisattva vehicles).

Pratyekabuddha-yāna—The vehicle of the "private Buddha." This is the course of those who serve as their own teachers and seek nirvāṇa for themselves. It contrasts both the Śrāvaka-yāna and Bodhisattva-yāna. The concept is found in many Buddhist texts, both Hīnayāna and Mahāyāna.

Pravāraṇā—The "Invitation" ceremony held at the end of the rainy season retreat. It dealt with purity during the rainy season, and was formally handled under one of the Karmavācanās.

pravrajyā—Literally "going forth"; contrasted with full ordination (upasaṃpadā), this is the initial ordination into the Buddhist monkhood. In practice it was regulated by a Karmavācanā and occupies a chapter in the Skandhaka portion of the Vinaya Piṭaka (the Pravrajyāvastu).

preta—Literally "hungry ghost"; one of the six destinies (gatis) into which one may be reborn. Knowing no peace, one in this realm is destined to constantly wander around searching for bits of food.

Prome—Main center of the Pyus (a Tibeto-Burmese speaking people) in northern Burma.

Pudgalavāda—Literally "Personalists"; a generic name indicating that group of Buddhists maintaining the doctrine of the pudgala (i.e., person). The pudgala doctrine states that what transmigrates is actually the pudgala, something neither indentical with nor different from the five skandhas. Many Buddhists felt this group to be heretical in the sense of violating the anātman doctrine.

Puggalapaññatti—"Description of Persons"; one of the books in the Abhidhamma Piṭaka of the Theravādins. It analyzes persons in terms of three basic personality types (lust, hatred, and delusion) and their subdivisions.

puṇḍarīka—A lotus flower; found in the title of the Saddharmapuṇḍarīka-sūtra, Sūtra on the Lotus of the True Teaching.

puṇyakarma—Literally "auspicious karma"; it usually refers to that stock of past good karma built up by those on the path to enlightenment.

Purāṇa—Monk who refuses to join the first council, explaining that he chooses to retain Buddha's doctrine and discipline as he remembers it to have been spoken by the Buddha.

Pure Land Sūtras—That body of literature dealing with discourses on the Pure Land of the Buddha Amitābha (often noted to be the Western Paradise), and consisting primarily of three texts: the Larger Sukhāvatī-vyūha-sūtra, the Smaller Sukhāvatīvyūha-sūtra, and the Amitāyur-dhyāna-sūtra.

Pūrṇa—Reputed to be, in the Tibetan tradition, the author of the Dhātukāya, one of the books in the Abhidharma Piṭaka of the Sarvāstivādins.

Pyus—A Tibeto-Burmese speaking people who, in the second century A.D. wandered into northern Burma. They established their main center at Prome.

Rāhula—Buddha's son whose name literally means "fetter," and who became a monk at age seven, later becoming chief of all novices.

Rājagṛha—During Buddha's time, the capital of Magadha. It was the location of the first Buddhist monastery and the site of the first Buddhist council allegedly held after Buddha's parinirvāṇa.

Ratnākaraśānti—Indian Tantric master who passed on the cycle of the Hevajra Tantra to the Tibetan 'Brog-mi.

Ratnakīrti—Buddhist logician around A.D. 1050 who was the pupil of Jñānaśrīmitra and who wrote the Apohasiddhi.

Ratnakūṭa—In Buddhist literature, a name given to a rather varied group of Mahāyāna sūtras, the Vimalakīrti-nirdeśa-sūtra being but one example. In the Tibetan and Chinese canons, this class of literature includes 49 Mahāyāna sūtras.

Reihai Seiten—"Service Book" of the Jōdo Shinshū School of Japanese Buddhism. It contains Fa-chao's "Nien-fo on Five Notes."

Revata—In the tradition of the second Buddhist council at Vaiśālī, Revata is a well respected monk who supports Yaśas in his stand against the vṛjiputraka bhikṣus.

Ṛg-veda—The first and most authoritative of the four Vedas. It consists of 1028 hymns to the various Hindu deities and was probably written around 1200 B.C.

Rhys Davids, Caroline Augusta Foley—Former student and later wife of the great Buddhologist Thomas William Rhys Davids. She was a vigorous editor and translator in her own right, and wrote several secondary books criticizing the traditional expositions on Buddhism as being products of monkish elitists. She propounded a Buddhism originally aimed at all people, and was regarded with some measure of criticism by many later scholars of Buddhism for supporting unsubstantiated theories.

Rhys Davids, Thomas William—Founder of the Pali Text Society in 1881, he was perhaps the most forceful figure in the editing and translating of the texts of the Theravādins. He was co-compiler (with William Stede) of a Pāli-English dictionary, now a standard for all students of Pāli. In addition, he wrote many books and articles and must be regarded as another "superstar" of Buddhology.

Rinzai (C. Lin-chi)—Japanese branch of Zen Buddhism derived from the Lin-chi branch of Chinese Buddhism. Brought to Japan by Eisai, it emphasizes the use of kōans and the doctrine of subitism.

Ritsu—One of the six academic traditions of Japanese "Nara" Buddhism which had been imported, without substantial modification, from China. It is the Vinaya School.

rNying-ma-pa—Sect of Tibetan Buddhism whose name literally means "ancient ones." They trace their lineage back to the foundation of Buddhism in Tibet. They seem to possess authentic Indian teachings and have tended to be less political than other Tibetan Buddhist sects.

Robinson, Richard Hugh—Founder of the Buddhist Studies Program at The University of Wisconsin (1961). Before his death, he was regarded as the foremost Buddhologist in America, having published the classic *Early Mādhyamika in India and China*, as well as several other books and numerous articles. Many of his translations are now being completed by his former students and will hopefully be published posthumously. He lived from 1926 to 1970.

rūpa—One of the five skandhas, dealing with those elements in the realm of "form." Since rūpa deals with the physical or form realm, it is of primary importance to Abhidharmists' analyses of existence.

Rūpakāya—In Hīnayānist terms, another designation for the "Form-Body" of Buddha, indicating his existence as a human.

Sadāparibhūta—"Ever Not-Condemn"; a Bodhisattva in the Saddharma-puṇḍarīka-sūtra who approached people saying, "I do not condemn you."

Saddharmapuṇḍarīka-sūtra—"Sūtra on the Lotus of the True Teaching"; a Mahāyānist sūtra which combated Hīnayāna doctrines as partial, shallow, and selfish, and presented a new view of the Buddha as eternal. It is a Vaipulya-sūtra, and often uses parables to illustrate its points.

Saichō—Buddhist monk in Japan who brought T'ien-t'ai Buddhism from

China to Japan (calling it Tendai in Japan) in the ninth century. He was posthumously given the name Dengyō Daishi.

sakṛdāgāmin—In the Hīnayānist stages of sanctification, this technical term means "once returner," and indicates that the person in question will attain enlightenment in one more lifetime.

Śākya—Tribe living in the foothills of the Himalayas, ruled over by King Śuddhodana and Queen Māyā, into which the future Buddha is born.

Śākyamuni—An epithet used to describe Siddhārtha Gautama, the historical Buddha, and meaning "sage of the Śākya (tribe)."

samādhi—Literally "trance" or "concentration"; the concentration of the mind on a single object with the resulting one-pointedness of mind. It also refers to steps 6 through 8 on the eightfold path (right effort, right mindfulness, and right concentration) and the fifth pāramitā or perfection.

Sāmaññaphala-sutta—A sutta in the Dīgha Nikāya of the Pāli Canon dealing with the "Fruits of the Life of a Recluse." It deals with the contemplative path in terms of withdrawal from sensory input in the progressive stages of trance (jhāna).

Samantabhadra—A well-known Bodhisattva who, in the Saddharmapuṇḍarīka-sūtra, protects the preachers of the Lotus Sūtra.

Samantapāsādikā—Voluminous Pāli commentary on the entire Vinaya Piṭaka.

samatha (S. śamatha)—Literally "calming down"; that portion of Buddhist meditation aiming at quieting the mind as a prerequisite to the careful observation of events called vipassanā (S. vipaśyanā) or "insight." The two practices are part and parcel of the meditational schema outlined in Buddhaghosa's Visuddhimagga.

Sāma-veda—The second Veda, the Veda of "Chants," takes many of the verses of the Ṛg-veda and reorganizes them so as to be applicable to the sacrificial ceremony.

Samayabhedoparacanacakra—Text written by Vasumitra containing much information on the sectarian movement in early Buddhism.

Saṃbhogakāya—According to Mahāyāna, the second of the three bodies of Buddha. This body, literally meaning "Enjoyment Body" or "Reward Body," is the preacher of the Mahāyāna sūtras and is seen by those on the Bodhisattva path. It is apparently a sort of quasi-material body mediating between the Nirmāṇakāya and Dharmakāya.

Saṃdhinirmocana-sūtra—A Mahāyānist text, generally identified with Yogācāra, whose title literally means "The Explication of Mysteries."

Saṃgha—Literally meaning "group," this term has been generally accepted as the designation for the Buddhist Order. It is the third in the Triratna or "Three Jewels."

saṃghabheda—Literally "schism in the saṃgha"; a term usually applied to the splitting up of sects. It is dealt with formally by one of the Karmavācanās.

saṃghakarma—Literally "act of the saṃgha"; the term applies to the means by which monastic business is transacted. Saṃghakarmas are, of course, regulated by the procedures of Karmavācanā.

saṃjñā—"Perception," the third of the five skandhas. It determines the characteristics of an object (without placing a "tag" or "label" on the object).

Sāṃkhya—One of the six classical schools (darśanas) of Indian Philosophy. They were clearly dualists, positing two eternals (prakṛti and puruṣa), and were frequently opponents of the Buddhists.

Saṃmitīya—One of the sects of Hīnayāna Buddhism classed in the Pudgalavādin category.

Saṃmitīyanikāya-śāstra—A Chinese translation of an Abhidharma text of the Saṃmitīya sect.

Sammohavinodanī—Buddhaghosa's commentary on the Vibhaṅga, one of the books in the Abhidhamma Piṭaka of the Pāli Canon.

saṃsāra—The cycle of perpetual flux, literally meaning "to wander through (or pass through) intensely," and used to designate the cycle of transmigration. It is frequently contrasted to nirvāṇa.

saṃskāra—The fourth skandha, literally meaning "mental constituents." It denotes the volitional aspects of the individual and "puts the mind in action."

saṃskṛta—"Conditioned"; used to designate those elements or dharmas which are originated through conditions.

samudaya—The Sanskrit term for the second of the Noble Truths, that of cause. This Noble Truth emphasizes that there is a cause for suffering, centered around the various forms of craving.

samurai—The military class in Japan who ruled during the Kamakura Period.

saṃvṛti-satya—Literally "worldly (or conventional) truth"; that which is contrasted with paramārtha-satya or ultimate truth. It reflects the two perspectives in which things may be viewed.

Saṃyuktāgama—"Linked Discourses"; the counterpart, in the Sanskrit Buddhist Canon, of the Saṃyutta Nikāya in the Pāli Canon.

Saṃyutta Nikāya—"Collection of Grouped Discourses"; the third section in the Sutta Piṭaka of the Pāli Canon.

Saṅgītiparyāya—One of the books in the Abhidharma Piṭaka of the Sarvāstivādins, reputed to have been written by either Mahākauṣṭhila or Śāriputra, which is a commentary on the Saṅgīti-sūtra and sets forth a résumé of Buddha's teaching.

San-lun—The "Three Treatise School," a classical school of Buddhism in China. It was founded by Kumārajīva (344–413) and organized by Tao-shêng (ca. 360–434), and corresponds to the Indian Mādhyamika School of Buddhism. The three treatises referred to are Nāgārjuna's Mādhyamika-śāstra, Dvadaśadvara, and the Śata-śāstra of Āryadeva.

Sanron (C. San-lun)—One of the six academic traditions of Japanese "Nara" Buddhism which had been imported, without substantial modification, from China. It corresponds to the Indian Mādhyamika and Chinese San-lun.

Śāntirakṣita—Famous Indian Buddhist who made two visits to Tibet, co-founding the Tibetan saṃgha and first monastery in Tibet. He is reputed to have been a noted logician.

Śāriputra—One of Buddha's chief early disciples who is said to have gained enlightenment simply by hearing a versified summary of Buddha's teaching. He is said to have been very learned in Abhidharma, and several Abhidharma texts of various schools bear his name in the title.

Śāriputrābhidharma—Chinese translation of an Abhidharma text, possibly belonging to the Dharmaguptaka sect.

Śāriputraparipṛcchā—Chinese translation of an Abhidharma text, possibly belonging to the Mahāsāṃghika sect.

Sārnāth—Famous place outside of which (in the Deer Park) Buddha preached his first sermon to the five ascetics. It is also the location of an Aśokan edict.

Sarvagāmin—In the tradition surrounding the second Buddhist council, this figure is an elder monk of Vaiśālī, said to have had Ānanda as his teacher. After being questioned by Śāṇavāsin concerning the ten points, the council convenes.

sarvam anityam—"All is impermanent;" statement of the second of the three marks of existence.

sarvam asti—Literally "all is," the terms from which the sect of the Sarvāstivādins take their name. In other words, they hold that "all is." The past is manifest in the present and the future is latent in the present by the transmission of dharmas.

Sarvāstivāda—"Holders of the Doctrine that All Is"; a sect of Hīnayāna Buddhism arising around 250 B.C. and holding to the doctrine of sarvam asti. They maintain that the 75 dharmas (in their own dharma list) had a permanent sort of existence through the three periods of time (past, present, future). In other words, the basic building blocks of existence change, but continuity is maintained. They became one of the most forceful of the Hīnayānist sects and endured about as long as Indian

Buddhism.

Sāsana (S. Śāsana)—A descriptive word meaning "Teaching" and used to denote the Buddhist religion.

Sa-skya-pa—Tibetan sect of Buddhism founded by 'Brog-mi, taking its name from the monastery he founded (Sa-skya) in 1073.

śāstra—Literally a "book" or "treatise"; usually applied to philosophical Buddhist texts which argued various points of interest in Buddhist philosophy.

Śatasāhasrikā-prajñāpāramitā-sūtra—The "100,000 Line Perfection of Wisdom Sūtra." The largest sūtra in this category of texts.

Śata-śāstra—The "Hundred Treatise" text, written by Āryadeva, which attacks various schools and expounds the doctrines of Mādhyamika, especially that of emptiness (śūnyatā).

sati (S. smṛti)—Literally "mindfulness"; the basis of Buddhist meditation seems to rest on the "setting up of mindfulness," as the Satipaṭṭhāna-sutta (S. Smṛtyupasthāna-sūtra) tells us.

Satipaṭṭhāna-sutta (S. Smṛtyupasthāna-sūtra)—A sutta in the Pāli Canon (No. 10 in the Majjhima Nikāya, No. 22 in the Dīgha Nikāya) which outlines the essentials of Buddhist meditation. It, of course, deals with the "setting up of mindfulness."

satori—Japanese technical term for enlightenment.

sattvaloka—In Buddhist cosmology the "world of beings."

Satyasiddhi-śāstra—A Hīnayāna text, written by Harivarman, which discusses emptiness. In some senses it bridges the gap between Hīnayāna and Mahāyāna.

Sautrāntika—A Hīnayāna Buddhist sect emphasizing the efficacy and authority of the sūtras. Vasubandhu's arguments in the Abhidharmakośa criticize the Vaibhāṣikas from a Sautrāntika viewpoint.

śayanāsana—Literally "bed and sitting"; that portion of furniture for the monk concerned with sitting meditation and sleeping facilities. The monk's possessions in the vihāra were meager and were regulated by the Karmavācanā procedure.

Sejo—Korean king who was a devout Buddhist during the Yi Dynasty.

Sejong—The fourth Korean king of the Yi Dynasty who reduced the number of Buddhist sects in Korea from seven to two.

sGam-po-pa—Important Tibetan Buddhist (1079–1153) who received the lineage of the bKa-rgyud-pa school from Milarepa. After sGam-po-pa, the sect split into four branches.

shakubuku—Literally "smash and flatten"; in Sōkagakkai Buddhism, it is an aggressive, persistent, and often violent conversion tactic meant to wear down one's resistance by constant religious assault.

Shan-tao—Chinese Patriarch (613–681) of the Ching-t'u sect of Buddhism, said to have written the Kuan-ching Chu.

Shê-lun—Chinese school of Buddhism based on the Mahāyānasaṃgraha-śāstra. It was later absorbed into the Hua-yen School.

Shên-hsiu—Chinese Buddhist monk (600–706) of the Northern Ch'an School who was identified as the Sixth Patriarch but had it removed by an imperial decision and properly awarded to his rival Hui-nêng of Southern Ch'an.

shikantaza (C. chih-kuan-ta-tso)—"Aiming at nothing except sitting"; a practice used in Sōtō Zen to "stop the mind" in the present moment by merely sitting.

Shin Arahan—Young Theravāda monk who taught and impressed King Anawratā of Pagan (1040–1077). He was put in charge of the saṃgha in unified Burma.

Shingon—School of Buddhism introduced into Japan by Kūkai (later named Kōbō Daishi). It is based on Chên-yên (the Chinese Tantric School of Buddhism), emphasizing Vairocana as the cosmic Buddha and adopting many Tantric practices.

shinkō shūkyō—Literally "New Religions"; a term used in Japan to denote those forms of contemporary, popular Buddhism which grew out of older, established forms but which diverge, in some respects, from the doctrine, practice, and goal of the parent group.

Shinran—Japanese Buddhist (1173–1262) who was a former disciple of Hōnen, but broke from traditional Jōdo Shū and founded his own school called Jōdo Shinshū (the "True Pure Land School").

Shintō—The native religion of Japan, existing before the entry of Buddhism. Throughout Japanese history, there has been much mutual influencing between the two groups.

shogun—Term for a military ruler in Japan. The shoguns reigned throughout the Tokugawa Period.

Shōman-gyō—The Japanese translation of the Śrīmālādevī-sūtra.

Shōmu—One of the most devout and energetic of all Japanese Buddhist sovereigns, under whom many new temples and works of art were created.

Shōsan Suzuki—One of the Buddhist monks during the stagnant and degenerate Tokugawa Period who helped to exemplify the very finest ideals of compassion.

Shōtoku—Prince Regent in Japan (d. 621) who was responsible for the early growth and development of Buddhism in Japan. Perhaps the counterpart of the Indian king Aśoka.

Shōtoku—Daughter of Emperor Shōmu who, like her father, was instrumental in promoting Buddhism.

Shun-tao—Monk who brought Buddhism into Korea from China around A.D. 372.

Siddhārtha—Literally "he whose aim will be accomplished"; name given to Gautama after the prediction by a sage that he would become either a universal monarch or a Buddha.

śīla—Broadly defined to mean morality (although there is no good English equivalent). It seems to be an internally enforced ethical guideline. The third, fourth, and fifth steps on the eightfold path (right speech, right action, and right livelihood) are often called (collectively) śīla, and it is also the second pāramitā or perfection.

skandha—Literally "heap" or "bundle"; the five aggregates which make up the individual. Since it deals with the makeup of the individual, it is of prime importance to Abhidharmists' analyses.

Skandhaka—That portion of the Vinaya Piṭaka containing a running history of the monastic order, revealed through a series of regulations pertaining to the organization of the saṃgha. It functions on the basis of the acts and ceremonies dictated by the Karmavācanās, and seems to be an outgrowth of this manner of transacting monastic business of all kinds.

Sōkagakkai—"Society for the Creation of Value"; one of the largest "new religions" of Japan. It draws much of its religious input from Nichiren Buddhism. It has much appeal to those socially and economically frustrated segments of society.

Soma—Substance consumed in Vedic times and said to produce divine ecstasy and magical powers. Some associate it with the psychotropic mushroom *amanita muscaria*. Later, it was deified, with Soma the god taking his place in the Vedic pantheon.

Sŏn—A Korean Buddhist Ch'an group that eventually broke into nine branches.

Sŏnjong—Buddhist meditation school in Korea which was composed of the Chinese schools of Vinaya, T'ien-t'ai, and Ch'an.

Sōtō—Japanese school of Zen Buddhism, derived from the Chinese Ts'ao-tung Ch'an. It was introduced into Japan by Dōgen, and emphasizes shikantaza ("just sitting") and gradualism.

śraddhā—Literally "faith" or "trust"; emphasizing faith in the Buddha, his Dharma, and his Saṃgha. It is not to be taken in the sense of "blind" faith but rather that which is quite open to the experiential realm.

śramaṇera—A novice Buddhist monk.

Śrāvaka—Literally a "hearer" or one who has heard Buddha's teachings directly. This title would thus apply to all of Buddha's early disciples.

The Mahāyānists use it in the pejorative sense to represent those who cannot understand the teachings of prajñāpāramitā.

Śrāvaka-yāna—The vehicle of the hearers or disciples. It represents that vehicle, according to the Mahāyānists, which includes those who must follow authoritative teaching to reach nirvāṇa. In other words, those who were Buddha's early disciples fall into this group. It is certainly negative in this usage.

srotāpanna—Literally "stream winner"; one who has entered the stream of Buddha's teachings and is on the path to enlightenment. It is the first stage of sanctification, and is attained by gaining insight into the Four Noble Truths.

Ssŭ-shih-erh Chang Ching—"Sūtra in 42 Chapters"; the earliest Buddhist text in China, said to have been imported by emperor Ming.

Stcherbatsky, Th.—Great Russian scholar of Buddhism. Well versed in the many Buddhist languages, as well as several European languages, Stcherbatsky translated many texts, perhaps his most noted being the Nyāyabindu (Vol. II. of *Buddhist Logic*). His book *The Central Conception of Buddhism and the Meaning of the Word "Dharma"* is one of the classics in the field.

Stein, Sir Mark Aurel—He followed the route of Alexander the Great and published *Serindia* (1921) and *Innermost Asia* (1928). He is partly responsible for the rediscovery of Tun-huang. He lived from 1862 to 1943.

Sthavira—Literally "Elder"; that title applied to the early schools of Buddhism who broke from the Mahāsāṃghikas. Sometimes, Sthavira is used as an inoffensive substitute for Hīnayāna.

Sthaviravāda—Literally "Holders of the Doctrine of the Elders"; that school emerging from the mahābheda and holding doctrines contrary to the Mahāsāṃghikas. Although the word transliterates to Theravāda in Pāli, it is not to be confused with this later school of Buddhism in Ceylon.

Sthiramati—An Indian Buddhist scholar whose commentary on Vasubandhu's Triṃśikā is one of the bases of the Chinese Fa-hsiang School of Buddhism.

sthūlātyaya—Literally "grave offense"; that category of offenses named after the completion of the root Prātimokṣa text (and consequently not admitted to it), but included in the Sūtravibhaṅga of the Vinaya Piṭaka.

stūpa—A memorial mound constructed over the relics of the Buddha or other important person. Around the turn of the Christian era, a cult grew around the worship of stūpas. To this day, stūpas remain worthy of reverence in Buddhist countries.

Śubhākarasiṃha—Buddhist who introduced Chên-yên, the Tantric School of Buddhism, into China in the eighth century.

Subhūti—A lesser known of Buddha's early disciples. In the Prajñāpāramitā literature, he emerges as the prime interlocutor, often exhibiting far greater insight than Buddha's foremost disciples.

Śuddhodana—Ruler of the Śākya tribe at the foothills of the Himalayas. He was Buddha's father, although apparently playing no role in the conception of the child.

Sukhāvatī—"Land of Happiness" or "Pure Land"; that special sphere over which Amitābha presides, located in the Western region. It is referred to as Gokurakukoku in Japanese and Chi-lo Kuo in Chinese.

Sukhāvatīvyūha-sūtras—Two Pure Land texts, a larger and a smaller, in which formal devotion to the Buddha (Buddha-bhakti) appears. The larger text emphasizes the large stock of merit necessary for rebirth in the Pure Land (as well as a description of the Pure Land), while the smaller emphasizes the use of sound, particularly Amitābha's name, as a means of gaining rebirth in the Pure Land.

Sung Dynasty—Chinese dynasty divided into two parts: Northern Sung (960–1127) and Southern Sung (1127–1279).

Sungjong—A Korean king during the Yi Dynasty who was a supporter of the Confucians and abolished the state supported ceremonies of the Buddhists.

śūnyā—Literally "empty" or "void"; see next entry.

śūnyatā—The doctrine of "emptiness' or "voidness," stressed in many Mahāyāna sūtras. It goes beyond the early Buddhist position of anātman (not-self), stating that even dharmas have no existence in their own right. Of course the relational aspect of existence is stressed here. Thus emptiness becomes an epistemological tool used to "unfreeze" the fixed notions of our minds. One must be careful to understand that śūnyatā is not an ontological state and that even emptiness is empty.

Śūraṅgama-sūtra—Buddhist text, usually identified with Yogācāra, emphasized in Ch'an.

sūtra—Literally "thread"; applied to Buddha's sermons. Thus, Buddha's sermons are called sūtras. In Hīnayāna schools, these sūtras are gathered together into a Sūtra Piṭaka. In Mahāyāna, they are more random, classified according to text type.

Sūtra Piṭaka (P. Sutta Piṭaka)—That portion of the Buddhist canon which gathers together all those sermons of the Buddha deemed canonical and authoritative. The Sūtra Piṭaka is broken down into five parts called Āgamas (Nikāyas in Pāli).

Sūtravibhaṅga—Literally "Analysis of a Sūtra"; that portion of the Vinaya Piṭaka which enlarges upon the offenses listed in the Prātimokṣa Sūtra.

It includes stories, commentaries, and exceptions to the rule lacking in the Prātimokṣa.

Sutta-nipāta—"Collection of Suttas"; the fifth book in the Khuddaka Nikāya of the Sutta Piṭaka of the Pāli Canon.

svabhāva—Literally "own-being" or "own-nature"; it is the svabhāva that dharmas are said to be lacking and which contribute to their being empty (śūnyatā). If a thing had "own-being," it would exist in itself, thus being outside dependent origination, and contradict Buddhist orthodoxy.

Ta Chih Tu Lun—A commentary, by Nāgārjuna, on the Pañcaviṃśati-sāhasrikā-prajñāpāramitā-sūtra, translated into Chinese by Kumārajīva.

Taihō—Reforms of 702 which set up the Japanese Buddhist saṃgha as a department of government.

T'ai-hsü—Buddhist (1890–1947) who helped promote a Chinese Buddhist revival in the twentieth century.

Taishō shinshū daizōkyō—Japanese edition of the Chinese Buddhist Canon published during the Taishō era in Japan.

Takuan—One of the Buddhist monks during the stagnant and degenerate Tokugawa Period in Japan who helped to exemplify the very finest ideals of compassion.

T'ang Dynasty—Dynasty in China from 618 to 907 which marked the high point in Chinese Buddhist history.

T'an-luan—Chinese Buddhist (476–542) who organized the Pure Land School of Buddhism in China. He is also reckoned as its first patriarch.

Tantra—Buddhist esoteric school originating in India, spreading to China, Japan, and Tibet, which emphasized techniques of spontaneity centered around use of mantras, maṇḍalas, and stirring psychological techniques.

Tao-an—An eminent Buddhist monk in China, living from 312 to 385, who condemned the expression of Buddhism in Taoist terms (by the ko-i method).

Tao-hsüan—Chinese Buddhist founding the Lu School of Chinese Buddhism.

Tao-shen—Chinese Buddhist who was instrumental in founding the Ti-lun School of Buddhism in China.

Tao-shêng—Chinese Buddhist monk who organized the San-lun School of Buddhism in China and debated with Hui-kuan on the controversy of whether enlightenment was obtained immediately or gradually.

Tao Tê Ching—"Standard Work on Tao (Way) and Tê (Virtue, Power)," supposedly written by Lao-tzŭ. It is the main Taoist text.

Tāranātha—Tibetan Buddhist historian, affording much in the way of the history of Buddhism.

Tathāgata—Literally the "Thus-Come"; epithet describing Siddhārtha

Gautama after he achieved complete, perfect enlightenment. Also used to describe other Buddhas.

Tathāgatagarbha—Doctrine found in Yogācāra which literally means the "womb of the Tathāgata" and functions as a synonym for the ālaya-vijñāna.

tathatā—Literally "suchness"; things as they really are. Perhaps a more modern rendering would be "is-ness." It functions as a synonym for enlightenment.

tat tvam asi—In Hinduism, the classic equation of the Upaniṣads, meaning "that thou are." It is essentially an identification of the individual ātman with ultimate reality (Brahman).

Tendai (C. T'ien-t'ai)—Mahāyāna school in Japan which is primarily based on the Lotus Sūtra. It was brought to Japan by Saichō early in the ninth century, and is modeled on the Chinese T'ien-t'ai.

Tenjur—In the Tibetan Buddhist Canon, this division contains the commentaries. Following the hymns of praise, we find two general types of commentaries: commentaries on the Tantras and commentaries on the Sūtras (and of course these are subdivided further).

Tetsugen—One of the Buddhist monks during the stagnant and degenerate Tokugawa Period in Japan who helped to exemplify the very finest ideals of compassion.

Thaton—One of the centers of the Talaing people in Lower Burma.

Thera-gāthā—"Verses of the Elders"; the eighth book in the Khuddaka Nikāya of the Sutta Piṭaka of the Pāli Canon.

Theravāda—"Those Who Hold the Doctrine of the Elders"; one of the traditional 18 sects of Hīnayāna Buddhism. This form of Buddhism emerged out of Mahinda's mission to Ceylon during Aśoka's reign. They are apparently very closely related to the orthodox Vibhajyavāda doctrine of Aśoka's time, and represent the sole remaining Hīnayānist sect today.

Therī-gāthā—"Verses of the Nuns"; the ninth book in the Khuddaka Nikāya of the Sutta Piṭaka of the Pāli Canon.

Thūpārāma Dāgaba—Stūpa in Ceylon said to contain the relic of Buddha's collar-bone.

T'ien-t'ai (J. Tendai)—School of Mahāyāna Buddhism in China which was organized by Chih-i (538–597). The basic text is the Lotus Sūtra. This school represented a Chinese attempt to establish a great eclectic school recognizing all froms of Buddhism. The school gets its name from T'ien-t'ai Shan, the mountain on which it was located.

Tilopa—The guru of Nāropa. He is described as being rather erratic, often only partially clothed and acting "crazy."

Ti-lun School—"School of the Stages"; it arose in the Liang Dynasty through the work of the Vinaya master Kuang, Hui-shun, Tao-shen, and others and is based on the Commentary on the Sūtra on the Ten Stages by the Indian monk Vasubandhu.

Toda, Jōsei—The second leader of the Sōkagakkai sect of Buddhism in Japan. He refined much of the teaching of the sect.

Tōdai-ji—Headquarters temple of the Kegon School of Buddhism in Japan, dedicated in 752 and built by Emperor Shōmu.

Tokugawa Period—Period in Japanese history (1603–1867) when Japan was completely isolated from the outside world and Buddhism, as well as all areas of life, was strictly controlled by the military shoguns.

Tokugawa, Iyeyasu—He seized control in Japan and set up a military dictatorship in 1603.

Toui—Korean Buddhist monk who went to China in A.D. 820 to study Ch'an Buddhism.

Trikāya—The doctrine of the Three Bodies of Buddha. They include the Nirmāṇakāya or Apparational Body, the Saṃbhogakāya or Enjoyment Body, and the Dharmakāya or "Essence Body."

Triṃśikā—The "Thirty Verses" by Vasubandhu which, in China, forms the basis of the Fa-hsiang School of Buddhism.

Tripiṭaka—The "Three Baskets" of the Buddhist Canon consisting of the Vinaya Piṭaka, Sūtra Piṭaka, and Abhidharma Piṭaka.

triratna—The "Three Jewels" of Buddhism including Buddha, Dharma, and Saṃgha. One of the elements in becoming a Buddhist involves taking refuge in the Three Jewels.

triśikṣā—Literally the "triple training"; as the eightfold path is usually subdivided, it falls into three classes: śīla, samādhi, and prajñā. It is these three that are referred to as the triple training.

Trisvabhāvanirdeśa—Literally the "Description of the Three Svabhāvas"; Yogācāra text by Vasubandhu outlining the three svabhāva theory.

tṛṣṇā—Literally "craving"; noted in the second Noble Truth to be the cause of suffering. Usually three kinds of craving are noted: kāma-tṛṣṇā (sensual craving), bhava-tṛṣṇā (craving for continued existence), and vibhava-tṛṣṇā (craving for extinction).

Ts'ao-shan Pên-chi—Chinese Buddhist (840–901) who was co-founder of the Ts'ao-tung "house" of Chinese Ch'an Buddhism.

Ts'ao-tung—One of the two (of the original five) "houses" of T'ang Dynasty Ch'an which have survived. It was founded by Ts'ao-shan Pên-chi and Tung-shan Liang-chieh and emphasizes chih-kuan-ta-tso and gradualism.

Tsong-kha-pa—Tibetan Buddhist (1357–1419) claiming to be in the lineage of Atīśa's bKa-gdams sect and founding three monasteries in Lhasa. He is the founder of the dGe-lugs-pa School of Tibetan Buddhism.

Tung-shan Liang-chieh—Chinese Buddhist (807–869) who was co-founder of the Ts'ao-tung "house" of Chinese Ch'an Buddhism.

Tun-huang—Place marking the entrance to China from Central Asia. Buddhism is likely to have made initial impact here, as many cave-temples, wall paintings, and valuable manuscripts have been retrieved from Tun-huang.

Tu-shun—Chinese Buddhist (557–640) who founded the Hua-yen School of Chinese Buddhism.

Tz'u-min—Chinese Buddhist monk (688–748) who attempted to harmonize the Ching-t'u and Ch'an School of Buddhism.

Udāna—"Solemn Utterances"; the third book in the Khuddaka Nikāya of the Sutta Piṭaka of the Pāli Canon.

Udraka Rāmaputra—The second teacher under whom Siddhārtha Gautama studied in his quest for enlightenment. Udraka's system taught the attainment of the "sphere of neither perception nor nonperception."

Unified Silla—Kingdom in Korea (668–935) in which Buddhism became a major institution.

Upadeśa-śāstra—An extensive commentary of the Vinaya of the Sarvāstivādins.

Upagupta—An alternate name for Aśoka's preceptor Moggaliputta Tissa. Around this time another figure named Upagupta is cited to be a patriarch of the Sarvāstivādin School of Buddhism, founding a community of monks in Mathurā.

Upāli—One of Buddha's leading disciples and a specialist on the rules of Vinaya. He was said to have recited the entire Vinaya at the first council, held at Rājagṛha. A text often identified with the Sarvāstivādins but being strongly influenced by Mahāyāna, bears his name: Upālipariprcchā.

Upaniṣad—Along with the Vedas and Brāhmaṇas, that literature of the Hindus regarded as śruti ("heard" or "revealed"). The word means "to sit down near to," and represents the teaching of ancient sages whose students gathered around to hear their pronouncements. The Upaniṣads represent highly speculative but non-systematic philosophy.

upāsaka—A male lay disciple in Buddhism.

upasaṃpadā—Full ordination into Buddhist monkhood. It follows the novitiate or śramaṇera stage, and is regulated by the Karmavācanā procedure.

upāsikā—A female lay disciple in Buddhism.

upāya—Literally "skill in means" or "skillful device"; those means by which Buddha (or Bodhisattvas) make the complex and difficult teachings of Buddhism understandable to persons of varying mental faculties. Buddha has often been regarded as a marvelous physician who, by his upāya, always dispensed the proper medicine in the appropriate dosage.

upāyakauśalya—Literally "skill in means." Like the previous entry, this term is used synonymously with upāya to represent Buddha's ability to know one's disposition and select the proper teaching device.

Vaibhāṣika—Hīnayāna Buddhist group in Kaśmīr that developed from the Sarvāstivādins and adhere primarily to two Sarvāstivādin texts, the Jñānaprasthāna and Abhidharmavibhāṣā-śāstra.

vaipulya—Literally "lengthy story"; a means by which Buddha taught the Dharma. This title is applied to various Mahāyāna sūtras, such as the Vajracchedikā-prajñāpāramitā-sūtra, and denotes them as "extended sūtras."

Vairocana—Literally "Shining Out"; a cosmic Buddha whose body is the emptiness of all things. In Chinese scholasticism he is sometimes regarded as the Dharmakāya of Śākyamuni.

Vaiśālī—Famous city in early Buddhism, perhaps best known for being the cite of the second Buddhist council following Buddha's death.

Vaiśeṣika-sūtra—Basic text of the Vaiśeṣika Darśana in Indian Philosophy, probably composed in the first century A.D.

Vajracchedikā-prajñāpāramitā-sūtra—Literally the "Diamond Sūtra"; a summary of the larger prajñāpāramitā sūtras which is said to contain the essence of their teaching.

vāsanā—In Yogācāra, the process of "perfuming," by which seeds from all other consciousness are deposited in the storehouse consciousness (ālaya-vijñāna). These seeds (bījas) in turn influence all future cognitions.

Vasubandhu—Great Buddhist commentator who originally wrote as a Sarvāstivādin, producing such works as the classic Abhidharmakośa, but was later converted to Yogācāra by his brother Asaṅga. Amongst his major contributions to Yogācāra, we can note his Karmasiddhiprakaraṇa, Viṃśatikā, Triṃśikā, and Trisvabhāvanirdeśa. With Buddhaghosa, he ranks amongst the most excellent of all Buddhist exegetes.

Vasumitra—Sarvāstivādin monk who served as "president" of the Buddhist council held by King Kaniṣka. He is the reputed author of the Samaya-bhedoparacanacakra and Prakaraṇapāda, the latter text being included in the Abhidharma Piṭaka of the Sarvāstivādins.

Vātsīputrīya—Hīnayānist sect often linked with the Saṃmitīyas, which broke from the orthodox Sthaviravāda doctrine. They may be classified as Pudgalavādins, accepting that the pudgala transmigrated, and rejecting the theory of the five skandhas.

Vaṭṭagāmaṇī—King who reigned in Ceylon from 29 to 17 B.C. He drove the Tamils from Ceylon, founded Abhayagiri monastery, and during his reign the Buddhist texts in Ceylon were committed to writing for the first time.

vedanā—Literally "feeling"; the second of the five skandhas. It derives from the contact of our physical and mental organs with objects in the external world.

Veḍḍa—Tribal group in ancient Ceylon living in the forests and hills and being predominantly hunters.

Veṇuvanārāma—"Bamboo Grove Park"; the first Buddhist monastery, donated to the saṃgha by Bimbisāra, king of Magadha during Buddha's lifetime.

Vesākha (S. Vaiśākha)—The full moon day of May; that day on which Buddha was born. This day was later turned into a great festival, celebrated in all Buddhist countries.

Vibhajyavāda—Literally "Distinctionist" or "Holders of the Doctrine of Distinctions"; that Hīnayāna sect thought to be orthodox by the time of Aśoka's council at Pāṭaliputra. The name seems to indicate that this group was called "distinctionist" because they made a distinction of phenomena in time into two categories: those that exist and those that do not. In the Theravāda records they gain supremacy over the Sarvāstivādins at Aśoka's council.

Vibhaṅga—Literally "Divisions"; one of the books in the Abhidhamma Piṭaka of the Pāli Canon.

Videha—Kingdom in India to the east of Kośala and north of Magadha which, although being a stronghold of Brāhmaṇical tradition, was strongly influenced by Buddha's teaching.

Vigrahavyāvartanī—One of the two major works of Nāgārjuna, founder of the Mādhyamika School of Buddhism, in which he sets out his basic doctrines.

vihāra—Originally a hut inhabited by a single monk during the rainy season retreat. As Buddhist monasticism developed, and the eremetical ideal was abandoned, the word came to denote an entire monastery.

vijñāna—"Consciousness," the fifth of the five skandhas. It represents the resultant activity when our mental and physical organs come into contact with objects in the external world, and the input derived therefrom is integrated, identified, and acted upon. Traditionally, there are six vijñānas: eye, ear, nose, tongue, body, and mind (but the Yogācārins enlarge this).

Vijñānakāya—Abhidharma text included in the Abhidharma Piṭaka of the Sarvāstivādins. It is reputed to have been written by Devaśarman and upholds the orthodox Sarvāstivādin concept of the existence of past and future in the present.

Vijñānavāda—Literally "Holders of the Doctrine of the Consciousness";

that title applied to the Yogācāra School of Buddhism which aims at being descriptive in terms of the doctrines held by the school. It refers specifically to Dharmapāla's viewpoint.

vijñaptimātra—In Yogācāra, the realization that our "normal" perceptions involve mental constructions and that all defined things are "apperception only."

Vimalakīrti—In Mahāyāna, a layman Bodhisattva who, in spite of his worldly ways, has great insight and attainment. A famous Mahāyāna text, the Vimalakīrti-nirdeśa-sūtra, was written about this figure, in which Vimalakīrti outshines all Buddha's great disciples in his understanding.

Vimānavatthu—"Stories About Heavenly Places"; the sixth book in the Khuddaka Nikāya of the Sutta Piṭaka of the Pāli Canon.

Viṃśatikā—The "Twenty Verses," written by Vasubandhu and representing an important Yogācāra text.

Vimuttimagga—Later Abhidhamma text, ascribed to Upatissa and having much in common with the Visuddhimagga of Buddhaghosa. It has been translated into Chinese.

Vinaya—That portion of Buddhist literature which deals with monastic discipline and the ethical dimension of Buddhism.

Vinaya Piṭaka—The first "Basket" in the Buddhist Canon, containing all the rules for monastic discipline, ethical considerations, and transacting monastic business.

Vinayasaṃgīti—Literally "chanting of the Vinaya"; a descriptive title sometimes applied to the first council, held at Rājagṛha.

Vinayavibhāṣā-śāstra—An extensive Vinaya commentary belonging to the Sarvāstivādin School of Buddhism.

vipassanā (S. vipaśyanā)—Literally "insight"; the second half of Buddhist meditational practice (the first being samatha) which leads to the experience of the four trances.

vīrya—Literally "vigor" or "striving"; the fourth of the pāramitās (perfections) practiced on the Bodhisattva path.

Viśākhā—A banker's daughter who was a famous lay follower of Buddhism. She excelled in performing social services for the saṃgha.

Visuddhimagga—The "Path of Purity," a classic Buddhist text written by Buddhaghosa. It has become a standard guide to Theravāda meditation and, as a compendium of doctrine, includes precepts, legends, miracle stories, etc., all of which glorify arhantship. It certainly ranks in brilliance with Vasubandhu's Abhidharmakośa.

Vītāśoka—The brother of King Aśoka who, as recorded in the Aśokāvadāna, was converted to Buddhism.

Vṛjiputraka bhikṣus—Buddhist monks in Vaiśālī who were observed by

Yaśas to be engaging in ten unlawful practices. On this basis, the famous council of Vaiśālī was held in which the evil practices of these monks were condemned and order restored.

vyākaraṇa—Literally "prediction"; received by the Bodhisattva (from a Buddha) who takes a vow to save all sentient beings, it notes when he will attain complete, perfect enlightenment.

Wang-shêng-lun Chu—"Commentary on the Essay on Rebirth"; a commentary by T'an-luan on the Amitāyuḥsūtrānyupadeśapratyājātipraṇidhānagāthā.

Warren, Henry Clarke—Scholar who lived from 1854 to 1899 and edited an edition of Buddhaghosa's Visuddhimagga, as well as publishing *Buddhism in Translations*, still perhaps the best anthology of translations from Theravāda texts.

watō (C. hua-t'ou)—"The head of a saying"; Watō is that which exists in the moment before thought arises; see hua-t'ou.

Wei-shih—Chinese school of Buddhism corresponding to the Indian Yogācāra.

White Lotus Society—An aristocratic sodality in Chinese Buddhism organized for meditating on the Pure Land. It was organized by Hui-yüan in 402.

wu—Chinese term literally signifying individual enlightenment.

Wu-mên Kuan—"The Gateless Barrier"; 48 dialogues compiled in 1228 by Hui-k'ai with his comments. It is well known in Ch'an Buddhism.

Wu-tsung—Taoist emperor who, in 845, vigorously suppressed Buddhism in China. His suppression effectively dealt a "death blow" to many Buddhist schools.

Yajur-veda—The third of the four Vedas. It deals specifically with the sacrifice and its performance.

yakkha (S. yakṣa)—Tree spirits whose function it was to "hover over" and guard man from evil. In pre-Buddhist Ceylon a tribal group called Yakkhas existed which worshipped spirits and snakes.

Yamaka—Literally "Pairs" or "Twin Verses"; one of the books in the Abhidhamma Piṭaka of the Pāli Canon.

Yaśas—In Buddha's time, one of his first conversions which led to the conversion of Yaśas' family and friends. One hundred years after Buddha's death a second person named Yaśas wanders into Vaiśālī, observes the Vṛjiputraka bhikṣus practicing ten evil practices, and starts the process which ultimately led to the second Buddhist council.

Yaśodharā—Wife of Siddhārtha Gautama (of course before he renounced worldly life).

Yaśomitra—Famous Buddhist commentator of about the eighth century

A.D.

yathābhūtam—Literally "things as they really are"; it is this that is the goal for all Buddhists, but particularly emphasized by the Mahāyānists. One can say that to see things as they really are is to be enlightened.

Yên Fo-t'iao—The first Chinese Buddhist monk.

Yi Hwaekwang—The leader of the Buddhist Sŏnjong national organization in Korea who went to Japan in 1910 and secretly consulted with Sōtō leaders regarding cooperation between Japanese and Korean Buddhists.

Yogācāra—Literally "Practice of Yoga"; Mahāyāna philosophical school founded by Asaṅga and innovating several new concepts in Buddhist thought, among them the eight consciousnesses, trisvabhāva doctrine, vijñaptimātra, and Tathāgatagarbha. With Mādhyamika, it represents the driving force in early Mahāyāna thought.

Yüan-wu—Chinese Buddhist monk (1063–1135) who compiled the Pi-yên Lu or "Blue Cliff Records."

Yuima-kyō—Japanese translation of the Vimalakīrti-nirdeśa-sūtra.

zazen—Literally "sitting in meditation"; with the notion that the person is already a Buddha, this realization being clouded only by his ignorance, the zazen provides for an opportunity in which one's inherent Buddha nature may manifest itself.

Zokuzōkyō—An augmentation to the Taishō shinshū daizōkyō, including pieces not present in this collection of the Chinese canon.

Bibliography

Adikaram, E.W. *Early History of Buddhism in Ceylon*. 2d impression. Colombo: M.D. Gunasena & Co., 1953.

Anesaki, Masaharu. *Nichiren, the Buddhist Prophet*. Harvard, 1916.

Aung, Shwe Zan, tr. *Compendium of Philosophy* (*Abhidhammaṭṭhasaṅgaha*). Reprint. London: Luzac & Company, for Pali Text Society, 1967.

Banerjee, Ankul Chandra. *Sarvāstivāda Literature*. Calcutta: D. Banerjee (Calcutta Oriental Press Private Limited), 1957.

Bapat, P.V., ed. *2500 Years of Buddhism*. Delhi: Government of India, 1956.

Bareau, André. *Les premiers conciles bouddhiques*. Paris: Presses Universitaires de France, 1955.

———. *Les Sectes Bouddhiques du Petit Véhicule*. Saigon: École Française D'Extrême-Orient, 1955.

———. *Recherches sur la biographie du Buddha dans les Sūtrapiṭaka et les Vinayapiṭaka anciens: de la quête du l'Éveil à la conversion de Śāriputra et de Maudgalyāyana*. Paris: École Française D'Extrême-Orient, 1963.

Barlingay, S.S. *A Modern Introduction to Indian Logic*. Delhi: National Publishing House, 1965.

Basham, A.L., ed. *Papers on the Date of Kaniṣka*. Leiden: E.J. Brill, 1968.

———. *The Wonder That Was India*. New York: Grove Press, 1959.

Bassagli, Mario. *Painting of Central Asia*. Translated by Lothian Small. Geneva: Editions d'Art Albert Skira; Cleveland: World Publishing Co., 1973.

Bechert, Heinz. *Buddhismus, Staat und Gesellschaft in den Ländern des Theravāda Buddhismus*. 2 vols. Berlin: Alfred Metzner, 1966–1967.

Bellah, Robert. *Tokugawa Religion*. Glencoe, Ill.: Free Press, 1957.

Beyer, Stephan V. *The Cult of Tārā: Magic and Ritual in Tibet*. Berkeley: University of California Press, 1974.

Bharati, Agehananda. *The Tantric Tradition*. Garden City, N.Y.: Anchor Books, 1970.

Bhattacharya, K., tr. "The Dialectical Method of Nāgārjuna" (translation of the Vigrahavyāvartanī), *Journal of Indian Philosophy*, 1 (1971): 217–61.

Blofeld, John. *The Tantric Mysticism of Tibet*. New York: E.P. Dutton & Co., 1970.

Bloom, Alfred. *Shinran's Gospel of Pure Grace*. Tucson: University of Arizona Press, 1965.

Bochenski, I.M. *A History of Formal Logic*. Translated by Ivo Thomas. Notre Dame, Ind.: University of Notre Dame Press, 1961.

Briggs, Lawrence Palmer. *The Ancient Khmer Empire*. Transactions of the American Philosophical Society, New Series Vol. 41, Pt. 1, 1951.

Burnouf, Eugène, tr. *Le Lotus de la Bonne Loi*. Paris: Imprimerie Nationale, 1852.

Bush, Richard C. *Religion in Communist China*. Nashville: Abingdon Press, 1970.

Chan, Wing-tsit. *A Sourcebook in Chinese Philosophy*. Princeton: Princeton University Press, 1963.

———. *Religious Trends in Modern China*. New York: Columbia University Press, 1953.

———. tr. *The Way of Lao-Tzu: Tao-te Ching*. Indianapolis: Bobbs-Merrill, 1963.

Chang, Garma Chen-chi. *The Buddhist Teaching of Totality: The Philosophy of Hwa-yen Buddhism*. University Park: The Pennsylvania State University Press, 1971.

———. *The Practice of Zen*. New York: Harper & Row, 1959.

Ch'en, Kenneth K.S. *Buddhism in China*. Princeton: The Princeton University Press, 1964.

Chi, Richard S.Y. *Buddhist Formal Logic*. London: Royal Asiatic Society of Great Britain and Ireland, 1969.

China Quarterly. No. 6 (April-June 1961): 1–14, Holmes Welch; No. 22 (April-June 1965): 14–30, Kenneth Ch'en, 143–53, Holmes Welch; No. 40 (October-December 1969), 127–36, Holmes Welch.

Clark, Charles Allen. *Religions of Old Korea*. New York: Fleming H. Reveil Co., 1932.

Coates, H.H., and Ishizuka, Ryugaku. *Hōnen, the Buddhist Saint: His Life and Teachings*. Reprint. Kyoto, 1949.

Coedès, Georges. *The Making of South East Asia*. Translated by H.M. Wright. Berkeley: University of California Press, 1966.

Conze, Edward, tr. *Abhisamayālaṅkāra, Introduction and Translation from original text, with Sanskrit-Tibetan Index*. Vol. 6 of Serie Orientale Roma. Rome: Instituto per il Medio ed Estremo Oriente, 1954.

———. *Buddhism: Its Essence and Development*. 6th printing. New York: Harper & Row Publishers, 1965.

———. *Buddhist Thought in India*. Reprint. Ann Arbor: The University of Michigan Press, Ann Arbor Paperbacks, 1967.

——— ed. and tr. *Selected Sayings From the Perfection of Wisdom*. London: The Buddhist Society, 1955.

———. *The Prajñāpāramitā Literature*. Vol. 6 of Indo-Iranian Monographs. 'S-Gravenhage: Mouton & Co., 1960.

———. *Thirty Years of Buddhist Studies*. Columbia: University of South Carolina Press, 1968.

Coomaraswamy, Ananda K. *History of Indian and Indonesian Art*. Reprint. New York: Dover Publications, 1965.

Corless, Roger J. *T'an-luan's Commentary on the Pure Land Discourse*. Ph.D. Dissertation, The University of Wisconsin, 1973.

Cowell, E.B., Müller, F. Max, and Takakusu, Junjiro, trs. *Buddhist Mahāyāna Texts*. Vol. 49 of Sacred Books of the East. Reprint. Delhi: Motilal Banarsidass, 1965.

de Bary, William Theodore, ed. *The Buddhist Tradition*. New York: Modern Library,

1969.

Demiéville, Paul. "À propos du concile de Vaiśālī," *T'oung Pao*, 40 (1951): 239–96.

———. "L'origine des sectes bouddhiques d'après Paramārtha," *Mélanges Chinois et Bouddhiques*, 1 (1931–32): 15–64.

de Visser, M.W. *Ancient Buddhism in Japan*. 2 Vols. Leiden: E.J. Brill, 1935.

Dumoulin, Heinrich. *A History of Zen Buddhism*. Translated by Paul Peachey. New York: Pantheon, 1963.

Dutt, Nalinaksha. *Aspects of Mahāyāna Buddhism and Its Relation to Hīnayāna*. London: Luzac & Co., 1930.

———. *Buddhist Sects in India*. Calcutta: K.L. Mukhopadhyay, 1970.

———. *Early History of the Spread of Buddhism and the Buddhist Schools*. London: Luzac & Co., 1925.

———. *Early Monastic Buddhism*. Calcutta: Calcutta Oriental Book Agency, 1960.

———. "The Second Buddhist Council," *Indian Historical Quarterly*, 35 (March 1959): 45–56.

Dutt, Sukumar. *Buddhist Monks and Monasteries of India*. London: George Allen & Unwin, 1962.

———. *Early Buddhist Monachism*. Rev. ed. Bombay: Asia Publishing House, 1960.

Earhart, H. Byron. *Japanese Religion: Unity and Diversity*. Belmont, Ca.: Dickenson Publishing Co., 1969.

Eliade, Mircea. *Shamanism: Archaic Techniques of Ecstasy*. Translated by Willard R. Trask. Princeton: Princeton University Press, 1964.

Eliot, Sir Charles. *Japanese Buddhism*. 3d impression. London: Routledge & Kegan Paul, 1964.

Ellwood, Robert S., Jr. *Religious and Spiritual Groups in Modern America*. Englewood Cliffs, N.J.: Prentice-Hall, 1973.

Foucher, Alfred. *La Vie du Bouddha*. English translation available as: *The Life of the Buddha According to the Ancient Texts and Monuments of India*. Middletown, Conn.: Wesleyan University Press, 1963.

Franke, R.O. "The Buddhist Councils at Rājagaha and Vesālī as Alleged in Cullavagga 11, 12," *Journal of the Pali Text Society* (1908): 1–80.

Frauwallner, Erich. *The Earliest Vinaya and the Beginnings of Buddhist Literature*. Vol. 8 of Serie Orientale Roma. Rome: Instituto per il Medio ed Estremo Oriente, 1956.

Geiger, Wilhelm, tr. *The Mahāvaṃsa or the Great Chronicle of Ceylon*. Reprint. London: Luzac & Company for Pali Text Society, 1964.

Gokhale, B. *Buddhism and Aśoka*. Baroda: Padmaja Publishers, 1948.

Gray, Basil, and Vincent, J.B. *Buddhist Cave Paintings at Tun-huang*. London: Faber & Faber, 1959.

Guenther, Herbert, tr. *The Jewel Ornament of Liberation (sGam.po.pa)*. 3d printing. Berkeley: Shabhala Publications.

Herrigel, Eugen. *Zen in the Art of Archery*. New York: Pantheon, 1953.

Hikata, R., tr. *Suvikrāntavikrāmī-prajñāpāramitā-sūtra*. Japan: Kyushu University, 1958.

Hoffmann, Helmut. *The Religions of Tibet*. Translated by Edward Fitzgerald. London: George Allen & Unwin, 1961.

Hofinger, M. *Étude sur la concile du Vaiśālī*. Louvain: Bureaux du Museon, 1946.

Hsiao, Ching-fên. *The Life and Teaching of T'an-luan*. Ph.D. Dissertation, Princeton Theological Seminary, 1967.

Humphreys, Christmas. *Sixty Years of Buddhism in England (1907–1967)*. London: The Buddhist Society, 1968.

Hunter, Louise. *Buddhism in Hawaii*. Honolulu: University of Hawaii Press, 1971.

Hurvitz, Leon. "Chih-i." *Mélanges Chinois et Bouddhiques* 12 (1962).

Inada, Kenneth K., tr. *Nāgārjuna, A Translation of his Mūlamadhyamakakārikā with an Introductory Essay*. Tokyo: The Hokuseido Press, 1970.

Jaini, Padmanabh. "*Śramanas:* Their Conflict with Brāhmaṇical Society." In Joseph Elder, ed., *Chapters in Indian Civilization*, vol. 1. Dubuque: Kendall/Hunt Publishing Company, 1970: 39–81.

Johansson, Rune. *The Psychology of Nirvāṇa*. Garden City, N.Y.: Anchor Books, 1970.

Jones, J.J., tr. *The Mahāvastu, translated from the Buddhist Sanskrit*. 3 vols. Vols. 16, 18, and 19 of *Sacred Books of the Buddhists*. London: Luzac & Company, 1949–56.

Kajiyama, Yuichi. *An Introduction to Buddhist Philosophy*. Memoirs of the Faculty of Letters, No. 10. Kyoto: Kyoto University, 1966.

Kapleau, Philip. *The Three Pillars of Zen*. Boston: Beacon Press, 1968.

Kennett, Jiyu. *Selling Water by the River: A Manual of Zen Training*. New York: Random House, 1972.

Kern, Jan Hendrik, tr. *The Saddharmapuṇḍarīka, or the Lotus of the True Law*. Vol. 21 of *Sacred Books of the East*. Reprint. New York: Dover Publications, 1963.

Kitagawa, Joseph. *Religion in Japanese History*. New York: Columbia University Press, 1966.

Lamotte, Étienne. *Historie du Bouddhisme Indien des origines à l'ère Śaka*. Reprint. Louvain: Publications Universitaires, 1967.

———, tr. *La Somme du Grand Véhicule d'Asaṅga* (*Mahāyānasaṃgraha*). 2 vols. Louvain: Bureaux du Muséon, 1938–39.

———, tr. *L'Enseignement de Vimalakīrti*. Louvain: Publications Universitaries, 1962.

———, ed. and tr. *Saṃdhinirmocana, L'explication des mystères, Texte tibetain édité et traduit*. Louvain: Bureaux du Muséon, 1935.

La Vallée Poussin, Louis de. "Cosmogony and Cosmology: Buddhist." In James Hastings, ed., *Encyclopedia of Religions and Ethics*, 4: 129–38.

———, tr. *L'Abhidharmakośa de Vasubandhu*. 6 vols. Paris: Paul Geuthner, 1923–31.

———. *Nirvāṇa*. Paris: Gabriel Beauchesne, 1925.

———. "The Buddhist Councils," *Indian Antiquary*, 37 (1908): 1–18, 81–106.

———. *The Way to Nirvāṇa: Six Lectures on Ancient Buddhism*. Cambridge: Cambridge University Press, 1917.

———, tr. *Vijñaptimātratāsiddhi, La Siddhi de Hiuan-Tsang, traduite et annotée*. 2 vols. Paris: Paul Geuthner, 1928–29.

Law, Bimala Churn. *A History of Pāli Literature*. 2 vols. London: Kegan Paul, Trench, Trübner & Co., 1933.

Leclère, Adhémard. *Histoire du Cambodge*. Paris: Paul Geuthner, 1914.

Lee, Peter H., *Lives of Eminent Korean Monks*. Cambridge: Harvard University Press,

1969.

Lévi, Sylvain, ed. and tr. *Asaṅga, Mahāyānasūtrālaṅkāra, exposé de la doctrine du grand véhicule selon le système Yogācāra*. 2 vols. Paris, 1907–1911.

———. "Notes sur les Indo-Scythes," *Journal Asiatique*, 8 (Novembre-Décembre 1896): 444–84; 9 (Janvier-Fevrier, 1897): 6–42.

Ling, Trevor. *Buddha, Marx and God*. New York: St. Martin's Press, 1966.

Lubac, Henri de. *La Rencontre du Bouddhisme et de l'Occident*. Paris: Aubier, 1952.

Malalasekera, G.P., et al. "Amita." In *Encyclopaedia of Buddhism*, Vol. 1, Fasc. 3 (1964): 434–63.

———. *The Pāli Literature of Ceylon*. Reprint. Colombo: M.D. Gunasena & Co., 1958.

Masunaga, Reihō. *A Primer of Sōtō Zen*. Honolulu: East-West Center Press, 1971.

McDermott, A.C.S. *An Eleventh-Century Buddhist Logic of "Exists."* Foundations of Language, Supplementary Series, Vol. 11. Dordrecht, Holland: D. Reidel, 1970.

McFarland, H. Neill. *The Rush Hour of the Gods*. New York: The Macmillan Company, 1967.

Mookerji, R. *Aśoka*. 3d ed., revised and enlarged. Delhi: Motilal Banarsidass, 1962.

Murti, T.R.V. *The Central Philosophy of Buddhism*. London: George Allen & Unwin, 1955.

Ñāṇamoli Thera, tr. *The Path of Purification* (*Visuddhimagga*). Colombo: R. Semage, 1956.

Ñāṇaponika Thera. *The Heart of Buddhist Meditation*. New York: Samuel Weiser, 1971. First published 1962.

Ñāṇatiloka Mahāthera. *Guide Through the Abhidhammapiṭaka*. Colombo: Bauddha Sāhitya Sabhā, 1957. First published 1938.

Nārada Thera. *The Buddha and His Teachings*. Colombo: Vajirārāma, 1964.

Needleman, Jacob. *The New Religions*. Garden City. N.Y.: Doubleday & Company, 1970.

Ngag-dbang Blo-bzang Ye-shes bstan-'dzin rGya-mtsho (His Holiness the 14th Dalai Lama). *My Land and My People*. New York: McGraw-Hill, 1962.

Nhat Nanh, Trich. *Vietnam: Lotus in a Sea of Fire*. New York: Hill and Wang, 1967.

Oldenberg, Hermann, ed. and tr. *The Dīpavaṃsa*. London: Williams & Norgate, 1879.

Pachow, W. *A Comparative Study of the Prātimokṣa*. In *Sino-Indian Studies*, Vol. 4, Pts. 1–4 and Vol. 5, Pt. 1, 1951–55.

Potter, Karl. *Presuppositions of India's Philosophies*. Englewood Cliffs, N.J.: Prentice-Hall, 1963.

Prebish, Charles S. *Buddhist Monastic Discipline: The Sanskrit Prātimokṣa Sūtras of the Mahāsāṃghikas and Mūlasarvāstivādins*. University Park: The Pennsylvania State University Press, 1975.

———. "A Review of Scholarship on the Buddhist Councils," *Journal of Asian Studies*, 33, 2 (February 1974): 239–54.

———. "The Prātimokṣa Puzzle: Fact Versus Fantasy," *Journal of the American Oriental Society*, 94, 2 (April-June 1974): 168–76.

———. "Theories Concerning the Skandhaka: An Appraisal," *Journal of Asian Studies*, 32, 4 (August 1973): 669–78.

Przyluski, Jean, tr. *La légende de l'empereur Aśoka dans les textes indiens et chinois*.

Paris: Paul Geuthner, 1923.

———. *Le Concile de Rājagṛha*. Paris: Paul Geuthner, 1926–28.

Rahula, Walpola. *History of Buddhism in Ceylon*. 2d ed. Colombo: M.D. Gunasena & Co., 1966.

———. *What the Buddha Taught*. 5th printing. New York: Grove Press, 1962.

Ray, Niharranjan. *Theravāda Buddhism in Burma*. Calcutta: University of Calcutta Press, 1946.

Reischauer, Edwin O., tr. *Ennin's Diary*. New York: Ronald Press, 1955.

———, tr. *Ennin's Travels in T'ang China*. New York: Ronald Press, 1955.

Renou, Louis, and Filliozat, Jean. *L'Inde Classique*. Tome 2. Paris: Imprimerie Nationale, 1953.

Rhys Davids, Thomas W., tr. *Buddhist Birth Stories*. London: G. Routledge & Sons, 1925.

Riepe, Dale. *The Philosophy of India and its Impact on American Thought*. Springfield, Ill.: Charles C. Thomas, 1970.

Robinson, Richard H. "Classical Indian Philosophy." In Joseph Elder, ed., *Chapters in Indian Civilization*, Vol. 1, pp. 127–227. Dubuque: Kendall/Hunt Publishing Company, 1970.

———. *Early Mādhyamika in India and China*. Madison: The University of Wisconsin Press, 1967.

———. *The Buddhist Religion*. Belmont, Ca.: Dickenson Publishing Co., 1970.

———, tr. *The Vimalakīrti Sūtra*. Madison: Department of Indian Studies, The University of Wisconsin, typescript, n.d.

Rockhill, W., tr. *The Life of the Buddha and the Early History of His Order*. Boston: J.R. Osgood & Co., 1885.

Saha, Kshanika. *Buddhism and Buddhist Literature in Central Asia*. Calcutta: K.L. Mukhopadhyay, 1970.

Sanghrakshita, Bhikshu. *A Survey of Buddhism*. 3d ed. Bangalore: The Indian Institute of World Culture, 1966.

Sansom, Sir George. *Japan, A Short Cultural History*. Rev. ed. New York: Appleton-Century-Crofts, 1962.

Schecter, Jerrold. *The New Face of the Buddha*. Tokyo: John Weatherhill, Inc., 1967.

Sekiguchi, Shindai. *Zen: A Manual for Westerners*. San Francisco: Japan Publications, 1970.

Seo, Kyun-bo. *A Study of Korean Zen Buddhism Approached Through the Chodangjip*. Ph.D. Dissertation, Temple University, n.d.

Shaku, Soyen. *Sermons of a Buddhist Abbot*. New York: Samuel Weiser, 1971. First published 1906.

Sharma, D. *The Differentiation Theory of Meaning in Indian Logic*. 'S-Gravenhage: Mouton & Co., 1969.

Slater, Robert. *Paradox and Nirvana*. Chicago: University of Chicago Press, 1951.

Snellgrove, David, and Richardson, Hugh. *A Cultural History of Tibet*. New York: Praeger, 1970.

Sprung, Mervyn, ed. *The Problem of Two Truths in Buddhism and Vedānta*. Boston: Reidel, 1973.

Starr, Frederick. *Korean Buddhism*. Boston: Marshall Jones Co., 1918.

Stcherbatsky, Th. *Buddhist Logic*. 2 vols. Reprint. New York: Dover Publications, 1962.

———. *The Central Conception of Buddhism and the Meaning of the Word "Dharma."* 2d ed. Calcutta: Susil Gupta, 1956.

———. *The Conception of Buddhist Nirvāṇa*. Leningrad: Publishing Office of the Academy of Science of the U.S.S.R., 1927.

———, tr. *Madhyāntavibhāga, Discourse on Discrimination between Middle and Extremes, ascribed to Maitreya and commented by Vasubandhu and Sthiramati. Bibliotheca Buddhica* 30 (1936).

Streng, Frederick J. *Emptiness: A Study in Religious Meaning*. Nashville: Abingdon Press, 1967.

Suzuki, Daisetz Teitarō. *Essays in Zen Buddhism*. Ser. 1, 2, 3. London: Rider & Co., 1949, 1953.

———. *Introduction to Zen Buddhism*. New York: Grove Press, 1964.

———. *Shin Buddhism*. New York: Harper & Row Publishers, 1970.

———. *Studies in the Laṅkāvatāra Sūtra*. London: George Routledge, 1930.

———, tr. *The Laṅkāvatāra Sūtra*. London: George Routledge, 1932.

———. *Zen and Japanese Culture*. New York: Pantheon, 1959.

Suzuki, Shunryu. *Zen Mind, Beginner's Mind*. Reprint. Tokyo: John Weatherhill, 1973.

Swearer, Donald K., ed. *Secrets of the Lotus*. New York: The Macmillan Company, 1971.

Takakusu, Junjiro. *The Essentials of Buddhist Philosophy*. 3d ed. Honolulu: Office Appliance Co., 1956.

Thapar, Romila. *Aśoka and the Decline of the Mauryas*. London: Oxford University Press, 1961.

Thomas, Edward J. *The History of Buddhist Thought*. Reprint of 2d ed. London: Routledge & Kegan Paul, 1963.

———. *The Life of the Buddha as Legend and History*. 3d ed., rev. London: Routledge & Kegan Paul, 1960.

Thomsen, Harry. *The New Religions of Japan*. Tokyo: Charles E. Tuttle, 1963.

Thubten, Jigme Norbu. *Tibet is My Country*. New York: E.P. Dutton & Co., 1961.

Trungpa, Chögyam. *Born in Tibet*. London: George Allen & Unwin, 1966. Penguin Books reprint with added Epilogue, 1971.

Tucci, Giuseppe. *Pre-Diṅnāga Buddhist Texts on Logic from Chinese Sources*. Gaekwad's Oriental Series, No. 49. Baroda: Oriental Institute, 1929.

Vajirañāṇa Mahāthera. *Buddhist Meditation in Theory and Practice*. Colombo: M.D. Gunasena & Co., 1962.

Viravong, Maha Sila. *History of Laos*. New York: Paragon, 1964.

Warren, Henry Clarke, tr. *Buddhism in Translations*. New York: Atheneum, 1963.

Wasson, R. Gordon. *Soma, Divine Mushroom of Immortality*. Popular edition. New York: Harcourt Brace Jovanovich, 1971.

Watanabe, Shoku. *Japanese Buddhism: A Critical Appraisal*. Revised edition. Tokyo: Kokusai Bunka Shinkōkai, Japan Cultural Society, 1968.

Welbon, Guy Richard. *The Buddhist Nirvāṇa and Its Western Interpreters*. Chicago: University of Chicago Press, 1968.

Welch, Holmes. *Buddhism under Mao*. Cambridge: Harvard University Press, 1973.

———. *The Buddhist Revival in China*. Cambridge: Harvard University Press, 1968.

———. *The Practice of Chinese Buddhism 1900–1950*. Cambridge: Harvard University Press, 1967.

White, James W. *The Sokagakkai and Mass Society*. Stanford: Stanford University Press, 1970.

Winternitz, Moriz. *A History of Indian Literature*. 2 vols. Calcutta: University of Calcutta, 1927, 1933.

Wright, Arthur F. *Buddhism in Chinese History*. Stanford: Stanford University Press, 1959. Paper, New York: Atheneum, 1965.

———. "Buddhism in Modern and Contemporary China." In Robert F. Spencer, ed., *Religion and Change in Contemporary China*. Minneapolis: Minnesota University Press, 1971.

Yamamoto, Kosho. *An Introduction to Shin Buddhism*. Ube, Japan: Karinbunko, 1963.

Yampolsky, Philip B., tr. *The Platform Sūtra of the Sixth Patriarch*. New York: Columbia University Press, 1967.

———. *The Zen Master Hakuin*. New York: Columbia University Press, 1971.

Yang, C.K. *Religion in Chinese Society*. Berkeley: University of California Press, 1967.

Yu, David C. "Buddhism in Communist China: Demise or Co-existence?," *Journal of the American Academy of Religion*, 39, (March 1971): 48–61.

Zürcher, Erik. *Buddhism, Its Origin and Spread in Words, Maps, and Pictures*. Leiden: E.J. Brill, 1959. New York: St. Martin's Press, 1962.

Index